W9-BOA-136

ECONOMICS
and
EDUCATION

THE FREE PRESS, NEW YORK
Collier-Macmillan Limited, London

DANIEL C. ROGERS
and
HIRSCH S. RUCHLIN

ECONOMICS

and

EDUCATION

Principles and Applications

The Free Press
A DIVISION OF THE MACMILLAN COMPANY
866 Third Avenue, New York, New York 10022

Collier-Macmillan Canada Ltd., Toronto, Ontario

Library of Congress Catalog Card Number: 74-143519

printing number

1   2   3   4   5   6   7   8   9   10

To Our Parents

Preface

THE aim of this book is to enable students of education and economics to comprehend economic research relevant to their field. Economics is in large part a way of thinking, a way of approaching problems. Economists have developed various tools and concepts which need to be learned before economic research can be understood. These tools are useful in analyzing diverse problems, not just educational ones. However, this book is focused on those economic tools and concepts which are necessary for analyzing educational problems. Economic tools will be applied to such problems as the determinants of the demand for education and the supply of educators; the market price (salary) of teachers; the production of education; the rate of return to investments in formal schooling and on-the-job training; the relationship between education and the alleviation of poverty; the efficiency and productivity of educational institutions; the role of education in economic growth and development; educational planning; the financing of education; and the competitive structure of the educational market. These are among the most prominent topics in the field of economics and education and we demonstrate the applicability of economic tools in generating information about these issues and in helping to formulate national policy for education.

In addition to developing specific economic tools necessary for an analysis of education, we reproduce a number of basic studies illustrating both the applicability (to education) of the economic concepts developed and the methodological and empirical problems encountered in doing research in the economics of education. In choosing studies for this text we were guided by the dual motives of both highlighting the way in which economists analyze educational issues and of selecting a relatively simple contribution in each area. Our selections are a minute sampling of the vast literature in the field of the economics of education. Although we do not always subscribe to the respective authors' assumptions and findings, the research presented is methodologically sound and ably demonstrates the application of economic theories to the real world of education.

Being members of a multi-disciplinary department we are fully aware of the limitations of analyzing a broad problem from the vantage point of only one social science discipline. Nevertheless we believe that economic studies of educational problem areas are vital in an age when educational needs far exceed the resources allocated to fulfill these needs. We do not suggest that the economic answer is *the* answer. Rather, it should be weighed along with the anthropological, psychological, political, sociological, and other findings about a problem. Even if the political aspects of a problem are deemed overriding in importance, it is important to know and understand the economic aspects of the question.

Theoretical and empirical research in the social sciences is becoming more and more mathematically and statistically oriented. Economics and education are not escaping this broad trend, neither should they endeavor to do so. We have appended to our text explanations of key mathematical and statistical concepts. Of course, many books have been written on these topics alone. It is our objective to bring together in as brief a manner as possible an introduction to those mathematical and statistical tools most commonly found in the economic study of education. We suggest that those students without any background in mathematics and statistics study these appendices carefully prior to reading the chapters dealing with demand and supply, and that the appendices be referred to as needed throughout the book. All mathematical and statistical terms appearing in the appendices are italicized, together with their definitions or descriptions. Thus the appendices can be used as a glossary by consulting the index and the appropriate appendix pages upon encountering unfamiliar mathematical or statistical terms.

We cannot begin to thank our own professors who introduced us to the realm of economics and acquainted us with the tools and research which we are attempting to impart. Suffice it to note that

with one or two minor exceptions we are presenting the work of
others. We are grateful to our colleagues and the students at Teachers
College, Columbia University, both in our basic economics of education
courses and in our seminar, who reviewed our work. In addition
special thanks are due to David Barkin, Susan Hall, Jeffrey Morris,
Harold Noah, Jacqueline Rogers, Charles Shami, Robert Stearns,
and Ray Whitman for their valuable comments on parts or all of
previous drafts of this manuscript. Needless to say, any remaining
errors and omissions are the responsibilities of the authors. Thanks
are also due to our wives, Jacqueline Rogers and Eleanor Ruchlin, for
their editorial assistance, Michael Righi for his bibliographic and
indexing assistance, and Barbara Battelle, Vicky Lackman, and Katy
Sullivan for typing the various drafts of the manuscript.

D.C.R.
H.S.R.

New York
June 1970

Contents

1
Economics and Education   1

4
Basic Studies in Educational Demand and Supply   63

5
Production   99

Tables

Figures

Appendix I

Appendix II

ECONOMICS
and
EDUCATION

Chapter 1 ECONOMICS AND EDUCATION

IN this chapter, we explore several aspects of the relationship between education and economics. These aspects include the common ground shared by educators and economists and the many economic attributes of education. We also analyze the role of government in providing education, define the nature of economics as a discipline, and discuss some basic methodological conventions that pervade economic theory and research. Together, these provide a general overview of the subject matter of this book.

INTERESTS COMMON TO ECONOMISTS AND EDUCATORS

Interest in the economics of education goes as far back as the times of Plato, Aristotle, and St. Thomas Aquinas.[1] From that era to the present man has been concerned with the role of education in society and the economic attributes of education. However, it is only since the second half of the twentieth century that the economics of education has become a subject in its own right. Since 1955 more than two thousand books and articles have appeared reporting the research of scholars in this area.

Interestingly enough, all this research, regardless of whether published in an economic or education medium, appears to converge around twelve major themes:

    1. International and intranational studies of expenditures on education.

Notes to Chapter 1 will be found on pages 363–364.

2. Financing education.
3. The demand for higher education.
4. Teacher supply and demand.
5. The production and distribution of education.
6. Efficiency in the educational organization.
7. Investment in education, investment criteria appropriate to education, and analysis of differential rates of return.
8. The role of education in the War on Poverty.
9. Education and economic growth.
10. Educational planning.
11. Educational obsolescence.
12. The competitive structure of education.

Although these themes have been discussed in past and continuing research, we believe that they will continue to head the list of future research. Therefore, they constitute the agenda of items to be discussed in this book.

EDUCATION AND KNOWLEDGE

Economists' interest in the area of education is not confined to education proper but encompasses the much larger category of knowledge. One prominent economist, Fritz Machlup, has written a monumental study in which knowledge as a whole, and education as one of its components, is investigated. Machlup states that there are two broad types of knowledge: the type that is designed to yield a large pay-off in the future and the type that gives its recipient immediate pleasure. Knowledge of either type can be acquired in numerous ways—at formal institutions like schools; through the written word as in books, magazines, and newspapers; or through audio and visual media such as radio, television, and the cinema.

Machlup justifies the entrance of an economist into an analysis of knowledge by noting that

The production of knowledge is an economic activity, an industry, if you like. Economists have analyzed agriculture, mining, iron and steel production, the paper industry, transportation, retailing, the production of all sorts of goods and services, but they have neglected to analyze the production of knowledge. This is surprising because there are a good many reasons why an economic analysis of the production of knowledge seems to be particularly interesting and promising of new insights.[2]

Machlup acknowledges that, among the major subdivisions of the knowledge industry, education is by far the most important. Education is not, however, a homogeneous category since there are multiple means of acquiring education. Education can be acquired in the home, in school, in church, in the armed forces, through the communications media, by training on the job, through self-education, and by learning from experience. Although we focus primarily on education in the school, the concepts we develop are equally applicable to other educational categories.

ECONOMIC BENEFITS OF EDUCATION

Aside from undertaking an economic analysis of education as an industry, economists are also interested in education for the various benefits that it contributes to society. In a study of the benefits of public education, Burton Weisbrod listed seven broad benefits attributable to education. They are:

1. Direct financial returns.
2. Financial options.
3. Hedging options.
4. Non-market returns.
5. Residence-related benefits.
6. Employment-related benefits.
7. Societal benefits.[3]

The first four of these refer to the returns to the individual, and the last three are benefits to others.

Direct financial returns stem from the positive correlation that all researchers find between educational attainment and earnings. Although part of this financial reward is undoubtedly due to ability, ambition, and a host of socioeconomic variables, no researcher has denied the positive role played by education. Financial options refer to the fact that each level of education prior to the highest achievable level provides an individual with the opportunity (the option) of acquiring yet additional education and reaping the extra benefits attached to that education. Education further provides a hedging option by increasing the probability that an individual will be able to adapt to the effects of technological change, either by remaining at a job and utilizing more sophisticated equipment or adapting to an entirely different job. Non-market returns result from all the do-it-yourself type of work that a person can perform as a result of his education.[4] Filing one's own income tax returns and helping one's children with their homework are but two examples of such non-market activity.

The preceding benefits are primarily of a private nature since individuals reap most, if not all, of the economic returns. The remaining three benefits are primarily social because society at large reaps the benefits of the individual's education. As these benefits are external to the individual (they are not captured primarily by him), they are known as external benefits or *externalities*. Residence-related benefits stemming from the physical juxtaposition of the beneficiaries and the educated individual consist of several types: those accruable to the current family and the future family of the individual, those reaped by the individual's neighbors, and those accruing to taxpayers at large. Employment-related benefits refer to the effects of the educated individual on the overall productivity of his colleagues, in situations where production involves cooperative effort. Societal benefits stem from the fact that literacy is a prime requisite for an intelligent citizenry, for a smooth organization of economic activity, and for economic growth. Furthermore, education reduces the financial burden on society by minimizing the need for corrective and welfare services.

THE ROLE OF GOVERNMENT IN PROVIDING EDUCATION

Within the American economic system government typically plays a very minor role in the productive process proper, although it assumes greater importance in the allocative sphere. Large and small private firms initiate, finance, and direct production. The owners of these firms invest their own capital, borrow from banks, attempt to raise money on the security (bond and stock) markets, hire labor, and produce goods and services in response to their reading of consumer desires. Although government defines the spectrum of legal activities, regulates the capital markets, and limits the conditions under which labor can be hired, it does not normally engage in the productive process itself.[5] Government does however play a much larger role in allocating the fruits of production by transferring some purchasing power from the relatively wealthy to the poor through taxation and welfare payments.

Under certain conditions a greater presence by government is called for in the production process.[6] The divergence of social and private benefits is one such case. If for any good or service the benefits to society are greater than the benefits accruable to the individual, private production would lead to a decrease of the benefit from society's viewpoint. As the representative of society's collective demand, government enters the picture to insure that production will be guided by society's, rather than the individual's, desires. Goods and services whose production entails such decisions are known as *merit wants*. Such goods and services are deemed so meritorious that their production is provided for through the public budget, either in its entirety or over and above what is provided for through private production.

Education is deemed to be a merit want. Due to the existence of externalities, as seen in the previous section, the social benefits of education exceed the private benefits. Governmental participation in this activity can take either of two forms: outright production and allocation on grounds other than financial ability (the establishment of a *public* system of education) or subsidization of private educational systems.

ECONOMICS DEFINED

Economics is concerned with two primary phenomena, desires and resources. Because desires are psychological and physical, economics deals with man; because resources are constructed from matter, economics deals with nature. Economic issues involve a basic confrontation between opposing forces: desires and resources, or man and environment. The confrontation is brought into being primarily because desires are infinite, whereas resources are finite. The history of civilization is a continuous illustration of man's wants exceeding his means; and it appears safe to predict that as affluent as our society may yet become there will always be unfulfilled wants.

The *raison d'être* of economics is man's desire to satisfy as many wants as possible within the existing stock of resources. This is achieved by using the stock of available resources as efficiently as possible so as to derive the greatest benefit from them. Economics does not prejudge society's desires. It is not a discipline concerned with morals. Rather it takes society's wishes as given and attempts to fill as many of these desires as possible with a minimum of resource input. Thus it is not uncommon to find economists engaged in research in such fields as military weaponry, space exploration, crime prevention, health, education, and poverty; together with the traditional areas of money, international trade, growth, and industrial organization.

Economics distinguishes between *free goods* and *scarce goods*. Free goods are those whose superabundance and easy availability decree that their price be zero. They are free. A classic case of a free good is air.[7] Scarce goods, which encompass just about all the goods we are familiar with, command a price because they are not easily and abundantly available. Whatever the source of scarcity, be it the limits of nature (there is a finite amount of fertile or habitable land) or the limits of human capacity (only so much can be accomplished in a day, week, year, or lifetime), the existence of scarcity coupled with unlimited wants sets the stage for an economist.

Economists build theories, devise ways to test the theories against the real world, and, depending on the results, accept, revise, or discard the theory. The basic assumption underlying all economic theory is that man has his self-interest at heart in *all* his endeavors. Of course, when so much is built on one assumption, that assumption must be broadly interpreted. It can include aesthetic as well as material factors. With economics one can investigate the decision and timing of having children, and how to educate them. One can study production, prices, crime, and love. All of this can be done and has been done simply by applying economic concepts and assumptions to whatever is being investigated.

BOUNDARIES OF THE DISCIPLINE

Economics as a discipline encompasses a broad spectrum of sub-areas. The American Economic Association has arranged these sub-areas into ten major groupings:

1. General economics, theory, history, systems.
2. Economic growth, development, planning, fluctuations.
3. Economic statistics.
4. Monetary and fiscal theory and institutions.
5. International economics.
6. Administration, business finance, marketing, accounting.
7. Industrial organization, technological change, industry studies.
8. Agriculture, natural resources.
9. Manpower, labor, population.
10. Welfare programs, consumer economics, urban and regional economics.

Economic analysis which is the term applied to the theoretical tools economists use regardless of the specialty areas, has traditionally been divided into two fields: macroeconomics and microeconomics. Macroeconomics deals with aggregate problems affecting the economy at large; microeconomics focuses on disaggregated problems specific to individual units or subsectors of the economy.

On a micro level economists may be concerned with the most minute detail of a person's economic existence, such as the goods he buys in the supermarket, the job he chooses, his pay rate, his decisions on family size, or the type and quantity of education he wishes for himself and his progeny. These same items of economic data may also interest a macroeconomist. From a macroeconomic standpoint interest would focus on factors affecting aggregate consumption patterns, job search and labor market knowledge, wage levels, population size and trends, and the national demand for educational services.

Economics of education, which cuts across several of the preceding categories, draws upon both macro and micro theory. Some topics in the economics of education—such as investment, financing, and productivity—utilize both macro and micro tools. Others, like the use of national income statistics and the application of economic growth theories, draw primarily upon the mainstream of macroeconomics, whereas questions of supply and demand and production functions have their theoretical foundations in microeconomic theory.

ECONOMIC ABSTRACTIONS

Economists, following in the footsteps of other researchers, have adopted many methodological and theoretical abstractions that appear time and again in economic writings and research. The three abstractions most important for our course of study will now be explored: rationality, markets, and competition.

Rationality

Economic doctrines, precepts, and theories usually postulate *rationality* on the part of the individual or group empowered to make economic decisions.[8] Rationality simply defined means being reasonable, reasonable in an economic sense. On the accepted assumption that economic goods provide pleasure rather than pain, economic rationality postulates that more is preferable to less. It also implies that if we are told that A is preferred to B, and B is preferred to C, A will be preferred to C. Rationality further implies that individuals and groups adopt measures that lead to a given goal with the use of a minimum of resources. Therefore maximization of gain, given a set of resources, or minimization of resource use (cost), given a goal, follow directly from our assumption of rationality.

Markets

Economists refer to *markets* in analyses of a wide variety of problems. It is not unusual to hear economists referring to the market for goods or services whether they are studying bread, books, bribes, or bombs. To an economist a market does not refer to a fixed structure in which trading takes place, although such a structure may house participants in the market. The members of the New York and American Stock Exchanges in the Wall Street area of Manhattan are part of the securities market, but do not constitute that market in its entirety. Rather, a market is a concept that incorporates all individuals or institutions that remain in contact concerning any economic good or service.

The only criteria for inclusion in a market are the ability and willingness to participate. Markets do not have fixed boundaries. Rather, they are delimited by time, distance, and personal and financial constraints. The market for a surgeon's services may be confined to a particular city or may be international depending on whether the patient is in need of an immediate operation or can wait a few days. This is an example of a variable time constraint. The public education market is circumscribed by geographical constraints. On the elementary level the market is usually the school district in which the child's family resides. On the secondary level the market may encompass a few townships or even a county. On the college and university level the market may be state, federal, or international. Personal factors determine the choice of attendance at religious or non-denominational educational institutions, whereas at all educational levels financial factors have a greater effect on the decision whether to attend private or public schools. From the point of view of the means test all those included in the market for private education are also included in the market for public education. Thus, there is a larger potential market for attendance at public educational institutions than at private ones.

It is not necessary to have purchased or sold an item to be part of the potential market for that item. Because his neighborhood library is physically available to an individual and he has the right to utilize its facilities, he can be part of the potential market for public library books even if he has never entered the library. However, he would not be part of the potential market if he were blind and the library had no books written in Braille. It is simple to describe a potential market, but for most markets it is quite difficult to specify exactly who is and who is not part of that market.

Economists conceive of the market as the supreme regulator of economic desires. Within the context of a market, demanders and suppliers make their respective desires known, and economic activity based on these data occurs. Consumers' demands, as registered in the market by purchases, prompt production and supply, while the availability of goods satisfies demands. The market becomes the unbiased arbitrator of desires and resources, signalling the need for an increase (when there is a shortage) or curtailment (when there is a surplus) in production and/or price in any specified area.

The market automatically adapts to changes in tastes and technology. For example, when the Russians launched their first orbital satellite (Sputnik) in 1957 and the United States found itself lagging behind in the space race, the United States' demand for engineers and scientists increased dramatically. Demand, however, exceeded the available supply. In response to this imbalance firms offered higher starting salaries to graduates with degrees in these areas and attempted to bid qualified engineers and scientists away from their competitors. Government funding for science education and space research increased significantly. In a matter of years the number of engineers and scientists increased dramatically as students responded to the improved opportunities in these fields. By the late 1960s, as military and domestic needs began to take precedence over science research and as the United States achieved a dominant position in the space race by being the first nation to land men on the moon, the need for additional engineers and scientists declined. The output of engineers and scientists did not decline proportionately; by 1969 a surplus of engineers and scientists existed; and the financial attractiveness of these professions declined. Consequently, a smaller proportion of college students are currently entering these fields.[9] All of this was accomplished automatically by the invisible hand of economic rationality guiding each person in the market to do that which would benefit him the most. We deal with these concepts in much greater detail in a subsequent chapter on the concepts of supply and demand.

Competition

Many types of markets are conceivable, ranging from those that are highly monopolistic (few sellers) to those that are highly competitive (many sellers). Economists, although noting the existence of many market structures, consistently refer to one basic type—the *perfectly competitive market*. This type, by definition, includes so many buyers and sellers that no participant can influence the overall outcome of the market by his offer or failure to offer to purchase or supply goods. It is the market as symbolized by the totality of all its participants, rather than any individual, that determines price and quantity of goods and services. Perfectly competitive markets lead to productive optima in that costs are kept to a minimum and output is maximized. With any other kind of market, an optimum productive solution may not be achieved.[10] Perfect competition is also the preferred market structure for resource allocation, because each factor of production is rewarded in proportion to its marginal contribution to production. Society, however, usually chooses to supplement the purchasing power of some groups at the expense of others. Taxation, the equal provision of public services regardless of means, charity, and welfare payments are the primary channels through which redistribution takes place.

ECONOMIC METHODOLOGY AND EMPIRICAL RESEARCH

The goals of economics, as well as of most other sciences, are explanation and prediction. These goals are achieved by combining theoretical and empirical research. Theorizing is based primarily on deductive reasoning and conceptualizations. Implications are then drawn based on the assumptions and the economic arguments of the theory. Empirical research is primarily inductive, since particular research findings are used to generalize about a larger group or population. The two research techniques are complementary in that theory provides a framework for conducting empirical research, and empirical research tests the explanatory and predictive power of a given theory.

Theory represents simplifications and generalizations of the real world. Theory never describes any particular situation or event completely, nor does it attempt to. To preserve its power of generalization and applicability to a host of situations, theory must concentrate on one, or a few, crucial characteristics that a broad group of events seem to have in common. By highlighting these crucial or pivotal characteristics theory becomes a useful framework for analyzing and interpreting events. Theories cannot and should not be judged on the basis of whether individuals assert that they act as a theory states they do. If the end result of their behavior conforms to the theoretical expectation, the theory is validated as useful. It is not what people say they do but rather what they actually do that is the important test of any theory's validity.

Theoretical arguments are formulated as models. Gardner Ackley captured the essence of models and theories in the following:

> A model...uses what we know or think we know about economic behavior patterns, technology, or institutions to permit us to make predictions—more or less specifically depending on how much or little we know....
>
> Economic models...are succinct statements of economic theory. Theory, in turn, is simply a generalization or abstraction of experience and observation. We see thousands of farmers producing and supplying wheat. We can observe many things about these farmers and their productive activities: the color of their eyes, the number of their children, their various productive techniques, the number of acres they farm, and millions of further details. We choose, however, to make one significant abstraction about their behavior. We select from among all our observations one relationship which we think is most relevant and significant—that they tend to grow more wheat at a higher than at a lower price. We throw away all the rest of our information (we could not, in any case, remember or record very much of it), and summarize our knowledge about the supply of wheat in a single function. Frequently, perhaps, our abstractions and generalizations from experience and observation are erroneous, or unnecessarily incomplete. But that is simply the difference between bad or inadequate and better or more complete theory.[11]

The function shown in equation (1)

$$S_w = f(P_w) \tag{1}$$

is a simplified model of the theory of supply and is read: The supply of wheat is a function of the price of wheat. A model can be specified either verbally or mathematically, although the latter technique is both more concise and readily amenable to empirical research. Once the elementary economic relationships are understood, it is possible to broaden the analysis both by adding variables to any one equation and by adding equations to incorporate larger and larger sectors of economic activity into a model.[12]

Because economics is a social science dealing with human beings, it is extremely difficult to undertake controlled experiments. A controlled experiment is one in which only one factor or variable is allowed to change, so that the effect of that one factor can be determined. To approximate controlled experiments, social scientists employ the *ceteris paribus* (other things equal) assumption. That is, the effects of changes in one variable are determined assuming that all other variables are held constant. This process can then be repeated to determine the effects of each of the other variables being considered. In theoretical work this is accomplished simply by thinking through the effects of the one variable on all other variables. In empirical work the effect of one variable alone is typically determined by statistical devices.[13] Thus, a multifaceted problem can be investigated in the absence of controlled experiments through the *ceteris paribus* assumption.

POSITIVE VERSUS NORMATIVE ISSUES

A fundamental distinction must be made between normative and positive issues. Normative issues are those that involve value judgments and, as a result of this factor, there is room for disagreement on these issues between men of reason.[14] Positive issues involve an analysis of what is, as opposed to what ought to be, and as such leave no room for disagreement. Unemployment either is or is not, for example, 4 per cent; the demand for college education is or is not increasing; the distribution of aggregate income is or is not unequal. In such instances economic theory and accepted and proven statistical tools should lead to uniform conclusions regardless of the political persuasion or ideology of the economist studying the problem.

To the extent that economic theory and statistical sources are not complete and statistics are not perfectly gathered, there may be differences even within positive economics. One area of research that illustrates such differences is the question of whether the costs incurred in obtaining a graduate education are repaid by subsequent earnings differentials.[15]

APPLICATION OF ECONOMIC MODELS TO EDUCATION

We recognize that education has many unique attributes differentiating it from the average stereotyped economic good. The aim of this book is to demonstrate that these unique characteristics notwithstanding, economic analysis can be profitably applied to the educational enterprise. In the theoretical chapters that follow we present the basic economic laws and theories utilized in analysis of education, frequently choosing examples from education for our illustrations. In the basic study chapters we further present the research of others as illustrations of how education is in practice incorporated into a pure economic framework. This research indicates how existing economic data can be used and how new data can be created to fill previous voids. The reader may not be willing to accept some of the assumptions or conclusions of the research reported. This is quite understandable given the newness of empirical research in the economics of education and the admittedly tentative nature of some of the research. What we hope will be evident to the reader is that economics has a positive contribution to make in analyses of educational issues.

QUESTIONS FOR DISCUSSION

1. What benefits do you expect to derive from your education? Which of these are primarily economic in nature?

2. What economic justification is there for government subsidization of private schools?

3. How did you define the higher educational market when you were considering your choice of a college and/or a graduate school? What factors determined your definition of the market?

4. Discuss the normative and positive attributes of the following:
   (a) school decentralization.
   (b) unionization of the teaching labor force.
   (c) equality of educational opportunity.

Chapter 2 NATIONAL INCOME CONCEPTS

NATIONAL income concepts are the basic framework for measuring and evaluating the performance of an economic system in terms of how rapidly it is growing, how stable it is, how its internal structure is changing over time, and how it allocates resources among its various sectors. National income accounts, which provide the basic data for such measures, are compiled and published regularly by the United States Department of Commerce. Because the source of funds for education and the employment of the output of the educational system—educated people—are dependent on the overall functioning of the economy, an understanding of national income is crucial for any student of the economics of education.

NATIONAL INCOME ACCOUNTS

There are many ways to gauge the economic well-being of society. One such indicator, the one most often utilized, is the annual total of goods and services produced by an economy. The basic national income account category used to measure annual total production of goods and services is called *Gross National Product* (GNP). It is defined as the total money value of final production of goods and services in the economy in any one year. It is important to stress that GNP is expressed in monetary units because money serves as the common denominator for the economic system. Simple addition of actual units of various products would pose severe problems, especially for comparative purposes. If a firm produces 4,000 desks and 1,000 blackboards in one

Notes to Chapter 2 will be found on page 364.

year and in another year produces 1,000 desks and 4,000 blackboards, in which year is the value of the produce greater? Converting desks and blackboards into their monetary values provides a ready-made comparative and additive device.

Although it may seem that the task of calculating GNP entails merely an addition of all the output of an economy in any one year, with the appropriate prices attached to each item, the actual process is not that simple. In practice one must distinguish between final products and intermediate ones. Final products are those that are sold to consumers, whereas intermediate products are those used in the production of other goods or services. To include the value of goods or services used as intermediate products would entail double counting. For example, in producing a book the ink and paper required in the production stage are considered intermediate products. In the computation of GNP the value of the book is directly included, but not the value of the paper and ink used to manufacture the book. The value of the paper and ink is already included in the cost (price) of the book because the producer of the book paid the producer of the paper and ink for these materials and included their costs in the price of the book. However, if paper and ink are final products in the sense that they are sold directly to consumers and not used as intermediate products in the production process of another good, they are included in GNP accounts.

A second methodological convention adopted in calculating GNP is the exclusion of the dollar value of any items that are sold second-hand. Such a sale entails only a *transfer* and not a production of goods. One man sells another man a used book and receives the money value of the used book as payment. This transaction does not reflect an addition to economic well-being because additional output was not created. However, the services of an agent or middleman who may have arranged this transaction are considered a productive activity, in that both the buyer and the seller consider themselves better off as a result of their trade. Thus, although the proceeds from the sale of a used item are omitted from the GNP accounts, the earnings or commissions of people engaged in selling such items are included.

GNP statistics can be derived in two alternate ways, either by summing the value of final output, or by summing the income generated at each stage in the production process. These two methods are referred to as GNP and GNI (Gross National Income), respectively. It must be stressed that GNP = GNI, as is shown in Table 2.1.

Final output (GNP) consists of four major component groups: consumption, investment, government, and net exports. This breakdown is based on the use to which the final production is put. GNI is based on the summation of the payments to the factors of production (traditionally classified as land, labor, and capital) and includes wages and salaries, rent, interest, depreciation, and profit. Profits are the balancing item for any activity in the sense that after the factors of production are remunerated, any remaining amount—which could be either positive or negative—is designated as profit and payable to the owners of the enterprise. The following hypothetical example illustrates this point.

Payment to the factors of production utilized in producing a book:

$$
\begin{aligned}
\text{land} &= \$1.00 \\
\text{labor} &= \$4.00 \\
\text{capital} &= \$1.50 \\
\hline
\text{Total} &\quad \$6.50
\end{aligned}
$$

If the book is sold for $7.50, a profit of $1.00 is made. If the book is sold for $6.00, a loss (a negative profit) of $.50 is realized.

Table 2.1 lists 1969 GNP estimates and illustrates the two alternative calculating approaches. It further lists some of the subdivisions of the major categories as illustrations of the relative importance of federal

Table 2.1

United States Gross National Product Accounts, 1969 (in billions of dollars)

GNP			GNI		
Personal consumption		576.0	Compensation of employees		564.3
Goods	333.4		Wages and salaries	509.9	
Services	242.6		Supplements to wages		
Gross domestic investment		139.4	and salaries	54.4	
Fixed investment	131.4		Proprietors' income		66.3
Changes in business			Rental income		21.6
inventories	8.0		Corporate profits		88.2
Net exports		2.1	Interest		30.6
Exports	55.3		Plus depreciation, indirect		
Imports	53.2		business taxes, and business		
Government purchases		214.6	transfer payments		162.1
Federal	101.9		Minus subsidies		1.0
State and local	112.7				
	GNP	932.1		GNI	932.1

Source: *Federal Reserve Bulletin* 56 (1970): A–68.

versus state and local units and goods versus services in overall consumption patterns. In addition to GNP the United States Department of Commerce publishes four national income account statistics. They are Net National Product (NNP), National Income (NI), Personal Income (PI), and Disposable Income (DI).[1] Each of these statistics is related to the GNP measure.

As the personal income statistic is widely utilized in discussions of the financing of education, it merits description in greater length. *Personal income* is defined as payments to the population from all sources: from businesses, government, households, and institutions. All forms of income from these sources are included in personal income: wages and salaries, other labor income, income of owners of unincorporated business (proprietors' income), rental income, dividends, interest, and transfer payments.[2] Table 2.2 lists these components of personal income, together with their 1969 dollar values.

Table 2.2

**United States Personal Income, 1969
(in billions of dollars)**

TOTAL PERSONAL INCOME	747.2	
Wage and salary disbursements		509.9
Other labor income		26.2
Proprietors' income		66.3
Rental income		21.6
Dividends		24.6
Personal interest income		59.4
Transfer payments		65.5
Less personal contributions for social insurance		− 26.3

Source: *Federal Reserve Bulletin* 56 (1970) : A–69.

Because the financing of public education is primarily derived from the taxes raised by state and local governments, and taxes are dependent on income and wealth (wealth being accumulated income), the income level of these governmental units is of importance. The income of a state or locality is conventionally defined as the sum of the personal income of its inhabitants. To adjust for the differing population sizes of various geographic units, per capita personal income is utilized. Per capita personal income is calculated by dividing total personal income by the population size. Table 2.3 lists total personal income and total personal income per capita by state for 1969. Two features of this table merit special attention. First, the per capita measure yields an entirely different ranking of states from that of the total personal income measure. The District of Columbia, which on a total basis ranks thirty-sixth, ranks first on a per capita basis. Second, the per capita income measure clearly highlights the wide difference in income levels between states.

Table 2.3

Personal Income and Personal Income per Capita by State, 1969

State and Region	Personal Income (in millions of dollars)	Personal Income per Capita
United States	$742,961	$3,680
New England	46,572	4,046
Maine	2,972	3,039
New Hampshire	2,491	3,474
Vermont	1,434	3,267
Massachusetts	22,623	4,138
Rhode Island	3,442	3,779
Connecticut	13,610	4,537
Mideast	176,264	4,160
New York	80,989	4,421
New Jersey	30,580	4,278
Pennsylvania	43,243	3,664
Delaware	2,167	4,013
Maryland	15,416	4,095
District of Columbia	3,869	4,849
Great Lakes	155,099	3,937
Michigan	34,574	3,944
Ohio	40,587	3,779
Indiana	18,891	3,691
Illinois	47,609	4,310
Wisconsin	15,437	3,647
Plains	56,555	3,496
Minnesota	13,350	3,608
Iowa	9,782	3,517
Missouri	16,086	3,459
North Dakota	1,852	3,011
South Dakota	2,011	3,051
Nebraska	5,278	3,642
Kansas	8,197	3,531
Southeast	128,084	2,896
Virginia	15,377	3,294
West Virginia	4,748	2,610
Kentucky	9,210	2,850
Tennessee	11,197	2,810
North Carolina	15,045	2,890
South Carolina	6,947	2,580
Georgia	14,108	3,040

Table 2.3—continued

State and Region	Personal Income (in millions of dollars)	Personal Income per Capita
Southeast—continued		
Florida	21,777	3,427
Alabama	9,062	2,567
Mississippi	5,174	2,192
Louisiana	10,413	2,780
Arkansas	5,027	2,520
Southwest	*52,797*	*3,211*
Oklahoma	7,872	3,065
Texas	36,401	3,254
New Mexico	2,876	2,894
Arizona	5,648	3,336
Rocky Mountain	*15,943*	*3,269*
Montana	2,168	3,124
Idaho	2,051	2,857
Wyoming	1,103	3,447
Colorado	7,492	3,568
Utah	3,129	2,994
Far West	*105,351*	*4,158*
Washington	13,046	3,835
Oregon	7,244	3,565
Nevada	1,992	4,359
California	83,070	4,272
Alaska	1,272	4,512
Hawaii	3,024	3,882

Source: *Survey of Current Business* 50 (1970) : 15, 16.

The interstate per capita personal income differentials have definite implications for public school financing. Reporting on the relationship between state personal income per capita and current public school expenditure per pupil, Charles Benson notes that in the 1929–30 and 1959–60 academic years per capita personal income differences accounted for 62 and 70 per cent, respectively, of the variation in expenditure per pupil.[3] Per capita personal income not only accounts for some of the variation in school expenditures, but it also is a prime determinant of an area's *ability* to finance educational expenditures, a concept that will be discussed in greater detail in a subsequent section of this chapter.

PRICE INDICES

Price changes can be the result of two factors. The first is changes in consumers' preferences among goods and/or changes in resources utilized in production. The second is changes in the value of the monetary unit, the dollar.

Because the national income account statistics are measured in money terms, economists are particularly interested in deflating or inflating these data to remove the effect of price changes that are solely due to changes in the value of the monetary unit. This is particularly important in a time series (longitudinal) analysis, because what is to be investigated are real changes net of changes in the size of the measuring unit. For example, in comparing any two years' GNP, the apparent changes in GNP may not be due to increases or decreases in production but rather to changes in the purchasing power of the dollar resulting from inflation or deflation. Therefore, economists often utilize national income accounts expressed in *real* terms, that is, in dollar units adjusted for price changes (constant dollars). This technique relies on the utilization of price indices.[4]

Published price indices are readily available. The three major types are the *consumer price index*, the *wholesale price index*, and the *GNP deflator*. Although the principles underlying the construction of these indices are similar, the items included in them differ, as their titles indicate. Owing to the different combinations of goods and services from which these indices are calculated, it is not uncommon to observe different rates of increase or decline among them. Generally, indices are derived by dividing current prices of selected items by the prices prevailing in a base time period and then multiplying this number by 100. The formula for a simple price index would be:

$$\text{Price Index} = \frac{\text{Price in Current Year}}{\text{Price in Base Year}} \times 100$$

The final step of multiplying by 100 is not mathematically necessary, but it simplifies the reporting and use of this adjusting tool. As the base period is assigned the value of 100, price increases are recorded by values in excess of 100 and price decreases by values less than 100. Table 2.4 shows the value of the GNP deflator for the period 1929–69, combined with GNP for that period in current year values. Dividing the GNP in current dollars by the GNP deflator and multiplying the quotient by 100 yields real GNP values. More specifically, as the GNP deflator is based on 1958 dollars, the derived GNP figures are shown in constant (1958) dollars.[5]

An analysis of changes in teachers' salaries over time provides another example of how price indices are used. Because teachers' salaries are reported in current dollars and because the purchasing

Table 2.4

Real GNP, 1929–69

Year	(1) GNP Current Dollars (in billions of dollars)	(2) GNP Deflator (1958 = base year)	(3)[a] Real GNP (in billions of 1958 dollars)
1929	103.1	50.6	203.6
1930	90.4	49.3	183.5
1931	75.8	44.8	169.3
1932	58.0	40.2	144.2
1933	55.6	39.3	141.5
1934	65.1	42.2	154.3
1935	72.2	42.6	169.5
1936	82.5	42.7	193.0
1937	90.4	44.5	203.2
1938	84.7	43.9	192.9
1939	90.5	43.2	209.4
1940	99.7	43.9	227.2
1941	124.5	47.2	263.7
1942	157.9	53.0	297.8
1943	191.6	56.8	337.1
1944	210.1	58.2	361.3
1945	211.9	59.7	355.2
1946	208.5	66.7	312.6
1947	231.3	74.6	309.9
1948	257.6	79.6	323.7
1949	256.5	79.1	324.1
1950	284.8	80.2	355.3
1951	328.4	85.6	383.4
1952	345.5	87.5	395.1
1953	364.6	88.3	412.8
1954	364.8	89.6	407.0
1955	398.0	90.9	438.0
1956	419.2	94.0	446.1
1957	441.1	97.5	452.5
1958	447.3	100.0	447.3
1959	483.7	101.6	475.9
1960	503.7	103.3	487.7
1961	520.1	104.6	497.2
1962	560.3	105.8	529.8
1963	590.5	107.2	551.0
1964	632.4	108.8	581.1
1965	684.9	110.9	617.8
1966	749.9	113.9	658.1
1967	793.5	117.6	674.6
1968	865.7	122.3	707.6
1969[b]	932.3	128.1	727.7

[a] Column 3 = Column 1 ÷ Column 2 × 100.
[b] Preliminary.

Source: *Economic Report of the President, 1970* (Washington, D.C.: U.S. Government Printing Office, 1970), tables C–1, C–2, C–3.

power of a dollar has declined in recent years, the real increase in teachers' salaries is less than a simplistic view of the salary schedules would indicate. Table 2.5 lists current and real average salaries paid to the total instructional staff in public schools from 1930 to 1969. Current salary data were adjusted for changes in the consumer price index, because this index best reflects changes in the overall cost of living. Thus, for example, what initially appears to be a 66 per cent increase ($3,255) from 1958–59 to 1968–69, is actually only a 32 per cent increase ($1,551) after the general cost of living increase is taken into account.

LIMITATIONS OF NATIONAL INCOME ACCOUNTING

Economists realize that the national income accounts as they are currently constructed are imperfect in that they do not take account of certain economic attributes and transactions which materially

Table 2.5
Average Salaries Paid Total Instructional Staff, 1930–69

School Year	Average Annual Salary (in current dollars)	Consumer Price Index (1957–59 = 100)	Average Annual Salary (in constant 1957–59 dollars)
1930–31	$1,440	53.0	$2,717
1932–33	1,316	45.1	2,918
1934–35	1,244	47.8	2,603
1936–37	1,327	50.0	2,654
1938–39	1,408	48.4	2,909
1940–41	1,470	51.3	2,865
1942–43	1,599	60.3	2,652
1944–45	1,846	62.7	2,944
1946–47	2,254	77.8	2,897
1948–49	2,846	83.0	3,429
1950–51	3,126	90.5	3,454
1952–53	3,554	93.2	3,813
1954–55	3,950	93.3	4,234
1956–57	4,350	98.0	4,439
1958–59	4,939	101.5	4,866
1960–61	5,449	104.2	5,229
1962–63	5,921	106.7	5,549
1964–65	6,465	109.9	5,883
1966–67	7,129	116.3	6,130
1968–69	8,194	127.7	6,417

Source: Salary data: National Education Association–Research Division. *Economic Status of the Teaching Profession, 1968–69* (Washington, D.C.: National Education Association, 1969), table 1; Consumer Price Index: *Economic Report of the President, 1970* (Washington, D.C.: U.S. Government Printing Office, 1970), table C–45.

affect society's well-being. Five major limitations to these measures exist.

First, the current accounts do not include most non-market activities such as the productive services of housewives, do-it-yourself work, and parents tutoring their children. If such work were purchased by hiring a housekeeper, governess, builder, repairman, or tutor, these transactions would be included in the national income accounts. Consequently, the current accounts are an underestimate of aggregate productive activity.

Second, the amount of leisure consumed by members of society has increased significantly during the last few decades. The reduction of the standard workweek from 60 hours at the turn of the century, to 48, 40, and now 37 hours has vastly increased the leisure time enjoyed by the average citizen. Leisure is definitely a part of economic well-being, but it is not accounted for in the national income accounts.

A third limitation is the lack of a comprehensive quality adjustment. The quality of goods and services has not remained uniform over time. Although some quality adjustments have been made, many others have not due to the great difficulty of evaluating them. Two examples where full quality adjustments have not been made illustrate this point. The quality of medical care has increased tremendously during the last half century while the quality (as judged by durability) of automobiles and homes has declined. Unless one assumes that overall quality changes are offsetting, with improvements cancelling deteriorations, GNP accounts are deficient because of this fact.

Fourth, national income statistics give no indication of the composition or distribution of total output. A distributional change away from military research to poverty and educational research may make society either better or worse off, yet national income data do not and cannot reflect this; nor do they reflect the distribution of income among the members of society. Although most citizens would agree that society's well-being increases as the inequality in the income distribution is lessened, national income accounts as currently constructed do not show any changes in income distribution.

Finally, national income statistics are overestimates of economic well-being to the extent that they do not take account of certain major disutilities that result from the production and consumption processes themselves. Although air and water pollution result directly from the production and utilization of modern transportation media, no adjustment is made for these negative attributes. Similarly, to the extent that urban overcrowding and crime result from industrialization, economic well-being is overstated by omitting a (negative) adjustment for these occurrences.

Before terminating the discussion of national income accounts, it should be noted that given all the imperfections in our system of national income accounts, these data nonetheless represent a major step forward in our stock of economic knowledge. They do provide a fairly comprehensive view of the economy which greatly facilitates empirical research. However, the national income accounts are an artificial system. Classifications and criteria for including or excluding certain types of economic activities are based on value judgments. The four major categories of GNP—consumption, investment, government spending, and net exports—could easily be subdivided or replaced. These four categories occupied economists' thinking in the 1930s when the national income accounts were formulated, and they were consequently emphasized. One could argue that as society adopts the goal of eradicating poverty, a new category emphasizing expenditures in this area should be explicitly included in the national income accounts. The realization that education is an important determinant of both economic growth and poverty supports the argument that educational expenditures should also be highlighted by a separate category rather than included in the consumption and government categories, as is current practice. As society's goals change, we should not be at all surprised to see changes in the construction of the economic accounts.

INEQUALITY IN INCOME DISTRIBUTION

The inequality in income distribution noted earlier has important implications for students of the economics of education, and for this reason merits further analysis. In the derivation of per capita personal income, total personal income was divided by the population size. The resulting per capita figures may give the mistaken impression that the income generated by an economy is divided equally among all the members of the economy. This is indeed not the case. Income is distributed far from equally. That is, the lowest x per cent of the population in terms of income commands less than x per cent of total income. For example, the lowest 30 per cent of the population commands less than 30 per cent of total income, and the lowest 99 per cent of the population commands less than 99 per cent of the income. Perfect income equality would imply that any x per cent of the population receives x per cent of the income.

Income inequality can be portrayed both statistically and diagrammatically. Table 2.6 depicts the income inequality prevailing in the United States during 1968. In all the groupings the top 5 per cent received more than 13 per cent of the income, and the lowest fifth (lowest 20 per cent) received less than 7 per cent of the income.

Diagrammatically, income inequality is shown by a *Lorenz curve*. As seen in Figure 2.1, a Lorenz curve is represented on a graph with the percentage of the population plotted on the horizontal axis and the percentage of income on the vertical axis. The graph is bisected by a diagonal which is the locus of points where the percentages of the two factors are equal. Thus, the diagonal represents a state of total equality. Income inequality is represented by a curve (Lorenz curve) divergent from the diagonal. The more unequal the distribution, the greater the disparity between the diagonal and the Lorenz curve. At the extreme, total inequality—where all the income is controlled

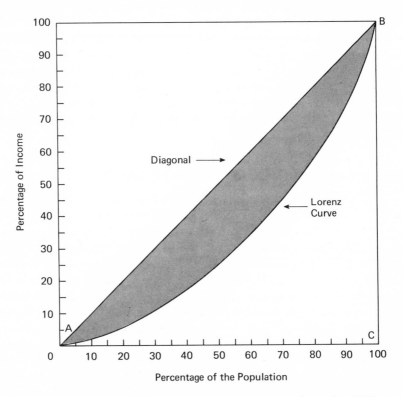

Figure 2.1   Lorenz Curve of United States Income Inequality, 1968

by one person—would be represented by a Lorenz curve following the right angle *ACB*. The Lorenz curve in Figure 2.1 depicts the income inequality prevailing in the United States in 1968 and is based on the data appearing in Table 2.6.

The *Gini ratio*, which is a numerical representation of the area between a diagonal and a Lorenz curve (the shaded area in Figure 2.1) relative to the total area below the diagonal (the area of triangle *ABC* in Figure 2.1), is a convenient statistical summary of income inequality. The closer the Lorenz curve is to the diagonal, the closer the Gini ratio approaches zero (the point of total equality); and the further the Lorenz curve is from the diagonal, the closer the Gini ratio

Table 2.6

**Percentage Share of
Aggregate Income in 1968[a]**

Income Rank	Percentage
All Families	
Percentage	*100.0*
Lowest fifth	5.7
Second fifth	12.4
Middle fifth	17.7
Fourth fifth	23.7
Highest fifth	40.6
Top 5 per cent	14.0
White	
Percentage	*100.0*
Lowest fifth	6.0
Second fifth	12.7
Middle fifth	17.7
Fourth fifth	23.4
Highest fifth	40.3
Top 5 per cent	14.0
Negro and Other Races	
Percentage	*100.0*
Lowest fifth	4.8
Second fifth	10.5
Middle fifth	16.5
Fourth fifth	24.6
Highest fifth	43.6
Top 5 per cent	16.1

[a] Received by each fifth of families ranked by income, by race of head, for the United States.

Source: *Current Population Reports*, Series P–60 (December 23, 1969).

Table 2.7
Years of School Completed by Persons 25 Years Old and Over, March 1969

	Total Population (in thousands)	Percentage Distribution Years of School Completed									Median School Years Completed
		Total	0–4	5–7	8	9–11	12	13–15	16	16+	
Total, All Races	107,750	100.0	5.6	9.4	13.7	17.2	33.5	9.8	6.5	4.2	12.1
Male	51,031	100.0	6.1	9.9	14.0	16.5	29.7	10.3	7.3	6.2	12.1
Female	56,719	100.0	5.1	9.0	13.5	17.9	36.9	9.3	5.8	2.4	12.1
Total, White	96,822	100.0	4.5	8.5	14.0	16.7	34.8	10.3	6.8	4.4	12.2
Male	45,989	100.0	4.8	9.1	14.3	16.1	30.6	10.8	7.7	6.6	12.2
Female	50,833	100.0	4.2	8.1	13.7	17.3	38.5	9.8	6.0	2.4	12.2
Total, Negro	9,918	100.0	15.5	18.3	11.5	22.4	22.3	5.4	3.1	1.5	9.6
Male	4,552	100.0	18.0	18.3	11.1	20.7	21.4	5.7	3.0	1.8	9.4
Female	5,366	100.0	13.4	18.3	11.9	23.9	23.0	5.1	3.2	1.3	9.8

Source: *Current Population Reports*, Series P-20 (February 19, 1970).

Table 2.8
Education of Head of Families[a]

	Total	Years of School Completed						
		Less than 8	8	9–11	12	13–15	16	16+
Number (in thousands)	47,197	7,018	6,326	8,088	14,681	4,919	3,386	2,779
Per cent	100.0	100.0	100.0	100.0	100.0	100.0	100.0	100.0
$1 to $1,999	5.1	13.5	7.3	4.8	2.8	2.2	1.2	1.4
$2,000 to $3,999	10.7	24.7	17.7	10.7	6.1	4.7	3.2	3.0
$4,000 to $6,999	19.5	27.4	26.0	23.3	18.1	13.2	7.8	6.8
$7,000 to $9,999	23.2	18.0	23.4	25.7	27.4	23.4	16.7	13.0
$10,000 to $14,999	25.8	12.3	18.1	24.5	31.2	32.7	33.8	31.1
$15,000 and over	15.7	4.0	7.4	10.7	14.5	24.0	37.3	44.6
Median Income	$8,865	$5,173	6,874	8,182	9,520	10,864	13,110	14,135

a With head 25 years old and over by total money income in 1968, by years of school completed.

Source: *Current Population Reports*, Series P-60 (December 23, 1969).

approaches one (total inequality). Over the period 1929 to 1967 the Gini ratio for the United States declined from .50 to .40, indicating a movement toward greater equality. However, the primary reduction in income inequality during this period occurred before the 1950s; there is little difference between income inequality today and at the end of World War II.

The distribution of education in the economy is also unequal, as seen in Table 2.7. The inequality is evident in breakdowns both by sex and race, with the difference between the races being an especially glaring one. The educational distribution is both affected by and affects the distribution of income and wealth. Members of poor families often cannot afford to continue their education beyond secondary school, and in some instances the elementary grades. These families cannot afford the tuition costs of institutions of higher learning, and more importantly, members of these poor families feel that they can no longer forgo employment which would enable them to contribute to the family budget. The greater the degree of poverty, the more limited educational opportunities become. With the passage of time, the limited educational opportunities available to the poor serve to perpetuate and accentuate the inequality in income and wealth.

The level of educational attainment is also a prime determinant of the level of income. Table 2.8 shows that on average the higher the educational attainment, the higher a person's lifetime income. The pioneering research of Herman Miller, Theodore Schultz, and Gary Becker has highlighted the quantitative relationship between education and earnings.[6]

NATIONAL INCOME CONCEPTS AND TAXATION

National income accounts are a basic data source for measures of state and local fiscal capacity and tax effort, two concepts with extremely important implications for school financing. Although in recent years the federal government has been assuming a larger responsibility for school financing, federal revenues still account for only approximately 10 per cent of the total educational budget. The state and local governments account for about 65 per cent of the budget, by far the largest share, while tuition and donations account for the remainder.

Analyses of state and local financing of education focus on questions of how much an area spends for education as opposed to how much an area *could* spend. Implicit in such discussions is the assumption that greater expenditures mean better education, *ceteris paribus*. The question of how much an area spends is a simple empirical one. The question of how much an area *could* spend hinges on its *fiscal capacity* and *tax effort*. The concept of fiscal capacity reflects the resources that can be taxed to raise revenue. The fiscal capacity of an area is primarily determined by the total resources of the area's population, its income, wealth, and business activity. Tax effort is simply the extent to which an area makes use of its fiscal capacity.[7]

There are two approaches to measuring fiscal capacity. The first approach focuses on income and analyzes measures of an area's income out of which taxes can be paid. The second approach focuses on an area's wealth and seeks to measure the tax base (the taxable resources) within an area in order to estimate the amount of revenue that could be raised under various levels of taxation. Whereas the second approach is preferable on theoretical grounds, the available data report income, and dictate the use of the first approach. Such measures of fiscal capacity seek to analyze what proportion of a state's or locality's resources are devoted to all public services, including education.[8]

Measures of capacity (ability) and effort can be calculated for educational expenditures alone. The National Education Association publishes annual reports containing school expenditure data for public school systems. Various governmental agencies, and particularly the Office of Education, periodically publish educational statistics containing data on school expenditures and revenues. Such data have been utilized to compare the relative position of states with regard to their effort and ability to finance educational expenditures.[9] We present below two indices of educational expenditures for 1968. Although our analysis focuses only on elementary and secondary school systems, we could have included higher education in the analysis.

School expenditures per student is a measure of a school system's *effort* in financing educational expenditures. The greater the expenditure, the greater the effort. In an attempt to obtain a comprehensive measure of state and local school expenditures per student we multiplied current state and local expenditure per pupil in average daily membership (a term synonomous to enrollment) by total public school enrollment to obtain a measure of total school expenditure.[10] This measure was then divided by the school age population (5 to 17 years old) to obtain a measure of school expenditures per potential student, which serves as an indicator of effort.

$$\text{EFFORT} = \frac{\dfrac{\text{Current Expenditures per pupil}}{\text{in A.D.M.}} \times \dfrac{\text{Public School}}{\text{Enrollment}}}{\text{School Age Population (5--17 years old)}}$$

$$= \frac{\text{Current Expenditures}}{\text{School Age Population}}$$

However, this measure does not adjust for the *ability* (fiscal capacity) of the states and localities. The greater the number of inhabitants 5 to 17 years old relative to the total personal income of the area, the lower its ability to finance each student's education. Similarly, the greater the number of inhabitants 5 to 17 years old relative to the total population of the area, the smaller the working population that can support school expenditures, and consequently the lower its ability. Multiplying the effort measure by the appropriate ratios representing the economic and demographic adjustments described above yields an *adjusted effort*—effort adjusted for ability—measure.

$$\begin{array}{l}\text{ADJUSTED} \\ \text{EFFORT}\end{array} = \frac{\text{Current Expenditures}}{\text{School Age Population}} \times \frac{\text{School Age Population}}{\text{Personal Income}}$$

$$\times \frac{\text{School Age Population}}{\text{Total Population}}$$

cancelling like terms yields:

$$\begin{array}{l}\text{ADJUSTED} \\ \text{EFFORT}\end{array} = \frac{\text{Current Expenditures}}{\text{Personal Income}} \times \frac{\text{School Age Population}}{\text{Total Population}}$$

A comparison between adjusted effort (a statistic that reflects what is being spent relative to the ability of a state to make those expenditures) and actual effort (a statistic that indicates what is actually being spent) highlights the effect of the adjustments. To make interstate comparisons possible the effort and adjusted effort measures were converted into indices, with the United States average serving as the base. The effort and adjusted effort indices were then ranked to simplify comparisons. The state indices and rankings appear in Table 2.9.

Before discussing the indices and rankings appearing in Table 2.9 two methodological choices affecting these measures deserve discussion. First, we chose to utilize as one of the adjustments for capacity the proportion of a state's population aged 5 to 17 years rather than the number of students in average daily attendance (ADA) because the latter inappropriately differentiates between those states which attempt to keep students in school longer and those which do not. A true capacity (ability) measure should be net of such factors. Second,

Table 2.9

Indices of Educational Expenditures for Elementary and Secondary Schooling, 1968

	EFFORT Index	Rank[a]	ADJUSTED EFFORT Index	Rank[a]		EFFORT Index	Rank[a]	ADJUSTED EFFORT Index	Rank[a]
Washington	157.4	1	104.2	26	Florida	99.7	26	96.2	34
Idaho	156.7	2	122.2	15	Rhode Island	99.5	27	87.4	42
Missouri	147.0	3	91.3	39	Virginia	92.2	28	103.4	29
New York	144.1	4	102.6	31	Massachusetts	92.1	29	72.5	50
Michigan	143.2	5	119.7	16	New Mexico	91.3	30	158.8	2
Kansas	143.0	6	103.9	27	Indiana	91.0	31	97.1	33
Wyoming	123.8	7	149.1	4	Ohio	89.0	32	90.5	41
Oregon	121.1	8	125.5	14	Oklahoma	87.1	33	82.1	47
Iowa	117.9	9	130.3	11	West Virginia	86.6	34	108.1	23
New Jersey	117.3	10	92.0	37	Utah	86.3	35	155.5	3
California	116.3	11	105.3	25	New Hampshire	85.3	36	84.6	46
Maryland	111.4	12	119.4	17	South Dakota	84.2	37	117.6	18
Nevada	110.6	13	103.2	30	North Dakota	82.5	38	132.6	9
Delaware	109.8	14	131.1	10	Georgia	82.2	39	103.5	28
Connecticut	108.4	15	74.3	49	Alabama	81.7	40	85.2	44
Minnesota	107.8	16	138.8	6	Louisiana	81.7	40	130.3	11
Alaska	105.1	17	198.1	1	Maine	81.2	42	109.8	21
Wisconsin	104.8	18	116.7	19	Nebraska	78.1	43	86.0	43
Arizona	104.5	19	135.8	7	Arkansas	76.8	44	102.2	32
Colorado	102.9	20	109.5	22	North Carolina	76.2	45	94.3	35
Pennsylvania	102.7	21	92.1	36	Kentucky	75.8	46	91.4	38
Vermont	102.5	22	126.3	13	Tennessee	75.6	47	90.7	40
Montana	101.6	23	139.9	5	South Carolina	72.7	48	115.9	20
Illinois	100.8	24	80.5	48	Texas	72.1	49	84.9	45
Hawaii	100.1	25	105.4	24	Mississippi	67.6	50	133.2	8
					United States	100.0		100.0	

[a] In case of a tie the same rank was assigned to both states and the succeeding rank was skipped.

Source: National Education Association–Research Division, *Rankings of the States, 1969 and 1970*. Research Reports 1969–R1, 1970–R1 (Washington, D.C.: National Education Association, 1969 and 1970). Tables 4, 5, 15 (1969 Report), and 111, 113 (1970 Report).

by focusing only on the public rather than the total (public *and* private) educational system we have biased the effort index because state expenditures earmarked for private schools were omitted. This omission, however, was dictated by the unavailability of comprehensive data on the private schools; it undoubtedly accounts for the poor showing of some of the larger and richer states which have relatively large expenditures for private schools.

The most striking finding drawn from the indices and rankings in Table 2.9 is the tremendous difference in the effort and adjusted effort rankings.[11] In only 11 states were the two indices within five rank points of each other, whereas in 21 states the rankings were at least 15 rank points apart.[12] Of those states that were in the top ten rankings

(1 to 10) based on effort, only one—Wyoming—was also in the top ten rankings based on adjusted effort. Of the ten states ranked lowest by effort (41 to 50) only three—Alabama, Nebraska, and Texas— were similarly ranked by adjusted effort. The sharpest contrasts were noticed for Mississippi, Missouri, Connecticut, and Utah, where the differences in ranking were 42, 36, 34, and 32 rank points respectively.

If the states are grouped geographically into south–nonsouth categories, one notes that the southern states were, by and large, at the lower end of the effort index spectrum. Moreover, the southern states were the majority among those states whose adjusted effort index exceeded their effort index. In the nonsouth category no predominant geographic pattern prevailed.

Although we are reluctant to draw policy conclusions from data for only one year and from an analysis that excludes private schools, comparisons of the type inherent in effort and adjusted effort discussions can be important considerations in devising formulas for federal grants-in-aid for educational purposes.[13] The value of the grant could be related to the differential between effort and effort adjusted for ability. In this way federal funds would complement rather than supplant state expenditures.

QUESTIONS FOR DISCUSSION

1. How would educational expenditures fit into the current major GNP categories: consumption, investment, government, net exports? In which category would you choose to place your own educational expenditures, and why?

2. What items would you include in the construction of an educational price index for elementary, secondary, and higher education?

3. What factors contribute to income inequality? Can and will education play a major role in equalizing income distribution?

4. Discuss the construction of the effort and adjusted effort indices. In what way could the theoretical conception of these indices be improved? Are the necessary data for these improvements available?

PROBLEMS

1. Given the following information calculate total profits if 50 units of a good are produced and each unit is sold at a price of $7.50:

wages	$100
rent	40
interest	50
materials	150

2. What were the money and real increases in average teachers salary during the period 1930–31 and 1968–69? (Refer to Table 2.5.)

3. Construct indices of teachers' salaries and Gross National Product for the period from 1951 to 1969.

Chapter 3 DEMAND, SUPPLY, AND THE THEORY OF THE FIRM

I N the brief discussion of markets in Chapter 1, we noted that prices are set in the market by the interaction of demand and supply. In this chapter we first analyze the basic forces determining market activity—demand and supply—and the interaction of these forces to determine market equilibrium. Next, we introduce and analyze the concept of elasticity as a measure of demand and supply response to changes. Finally, we derive elements of the theory of the firm utilized in analyses of educational institutions as economic enterprises. A discussion of utility theory and cost curves—concepts used in a rigorous derivation of demand and supply respectively—are appended to the chapter. In the next chapter the tools and concepts developed here are applied to analyses of major educational issues.

In demonstrating the relevancy of the demand, supply, and equilibrium concepts to educational problems, we focus attention on one area of the school curriculum, physical education, and illustrate the applicability of these concepts to the question of obtaining an item of athletic equipment: basketballs. Obviously, the ensuing discussion is applicable throughout the educational system and the economy.

DEMAND: SCHEDULES, CURVES, AND DETERMINANTS

Economists define *demand* as a schedule indicating the amount of a particular good or service that consumers are willing and able to buy at each price in a set of possible prices during a specified time

Notes to Chapter 3 will be found on pages 365–366.

period. A hypothetical demand schedule of a physical education department for basketballs, appearing in Table 3.1, portrays a series of possible price-quantity alternatives. The terms "willing" and "able" are used in the definition to stress that only *effective demand* is being considered. Although all physical education departments may be willing to purchase basketballs, they may not all have the economic ability. If they do not possess the necessary funds and do not have access to credit sources, their willingness alone will not suffice. Hence, only those that are both willing and able to make a purchase are considered relevant demanders.

Table 3.1

Demand Schedule

Point	Price	Quantity Demanded
A	$30	6
B	24	18
C	18	24
D	12	30
E	6	36

A fundamental characteristic of demand is the inverse relationship between price and quantity; that is, as price increases the quantity demanded decreases, and as price decreases the quantity demanded increases. This relationship is commonly referred to as the *Law of Demand*.

This law can be explained and justified on empirical and intuitive grounds. An empirical study of the law of demand as applied to education appears in the next chapter. Intuitively we know that the higher the price of a good or service, the fewer the number of people who can afford to purchase it. Thus, the number of potential purchasers decreases as the price of the item increases. People who are already demanders of an item may decide to decrease the number of units purchased as the price increases. At a low price one may buy several units; at a higher price less may be purchased. For example, a school system may have earmarked a sum of $500 a year for basketballs. If the cost of basketballs increases, the school system can no longer buy the same number of basketballs. The resultant decline in ability to purchase basketballs is a decrease in real income—the *income effect*—and prompts the purchasing of fewer units of the good or service. In practice the effect of this decline in income may not be entirely directed at the item whose price increased but may be apportioned over the entire range of goods and services bought.

The decline in purchases may also result from the substitution of cheaper items for the one whose price rose—the *substitution effect*. An example will illustrate this substitution. Given the $500 budget, a physical education department may decide to schedule five basketball games and five calisthenics sessions per day, purchasing the necessary athletic equipment with the $500. If the price of athletic equipment increases, the physical education department may decide to substitute the cheaper activity—calisthenics—for the more expensive one—ball games. Thus, both the income and substitution effect lead to a smaller quantity demanded at higher prices. Similarly, were the price to fall a greater quantity would be demanded.[1]

The inverse relationship described by the law of demand can be portrayed diagrammatically in a two-dimensional diagram as a line sloping downward from left to right. The demand curve in Figure 3.1 is a graphic representation of the demand schedule appearing in Table 3.1. (By convention, price is indicated on the vertical axis and quantity is indicated on the horizontal axis.) By drawing a perpendicular line from any point of the price axis to the demand curve and a second perpendicular line from this point of intersection to the quantity axis, one ascertains the quantity that will be demanded at a given price. A perpendicular line from $24 on the price axis to the demand curve intersects the curve at *B*. Drawing a second perpendicular line from *B* to the quantity axis indicates that 18 units will be demanded at a price of $24. Repeating this exercise from a price of $12, a quantity of 30 is found (point *D* on the demand curve represents this price quantity combination). These two price-quantity combinations illustrate the law of demand.

Because the time element is an important factor in demand discussions, quantity demanded must have a time dimension. For example, the number of basketballs demanded at a given price during a year is much greater than during a week or month. Consequently, whenever reference is made to demand, a specific time dimension is implicitly assumed.

The demand curve portrayed in Figure 3.1 was derived in terms of the demand schedule of an individual or small group. Since the whole equals the sum of its parts, the aggregate demand curve for any group of people (all the physical education departments in a school district) for a specific good or service (basketballs) is the sum of all the individual demand curves, the summation being of a horizontal nature. That is,

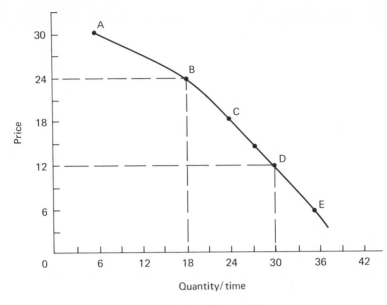

Figure 3.1   Demand Curve

for an aggregate demand curve the scale of the price axis remains the same, but the scale of the quantity axis is inflated to accommodate the universe under discussion $(D_A + D_B = D_C$, as seen in Figure 3.2).

The law of demand postulates an inverse relationship between price and quantity, emphasizing the importance of price as a determinant of quantity demanded. However, other factors, such as tastes, income, and prices of substitute goods (basketballs versus volleyballs) and complementary goods (basketballs and baskets) also influence demand. Although changes in the price of the good or service determine the corresponding changes in quantity demanded, represented by movements *along the curve*, changes in the remaining factors determine shifts in demand, represented by *shifts in the position of the curve*. An examination of the effect of changes in each of these three determinants of the school's demand for basketballs will illustrate this point.

A change in tastes in favor of basketball due to advertising, for example, will mean that more basketballs will be demanded at each price—demand curve DD in Figure 3.3 shifts to the right, to D_2D_2. A shift in tastes away from basketball would result in less overall demand —a shift from DD to D_1D_1. An increase in the school budget makes possible the purchase of both a greater variety of items and additional units of items already in the budget. Increased purchases of basketballs due to this factor are represented by a shift from DD to D_2D_2. A reduction in the school budget has the opposite effect.[2]

A decline in price of a substitute good, such as volleyballs or footballs would shift the demand curve for basketballs down from DD to D_1D_1 as the former items are substituted for the latter. Alternately, an increase in the price of substitute goods would shift the demand curve for basketballs up to D_2D_2, signifying that more basketballs would then be bought. In the case of complementary goods (goods often or typically used together, like basketballs and baskets or bread and butter) a rise in the price of the complementary good leads to a decrease in the demand for the original good (a shift from DD to D_1D_1) because the entire activity—playing basketball—becomes more expensive. Alternately, a decline in the price of the complementary good leads to an increase in the demand for the original good (a shift from DD to D_2D_2), as basketball games become a cheaper activity.

A *change in demand* must not be confused with a *change in quantity demanded*. Mistakenly calling these two by the same name is one of the most common errors found in popular usage of economics terms. A change in demand refers to shifts in the demand curve resulting from changes in tastes, income, and prices of related goods. A change in quantity demanded refers to a movement along a given demand curve and results from a change in the price of the good under discussion

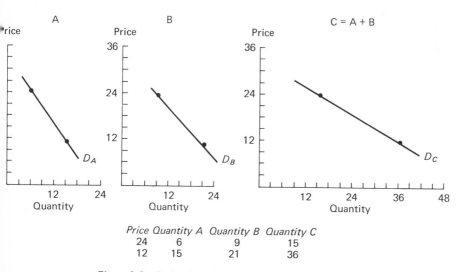

Figure 3.2   Derivation of an Aggregate Demand Curve

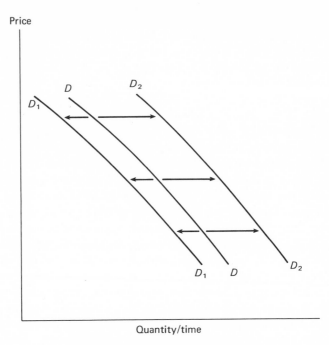

Figure 3.3 Shifts in the Demand Curve

with all other factors held constant. Referring to Figure 3.1, a price change from $24 to $12 induces a change in quantity demanded from 18 units to 30 units, a change that occurs along the demand curve; whereas changes of income, tastes, or prices of other goods induce changes in demand as illustrated in Figure 3.3.

The application of demand theory to decisions to purchase education is straightforward. More education will be purchased at lower prices and less education at higher prices, *ceteris paribus*. It is in defining the price of education that problems may arise. Most people tend to think of the price of education as being tuition costs, if any, and possibly the cost of school supplies and transportation. However, these are but one component of the cost of education and, in the case of secondary and higher education, the smaller component. The process of acquiring education takes time, a considerable amount of time. The time devoted to school attendance cannot be used for alternate purposes such as working for pay. The income forfeited while attending school is a cost of acquiring education. Thus, the total cost of education is composed of *direct costs* (tuition, supplies, and the like) and *indirect* or *opportunity* costs (foregone earnings).[3] It has been estimated that opportunity costs for secondary and higher education account for approximately three-fifths of the total cost of acquiring education.[4]

SUPPLY: SCHEDULES, CURVES, AND DETERMINANTS

Supply is defined as a schedule of various amounts of a good or service that producers are willing and able to sell at each specific price in a set of possible prices during a specified time period. A hypothetical supply schedule for one firm producing basketballs is shown in Table 3.2. It portrays a schedule of alternatives, just as the demand schedule does. But whereas the price-quantity relationship in demand is an inverse one, in supply it is a direct one. At a higher price more will be supplied; at a lower price less will be supplied. One is tempted to denote this direct relationship by calling it the Law of Supply, but a classic exception prevents this.[5] Figure 3.4 is a diagrammatic representation of Table 3.2 and exhibits the price-quantity relationship attributed to traditional supply curves.

Table 3.2

Supply Schedule

Point	Price	Quantity Supplied
A	$33	51
B	27	42
C	18	24
D	15	18
E	6	9

The direct price-quantity relationship is illustrated by noting the quantity changes as the price rises from $15 to $27. By drawing perpendicular lines from the price axis to the supply curve and from the supply curve to the quantity axis, one notes that at a price of $15, 18 basketballs would be supplied (point *D*) and at a price of $27, 42 would be supplied (point *B*). Thus, a price increase of $12 causes a corresponding increase of 24 units in the quantity supplied.

In calculating supply definite time values are implicitly attached to the quantity measures. The reasoning behind this methodological step is similar to that given in the demand section—*i.e.*, the quantity

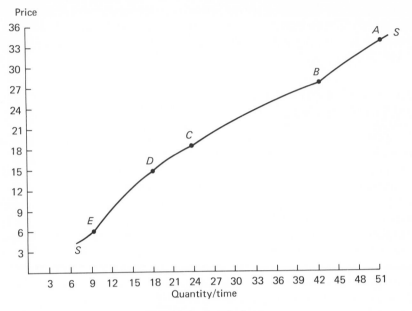

Figure 3.4 Supply Curve

supplied depends on the duration of the period. The supply of basket-balls produced in one week is a fraction of the supply produced in a month or a year. Similarly, the aggregate (industry) supply curve for an item is a horizontal summation of all the individual (firm) supply curves.

Paralleling the exposition in the demand section, the positive price-quantity relationship of supply can also be explained on intuitive grounds. At a given price only a certain number of firms can cover costs and hence, will produce the good (basketballs). But at a higher price, firms of lower efficiency will be able to cover costs and will enter the market. Whether these new firms have switched from producing a different, less profitable, item or are new organizations responding to the new conditions, their effect on supply is the same. In addition firms that were already suppliers of basketballs may increase their production in response to a higher price. Prior to the price increase such an action would not have been profitable. All of these increases in production result in increased supply.

The sole determinant of the supply of a good or service is not its price. Although price is singled out for special emphasis, additional factors also influence supply. Primary among them are technology, prices of the factors of production, and prices of related goods. Although changes in the price of the good to be supplied determine movements along the supply curve, changes in the three variables just enumerated determine shifts in the supply curve. The nature of such shifts is illustrated in Figure 3.5.

Technology and the prices of the factors of production together determine the costs of production. Technology refers to the state of the arts in production and denotes technological knowledge about the various ways of combining the factors of production to produce an item. However, technological factors by themselves do not determine the method of production. Cost data for the alternative techniques of production are needed to determine which system is most economic. Thus, technological factors in conjunction with data on the costs of the factors of production influence supply. If new technological advances reduce costs or if the prices of the factors of production decline, the supply of basketballs will increase. This is shown by a shift of the supply curve to the right from SS to S_2S_2. If prices of the factors of production increase, the quantity of basketballs supplied at any given

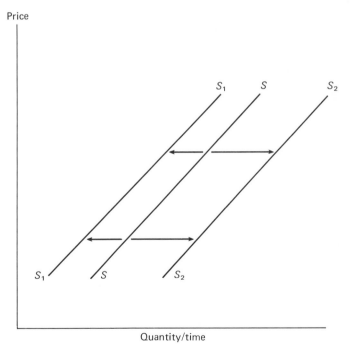

Figure 3.5   Shifts in the Supply Curve

price will diminish because of the higher production costs. This is portrayed by a shift of the supply curve to the left, from SS to S_1S_1.

Changes in the prices of related goods will also lead to shifts of the supply curve. An increase in the price of a good to which the current resources of any supplier can be easily adapted, for example, footballs, will cause a drop in the supply of the good originally produced, since the producer is motivated to shift his production to the related good. This is shown by a shift from SS to S_1S_1. A decrease in the price of related goods will motivate firms whose resources can be adapted to the production of basketballs to do so, thereby increasing the supply. This is shown diagrammatically as a shift from SS to S_2S_2.

We emphasize again that movements along a curve must be differentiated from shifts of the curve. A change in the price of the good to be supplied will cause a change in the quantity supplied, which is a *movement along the supply curve* (see Figure 3.4). A change in the costs of production and prices of related goods will result in a *shift of the supply curve* either to the left or right (see Figure 3.5).

EQUILIBRIUM

Demand and supply have been discussed separately. However, it is the interaction of these two forces which determines the price of any good or service. Neither blade of a pair of scissors can do the job alone. The same can be said about demand and supply in relation to the functioning of the market mechanism. Simply defined, *equilibrium* is a psychological or physical state in which, once attained, there is no impetus for change. A useful illustration of an equilibrium condition is two children of equal weight perfectly balanced on a seesaw. If one child moves forward or backward or if a heavier child is substituted for a lighter one, movement will take place until a compensating change is made, yielding a new equilibrium.

By combining the demand and supply curves appearing in Figures 3.1 and 3.4, we can see how a typical market would operate. These two curves are reproduced and combined into one diagram, Figure 3.6. Because we are dealing with a market situation, all quantity measures are multiplied by a factor of 1,000 to reflect the greater volume characteristic of market situations. Given the demand and supply data as shown in Figure 3.6, assume that an initial price of $6 prevails. Drawing perpendicular lines from the price axis to the curves and from the curves to the quantity axis, we note that at a price of $6 demanders want 36,000 basketballs while suppliers are willing to supply only 9,000. Demand exceeds supply by 27,000 units; such a situation is referred to as a *sellers' market*. Either one of two things can now happen: basketballs will have to be rationed, or the price will have to rise. If basketballs are rationed, the market mechanism is supplanted by legal institutional arrangements. Rationing can work, but it is not entirely viable, as the rapid development of black markets that usually accompany rationing attests. On the other hand, a price increase is a market solution. As the price rises, the number of persons willing and able to demand basketballs decreases, and the number willing and able to supply the good increases. The price rise will continue until a price of $18 is reached. At that price demand equals supply, a quantity of 24,000 basketballs will be both demanded and supplied, and an equilibrium situation (point *E*) will have been reached.

Similarly, if the initial price were $30, we can see by drawing the appropriate perpendicular lines that the quantity demanded, 6,000 basketballs, falls short of the quantity supplied, 45,000 basketballs, by 39,000 units. A surplus, or *buyers' market*, exists. The only way that such a surplus can be disposed of, short of destroying it, is by reducing the price. (Department store clearance sales are an example of the

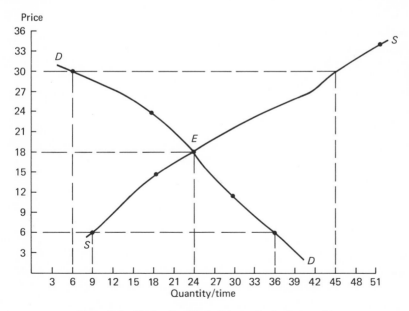

Figure 3.6 Market Equilibrium (quantity in thousands)

reaction to such a situation.) As the price declines, the number of demanders increases and the number of suppliers decreases until, at a price of $18 and a corresponding quantity of 24,000 basketballs, an equilibrium situation is reached (point E). We have described the achievement of equilibrium as an iterative process with one final market clearing price, that is, an auction situation. But actually, equilibrium is achieved through a succession of nonclearing prices, each prompting further price changes in the direction of equilibrium.

The equilibrium price, once established, prevails for all units. At the equilibrium price the market is cleared, that is, at this price all those demanding the good or service can obtain it and all sellers can find buyers. Those consumers who would have been willing to pay a higher price and those firms who would have been willing to supply the item at a lower price benefit from the equilibrium price. These consumers reap a *consumers' surplus* in the sense that they can buy at a lower price than the maximum they would have been willing to offer, and these producers reap a *producers' surplus* owing to the price being higher than the minimum at which they would have been willing to sell. Consumers who are not willing to pay a price as high as the equilibrium price and producers who are not willing to sell at a price as low as the equilibrium price are excluded from the market.

In most economic models, although equilibrium may not be reached instantaneously, given sufficient time, it will be reached.[6] Once equilibrium is attained there is no economic incentive for additional changes. However, in a dynamic economy, change is constantly occurring and equilibrium may never be attained. This is no fault of the market mechanism, nor does it detract from the usefulness of the market system. What counts is that the market, if functioning properly, will be an unbiased arbitrator of economic desires, constantly guiding economic activity toward equilibrium. It is as if an invisible hand were directing the entire economy in the quest for maximizing aggregate well-being.

ELASTICITIES

The information contained in demand and supply curves indicates that consumers will react to a decrease in price by increasing the amount demanded, and producers by decreasing the amount supplied. Similarly, a price increase will cause demanders to reduce their purchase offerings and suppliers to increase theirs. But by how much? The concepts of *elasticity*, defined as the percentage change in quantity divided by the percentage change in price, is used to answer this question. If, in percentage terms, the price change exceeds the resultant quantity change, the demand or supply is said to be *inelastic*. If the reverse is true, then the demand or supply is said to be *elastic*. Finally, if the resultant quantity change is equal in percentage terms to the price change, the demand or supply is said to be of *unitary elasticity*.

The following criteria define the elasticity range:

Elasticity Value	*Elasticity Description*
Less than one	Inelastic
One	Unitary elasticity
Greater than one	Elastic

Measures of elasticity bear a direct relationship to revenue considerations. *Total revenue* (*TR*) for any transaction is defined as the price charged per item (*P*) times the quantity sold (*Q*), that is, $TR = P \cdot Q$. For any given price change the following relationship between demand elasticity and total revenue prevails.

	Total Revenue After a Price	
Demand Elasticity	*Increase*	*Decrease*
Elastic	Decreases	Increases
Unitary	No change	No Change
Inelastic	Increases	Decreases

By definition, an elastic demand curve (or section of a demand curve, since elasticity usually varies over the range of a given curve) implies that the quantity change is proportionately larger than the price change. By referring to the total revenue formula and recalling the price-quantity relationship for a demand curve, one can see that total revenue will decrease when price increases and increase when price decreases. Similarly, by applying the appropriate price-quantity relationships for unitary elasticity and inelasticity, one can easily derive the results seen above.

Elasticity (*e*) is calculated by the use of the following formula

$$e = \frac{\text{percentage change in quantity}}{\text{percentage change in price}}$$

$$= \frac{\text{change in quantity}}{\text{original quantity}} \div \frac{\text{change in price}}{\text{original price}}$$

Substituting the symbol Δ for the term change in, Q for quantity, and P for price, the elasticity formula can be written as

$$e = \frac{\Delta Q}{Q} \div \frac{\Delta P}{P}$$

or

$$e = \frac{\Delta Q}{\Delta P} \cdot \frac{P}{Q}$$

In the case of demand elasticity, the formula becomes

$$e = -\frac{\Delta Q}{Q} \div \frac{\Delta P}{P}$$

The minus sign is introduced so that the value of the elasticity coefficient will be positive, which is desirable for the sake of consistency with supply. In the absence of such an adjustment the inverse relationship between price and quantity characteristic of demand would have yielded a negative elasticity value.

The elasticity coefficient can be calculated in one of two ways, depending on the data available. If an equation for a demand or supply curve is known and one wants to calculate an elasticity coefficient at a given price-quantity combination, *point elasticity* is the appropriate measure. The formula for point elasticity (e_p) is

$$e_p = \frac{dQ}{dP} \cdot \frac{P}{Q}$$

where d is a notation representing differentiation.[7] Given the following demand equation

$$Q = 200 - 20P$$

the point elasticity at any given price or quantity can be calculated. For example, at a quantity of 100 units, price elasticity is 1.[8]

If an equation for the demand or supply curve is unknown and one has information only on two price-quantity combinations, an *arc elasticity* coefficient can be calculated. The formula for calculating arc elasticity (e_a) is

$$e_a = \frac{\dfrac{\Delta Q}{\dfrac{Q_1 + Q_2}{2}}}{\dfrac{\Delta P}{\dfrac{P_1 + P_2}{2}}}$$

Considering the following two price-quantity combinations extracted from Table 3.1

Point	Price	Quantity
B	24	18
C	18	24

the arc elasticity is found to be one, indicating unitary elasticity over this range.[9] In calculating arc elasticities neither point B nor point C was used as the base from which a price and quantity change occurred. Rather, an average of the two points was used. If point B were chosen, e_a would equal 1.33, and if point C were chosen, e_a would be .75.[10] This problem is overcome by using an average as the base.

The elasticity discussion up to this point has been in terms of *price elasticities*—the response in quantity to a change in price. Elasticity measures can be applied to practically any type of economic data with the resulting values interpreted along the lines set forth above. Two major elasticity measures, in addition to price elasticity, bear mentioning. The first is *cross elasticity*, which measures the change in quantity of some good, basketballs (B), in response to a change in the price of some other good, volleyballs (V) $[\Delta Q_B/Q_B \div \Delta P_V/P_V]$. The sign of the cross elasticity coefficient indicates whether the two goods are substitutes (positive sign) or complements (negative sign). The greater the absolute value of the cross elasticity coefficient, the greater the substitutability or complementarity. The second is an *income elasticity* measure $[\Delta Q/Q \div \Delta Y/Y$, where Q = quantity and Y = income] which is interpreted as the relative change in quantity in response to a relative change in income. (In the following chapter we present some research findings on the relationship between a measure of national income and the demand for higher education in the United States.)

ELEMENTS OF THE THEORY OF THE FIRM

Researchers are beginning to analyze educational institutions as firms producing education, and they are applying concepts associated with the *theory of the firm* to education. Consequently, an excursion into this area of microeconomics is useful.

The term *firm* is used in the economics literature to cover all forms of business enterprise ranging from a small business employing only one worker and very little capital to the largest corporate enterprises. The economic characteristic of firms is that they engage in and control the production of goods and services. Having decided to enter a particular field, firms must then decide upon the appropriate size of the enterprise suiting their needs and upon the output level they intend to produce. In reaching these decisions the firms' directors (whether they be the owner(s), the stockholders, or the board of directors) must consider the benefits and costs of each course of action. In conventional economic analysis the benefits of an enterprise are measured by the total revenue obtained from selling the output, and *profits* are the residual after costs are subtracted from benefits. The importance of the theory of the firm is that it provides a framework for the analysis of and a rule for profit maximization. Before the profit maximizing rule can be explained, a discussion of revenue and the cost of production is in order.

Total revenue (TR), as defined previously, is the price charged per item (P), times the quantity sold (Q); or $TR = P \cdot Q$. Once a firm determines the price at which its product will be sold, it can predict with some degree of accuracy the quantity that will be demanded and can then ascertain its total revenue by multiplying this quantity by the price to be charged. However, for purposes of defining its optimum production level, a firm is interested in knowing what additional revenue it will be receiving as it expands its production. Having decided to enter into production, the question of importance is: Should production be carried up to x units, or should it be extended to $x + 1$, $x + 2$, or $x + n$ units? The answer to this question depends, in part, on the additional or *marginal revenue* that can be obtained from additional production.[11] However, revenue considerations account for only half the picture. Cost considerations are also a determinant of the level of production.

Just as the decision makers in the firm want to know the marginal revenue accruing from added production, they also want to know the additional or *marginal cost* that will be incurred by expanding production.[12] It is only when the added costs and revenue can be contrasted that a decision can be reached on whether profits will be increased by expanding production; and only when profits can be increased should added production be undertaken.

The preceding discussion can be generalized into the following rule of production: Produce up to the point where marginal revenue equals marginal cost. If marginal revenue exceeds marginal cost, the returns from the sale of the additional item produced exceeds the cost of production. A profit is being reaped on the production of this marginal unit, and production should be expanded so long as additional profit can be made. Alternately, if marginal cost exceeds marginal revenue, the cost of producing the marginal unit exceeds the added revenue from its sale, a marginal loss is being incurred, and production should be curtailed until such losses are eliminated. Having reached a production point where marginal revenue equals marginal cost, a firm cannot increase its total profits by either expanding or curtailing output. This point on the production scale, where marginal revenue equals marginal cost, is thus an *equilibrium* situation from the vantage point of the firm.

The theory of the firm is frequently challenged as a good prediction of a firm's behavior. The argument that is usually advanced is that many firms do not attempt to maximize only profits. Some firms may be willing to sacrifice some profits for size or control of a market, thus expanding production beyond the most profitable point. Others may value consumer goodwill and may deliberately sacrifice a degree of profitability (by either keeping price too low or quantity too high) to maintain it. These criticisms of the theory, although valid, do not destroy the usefulness of the theory of the firm as a guide to production, namely, produce up to the point where the marginal return equals the marginal cost. If profit maximization is not considered to be the sole object of production, then size, goodwill, or any other desired factors can be chosen as the goal of production. Once the goal has been specified, the equating of marginal benefits to marginal cost insures the maximization of whatever goal is adopted.

How applicable is the theory of the firm to educational decision making? Although there appears to be basic agreement on what are the total costs of operating an educational institution and attempts can be made to quantify them, the issue of an educational institution's revenue is an unsettled one. Can revenue be narrowly equated with tuition? Undoubtedly not, for if it were, there could be no justification for scholarships, fellowships, and other forms of financial aid. Expanding the revenue function to include research contracts from public and private sources, donations from alumni and the public at large, and still other sources of revenue may be a more satisfactory and realistic view of school revenue. If this view is adopted, revenue estimates can indeed be made.

What do educational institutions attempt to maximize? Size, endowment funds, research, or service to the community or the nation at large? Which group, or groups, in the educational institution make these decisions: the trustees, administrators, faculty, or students? These questions are indeed difficult and crucial, and the controversies that they generate underlie much of the recent turmoil in our educational institutions. Nevertheless, many researchers have utilized the basic framework of the theory of the firm to analyze the operation of educational institutions. We refer to this research in the next chapter, illustrating one attempt to cast educational decision making within the mold of an economic firm. The excerpt on student unrest appearing in Chapter 11 is yet another illustration of the applicability of this body of economic theory to educational issues.

Appendix **A** Chapter **3**
Utility Analysis and Consumer Choice

THE discussion of demand theory at the beginning of Chapter 3 was based mainly on intuitive notions. Two additional bodies of economic theory are frequently employed in deriving the law of demand: utility theory and indifference curve theory. Because utility theory and the terminology to which it has given rise are beginning to appear more frequently in research in economics of education, we briefly present the essentials of this method of analysis.[13] Utility theory will then be utilized to illustrate the establishment of consumer equilibrium.

A major assumption underlying the law of demand posits that whereas consumers' total wants may be infinite, wants for specific goods and services are finite, and hence ultimately satiable. In any given time period, if tastes remain unchanged, the greater the quantity of a specific good or service a consumer obtains, the less desirous he becomes of obtaining yet additional units. This can readily be seen by reference to an item of food—a hamburger. The first hamburger consumed at a given time provides tremendous psychological and physical satisfaction. Additional hamburgers continue to make positive contributions to the person's overall sense of well-being, but the additional or marginal contribution of each succeeding hamburger becomes less and less. Ultimately, a stage will be reached when one more hamburger produces revulsion rather than satisfaction.

This phenomenon is known as the *Law of Diminishing Marginal Utility*, where the term utility represents want satisfying power. Utility does not necessarily represent functional usefulness, because it is subjective in nature. For example, a diamond ring may provide enormous utility to a woman, but no utility at all to a little girl. Since the law of diminishing marginal utility implies that successive units of a good or service yield smaller and smaller amounts of utility, the basic assumption of economic rationality leads to the assertion that at a point in time the consumer will increase his consumption of a good or service only if its price falls. Because it is possible to purchase various bundles of goods and services with a specific sum of money, the rational economic man would buy additional units of an item, given the law of diminishing marginal utility, only if the price of successive units declines.[14]

Utility analysis can also be applied to illustrate general consumer equilibrium. The following assertions are basic to the forthcoming analysis:

1. A consumer wants to maximize his utility; stated differently, he wants to get the most for his money.
2. He has a consistent set of preferences that are known to him.
3. His income is limited.
4. All goods and services must be purchased; they are not free.

Given considerations (3) and (4), a consumer will be willing and able to purchase only a limited amount of goods and services. Considerations (1) and (2) decree that purchasers will not choose randomly, but rather on the basis of a systematic scheme aimed at achieving (1). Total satisfaction from aggregate consumption is maximized when money resources are allocated so that the last dollar spent on any item in the overall consumption bundle yields the same amount of marginal (extra) utility as the last dollar spent on any other item. The situation is depicted algebraically as:

$$\frac{MU_a}{P_a} = \frac{MU_b}{P_b} = \cdots = \frac{MU_z}{P_z}$$

(MU = marginal utility; P = price; $a \cdots z$ = the spectrum of goods and services consumed)

and states that the ratio of the marginal utility to price of all goods and services purchased must be equal.

If this equality does not hold, a consumer can maximize his satisfaction by shifting consumption away from goods or services whose MU/P ratios are low to those whose MU/P ratios are high. A high MU/P ratio indicates that the satisfaction reaped from consuming these items is high relative to their price. By consuming more of these goods or services, total satisfaction is increased. However, as additional units of goods and services with relatively high MU/P ratios are consumed, the value of these ratios declines. The law of diminishing marginal utility postulates an inverse relationship between marginal utility and quantity consumed. Thus, additional consumption of these items entails consuming units with lower and lower marginal utility values thereby depressing their MU/P ratios.[15] Similarly, the reduction in the consumption of those goods or services with relatively low MU/P ratios causes their ratios to increase. When the consumption of any good or service is curtailed, the marginal utility of the remaining units of the item consumed is higher than the marginal utility of the units given up. Consequently, by shifting consumption away from those items with low MU/P ratios to those with high MU/P ratios, consumer satisfaction is increased. When a point is reached where the consumer cannot gain anything from shifting a dollar from the purchase of one item to that of another, an equilibrium point has been achieved and consumer satisfaction is maximized. In practice consumer equilibrium may be reached at a point where the MU/P ratios of all the goods or services consumed are not precisely equal. However, since minute adjustments cannot be made due to its usually being impossible to buy a fraction of a unit (for example, 1/2 of a car), this is the best that can be done.

A numerical example will help to clarify the utility maximizing rule. Assume an entertainment budget of $22 and two sources of entertainment: the theater (T) and the ballet (B). Suppose that a typical consumer states, on response to a query, that his marginal utility schedules for T and B are as follows.

T		B	
	Units of Marginal		Units of Marginal
Unit	Utility	Unit	Utility
1st	110	1st	60
2nd	80	2nd	35
3rd	40	3rd	20
4th	5	4th	10
5th	0	5th	0

If tickets per performance cost $8 for T and $6 for B, utility maximization would be reached with the purchase of $2T$ and $1B$, for only at that combination is the rule of $MU_T/P_T = MU_B/P_B$ satisfied. Purchasing $1T$ and $2B$ yields only 205 units of utility, as compared to 250 units of utility when $2T$ and $1B$ are consumed. Other combinations composed of more than $2T$ and $1B$ are not feasible given the assumed prices of T and B and the budget constraint of $22. Should the marginal utility schedule change as a result of changes in taste for either T or B or both, or should the price of T or B change, a new utility maximization combination would result.

Economists realize and readily admit that the utility concept is a theoretical one, and it is not easily converted into operational terms because no precise measure has been devised to determine utility. However, most people do typically follow what we can describe as the system of marginal utility calculus. The teacher who asks himself whether he should assign book A or book B as a text for his course, given that the former costs \$2 more, is indulging in marginal utility analysis. Albeit in a loose fashion, we are all marginal utility estimators and marginal utility/price analysts.

Appendix **B**   Chapter **3**
Cost Curves

IN this appendix the nature of the supply curve is developed in a more rigorous manner than that presented in Chapter 3. Here cost curves are developed to show the underlying reasons for the particular shape of any supply curve. A knowledge of the structure of these curves is useful for understanding problems of cost and supply.

The basic consideration determining the ability and willingness of a firm to supply a good or service is the cost of its production. One important factor determining the costs of production is the time horizon considered. The longer the time period, the greater the possibility of making adjustments and changes in the production process, and thus reducing costs. Whereas most labor resources used in production can be varied quickly and easily, capital resources are not as flexible. Existing machinery can be used more or less intensively, but new machinery often cannot be ordered and assembled without experiencing a delay of months. Due to this time factor, economists differentiate between the *short run* and the *long run*. The short run is defined as the period during which adjustments can be made only in the labor resources and materials used in production.[16] Calling labor a variable factor and capital a fixed factor, we can redefine the short run as the period when only the variable inputs can be changed and the long run as the period when variable and fixed factors can both be changed. Thus, new firms cannot begin production during the period defined as the short run. While firms can cease production in the short run, they can terminate their existence only in the long run, because time is required for the liquidation of fixed factors of production.

The ensuing discussion and derivation of hypothetical cost curves is focussed on the short run period. Cost curves similar to those to be derived for the short run can be derived for the long run, with the long run cost curves having shapes and characteristics similar to their short run counterparts. In the long run a distinction between variable and fixed costs is irrelevant because all costs are then variable.

Costs of production are determined by multiplying the number of units of each factor used in production by their respective costs. Costs arising from the utilization of fixed factors are known as *fixed costs*; costs arising from the utilization of variable factors are known as *variable costs*. The relationship between costs and output is not a constant one, as seen in the first two columns of Table 3.3. As production begins *variable costs* and *total costs*, where total costs are the sum of the variable and fixed costs, increase at a decreasing rate. For example, if the variable cost for one unit is 40, the variable cost for two and three units might be 75 and 105, the increase falling from 40 to 35 to 30. This phenomenon is often ignored because it is probably applicable only to a limited quantity range, and it would generally be irrational to produce quantities in this range of decreasing average variable cost. After a point (the fourth unit of output in our example), they begin to increase at an increasing rate. (This is owing to the Law of Decreasing Marginal Returns to a Factor, which is presented in Chapter 5.) This cost relationship is shown diagrammatically in Figure 3.7.

Table 3.3

Total, Average, and Marginal Cost Schedule

(1) Units of Output	(2) Total Cost	(3) Fixed Cost	(4) Variable Cost	(5) Average Total Cost	(6) Average Fixed Cost	(7) Average Variable Cost	(8) Marginal Cost
0	$200	$200	$ 0				$ 40
1	240	200	40	$240.00	$200.00	$40.00	35
2	275	200	75	137.50	100.00	37.50	30
3	305	200	105	101.67	66.67	35.00	25
4	330	200	130	82.50	50.00	32.50	30
5	360	200	160	72.00	40.00	32.50	35
6	395	200	195	65.83	33.33	32.00	45
7	440	200	240	62.86	28.58	34.28	60
8	500	200	300	62.50	25.00	37.50	80
9	580	200	380	64.44	22.22	42.22	100
10	680	200	480	68.00	20.00	48.00	

Average cost schedules can easily be derived from the total schedules by dividing total costs by the number of units produced. Average cost schedules depict in a clearer manner the cost developments as production increases. The fifth, sixth, and seventh columns of Table 3.3 present the average total, average fixed, and average variable cost schedules corresponding to the three total cost schedules. Figure 3.8 contains a diagrammatic exposition of the average cost curves.

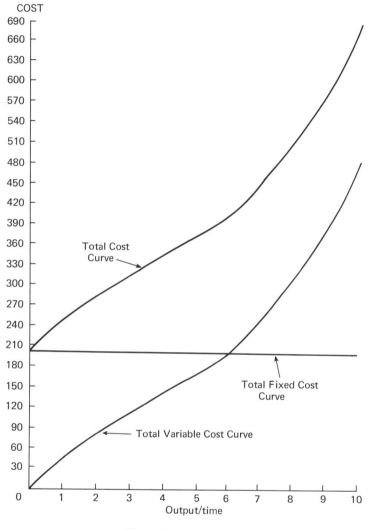

Figure 3.7   Total Cost Curves

Average fixed costs decline as output increases because the given fixed costs are divided among more and more units as production continues. *Average variable costs* decline at the beginning, reflecting that part of total variable costs that increases at a decreasing rate. Beyond a point, they begin to increase. *Average total cost* is simply the vertical summation of average fixed and average variable costs. Average total costs

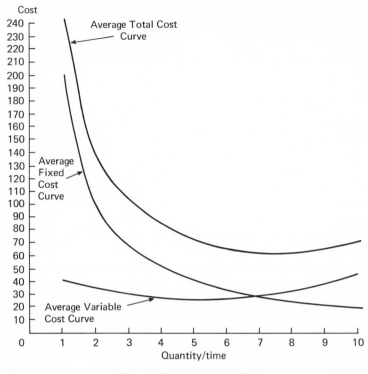

Figure 3.8 Average Cost Curves

decline as production begins, reflecting the greater weight at that stage attributed to the declining average fixed costs. However, a point is reached where the rate of decline of average fixed costs is outweighed by the increase of average variable costs, and thereafter average total costs also increase.

One final cost curve must be derived before we have the necessary economic tools to explain the upward sloping shape of the supply curve. This cost concept is called *marginal cost*. The word marginal here, as elsewhere, connotes additional or extra so that marginal cost is the addition to total costs from an additional unit of output. Marginal costs are presented in the last column of Table 3.3 and are shown diagrammatically in Figure 3.9 together with the corresponding average cost curves. One interesting property of production costs is immediately noticeable from Figure 3.9, namely, that the marginal curve crosses both the average total cost and average variable cost curves at their lowest points. This marginal-average relationship results from mathematical rather than economic precepts.

The marginal cost curve resembles the supply curve and, with but one qualification, it is the supply curve. The qualification is that the segment of the marginal cost curve below the intersection of the marginal cost and average variable cost curves is excluded because the firm would not produce, in either the short or long run if variable costs could not be covered. Producing would entail losses equal to fixed costs plus that part of variable costs that are not recouped, whereas halting production would entail losses equal to fixed costs only.

The cost concepts and hypothetical curves developed in this appendix are frequently used in analyses of the operating costs of educational institutions and in studies of educational productivity. Many of the concepts presented in Chapters 5 and 6 are closely connected with these cost curves.

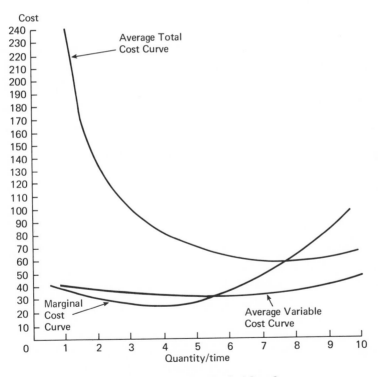

Figure 3.9   Average and Marginal Cost Curves

QUESTIONS FOR DISCUSSION

1. What factors determine a school system's demand for a particular set of mathematics books? Changes in which of these factors would represent a movement along the school's demand curve for mathematics books, and which represent a shift in the school's demand curve?

2. Given that all children in the United States are legally required to attend school, in what sense might families' demands for education differ?

3. What factors determine the supply of private education? How applicable is supply theory to the question of providing private educational facilities?

4. Is the market for higher education in equilibrium? Why?

5. What is the marginal cost of educating one more pupil at your university? One hundred more pupils? One thousand more pupils? Does your university appear to equate marginal costs and marginal revenue in any of its policy decisions? In what additional areas can it apply this decision rule?

PROBLEMS

1. Given the demand schedule in Table 3.1, how much revenue would be generated from the sale of 18 units?

2. Basing your calculations on the price-quantity data appearing in Table 3.1, calculate the arc elasticities over ranges *AB* and *DE*.

3. Plot the following demand and supply schedules:

Demand		Supply	
Price	*Quantity*	*Price*	*Quantity*
$8	6	$7	25
5	9	5	18
4	12	3	10
2	20	2	4

What are the equilibrium price and quantity (approximately)?

Chapter 4 BASIC STUDIES IN EDUCATIONAL DEMAND AND SUPPLY

THE economic theories and tools developed in Chapter 3 have wide applicability in the educational enterprise. Interesting research is appearing that treats educational institutions as firms producing education.[1] Such research attempts are still in their infancy and are not reproduced here. The concepts of demand, supply, and market equilibrium, however, have long been utilized by educational researchers with interesting results. Three illustrations are the projection and interpretation of trends in the demand for education, an analysis of the supply of and the demand for faculty, and an analysis of the effects on higher education enrollment of a graduated tuition program in state universities. The articles reprinted below illustrate conceptual and empirical approaches to these research areas and highlight crucial issues confronting educational administrators and policy-makers.

The Campbell and Siegel article, "The Demand for Higher Education in the United States, 1919–1964," develops a demand model for explaining fluctuations in the demand for higher education in the United States during the period 1919–1964.[2] The demand model in this article is based on conventional demand theory, highlighting the role of income and prices in consumer decision making. Real disposable income per household, where disposable income is defined as personal income minus income taxes, and an index of tuition costs are used by the authors as their income and price variables, respectively.

In the empirical section of their article Campbell and Siegel, by utilizing regression analysis, test the hypothesis that the demand for higher education is a function of income and price. This statistical

Notes to Chapter 4 will be found on pages 366–371.

tool attempts to explain the variance in one variable (demand) based on the corresponding variance in a set of other variables (income and price).[3] The authors implicitly assume that proportional changes in price and income will have proportional effects on demand. That is, a given percentage increase in the determinants of demand, income and price, will always have the same effect on demand in percentage terms. For example, a 10 per cent change in income will have the same percentage effect on demand whether income was initially at a level of 10 or 1,000 units. Although a 10 per cent increase in the former case is an increase of 1 unit, and in the latter case an increase of 100 units, the effect in terms of an increase in demand is the same. As a result of this assumption, an *exponential* demand model in the form of $D = f(Y^a P^b)$ is postulated because exponentials exhibit the type of relationship described above. Because conventional regression analysis can be performed only on linear equations, a logarithmic transformation of the demand model is required.[4] This transformation yields a linear demand equation of the following form: $\log D = a \log Y + b \log P$, where D, Y, and P are demand, income, and price, and a and b are the regression coefficients to be estimated.

Given the data on prices, income, and enrollment for the period being investigated, the value of the parameters (a and b) are estimated. The values of the coefficients of the income and tuition (price) variables derived from the regression analysis are estimates of the effect of a given percentage change of those variables on demand. For example, the coefficient of income ($\log Y$) is found to be $+1.2036$. Therefore, a 10 per cent increase in income will lead to a 12.036 per cent (1.2036×10 per cent) increase in demand. Because the equation was specified in logarithmic form, the coefficients of the income and price variables are also income and price elasticities of demand.[5]

The Campbell and Siegel model and the results derived from a statistical analysis of the historical data can be used to predict changes in the demand for higher education by projecting changes in income and price (tuition), inserting these projections into the model, and deriving the implied demand.[6]

The Cartter article, "The Supply and Demand for College Teachers," utilizes the concepts of demand and supply to analyze aspects of disequilibrium in the higher education market for faculty with doctorates. Cartter begins his analysis by noting that the extensive literature on the subject of faculty shortages prepared by the National Education Association (NEA) reports only one component of the total supply—new faculty receiving their doctorates. Persons who were teaching before receiving their doctorates who remain in teaching and doctorate transfers into teaching from other occupations are omitted thus biasing the NEA reports.

Cartter constructs a demand and supply model for projecting the number of faculty with doctorates. This model is claimed to be an extension of and an improvement over the one used by the U.S. Office of Education. Cartter generates a new data series based on his model of the projected number of faculty with doctorates from 1965 through 1985 and finds that the NEA's conclusion of a continuing shortage of faculty with doctorates in higher education is erroneous. Cartter predicts a surplus rather than a deficit.[7] Interesting implications for (graduate) educational planning and the relative economic status of college faculty emerge from Cartter's findings.

The Burns and Chiswick article, "Analysis of the Effects of a Graduated Tuition Program at State Universities," analyzes a hypothetical reestablishment of market equilibrium in the higher education market after state universities substitute graduated tuition—tuition directly related to wealth—for the current system of free or nominal tuition. The authors present their analysis against the background of increased demand for higher education since World War II and the concurrent increase in educational costs, factors that prompt the serious consideration of a graduated tuition scheme.

Burns and Chiswick attempt to formulate their analysis along the lines of the theory of the firm, highlighting profit maximization as the goal of production. Within the context of an educational institution, profit maximization is interpreted rather broadly and imaginatively with interesting results. The authors note that whereas price (tuition) does not function as a market regulator in education, rationing of enrollment must occur. Two rationing criteria are posited: fixed minimum quality and fixed maximum quantity. Under both rationing criteria the authors postulate changes in the composition of the student body attending private and public universities, level of state control over public institutions, and the degree of student freedom resulting from the implementation of a graduated tuition program. The article raises many crucial educational questions and demonstrates how one can theorize about an educational problem in economic terms.

THE DEMAND FOR HIGHER EDUCATION IN THE UNITED STATES, 1919–1964

ROBERT CAMPBELL AND BARRY N. SIEGEL

This is a study of the demand for higher education in the United States for the period since World War I. The study is based upon aggregate enrollment data and it uses the rather common economic variables of income and price (tuition) to explain the movements of demand during the period. To anticipate our conclusions, we have found that these two variables explain some 87 per cent of the variation of demand for higher education as we have measured it. In addition, we have found that demand responds positively to changes in income and negatively to changes in price. We believe that these results have important implications for the theory of educational demand and for the conduct of national educational policy.

THEORETICAL BASIS OF DEMAND ESTIMATES

Our results make sense only if we can put them in touch with a reasonable theory of educational demand. There are two not necessarily mutually exclusive approaches to such a theory. One approach views the decision to enroll in an institution of higher education as an investment decision, while the other views it as a current consumption decision. Both of these approaches can be integrated for the purposes of this paper.

The investment approach[8] to the theory of educational demand asserts that an individual will purchase a college education if the present value of the expected stream of benefits resulting from the education exceeds the present cost of the education.[9] The expected stream of benefits includes two elements: the additional lifetime money income resulting from higher education and the additional social and intellectual amenities which a person might expect to receive as a result of having gone to college. The first benefit makes a college education similar to a producer durable, while the second causes it to resemble a consumer durable, whose yield is real rather than monetary.

The cost of a college education must also be viewed rather broadly. It includes direct money outlays in the form of tuition and fees, books, differential living costs, and other outlays incident to going to school. An enrollment also entails indirect financial burdens in the form of oppor-

Reprinted from the *American Economic Review* 57 (1967): 482–94. Copyright © 1967 by The American Economic Association.

tunity costs, as measured by the loss of income incurred while in school. Finally, there are non-monetary costs which include such things as the burden of study and, for some students, the pain of being away from home.

As with other investments, purchase of an education entails risks. The expected stream of benefits may fail to materialize, either because the student may fail to complete his education or because expected posteducational opportunities may not materialize.

An individual facing an enrollment decision presumably makes his decision in the light of the expected benefits and costs involved in an enrollment. For any given set of benefits and costs there will be an implied rate of return on the educational investment. The rate of return will be composed of two parts, one relating to the stream of monetary benefits and costs and another relating to the nonmonetary benefits and costs. Conceptually, these two elements are incommensurate; hence, we must imagine that the individual places some sort of monetary valuation upon the real part of the stream of benefits and costs. Whether or not individuals actually do this is, of course, an open question. Indeed, it is difficult to imagine how, in principle, such valuations can be made. The value to the individual of the stream of expected real benefits should equal the minimum compensation the individual would accept in order to induce him to give up those benefits but still undertake his education. In a similar vein, the real costs of an education may be valued by the maximum amount of money a person would pay to avoid them, while still expecting to receive the future stream of benefits. Such a procedure implies that real benefits can be sold and that relief from real costs can be bought. It is hard to see how this can be done. Fortunately, it is not our purpose here to measure the expected rate of return on an educational investment. Nevertheless, since such a concept is crucial to the investment approach, we shall assume that individuals act according to estimates of such a rate of return, with due allowance for the riskiness of their investments.[10]

Ordinary investment theory would have the individual compare his expected rate of return with some appropriate interest rate. An education will be purchased if the expected rate of return exceeds the rate of interest. The education will not be purchased if the interest rate exceeds the rate of return. An aggregate demand schedule for enrollments may then be derived by arraying individuals according to their expected rates of return (from highest to lowest). The total number of enrollments demanded will equal the aggregate of all enrollments for which the rate of return exceeds the rate of interest. Variations in the rate of interest will lead to inverse variations in the number of enrollments demanded.

This theory of enrollment demand depends heavily upon the assumption that loan capital will be available to all those who wish to purchase an investment. Although the situation is changing rapidly, this assumption is a bad one. The supply of credit for educational lending is still highly imperfect, and most individuals must depend upon personal or family resources, personal loans, or gifts and scholarships. For this reason, we should expect the actual demand schedule for enrollments to be below the schedule described above, since there will be many profitable educational investments which cannot be made for lack of finance. We should also expect aggregate demand to be relatively insensitive to changes in market rates of interest.

Variations in enrollment demand are related to variations in the factors affecting the expected rate of return. A general rise in expected money income, or a reduction in the uncertainty of acquiring the income, from educational investments, should increase the demand for higher education. An increase in the cost of educational investments, either in the form of an increase in opportunity costs or in the form of increased direct money outlays, should lead to a reduction in educational demand. Finally, because people must substitute personal for borrowed resources, we may expect the demand for education to vary directly with disposable family or household income.

Turning to the consumption approach to educational demand, we have already argued that a college education can be considered as a consumer durable, yielding a stream of future services over the lifetime of the individual. It is also true that an enrollment may bring current consumption benefits. These benefits include the many social, intellectual, and athletic activities available in most colleges and universities in the United States. We cannot directly measure the value of these benefits, but we may suppose that it is in some approximate sense measured by the outlays an individual would have to make to buy a substitute bundle of goods and activities outside of college. This method of valuation implies that the cost of current consumption benefits varies directly with the prices of consumer goods in general.

The consumption approach supplements and enriches the investment theory of educational demand in several ways. First, it allows us to offset part of the current costs of enrollment with a positive current benefit. Second, it allows us to strengthen the predicted effect of income upon the demand for enrollments. If both future and present consumption benefits from education are normal goods, an increase in income should lead directly to an increase in enrollment demand. This income effect is quite separate from the earlier effect mentioned in connection with the lack of loan capital.

Finally, the consumption approach allows us to argue that educational demand is sensitive to the money costs of an enrollment relative to current consumer goods prices. For, consider a rise in the price level of all consumer goods relative to current tuition charges and other enrollment costs. Such a rise implies a reduction in the cost of the future consumption benefits from an education relative to the cost of present consumption goods in general. Conventional demand theory suggests that such a reduction will lead to the substitution of future consumption (through increased enrollments) for present consumption. An additional effect, working in the same direction, arises from the fact that the current consumption benefits from enrollments are valued by their substitutes among other consumer goods. The increase in consumer goods' prices raises the value of the current consumption benefit from enrollments. Since the value of the current consumption benefit offsets the money and real costs of an enrollment, the net cost of enrollments should fall. This, in turn, works to raise the expected rate of return from education and, hence, to increase enrollment demand.

In summary, our theory argues that, for a given population, enrollment demand should vary positively with expected money and real yields from education, positively with income, positively with the consumer price index, and negatively with the money and real costs of education. We now proceed to the empirical specification of the demand model.

MEASUREMENT OF DEMAND

Enrollment data provide the most obvious source of information on demand. It is customary to express enrollment as a ratio of some relevant population group in order to measure the intensity or pervasiveness of demand for higher education within the relevant group. The U.S. Office of Education, for example, publishes widely used ratios of enrollments of various types (undergraduate, graduate, etc.) to both the 18–21 and the 18–24 year old age groups [8, p. 76]. While such ratios may be useful for some purposes, they are not useful for ours. We need a measure which relates enrollments to those in a position to choose to go on to college at any particular point in time. People lacking a high school diploma or its equivalent, for example, are rarely in a position to enter an institution of higher education of any sort. Neither is it possible for people who are institutionalized, immobilized for reasons of health, or who are members of the armed forces to go to college, even if they possess high school diplomas. It is for these reasons that we have chosen to measure demand with the ratio of undergraduate enrollment to those in the 18–24 year age group who possess high school diplomas and who are not in the armed forces. We shall call this group the *eligible college age population* or, for short, the "eligibles." [11]

Figure 4.1 plots the movements of enrollments, eligibles, and the 18–24 year population on a semilogarithmic scale for the years 1919 to 1964. For reasons which will be explained below, we have chosen to use resident undergraduate degree enrollment in four-year institutions as our measure of demand. Movements of the enrollment ratio as we would measure it can be inferred from the vertical distance between the top two series. The ratio published by the Office of Education is measured by the vertical distance between the top and the bottom series. The chart shows that the ratio of enrollment to the total 18–24 year group has risen continuously and extensively since 1919, whereas the ratio of enrollment to the eligible college age population has had no trend during the same period.[12] The rise in the Office of Education ratio is evidently due to the increase over the period in the proportion of people in the 18–24 year group who have completed a high school education. We do not know if this long run increase in demand for high school diplomas is derived from the demand for higher

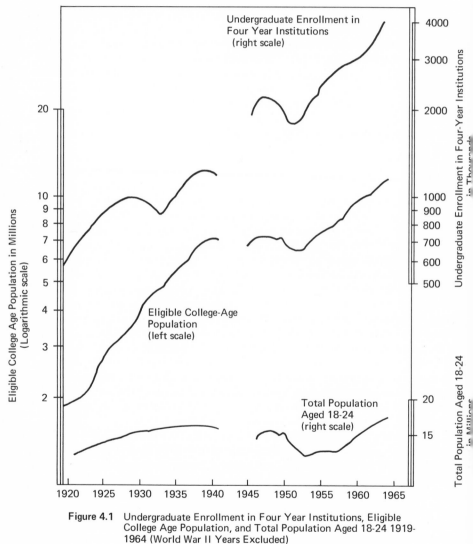

Figure 4.1   Undergraduate Enrollment in Four Year Institutions, Eligible College Age Population, and Total Population Aged 18-24 1919-1964 (World War II Years Excluded)

Sources: See Appendix

education, or from a combination of factors including the demand for higher education. We do believe, however, that the demand for high school diplomas is sufficiently complex to warrant a separate study. Here we confine ourselves to the problem of the demand for higher education among those who are in a position to make a choice for or against going to college, *i.e.*, among those we have defined as the eligible college age population.

Although there was no trend in the ratio of undergraduate enrollment to the eligible group during the 1919–64 period, Figure 4.1 does reveal that the ratio fluctuated during the period. It began to fall in the late 1920s and remained depressed during the 1930s. After World War II the ratio increased and fluctuated around its level for the 1920s. While the absence of trend in the ratio suggests that there has been no basic change in the taste for higher education among those in a position to choose to go to college, the fluctuations in the ratio strongly suggest the existence of a relationship between the demand for higher education and the economic variables discussed above.

FORMULATION OF THE EMPIRICAL DEMAND MODEL

Ideally, a statistical test of the theory of enrollment demand would require data on both educational costs and finance as well as expected differential income streams for those eligible to enroll. We do not have all the necessary data, even to an approximation, in the form of continuous time series. We do have, however, some data which can be related to elements in the earlier described model.

The financial costs of investing in college enrollment can be represented by an index of tuitions, deflated by the consumer price index.[13] Since this is equivalent to introducing the familiar relative price variable of demand analysis, it should also help to explain the demand for enrollments as present and future consumer goods. Similarly, consideration of both the producer and consumer good aspects of an enrollment requires data on both the amounts and sources of funds used to purchase enrollments. Since we have limited information on such matters for the period of time of the study, we have chosen to use estimates of real disposable income per household. We assume that other financial resources vary with this measure.[14]

The model also calls for some measure of opportunity costs. We have not included such a variable primarily because it is difficult to find a satisfactory measure. Income from jobs available to high school graduates provides, to be sure, a measure of opportunity costs. To some extent, this measure is already included in our household income variable. Nevertheless, it is still not clear that the availability of such jobs works consistently in the direction of reducing enrollment demand. Students who work draw their incomes from jobs very similar to those available to young high school graduates who do not enroll in college. Hence, an increase in such opportunities may well work to increase, as well as to decrease demand. Because of this ambiguity, we have decided to exclude opportunity costs from the test of the model.

A formal statement of the model is given by equation (1):

$$N_t = f_1(Y_{Ht}, P_t, E_t) \qquad (1)$$

where N_t is undergraduate degree enrollment in 4-year institutions in year t, Y_{Ht} is real disposable income per household in year t, P_t is average real tuition in year t, and E_t is the number of 18–24 year old eligibles in year t.

For equation (1) to provide a test of our demand model, certain conditions must be satisfied. The most inportant is that enrollments not be constrained by institutional restrictions, *e.g.*, entrance requirements beyond the minimum requirement of a high school diploma. Since N_t is the aggregate of undergraduate enrollments in 4-year institutions, we believe that we can assume such constraints away. In the United States, there is probably an institution of higher education for virtually anyone who both possesses a high school diploma and has the necessary financial resources.[15]

In addition, we assume: (a) that the enrollment demand function is homogeneous,[16] and (b) that eligibles over the period of the test have not, on the average, changed their tastes for higher education.

Since we wish to study the *ratio* of enrollments to eligibles, we can convert equation (1) into the general form

$$\frac{N_t}{E_t} = R_t = f_1(Y_{Ht}, P_t). \qquad (2)$$

Note that equation (2) requires f_1 to be homogeneous of degree one in E_t, *i.e.*, that changes in E_t do not carry with them compositional changes in the population of eligibles which might affect R_t. Among such changes, for example, would be relative increases in eligible individuals who have strong preferences for higher education. We believe that our statistical results support this assumption and turn now to the estimation of the demand function.

ESTIMATION OF THE DEMAND FUNCTION

Figure 4.2 presents on a logarithmic scale the raw materials for our test: (1) the ratio of undergraduate enrollment in 4-year institutions to eligible 18–24 year olds; (2) real disposable income per household; and (3) an index of tuition costs deflated by the consumers' price index. Note that only nine observations for the period 1927–63 appear in the figure. While we have more complete data on the enrollment ratio and real disposable income per household, ready estimates of tuition costs are available only for the nine years indicated.[17]

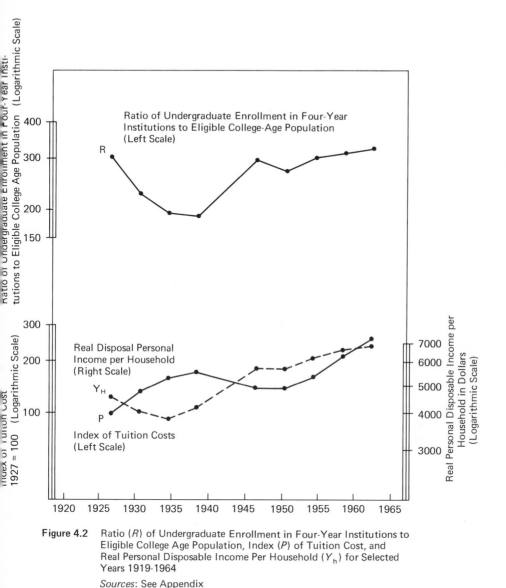

Figure 4.2   Ratio (R) of Undergraduate Enrollment in Four-Year Institutions to
Eligible College Age Population, Index (P) of Tuition Cost, and
Real Personal Disposable Income Per Household (Y_h) for Selected
Years 1919-1964

Sources: See Appendix

Inspection of Figure 4.2 appears to support our hypotheses about the
behavior of the demand for education. The enrollment ratio tends to vary
directly with variations in real household income and inversely with the
index of relative tuition costs. In the 1950s and 1960s the enrollment ratio
approximated its value in the 1920s. Without our hypothesis concerning

the importance of price, this would be puzzling behavior. Real household income was much higher in the 1950s and 1960s than it was during the 1920s, and one would have expected higher income to have a positive effect on the ratio. We believe that the absence of an upward trend in the enrollment ratio during 1919–64 was due to the negative influence of price offsetting the positive influence of income on the demand for higher education.

Although only nine observations[18] were usable for regression analysis, we feel these years to be sufficiently representative of the period as a whole to justify such an analysis. Our regression took the form:

$$R_t = b Y_{Ht}^{\alpha} P_t^{\beta} \text{ or taking logarithms,} \tag{3}$$

$$\log R_t = \log b + \alpha \log Y_{Ht} + \beta \log P_t \tag{3a}$$

The regression tests our hypotheses (1) that the income effect upon R_t is positive (that $\alpha > 0$) and (2) that the price effect is negative (that $\beta < 0$). The results are consistent with these hypotheses (standard errors are in parentheses):

$$\log R_t = .7425 + 1.2036 \log Y_{Ht} - .4404 \log P_t \tag{3b}$$
$$(.3702)* \quad (.1942)\dagger \qquad (.1506)\ddagger$$

$$\text{Coefficient of Multiple Correlation} = .9316$$
$$F = 19.701$$
$$F_{.01} = 10.92$$

Unfortunately, our results do not permit a verification of our belief that R_t was trendless during the 1919–64 period because of the offsetting effects of income and price. Although α and β possess the necessary signs, the rather large standard errors associated with their estimated values rules out a precise prediction of R_t. At the same time, while we have not verified our hypothesis, we certainly have not rejected it.

TWO-YEAR COLLEGE ENROLLMENTS

The estimated demand function—equation (3b)—relates the ratio of undergraduate enrollment in 4-year institutions to the eligibles in the 18–24 year old age group. The calculations exclude both graduate students and students enrolled in 2-year institutions. It is perfectly legitimate to exclude graduate students, since both the age levels and eligibility requirements for graduate work differ sharply from the age levels and eligibility requirements for undergraduate work.

* Not significant, using $t_{.05}$ in a two-tailed test.
† Significantly greater than zero, using $t_{.005}$ in a one-tailed test.
‡ Significantly less than zero, using $t_{.025}(= 2.447)$ in a one-tailed test.

The exclusion of enrollments in 2-year institutions, however, does not have equal legitimacy. To be sure, a high school diploma is not necessary for matriculation in many of these institutions and vocational training, not ordinary college work, is the objective of many students in these institutions. Nevertheless, we are uncomfortable with the exclusion of enrollments in 2-year institutions, since an enrollment in a 2-year institution can be a substitute for an enrollment in the freshman and sophomore level in a 4-year institution.

Since there is no firm basis for separating students who seek vocational training from those who use a 2-year institution as a substitute for a 4-year school,[19] these students can be treated in only two ways: (a) we can exclude them from the enrollment ratio, as we have done, or (b) we can include them in the ratio and seek an interpretation of the change in the ratio.

If enrollments in 2-year institutions are included in the numerator of the enrollment ratio, a definite upward trend appears. As Table 4.1 indicates, most of the trend appears after World War II, a period during which the number of junior colleges and community colleges expanded rapidly.

If we choose to regard the bulk of enrollments in 2-year institutions as substitutes for enrollments in the first two years of 4-year institutions, the theory outlined above can easily explain the resulting upward trend

Table 4.1

Enrollment Ratios for Undergraduates, Selected Years 1919–64

Year	2- and 4-Year Institutions (1)	4-Year Institutions Only (2)	Difference Between (1) and (2)
1919	.328	.323	.005
1927	.320	.305	.015
1931	.246	.225	.021
1939	.201	.179	.022
1947	.332	.299	.033
1951	.309	.276	.033
1952	.321	.277	.044
1953	.339	.290	.049
1954	.348	.299	.049
1955	.356	.305	.051
1956	.377	.323	.054
1957	.382	.326	.056
1958	.382	.326	.056
1959	.371	.316	.055
1960	.368	.311	.057
1961	.372	.310	.062
1962	.384	.317	.067
1963	.393	.326	.067
1964	.395	.326	.069

Sources: See Appendix.

in the enrollment ratio. Two-year colleges are usually low cost institutions—in terms of living costs, tuition, and fees—relative to most competing 4-year institutions. In addition, their closeness to students' homes and their flexible programs make it relatively easier for students to acquire part-time employment. Finally, the presence of many low quality students in these institutions reduces competition for able students. The combination of easier financial burdens plus less intensive competition reduces the risk of not completing schooling anticipated by many students in the first 2 years of college. Lower costs, easier work opportunities, and reduced risk all work in the direction of increasing the demand for higher education.

CONCLUSION

Our empirical results are easily summarized in two propositions: (1) Since 1919 there has been no trend in the ratio of enrollments in 4-year institutions to the eligible population; and (2) the fluctuations in the ratio which have taken place are associated with fluctuations in disposable income per family and an index of tuition as deflated by the consumer price index. The income and price elasticities of demand (using the enrollment ratio as a measure of demand) are $+1.20$ and $-.44$. Although both of these elasticities were statistically significant when tested against the null hypothesis, we are well aware that our small sample of observations has prevented us from making reliable estimates of the elasticity coefficients. It follows that the results of the study are less useful for forecasting purposes than they might have been with a larger sample. We do believe, however, that the results substantiate, at least in part, the model of educational demand we postulated in the paper. Unfortunately, however, the model we used was a hybrid investment-consumption model, and our results cannot be used to separate out the contribution of each of these elements to the demand for higher education. Such a separation is, in our minds, a useful area for further research.

References

1. G. S. BECKER, *Human Capital: A Theoretical and Empirical Analysis*, New York 1964.
2. M. BLAUG, "The Rate of Return on Investment in Education in Great Britain," *Manchester School*, Sept. 1965, *33*, 205–51.
3. ——, "An Economic Interpretation of the Private Demand for Education," *Economica*, May 1966, *33*, 166–82.
4. A. CARRTER AND R. FARRELL, "Higher Education in the Last Third of the Century," *Educ. Record*, Spring 1965, *46*, 119–31.
5. B. A. JAFFE AND W. ADAMS, "Trends in College Enrollment," *College Board Review*, Winter 1964–65, *55*, 27–32.
6. J. LANSING, T. LORIMER, AND C. MORIGUCHI, *How People Pay for College.* Ann Arbor 1960.

7. T. W. Schultz, "Investment in Human Capital," *Am. Econ. Rev.*, March 1961, *51*, 1–17.
8. U.S. Office of Education, *Digest of Educational Statistics*. Washington 1964.

Appendix: Sources and Methods of Statistical Estimates

1. *Eligible College Age Population.* With certain exclusions, this group was estimated from 7-year cumulative totals of high school graduates, beginning with the seventh year prior to the year for which the estimate was required. *Historical Statistics of the United States, Colonial Times to 1957* (1960) and the *Statistical Abstract of the United States* (both published by the U.S. Department of Commerce) provided data for most of the years. Since graduation data appeared biannually for most of these years, it was necessary to interpolate for the missing years. The elements of the cumulative totals were adjusted for death rates. Armed service high school graduates in the 18–24 age group were estimated for 1940 to 1964 by taking the ratio of the 7-year cumulative total to the total 18–24 year age group and multiplying the result by the number of 18–24 year servicemen (calculated from the *Current Population Report*, P-25, #98, U.S. Bureau of the Census). Since age breakdowns of servicemen prior to 1940 are not available, the ratio was multiplied by the total number of enlisted men for these years, on the assumption that this group comprised the bulk of servicemen in the appropriate age group. Official data on the age and educational composition of the armed forces are extremely sketchy, especially for earlier years. Nevertheless, perusal of *Selected Manpower Statistics* (Directorate for Statistical Services, Office of the Secretary of Defense, 19 February, 1965) will show that our assumptions are warranted for the years since 1948. As noted in the text, we did not have estimates of the institutionalized population in the appropriate age group. More important, we did not exclude people in the 18–24 age group who had already received college degrees. We do not think that the year-to-year variation in the enrollment ratio will be much affected by the inclusion of this group. In any event, we had no hard data on the age distribution over time of college graduates.

2. *Enrollment Data.* *Historical Statistics* and the *Digest of Educational Statistics* [8] provided the basic sources for our estimates. It was necessary to splice together earlier and later enrollment estimates in order to put them on a comparable basis. Those presented in *Historical Statistics* for 1919–53 were based upon cumulative estimates for the academic year. Those presented in the *Digest* were for Fall enrollments, 1939, and 1946–64. The Fall enrollment figures were "blown up" by a factor relating the Fall and cumulative enrollments in four common years. In addition, in order to derive undergraduate enrollments it was necessary to estimate graduate student enrollments for a number of years.

The quality of the pre-World War II enrollment figures has long been suspect by students of higher education. Jaffe and Adams [5], for example, chose to work with backward projections of census data rather than enrollment data for this reason. We did not do so because such a method would not have yielded enough years to be useful in estimating the demand function. In any event, it is striking that our method comes to much the same conclusion about trends in the enrollment ratio that Jaffe and Adams came to. Our confidence in the usability of the official enrollment data has been increased by the Jaffe-Adams study.

3. *Tuition. The Fact Book on Higher Education* (Washington: American Council on Education) publishes various indexes on tuition and other student costs in looseleaf form. We constructed an index weighted by the number of students enrolled in public and private institutions and based upon the indexes of tuition and fees presented on page 263 (dated March 1964) of the *Fact Book* for 99 private and 33 public institutions. As noted in the text, only 9 years of estimates are available from this source for the period of the study.

4. *Disposable Income per Household.* Based upon data in *Historical Statistics, Statistical Abstract,* and the *Annual Report of the President's Council of Economic Advisers,* 1965 (Washington, 1965). We would have preferred to use estimated income per family, especially in those families where the head is 35–55 years of age and income exceeded a specified minimum. Such detailed income distribution data is not available for the pre-War period, except for 1929 and 1935–36.

THE SUPPLY OF AND DEMAND FOR COLLEGE TEACHERS

ALLAN M. CARTTER

Considering the importance of the problem to higher education, and the many hundreds of millions of dollars appropriated by the federal government for the expansion of graduate education over the last few years, it is rather astonishing that we know so little about the present and probable supply and demand of college teachers. The consensus today, as expressed by several federal agencies, the National Education Association, and many college and university presidents and graduate deans, seems to be summed up in the following three propositions: (a) persons trained at the doctoral level are in increasingly short supply; (b) the quality of faculty (as measured by highest degree attained) in the nation's colleges and universities is deteriorating; and (c) the situation will worsen over the coming decade as a consequence of burgeoning undergraduate enrollments. Over the last few years various distinguished educational spokesmen have used such terms as "disastrous shortage," "serious crisis," the nation standing "virtually paralyzed," "frightening figures," and "a major national scandal" to describe the supply of college teachers and have called for

Reprinted from the *Journal of Human Resources* 1 (1966): 22–38. Copyright © 1966 by the Regents of the University of Wisconsin. (A slight error in the formulation of the model and the data generated therefrom have been corrected by the editors.—Eds.)

"heroic efforts," "crash programs," and new degrees short of the doctorate to stem the tide.

At the risk of flying in the face of commonly held opinion, I wish to argue the reverse of the above propositions: namely that (a) the "sellers market" in academic personnel is likely to disappear over the coming decade; (b) the quality of faculty in the nation's colleges and universities has improved, not deteriorated, over the last ten years; and (c) the situation is moderately well in hand now and will improve dramatically in the 1970s. In an attempt to support these views, the paper will first summarize events of the last ten years and then present a growth model helpful in projecting supply and demand conditions ahead to 1985.

THE LAST DECADE

The belief that things are getting worse rather than better is largely attributable to the biennial research bulletins issued since 1955 by the National Education Association on "Teacher Supply and Demand in Universities, Colleges and Junior Colleges."[20] The first report presented a distribution of total staff by highest degree for 637 reporting institutions in 1953–54. Successive reports, however, have only inquired as to highest degree of *new* teachers. The figures shown in Table 4.2, taken from the various NEA reports, have led some readers to believe that a rapid deterioration in faculty quality was in fact occurring.

Table 4.2

Percentage of Total Staff in 1953/54 and New Teachers in Successive Years Who had the Doctorate

Total Staff in 1953/54	40.5%
New teachers in 1953/54	31.4
1954/55	28.4
1955/56	26.7
1956/57	23.5
1957/58	25.3
1958/59	23.8
1959/60	25.9
1960/61	25.8
1961/62	27.3
1962/63	25.4
1963/64	28.3
1964/65	27.2

Source: "Teacher Supply and Demand in Universities, Colleges and Junior Colleges, 1963/64 and 1964/65," *NEA Research Report 1965 R–4*, Table 2.

A few critics of these reports have noted that it is improper to compare average and incremental ratios, but no attempt has been made to estimate the magnitude of this distortion. Table 4.3 is an attempt to correct this procedure, using additional data from the NEA reports. Columns 1 and 2 are the data used by Maul to obtain the percentages in Table 4.2. In addition, however, the biennial reports give the number of new doctorates each year who "continue in teaching," and thus do not show up in the "new teacher" series.[21] These are shown in column 3 of Table 4.3, and a ratio of new doctorates in teaching to new teachers is computed in Column 4. Now a meaningful comparison can be made between the average ratio

Table 4.3

Additions to College Teaching Staff and to Doctorates in Teaching 1953–65

Year	New Teachers (1)	New Teachers With Doctorate (2)	Continuing Teachers Receiving Doctorate (3)	Ratio of New Doctorates in Teaching to New Teachers (4)
(Total Staff in 1953/54)	(58,719)	(23,768)	—	(.405)
1953/54	4,232	1,329	na	na
1954/55	4,694	1,333	822	.460
1955/56	6,337	1,695	856	.403
1956/57	8,308	1,953	1,528	.419
1957/58	9,293	2,354	1,529	.418
1958/59	9,100	2,254	1,825	.448
1959/60	10,221	2,650	1,894	.447
1960/61	11,184	2,886	1,987	.436
1961/62	10,439	2,851	2,115	.476
1962/63	12,186	3,092	2.334	.445
1963/64	13,562	3,833	2,732	.484
1964/65	16,059	4,361	3,084 est.	.463 est.

Source : Columns 1 and 2 from *NEA Research Report 1965-R-4*. Column 3 computed from Table Y of 1965 Report and comparable tables in earlier reports in the series. Column 4 is col. 2 + 3 ÷ col. 1.

for 1953–54 and the incremental changes in both the number and degree level of college teachers. This series suggests a slight improvement in the proportion of senior college faculty with the doctorate.

One further factor should be considered which is also favorable to the view that the quality of faculty (as measured by highest degrees attained) has not deteriorated. *A priori* one would assume that teachers with the doctorate are more likely to make a lifetime career of teaching than those without a doctorate. It would be reasonable to assume that there is a differential net transfer rate for the two groups. A recent Office of Education study, to be published later this year,[22] indicates that for 1962–63 the rate of those leaving college teaching for reasons other than death or retirement was 3.1 per cent for doctorates and 7.1 per cent for nondoctorates. Other data, discussed below, further indicate that the net transfer rate of doctorates into and out of teaching has been approximately zero in recent years—that is, that the in-transfer rate of doctorates from other employment was also about 3 per cent. To illustrate the effect of a difference in the net transfer rate, assume that the rate is zero for Ph.D.'s and a 5 per cent annual net loss for non-doctorates. For the 1963–64 class of new teachers, with an initial ratio of .484, five years later the ratio of doctorates to total continuing teachers would rise to .548. Unfortunately, we have only one fragment of data from the COLFACS study to judge by, so this example is suggestive only; presumably the separations rate for non-doctorates is positive but not greater than seven per cent.

If the data in Table 4.3, and its accompanying speculations, were the entire basis of the thesis that the percentage of college faculty with doctorate has been rising over the last decade, it would rest on a slender reed indeed. But this view is now supported by two new studies. One was recently presented by this author, drawn from data collected quadriennially by the American Council on Education.[23] The findings are summarized in the first two columns of Table 4.4. The other is a soon-to-be-published study (COLFACS) by the Office of Education, whose findings are summarized in column 4 of Table 4.4. Whether one views the comparison between total

Table 4.4

Percentage of Doctorates Among Four-Year College and University Faculty

Type of Institution	All Instructional Staff		Full-Time Instructional Staff	
	1950–51 (ACE)[a]	1962–63 (ACE)[a]	1953–54 (NEA)[b]	1962–63 (OE)[c]
Public universities	36.0	44.9	44.0	58.4
Private universities	37.3	43.8	51.9	59.6
Public colleges	28.2	33.5	30.7	42.6
Private colleges	29.7	35.4	35.2	42.7
All institutions	32.3	39.4	40.5	50.6

[a] Cartter "A New Look . . . ," *op. cit.*
[b] "Teacher Supply and Demand in Degree Granting Institutions," *NEA Research Bulletin*, XXXIII, No. 4 (December 1955), 138.
[c] "Doctorates among Teaching Faculty," *op. cit.*, Table III.

or full-time instructional staff, it seems clear that the percentage of doctorates has been rising for each type of institution. This conclusion is consistent with the NEA data as presented in Table 4.3 above, although it is just the opposite of the conclusion which NEA drew from its own material.

FACULTY FORECASTING MODELS

Projections of the demand for college teachers made over the last decade have varied widely, and most have been such poor predictors of actual developments as to call for careful scrutiny of the basis on which the projections were made. The best known model is that developed by Ray Maul in the 1959 NEA report,[24] and now used by the Office of Education.[25] The model consists of three ingredients: (a) an independent projection of future enrollment; (b) an assumed student/staff ratio; and (c) an assumed replacement rate for faculty deaths, retirements, and shifts to other employment sectors. In the most recent presentation by the Office of Education, the student/staff ratio is estimated to average 14:1 for the next decade,[26] and the replacement rate is assumed to be 6 per cent. The choice of the latter percentage apparently derives from the earlier Maul model.[27] The result of this model, when applied to Office of Education enrollment projections, is to predict an aggregate need for some 556,000 new college teachers over the next ten years. Assuming constant quality of faculty, the Office of Education predicts a probable "deficit" of more than 120,000 doctorates by 1973/74.[28]

There are a number of aspects of the current OE model which I believe lead to a considerable exaggeration of future faculty needs. First, the projected student/staff ratio (18:1, based on total instructional staff) is lower than the experience of the last decade would indicate. Table 4.5,

Table 4.5

Average and Marginal Faculty Coefficients 1953/54–1963/64

	E	ΔE	F	ΔF	$\frac{F}{E}$	$\frac{\Delta F}{\Delta E}$	ΔE:ΔF
1953/54	2,236		182.0		.084		
1955/56	2,660	424	197.8	15.8	.076	.037	26.8:1
1957/58	3,047	387	226.5	28.7	.074	.074	13.5:1
1959/60	3,377	330	244.5	18.0	.072	.055	18.2:1
1961/62	3,861	484	266.6	22.1	.069	.046	21.7:1
1963/64	4,495	634	298.9	32.3	.066	.051	19.6:1
1953/54 to 1963/64		2,259		116.9		.0517	19.3:1

Source: "Projections of Educational Statistics to 1973/74" (*OE-10030*, 1964), pp. 8 and 24. Faculty considered here are members of the Instructional Staff at the level of Instructor or above. The extreme high and low ratios for 1955/56 and 1957/58 may result from errors in reporting by institutions.

using Office of Education data, shows the increment of enrollment (ΔE) and the increment in total instructional staff (ΔF) since 1953/54.[29] It has averaged 19.3:1 and there is no clear trend upward or downward. On reflection, this does not seem an unusually high marginal ratio, for a number of reasons. First, junior colleges, where the averate ratio is 20:1 or greater, represent a larger portion of increments in enrollment than they do of the current total (nearly 30 per cent of the annual increases, as compared to less than 15 per cent of the total). Second, enrollment in public institutions, where the ratio is moderately high, is expanding more rapidly than in private colleges and universities. Third, much of the expansion is occurring in already existing institutions, and one would expect there to be some manpower economies of scale associated with such growth. Finally, modest changes in technology (language laboratories, educational television, independent study, etc.) presumably work to increase the ratio despite enrollment expansion. A continuing *marginal* ratio of nearly 20:1 would mean that the *average* ratio will rise from 15.3:1 today to 17.3:1 by 1985. The Office of Education choice of an 18:1 ratio, therefore, appears to overstate the expansion needs by nearly 10 per cent.

A second, and more major, criticism is the use of a 6 per cent replacement rate for faculty, for I believe it overstates replacement needs by a factor of three, for the following reason. If one applied this model to the last decade, beginning with 1953/54, then we should have experienced a decline in the percentage of doctorates on teaching faculties from about 40 per cent to 30 per cent; instead, as Table 4.4 indicated, it has risen by seven to ten percentage points for four-year institutions. As I have indicated in another paper, the actual experience in the last ten years is consistent with a replacement rate of *slightly less than 2 per cent.* Judging by the age distribution of present faculty (1962/63), applying appropriate mortality rates, and estimating retirements, my calculation of the actual replacement rate for the coming decade is given in Table 4.6.[30]

Table 4.6

**Estimated Annual Replacement Rate
for College Faculty**

Losses annually due to:

Deaths	.69%
Retirements	1.12
Net Transfer to Other Enployment	.11
Total Annual Losses	1.92

A third objection to the OE model is that included in full-time equivalent staff are personnel for administrative services (few of whom, below the level of academic deans, would be expected to have the doctorate), junior instructional staff (who by definition are teaching assistants without the doctorate), and a large number for "research." Since research personnel needs are determined by factors largely independent of the purely educational function, and doctorates are probably not a large fraction of the other two categories, it seems much more appropriate to concentrate just on the needs for teaching faculty. As a corollary, this requires counting only new doctorates who enter teaching as a component of supply, rather than the number who enter higher education in all of its various facets.

So much for the Office of Education forecasts; as a stone-thrower I should at least create my own glass house as a target for others. The starting point is a projection of college enrollments (E) and doctoral degrees (P) to 1985 in Table 4.7. The enrollment projection is similar to that of the Office of Education through 1974 and assumes that the ratio of under-graduate enrollment to the 18–21 age group rises to .55 by 1985.[31] (It is now approximately .40.) The doctoral projection is that of the author, and while it is moderately higher than the most recent Office of Education projection, it is below that of the National Science Foundation.[32] If the projections turn out to be accurate—and I believe they are about as good a guess as can be made—one can then attempt to analyze the staffing implications of such a future growth path.

Table 4.7

Total College Enrollment (E) and Doctoral Production (P), Actual 1953–64 and Projected to 1985 (thousands)

	E	ΔE	P
1953–54	2,207		9.0
1954–55	2,421	214	8.8
1955–56	2,627	206	8.9
1956–57	2,891	264	8.8
1957–58	3,009	118	8.9
1958–59	3,195	186	9.4
1959–60	3,344	149	9.8
1960–61	3,536	192	10.6
1961–62	3,804	268	11.6
1962–63	4,124	320	12.6
1963–64	4,433	309	14.5
1964–65	4,744	311	15.0
1965–66	5,185	441	16.1
1966–67	5,641	456	16.8
1967–68	6,064	423	18.0
1968–69	6,382	318	19.5
1969–70	6,676	294	21.4
1970–71	6,982	306	23.2
1971–72	7,315	333	26.0
1972–73	7,671	356	28.9
1973–74	8,027	356	31.5
1974–75	8,401	374	33.6
1975–76	8,750	349	35.7
1976–77	9,082	332	37.9
1977–78	9,369	287	40.4
1978–79	9,644	275	43.1
1979–80	9,936	292	46.0
1980–81	10,148	212	47.9
1981–82	10,288	140	49.7
1982–83	10,428	140	51.6
1983–84	10,487	59	53.2
1984–85	10,598	111	54.7

Source: Actual figures from Office of Education data; Projections by the author. (See A. M. Cartter and R. Farrell, "Higher Education in the Last Third of the Century," *The Educational Record* (Spring 1965), 119–28.)

If we are to assess the quality of instructional staff by highest degree obtained (a rough but useful measure), we need to know the total size of faculty required and the likely number of teachers who will have the doctoral degree. Given the enrollment projection, the total faculty will expand as follows:

$$F_t = F_{t-1} + f(E_t - E_{t-1}) \qquad (1)$$

where F is faculty, E enrollment, and f the faculty coefficient (the inverse of the student/staff ratio). As indicated in Table 4.5, f has averaged .0517 over the last decade, and for the moment I will continue to assume that it remains constant.

Given the present number of doctorates on instructional staffs, and the doctoral projection in Table 4.6, the number of doctorates in teaching will grow in the following manner:

$$D_t = [1 - (c + m + r - a)]D_{t-1} + bP_{t-1} \qquad (2)$$

where the following new terms are introduced: a = the accretion, or in-transfer, rate of persons with the doctorate who enter teaching from other employment; c = the loss, or out-transfer, rate of doctorates leaving teaching for other employment; m = the mortality rate of present teachers; r = the retirement rate of present teachers; b = the percentage of new doctorates who enter teaching; and P = the number of doctoral degrees awarded. (Using academic years as periods, the number of new Ph.D.'s entering teaching in year t depends upon doctoral output in year $t - 1$.)

Given the values of the respective coefficients, equations (1) and (2) indicate how total faculty and doctorates in teaching will grow. In order to see the effect of various values for the coefficients, it may be useful to construct a supply and demand equation:

$$bP_{t-1} = (c + m + r - a)D_{t-1} + qf(E_t - E_{t-1}) \qquad (3)$$

Here, one new coefficient, q, the percentage of new teachers with the doctorate, has been added. This equation represents a supply-demand identity, the lefthand term representing the quantity of new doctorates supplied, and the two righthand terms the replacement and expansion demand components.[33] From various studies we can estimate the approximate values of each of these variables for recent years.

b = .50 (the NEA reports indicate an average of about .48 over the decade, closer to .50 for the last four years)

m = .0069 (calculated from the age distribution of faculty in the COLFACS study)

r = .0112 (calculated from COLFACS data)

c = .0321 (the rate at which doctorates intended to leave higher education, from COLFACS data)

$a = .0310$ (estimated on the basis of Table 4.6 above, which indicates that the net transfer rate $(c - a)$ has been approximately $.0011$)

$q = .33$ (the estimated value over the past decade)

$f = .0517$ (from Table 4.5 above)

$D =$ approximately 90,000 in 1963/64

The combined factors which go to make up the replacement rate are equal to .0192, as indicated in Table 4.6. These factors are small in magnitude and appear to have been relatively stable in recent years—although $(c - a)$ obviously responds to changes in the relative salary level of academic personnel. The three significant coefficients are b, q, and f. Of these, f has remained relatively constant since 1958 at about .05 and is stable in the sense that it is the result of conscious decisions on the part of college and university administrators to determine the staff/student ratio. The percentage of new teachers hired with the doctorate, q, reflects the aspirations of the institutions, for most institutions equate a high q with excellence

Table 4.8

Projected Percentages of New Doctorates Entering Teaching *(b)* and New Teachers with the Doctorate *(q)* for "Constant Quality" and "Absorption" Growth Models; 1965–85

	Values of	
	b $(q = .33)$	q $(b = .50)$
1965–66	63%	25%
1966–67	61	26
1967–68	56	29
1968–69	43	41
1969–70	38	48
1970–71	36	52
1971–72	36	52
1972–73	35	55
1973–74	32	62
1974–75	31	64
1975–76	28	73
1976–77	27	82
1977–78	24	100
1978–79	23	111
1979–80	23	111
1980–81	19	164
1981–82	16	256
1982–83	16	263
1983–84	14	643
1984–85	16	349

Note: Based on assumed continuing values: $f = .0517$ and $(c + m + r - a) = .02$.

and a low q with deterioration of faculty quality. The percentage of doctorates who enter college teaching reflects the aspirations of graduate
students, for a majority enter graduate school with the intention of becoming
college teachers.[34] Both b and q are highly variable, depending upon yearly
market conditions for new Ph.D.'s.

Using the projections for E and P for the next twenty years, assuming
a constant faculty coefficient ($f = .0517$) and a constant replacement rate
(rounded off at $[c + m + r - a] = .02$), what behavior might we predict
for b and q? Column 1 of Table 4.8 gives the predicted values for b if q
remains constant—that is, the percentage of new Ph.D.'s who would have
to enter college teaching in order to maintain a constant ratio of doctorates
in teaching to total faculty. We might call this the "constant faculty quality"
model.[35] Over the coming three years, the required value of b is higher
than we have experienced or can reasonably expect; therefore the quality
of faculty is unlikely to be maintained. However, after 1968, b will steadily
decline (to a low of less than 12 per cent for the 1980–85 period) and will
probably be lower than it has ever been in history.

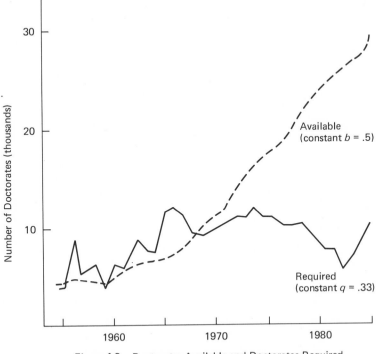

Figure 4.3   Doctorates Available and Doctorates Required
to Maintain Constant Quality of Faculty at
1963/64 Level.

Alternatively, column 2 of Table 4.8 projects an "absorption" model, assuming that the percentage of new doctorates entering teaching (b) remains constant at 50 per cent and that all such available doctorates become employed in college teaching. The ratio of new teachers with the doctorate to annual additions to the instructional staff ($q = \Delta D/\Delta F$) rises steadily. Assuming a constant b, by 1977/78, *every* new college teacher would possess the doctorate; after that year the absolute number of non-doctorates would fall rapidly, as doctorate-teachers displaced non-doctorates faster than the latter were reaching retirement age. Figure 4.3 illustrates dramatically the relationship between the available supply, if b remains constant, and the annual requirement for new doctorates in teaching for constant quality. After a temporary deficit in the 1965–68 years, the available supply begins to exceed demand by a rapidly growing amount, sharply altering the market conditions for college teachers.

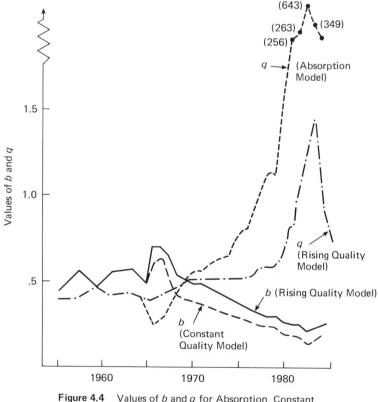

Figure 4.4   Values of b and q for Absorption, Constant Quality, and Rising Quality Models

The "absorption" and "constant quality" versions of the model seem to me to represent the outside limits; actual experience will probably lie somewhere between. Figure 4.4 shows the outer boundaries and illustrates an intermediate case similar to the experience of the last decade discussed in the first section of the paper. In this example, it is assumed that the overall ratio of doctorates to faculty continues to rise by one-half of one percentage point each year. The two intermediate lines indicate the values for both b and q (given the projections of E and P) for a steadily rising quality model. In this case, q rises to about unity (its logical maximum), and b gradually declines to one-fifth.

CONCLUSIONS

The preceding analysis suggests that educators have been much too pessimistic about the adequacy of both the present and future supply of college teachers. We seem to have learned little from the experience of the 1950s, when the National Education Association and most public school officials were maintaining that there was a critical shortage of school teachers, only to find by the end of the decade that both the number and quality (as measured by formal preparation) of teachers had been steadily rising. Similarly, the despairing cries about the rapidly deteriorating situation on the college level have now proved to be in error, and the future looks bright beyond the next three to five years.

If the projections of total college enrollment and of doctorates to be awarded are even approximately correct, the sellers' market for college faculty will quickly disappear in the early 1970s. This has many implications for public policy and for the nation's colleges.

Given the time lag between entrance to graduate school and completion of doctorate, it is conceivable that graduate education facilities might be expanded too rapidly by basing decisions on degrees awarded in the recent past. The *present* faculty and facilities, at their current level of utilization, would turn out about 20,000 doctorates a year in a stable system. That is to say, because we are rapidly expanding, we occasionally forget that the fifteen thousand doctorates awarded this year reflect the teaching capacity of the graduate schools about 1960. If, as the model suggests, the demand for new doctorates in teaching will stabilize or even decline after 1968, as a consequence of the declining rate of growth of the total system, then a serious question of public policy may be whether or not it is desirable to encourage many new institutions to enter the doctoral field. Four-fifths of the nearly 250 universities presently awarding the Ph.D. are too small to be educationally or economically efficient. We might well ask whether public policy would be better served by consolidating and strengthening our existing graduate schools, rather than by encouraging another ten or twelve new doctoral-granting institutions to join the university ranks each year, as is now occurring.[36]

The model also has serious implications for the future level of academic salaries. For the next three years, the market will remain fairly tight, and the succeeding several years may be needed to regain temporarily lost ground. The 1970s, however, may usher in a "buyers' market," and academicians may experience again a decline in their *relative income* position. The model above assumed that the replacement rate remained constant over the next twenty years, but this is unlikely in a market where supply is relatively abundant. There may develop a trend for colleges to lower mandatory retirement ages (thus raising r), and the transfer rate of senior staff $(c - a)$ will probably rise a few percentage points. For example, a tendency for b to fall as a result of a decrease in demand would tend to depress beginning academic salaries. As the upward pressure on salaries of new Ph.D.'s diminishes, colleges may let out-transfers increase and reduce in-transfers of older doctorates (*i.e.*, $[c - a]$ would rise), partly stemming the decline in b. Junior and senior faculty are relatively good substitutes, from the point of view of performing the teaching function. Alternatively, the slack might be taken up by a rising faculty coefficient (a reduced marginal student/staff ratio).

If I were to hazard a guess fifteen or so years ahead, I would predict a fairly constant marginal faculty coefficient (f), a gradually diminishing percentage of new Ph.D.'s entering teaching (b) after 1970, a continuing modest improvement in the percentage of faculty with the doctorate $(q > D/F)$, a positive net out-transfer rate $(c > a$, and gradually rising), and a slowing down in the upward drift of academic salaries, becoming noticeable in the early 1970s. It may well be that the real challenge to Committee Z of the American Association of University Professors will come in the 1970s, when in all probability market forces will oppose rather than uphold efforts to improve the relative income position of college teachers.

The discussion above has ignored field-by-field differences, partly in the interests of brevity and partly because the aggregate data are better than that for individual disciplines. There are wide variations in the values of each of the coefficients from field to field,[37] but the demarcations between fields are too fuzzy to permit the application of such a model with any degree of precision to individual disciplines. Certainly, shortages in many fields will continue beyond 1970, but the general outlook appears to be favorable for the continued expansion and improved quality of higher education in the United States.

ANALYSIS OF THE EFFECTS OF A GRADUATED TUITION PROGRAM AT STATE UNIVERSITIES

JOSEPH M. BURNS AND BARRY R. CHISWICK

I. INTRODUCTION

The demand for higher education, especially for state colleges and universities, has increased greatly since the end of World War II. During this same period the costs of operating a university have increased substantially, due in part to the increased cost of faculty services and the greater emphasis on physical sciences and graduate education.[38] Confronted with both a rising demand and rising costs, state universities have tended to increase tuition charges and/or student fees.[39]

In recent years there has also been increasing recognition of the difficulty on the part of the poor of borrowing funds to finance the direct and opportunity costs of schooling. This view, together with rising tuition, has resulted in an increase of interest in graduated tuition programs, or scholarships which vary inversely in magnitude with the student's family income.[40] Both state and private institutions appear to be adopting such programs.[41]

There are two arguments based on the economic self-interest of public and private universities which are consistent with graduated tuition. First, if students from poorer families have a more elastic demand than wealthier students for schooling at any particular institution, the universities, being able to effectively separate the market on the basis of wealth, may be engaging in monopolistic price discrimination as a profit-maximizing technique.[42] Second, high ability poor students may be productive in generating revenue for the university by increasing the quality (academic, athletic, etc.) of the student body. These funds could come from the state, private donors, or a higher demand by wealthy students for education at that institution.

The economic rationale in terms of social efficiency of a graduated tuition program at a state university has been considered elsewhere.[43] The effects of a change from zero (or nominal) tuition to a graduated tuition program at a public university have been virtually ignored in the literature. This article examines the effects of the adoption of such a program. In particular, it analyzes the effects on the composition of students—in terms of wealth and ability—at state and private universities.

Reprinted from the *Journal of Human Resources* 5 (1970): 237–45. Copyright © 1970 by the Regents of the University of Wisconsin. (Nontechnical words have been substituted for two linear algebra terms.—Eds.)

In this article, "public" universities are distinguished from "private" ones. In analyzing the effects of the adoption of graduated tuition at a particular public university, all other universities, whether public or private, are considered private. The analysis is for first-order effects, since private universities are assumed to be passive. In addition, the analysis is developed for two homogeneous income groups (poor and wealthy) and two homogeneous ability groups (low and high).

Section II presents some prefatory comments on university admissions policies because of their bearing on the nature of the effects of the adoption of graduated tuition. Section III analyzes the direct effects on the level of wealth and quality of students at both public and private universities. Section IV considers indirect effects of the program and is, in particular, concerned with the degree of state control over the public university and student independence. Section V is a conclusion.

II. UNIVERSITY POLICIES

The effects on the composition of students of adopting a graduated tuition program at a state university depend on the type of admissions policies at the state and private universities. The universities' admissions policies may be viewed in terms of a tradeoff between higher university revenue from a market-clearing tuition set of prices and lower university revenue from a less-than-market clearing tuition set of prices with the university administrators rationing the supply of admissions on some basis.[44]

Some schools do in fact charge market-clearing prices. Barbering and secretarial schools, as well as Parsons College, are examples of such institutions. At most schools, however, the price of instruction (i.e., tuition) is uniform and is less than the market-clearing price.

There are two hypotheses consistent with university administrators' charging a less-than-market clearing price. First, the administrators' behavior could be explained by assuming that they are utility maximizers whose pecuniary incomes are regulated by public (or alumni) censure.[45] The administrators can, however, use their official positions to increase their nonpecuniary or pecuniary incomes elsewhere. Indeed, many former college administrators have obtained prestigious and lucrative off-campus employment. Thus, administrators could seek to increase their real incomes through the prestige of being associated with a "high quality" university, where quality has a large number of dimensions, as indicated below. For this reason, administrators might opt for a less-than-market clearing tuition price.

Second, the administrators' behavior could be explained by long-run profit considerations for their respective universities. In this connection, the supply of faculty services, governmental grants, private donations, and future students' demands for education at a particular university are positively related to the quality of its students. That is, high quality students can result in lower factor costs and/or larger revenues from sources other than current tuition. In this way, quality rationing may be consistent with profit maximization.

To simplify the analysis, only two types of university admissions policies are considered— fixed minimum quality and fixed maximum quantity of students.[46] Both types imply the rationing of admissions. If it were assumed that the distribution of ability were the same across age groups, variations in the size of the group would produce variations in the number of students of a given level of ability. A fixed minimum quality would permit admissions that vary with the size of the age group as well as with the distribution of ability. Such a policy, however, would result in fluctuating enrollments.

In this article, the students' "ability," or "quality," is assumed to be the mechanism through which administrators ration the supply of admissions among the demanders. Each student is evaluated by the university in terms of his characteristics. The elements in the set of student characteristics include, inter alia, academic ability, race, religion, sex, social class, location of residence, and athletic ability. The set of a student's characteristics can be thought of as being multiplied by the set of weights assigned by the university. The resulting value indicates the student's "ability," or "quality," as measured by that school. It is this value which is used in the nonprice rationing of admissions.

The weights attached to the students' characteristics are a function of the preference of, and the opportunity sets confronting, the administrators. Since both preference and opportunity sets vary among administrators, the weights attached to these characteristics will also vary from one campus to another. This variation in weights is one factor explaining differences in the composition of student bodies across campuses as well as at a given campus over time. For example, recent changes in attitudes toward minority groups have affected the weights administrators attach to student characteristics, with subsequent changes in the composition of student bodies. The greater the cross-sectional variation in these weights, the greater will be the apparent variation in the characteristics of students at different schools both before and after the adoption of graduated tuition.

III. DIRECT EFFECTS

The adoption of a graduated tuition program at a state university directly affects the composition of both its students and those at private universities.

Wealth of Students

The change from a zero or nominal tuition to a graduated tuition program at a state university would have direct effects, at the margin, on both wealthy students attending the state university and poor students not attending it. Faced with a higher price at the state university, wealthy students would decrease the amount demanded of this type of education.[47] In particular, some of high ability would seek to transfer to private institutions, while some of low ability would drop out of school.

Poor students who had been attracted to private universities through large scholarships would be faced with a lower (and perhaps negative) price at the state university under graduated tuition. For them, the relative advantage of attending the state university would have increased, thereby inducing some to transfer.[48] Also, some poor students who would otherwise not attend, would now enter school.

Thus the adoption of graduated tuition at a state university would necessarily make the private university more of a "rich man's" school and the public university more of a "poor man's" school. For the educational system as a whole, there would be an unambiguous decrease in the average wealth of students' families.[49]

Quality of Students

The effects of the graduated tuition program at a state university on the quality of students at the public and private institutions are not *a priori* clear: at each type of institution, some students may be leaving (either as transferees or dropouts) and some may be entering (either as transferees or new entrants). The nature of the effects at each type of institution depends on the admissions policy of the universities.

Admissions Policy: Fixed Minimum Quality. For the educational system as a whole, the adoption of graduated tuition at a state university would induce some low-ability wealthy students to leave and some high-ability poor students to enter. Therefore, if the quantity of entering and departing students were the same, the average quality of the students in the educational system would necessarily improve. If, however, the quantity of entering and departing students were not the same, the effect on the average quality of the students would be ambiguous. Indeed, if the average quality of the entering students were above that of the departing ones but below that of the students not affected by the change in tuition, and if the number of entering students were greater than the number of departing students, the average quality of the student bodies might deteriorate. It seems likely, however, that the average quality of university students would improve.

For the state university, the adoption of graduated tuition would induce some high-ability and low-ability wealthy students to leave and some high-ability poor students to enter. Thus the average quality of the entering students is likely to be above that of those departing. For this reason it seems likely that the average quality of students at the state university would improve.

For the private universities, some high-ability and low-ability wealthy students would be induced to enter, while some high-ability poor students would be induced to leave. Thus the average ability of the departing students is likely to be above that of the entering ones. For this reason, it seems likely that the average ability of students at the private universities would deteriorate.

Admissions Policy: Fixed Maximum Quantity. If the university admissions policy were geared to a fixed maximum quantity of students, the analysis would differ only slightly from that presented above. The essential difference is that the minimum quality standard at both institutions would now have to be varied in such a way as to equate the given supply of schooling to the quantity demanded. In particular, the minimum acceptable quality would have to increase if the quantity of potential entering students were greater than that of potential departing students, and it would have to decrease if the quantity of potential entering students were less than that of potential departing students. If the adoption of graduated tuition induced an equal number to enter and leave each type of institution, the minimum acceptable quality of students would not have to change.

Given the fixed number of admissions at both private and public universities, the average quality of students would necessarily improve for the educational system as a whole. The only net changes in the system would be the entrance of high-ability poor to the public university and the departure of low-ability wealthy from the public university. Unlike the situation prevailing with the minimum quality standards, the average quality of students cannot decline at both institutions. At the public university, the average quality of students would probably increase; but at the private universities, the change in average quality would be less certain.

IV. INDIRECT EFFECTS

The adoption of graduated tuition at a state university would also have indirect effects on the students, a consequence of the students' response to change in factors other than the money price of education. The non-price factors that affect students' demands for schooling include the degree of state control over the university, the degree of uncertainty over the university's budget, the quality of faculty and administration, and the degree of student freedom.

The degree of direct and indirect control over the policies of a public university is likely to be directly related to the state's relative contribution to the university's resources. With the adoption of a graduated tuition program, the state's relative contribution would probably diminish: the increments in revenue available to the university from nonstate sources (*i.e.*, tuition charges plus donations) would probably exceed the decrements in resources due to the increase in scholarship assistance.[50]

There are two reasons why the decrease in reliance on public funds may increase the magnitude of donations. First, university administrators are likely to increase the magnitude of resources devoted to the procurement of donations.[51] Second, donors are less likely to feel that their gifts are a substitute for public funds, and consequently they can be expected to increase their contributions.[52] On the assumption that the contributors to the university's resources have proportionate control over the allocation of funds, the relative decrease in the state's contribution would mean a smaller degree of state control over the university.[53]

The adoption of graduated tuition is also likely to entail a smaller degree of uncertainty over the total volume of funds available to the university. This conclusion is based upon an application of the law of large numbers. That is, the relative variance in the distribution of funds derived from a large number of independent or partially independent sources (*i.e.*, the state, the student, and the donors) is likely to be smaller than that derived from a small number of independent sources (*i.e.*, the state). Both the smaller degree of state control and the smaller degree of uncertainty over the university's total resources would increase the students' demand schedule for schooling.

It seems plausible to assume that the supply schedules of faculty and administrative services are inversely related to the degree of uncertainty over the total volume of funds available to the university and to the level of actual or imagined state control (both monetary and non-monetary) over the university.[54] Therefore, the adoption of graduated tuition would increase the supply schedules of faculty and administrative services to the public university, thereby improving the quality of the faculty and administration for a given budget. Since the demand schedule of students for schooling at a particular university is directly related to the quality of the faculty and administration, the improvement in the latter quality would increase the students' demand schedule for schooling.

The graduated tuition program could also affect the control universities and parents have over students as individuals. Since, as argued above, the school is likely to be more dependent on students' funds under the new program, the university's control over students' activities would decline.[55] Since a student's demand for schooling is likely to be negatively related to the extent of university control over his activities, the decline in control would increase the demand schedule for schooling at that institution.

The change to graduated tuition would compel students from wealthy families to finance a larger share of their educational costs, whereas the converse would hold for poor families. Thus students from wealthy (poor) families would be more (less) dependent on parental and less (more) dependent on state financial support. Many students feel that parental control over a given amount of funds is more onerous than state control.[56] If this is a general characteristic, then those from wealthy families would experience a loss of freedom, whereas those from poor families would experience a gain of freedom. The opposition of middle income and wealthy students to the adoption of graduated tuition by state universities may be a consequence of the expected loss of freedom as well as the adverse effect on their families' wealth. It is interesting to note that those who would experience the largest gain in wealth and freedom are least represented on state university campuses.

V. CONCLUSION

A change from a low or zero tuition to a graduated tuition system at a state university affects the composition of students at both the state and private universities. The direction and magnitude of the changes in the composition of students depend on the universities' admissions policies with respect to the quality and quantity of students, as well as the elasticity of demand for schooling and the extent of the price change for the various income and ability groups.

For the educational system as a whole, there would be a decrease in the average wealth of students' families and most likely an increase in the average quality of students. The state university, however, would become more of a "poor man's" school and the private university more of a "rich man's" school. Many would consider this increased homogeneity to be contrary to the objectives of a democratic society and detrimental to the educational process. The increased homogeneity would be mitigated if private universities increased their scholarship assistance to students from poor families.

The expansion of zero or low tuition public universities subsidized by state treasuries has reduced the ability of private universities to attract high ability and wealthy students. The result has been a decline in the competitive position of private institutions.[57] Graduated tuition would reduce and alter the composition of the public subsidy to state universities. In so doing, it would increase revenues to private universities from current tuition, but might decrease revenues from other sources due to the exodus of some high-ability poor students Although the net effect on the competitive position of private universities is not a priori clear, it seems likely that the competitive position of most of the institutions would be improved.

A graduated tuition program at a state university would decrease the university's reliance on the state for financial support. As a result there would be greater certainty as to the magnitude of the university's resources in a given year, and less actual and potential state control over the university's allocation of funds and regulations. Students, faculty, and administrators would share this greater freedom, especially if the scholarships were not tied to the students' behavior or consumption. Finally, due to a redistribution of the source of subsidy from the state to their parents, students from wealthy families are likely to experience a loss of freedom, whereas students from poor families are likely to experience a gain of freedom.

QUESTIONS FOR DISCUSSION

1. Would it be correct for a single college or university to estimate the effect of a tuition increase on the number of applications it would receive on the basis of the price elasticity that Campbell and Siegal found? Why?

2. What factors other than those listed by Cartter (on pp. 78–90) might have contributed to the difficulties that were observed in 1969–70 of graduate students finding teaching positions?

3. In what ways might the publications by the NEA have created the over-supply that Cartter predicted?

4. What effect would you predict open enrollments in state universities would have on public and private institutions of higher learning?

5. Would a graduated tuition program at state universities be preferable to a high uniform tuition charge accompanied by liberal loan provisions? Why?

Chapter 5 PRODUCTION

PRODUCTION is one of the essential activities of mankind. Without production there would be no food to eat, no clothes to wear, and no houses to live in. Even fruit that grows wild is "produced" in the sense that it must be found and gathered. In Chapter 3 the supply and demand for goods, services, and factors of production and the theory of the firm were introduced. In that chapter the firm was the smallest unit considered. This chapter presents an investigation and systematization of the production process and the elements that enter into it from a more micro viewpoint; here an individual unit of a good, of labor, and of capital is the smallest element considered. The elements that enter into the productive process and the products resultant therefrom are generally reduced to a common denominator, money. As was explained in Chapter 2, the use of dollars as a common denominator is a necessary procedure for most problems but does have its cost in distortions of reality.

The factors put into production are usually abstracted into three categories: land, labor, and capital.[1] Entrepreneurship is considered to be a separate factor of production by some economists. It is variously defined, but the most important attributes of an entrepreneur are that he innovates and therein takes risks. He is a person who introduces a new way of doing things—perhaps inventing it, perhaps only popularizing it. Examples of entrepreneurship in education include the organization of the first Montessori schools in the United States and the popularization of computer-aided instruction. Both of these involve new methods of education and risk of the capital and labor of the entrepreneurs. For simplicity, we limit the presentation here to three factors.

Notes to Chapter 5 will be found on page 371.

99

Land, labor, and capital can all be accurately denominated in dollars since they are traded in the market place—either sold outright (capital and land, but not labor since a man may not legally sell himself) or the services sold (all three). Some outputs, such as government services and education, are less neatly denominated in dollars because they are neither sold nor rented in the market place. Nevertheless, they are evaluated in dollar terms on the basis of the cost of the inputs that enter into their production, that is, such things as the salaries of teachers, administrators, and clerical staff and the price of books, desks, and paper.

THE FACTORS OF PRODUCTION: LAND, LABOR, AND CAPITAL

The term *land* is a shorthand for *all natural resources*. Together with labor, land is considered a primary factor of production, primary in the sense that land and labor are not in any way products of the economic system but rather they are products of nature. The quantity of land, in its narrowest sense, is more or less fixed. We say more or less because man has managed to both create (*e.g.*, through land-fill in bogs and on ocean fronts) and destroy (*e.g.*, the vaporization of land to create harbors through bomb explosions) land. Other natural resources included in the land rubric, such as coal, iron ore, and oil, are of course easily used up.

Land, in the narrow sense, enters into production in many different ways. First, it is a basic element in farms which produce food, fiber, and materials for our personal consumption and for our industries. Second, houses, schools, and factories are built on land. Finally, man takes recreation on land of all kinds—seashore, desert, mountains, forests, and so on. The composition of the land, its minerals and substance, is also exploited for man's ends. Minerals valuable in various productive processes are mined from it, and it is moved and shaped to form dams and roads.

Labor is the effort of man. However, when discussing labor as a factor of production, certain qualifications are necessary. In official statistics only efforts which contribute to the production of goods or services and for the most part only efforts which, directly or through the goods they produce, pass through the market place are counted as labor.

Labor is measured either in terms of time or of dollar value. In the time dimension, man-years and man-hours are the most common units. The number of man-years worked in an economy in a given year is determined by several factors. The most important of these are the size and age distribution of the population, the labor force participation rate,[2] the state of the economy (*i.e.*, boom or recession), and how much work is normally considered full time employment. The man-hour unit measurements are aggregated over very different types of labor, all the way from unskilled laborers to surgeons. The dollar measurement of labor, the total amount of wages and salaries paid in a year, takes some account of the differences between the labor of different people which the man-hour measure does not since the latter weights all labor man-hours equally regardless of the type of labor, as seen in Table 5.1. Man-years and payments to labor changed over time in different patterns. Real wages more than doubled whereas hours worked grew by only one-third during the 23-year period covered in the table. If individuals were paid exactly what they contribute to the productive process, using the dollar cost of the labor would be unimpeachable. However, wage payments sometimes reflect factors other than productivity, such as friendship, social status, minimum wage legislation, and unionization. In many cases we assume these problems away to facilitate analysis, as we shall see below.

Many attributes of men affect the quality of their labor. All of these are ideally mirrored in their wages and hence taken account of in

Table 5.1

Total Man-hours and Real Wages of Production and Non-Supervisory Workers on Private Payrolls

Year	Man-hours[a]	Real Wages[b]
1947	70,718	102,810
1949	67,936	104,370
1951	75,160	120,430
1953	77,620	134,090
1955	77,220	141,530
1957	77,445	149,340
1959	77,228	153,670
1961	76,250	156,580
1963	79,804	170,510
1965	85,364	190,290
1967	89,254	205,670
1969[c]	94,069	223,940

[a] In millions.
[b] In millions of dollars at 1957–59 prices.
[c] Preliminary.
Source: United States Department of Labor, *Manpower Report of the President: 1970* (Washington, D.C.: U.S. Government Printing Office, 1970), pp. 267, 271, 272, and 328.

the dollar measurement of labor. There are obvious physical differences between workers. For some occupations physical strength makes a difference in productivity; for others it does not. Additional factors affecting productivity in many occupations are psychological well-being and intelligence or mental ability, different types of mental ability being important for different activities. Last, but certainly not least, training and education contribute to the quality of labor. These are added to the basic natural quality of the labor and can be and are analyzed separately under the rubric of *human capital* (a term that is discussed below). It is the total package of these attributes that is so neatly summed into the dollar cost of the labor.

The final basic factor of production is capital. The term capital can be confusing because it is used for two distinctly different things. Capital, when referring to a factor of production, is a physical thing—machines, buildings, and so forth—that contributes to production. The other use of the term capital is in reference to a monetary asset such as a bond or a bank account. In this latter sense capital is merely a legal claim for someone's debt. The two meanings of capital are often used interchangeably because businessmen can easily convert a claim to resources into the actual resources. One type of capital is as good as the other for their purposes. However, in this chapter the word capital is used in its physical rather than monetary sense.

Capital is used in a third way in the term human capital. It refers to the investment embodied in individuals. It is investment (in the form of education and training) that makes the difference between a very intelligent unskilled laborer and a surgeon. Such human capital can be thought of as a long-lived factor of production just like a machine. The concept of human capital will be elaborated upon considerably in coming chapters.

Capital is an intermediate factor of production because it is produced through the application of labor and natural resources. It is the indirect method of production using the intermediate factor, capital, which leads to increased labor productivity. The use of labor and materials in the production of an adding machine is a process of capital formation. The adding machine is a capital good that will be used together with other labor and materials in the production of final goods and services. The investment in the production of the adding machine leads to a greater output than would have been possible if all the labor had been directly expended on the formation of the final good. Think of how many calculations can be performed with an adding machine relative to what could be done with pencil and paper or simply in one's head. However, it must be remembered that any increase in capital is achieved only at the expense of less consumption in the present since the resources which are utilized in producing the capital could have been utilized for the production of goods or services to be consumed in the present.

Capital, too, can be aggregated in dollar units. For this purpose the dollar cost of producing the capital good is taken as capital's value. Over time, wear and tear decrease the value of the capital goods. In order to aggregate capital of various ages (what has become known as "vintages"), the capital goods are *depreciated* as they grow older. That is, a certain dollar amount is deducted from the value of the capital good each year. Another factor affecting the dollar value of capital after it is produced is technological progress that leads to obsolescence of existing capital. The dollar value of capital in the form of a factory for the production of horse-drawn carriages fell drastically after the horseless carriage was invented. The necessity to make judgments on how much depreciation and obsolescence of the capital stock has occurred makes the figures on the capital stock extant as arguable as most of the other figures we have discussed.

THE PRODUCTION POSSIBILITY FRONTIER

Two important concepts are described in this section: the law of increasing costs and the concept of efficiency. These are vital to the understanding of the production possibility frontier and are therefore discussed in conjunction with it.[3] In Chapter 2 GNP, the aggregate of all the goods and services produced in the economy in a given year, was defined and discussed. Suppose that instead of producing many goods, all our factors of production were directed to the production of a single good, say desks. All workers leave their jobs and go into the forests to cut lumber or into factories to put together desks. If this were to happen, there would be a number of desks produced that would be the maximum possible in the given economy, say 80 billion. The value of the desks produced would be GNP. Alternatively, suppose all resources are utilized for the production of blackboards. Again, there is a maximum number that could be produced, say 40 billion. Neither of these alternatives is very attractive. With no desks, students would have to sit on the floor. With no blackboards, teachers could not demonstrate points very easily. Therefore, anyone would prefer that some of each of the goods be produced. Now suppose that half the available resources were devoted to the production of each of the two goods. How many blackboards and desks could be produced? Actually, output would be more than half of the above mentioned potentials of each, say 48 billion desks and 26 billion blackboards. (Figure 5.1 shows these three possible combinations of blackboards and desks as points D, F, and E: point D is 80 units of desks and zero units of blackboards, E is 48 units of desks and 26 units of blackboards, and F is 40 units of blackboards and zero units of desks.) This is accounted for by the general principle known as the *Law of Increasing Costs: We have to give up more and more of good* A *in order to get an additional unit of good* B *as we have more and more of good* B. It is possible to produce more than half of each of the totals for desks and blackboards alone when only half the resources are devoted to each because those resources best suited for making blackboards are transferred into the production of blackboards on the one hand and, on the other hand, those resources best suited for making desks are transferred into the production of desks. Thus, miners work on producing slate for blackboards rather than making desks where they added very little to output, and farmers work on tree production for desks rather than on blackboards where they would contribute little.

Refer again to Figure 5.1. When both blackboards and desks are produced at point E, we can give up 14 units of desks and add 7 units of blackboards to our production (from E to G). To get still another 7 units of blackboards, 34 units of desks (from point G to point F) would have to be foregone. The locus of points that shows the maximum number of desks that can be produced for each number of blackboards is called the *production possibility frontier*.[4] In the case of three (or n) goods, the production possibility frontier would be three (or n) dimensional. The difficulty of drawing three (and n) dimensional figures is one rationale for limiting discussion to a two-product case.[5]

Does one of the points on the production possibility frontier indicate how much will actually be produced in a given year? Undoubtedly, no. The production possibility frontier tells how much *could* be produced, given the best and most efficient utilization of all the resources. Unfortunately, it is quite rare to find all resources being utilized in the most efficient manner possible. Producing a quantity of goods represented by any point on the production possibility frontier is being *efficient*. Typically, the economy will produce some combination of goods represented by a point such as J on Figure 5.1. This point, like all other points inside the production possibility frontier, is inefficient. To complete the taxonomy, any point such as K which is outside the production possibility frontier is *unfeasible;* that is, it represents a

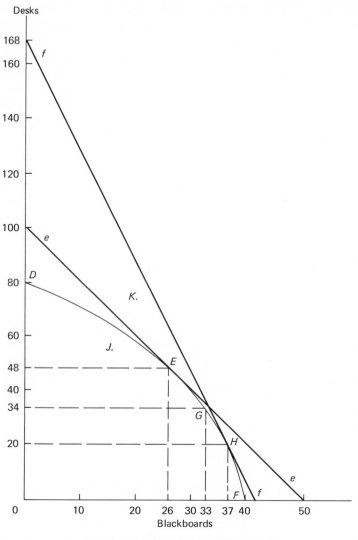

Figure 5.1   Production Possibility Frontier

combination of goods which is beyond the capabilities of the economy to produce. Efficiency in economic terms is a very narrow, strictly technical word. One can be efficient while producing nothing but blackboards (point *F* on Figure 5.1) even though everyone must write on his lap.

One can indicate, however, what combination of goods *should* be produced. Ideally, of course, we would produce efficiently. But that only says that production should be on the production possibility frontier, and that frontier is made up of an infinity of points. The point that is *optimum* (that is, *efficient and most desirable*) is the point representing the combination of goods that has the greatest value. The optimum combination of goods is the one that would ideally be produced. The optimum point can easily be found by taking the price rates of the two goods and drawing the tangent to the production possibility frontier that has a slope representing that price ratio.[6] The tangent line *ee* in Figure 5.1 represents such a situation. If the price of blackboard units were twice the price of desk units, say $20 for a blackboard and $10 for a desk, the relative price line would have a slope of 2 since a given amount of money can purchase twice as many desks as blackboards. The largest GNP value would be derived by producing 48 desks and 26 blackboards, as represented by point *E* on tangent line *ee*. The value of this combination of goods would be $1,000 [(26 × $20 = $520) plus (48 × $10 = $480) equals $1,000]. All other combinations of goods have lower values. For example, point *H* representing 20 desks and 37 blackboards has a value of $940, point *F* representing 40 blackboards and zero desks has a value of $800, and point *J* representing 40 desks and 20 blackboards has a value of $800. Thus, the point of tangency between the production possibility frontier and the line with a slope representing the price ratios of the two goods defines the optimum point of production. Whereas it is simple to define and find the optimum output combination in theory, it is very difficult to do so in practice because it requires so much data.

A TWO-FACTOR MODEL OF PRODUCTION

Now that factors of production and the production possibility frontier have been defined and described, we shall investigate the processes by which the factors of production are transformed into the final goods that go to make up the production possibility frontier: the production function. For reasons of simplicity this will be done in terms of only two factors of production, as was explained when the production possibility frontier was developed.[7] In examining this two-factor model, the main laws of production—decreasing returns to a factor and economies and diseconomies of scale—will be evolved.

A *production function* is a relationship between inputs and outputs. It can be in a generalized functional forms such as

$$Q = f(K, L) \tag{1}$$

or a specific form such as

$$Q = 50K + 20L \tag{2}$$

where Q stands for units of output, K stands for units of capital, and L stands for units of labor. The first formulation, equation (1), reveals only that the amount of output is a function of or depends upon the amount of capital and labor employed. It does not disclose the exact form of that dependence; the second formulation (2) does. Production functions such as equation (2) are derived empirically; various amounts of capital are employed with various amounts of labor, and the amounts of output resulting are recorded. Suppose it were found that the outputs shown in the hypothetical production schedule (Table 5.2) were produced when one to four units of capital were combined with one to eight units of labor. For example, when two units of capital (say, two machines) were combined with three units of labor (say three 100-man-hours), 245 units of output (say, desks) were produced. Such empirical findings as are described in Table 5.2 may or may not be summarizable in a neat formula such as equation (2). In our example, because the numbers in Table 5.2 were not derived empirically, they are perfectly summarized (except for rounding) by the following production function

$$Q = 100\sqrt{K \cdot L} \tag{3}$$

Actual empirical results would undoubtedly require a much more complex formulation.

Table 5.2

Output in a Two-Factor Production Model

Capital									
4	0	200	283	346	400	447	490	529	566
3	0	173	245	300	346	387	424	458	490
2	0	141	200	245	283	316	346	374	400
1	0	100	141	173	200	224	245	265	283
0	0	0	0	0	0	0	0	0	0
	0	1	2	3	4	5	6	7	8	Labor

An examination of these numbers will reveal some interesting characteristics. First, they show what effect increasing all factors of production by the same scale-factor has on output. Take, for example, the following three combinations of labor and capital: 1 capital with 2 labor, 2 capital with 4 labor, and 3 capital with 6 labor. Except for rounding differences, the outputs for the latter two bundles of factors are exactly two and three times that of the first: 141, 283, and 424. That is, as the amount of the factors of production is doubled or tripled, output is doubled or tripled. Since this result is found for every set of factor inputs, one can conclude that this production function demonstrates constant returns to scale. *Constant returns to scale is defined as a condition wherein when all factors of production are increased by the same multiple, output is increased by that multiple.*

Constant returns to scale is not a general economic law. Cases of decreasing and increasing returns to scale are also common. *Decreasing (increasing) returns to scale is defined as a condition wherein when all factors of production are increased by the same multiple, output is increased by a smaller (larger) multiple.*[8] A small manufacturer increasing his scale of operations to the point that he can use automated machinery is an example of where economies of scale can be seen. Many machines just cannot be made in all sizes, *e.g.*, small blast furnaces simply do not exist. A certain critical minimum operation is necessary for their employment. When such capital is utilized, output goes up by an amount more than proportional to the increase of labor and capital. On the other side of the spectrum, a size is sometimes reached that is so great that additions to capital and labor achieve a less than proportional increase in output. Some would say that the federal government is at this stage, others that the New York City school system is. In both cases the claim is that the bureaucracy becomes too large and ungainly to be managed properly.[9]

There are those who argue that neither economies nor diseconomies of scale actually exist. If one seems to observe diseconomies of scale as a firm grows larger, it is merely due to a lack of increasing the managerial input to scale, perhaps in both quantity and quality. The claim is that if one seems to observe economies of scale, it is rather indivisibility of certain capital items. If all factors of production were completely divisible so that one *could* actually increase all of them to scale, there would be no economies of scale observed. These arguments have some validity. In a technical sense the argument against economies of scale may be correct, but if so, it is merely a definitional destruction of economies of scale. The argument against diseconomies of scale is one that is difficult to prove one way or the other because the quality of management can be only subjectively evaluated.

The second attribute of this production function is that it demonstrates the *Law of Decreasing Marginal Returns to a Factor: As we add more and more of one factor, holding all others constant, there will be less and less additional output produced.*[10] Take any amount of capital or labor, say 2 units of capital, and observe how much output is produced as the other factor is increased by one unit at a time holding the amount of capital constant. Referring to production function (3) represented by Table 5.2, it is seen that the first unit of labor increases output from zero to 141 units, an increase of 141 units. The second unit increases output to 200, an increase of 59 units. The third unit of labor increases output to 245, an increase of 45 units. The fourth, fifth, sixth, seventh, and eighth units of labor add 38, 33, 30, 28, and 26 additional units of output, respectively. Each additional unit adds a smaller amount to total output. One could find the same type of result from adding labor (capital) to any base amount of capital (labor). Thus, production function (3) demonstrates decreasing marginal returns to a factor of production.

The fact that production function (3) has as an attribute decreasing returns to a factor is interesting, but what is the logic behind this phenomenon? Is it merely a mathematical quirk of the hypothetical production function chosen or, rather, a reasonable economic law? Imagine a library with a certain amount of equipment and books. Without any labor there will be no output where output is defined as people checking out books and otherwise utilizing the library's potential services. When one librarian is added (1 unit of labor), some output will be produced. When a second librarian is added, there will be a greater quantity of output. As librarians are continually added, there will be more and more output. The crucial question is: How much will output increase for each additional librarian? The logical and observable answer is that each librarian will contribute less and less *additional* output to the total, that is, diminishing marginal returns to the factor occurs. This is due to the amount of books and equipment being fixed. Each additional librarian can add something to output by reshelving books more quickly, cataloging more quickly, knowing more thoroughly the books of various types, and so on. However, the marginal contribution of each new librarian is bound to fall because the tasks he performs are less and less important. They will indeed be less and less important because the first librarian is certainly going to perform the most important activity, the second librarian the next most important one, and so on. Another way of looking at this phenomenon is that each librarian has less of the fixed resources of books and equipment to work with than before as the fixed stock of capital and materials is spread over more and more labor. Naturally, the last librarian will not be able to produce as much as the previous one. The effect that decreasing marginal returns to a factor describes can also be characterized by the phrase *diminishing marginal produc-tivity.*[11]

The possibility of exceptions to the law of decreasing marginal returns to a factor does exist. At the onset of production one could imagine increasing returns to a factor. For example, in the case of the library, with a given amount of capital and one librarian the single worker would have to undertake each of the activities involved in a library. He would have to catalog, check out books, order books, keep the accounts, shelve books, give reference aid, and so forth. The addition of a second librarian would permit specialization and hence greater productivity. Thus, the output of the two men could be more than double the output of one. However, such instances of increasing returns to a factor are generally ignored because no one is going to produce at a point where increasing returns to a factor is possible. More and more of that factor will be hired until production is carried beyond this range. At the other end of the spectrum, there is a tech-nological possibility of observing negative marginal returns to a factor: As an additional unit of labor, for example, is added to a fixed amount of capital and land, the total output decreases. An example of negative marginal returns would be the addition of labor into a library to the point where the librarians were so crowded that they bumped into one another while attempting to work thus causing everyone's work to suffer. It is easy to see that this is not a practical problem, which is why the possibility of negative returns to a factor is normally ignored also.

One point must be stressed because it is so often confused by students: There is no inconsistency between *constant* returns to scale and *decreasing* returns to a factor. It was seen in Table 5.2 that both of these characteristics were present in the same production schedule. There is no logical conflict. Constant returns to scale refers to a situa-tion where all the factors of production are being increased by the same multiple. Decreasing returns to a factor refers to having one factor increase while all the others remain fixed.

An additional concept utilized in discussions of production is that of an *isoquant*. An isoquant is a line of equal quantities. In the context of a production function, it is a line representing various combinations of labor and capital which yield the same amount of output. Referring again to Table 5.2, it can be seen that an isoquant representing 200 units of output would pass through the points represented by 4 capital and 1 labor, 2 capital and 2 labor, and 1 capital and 4 labor as depicted in Figure 5.2. Similarly, the isoquant representing 283 units of output goes through the points: 4 capital and 2 labor, 2 capital and 4 labor, and 1 capital and 8 labor. It can be surmised that any other point on the isoquant is a possible combination of labor and capital that would yield the same output.

Efficiency in production is defined as the achievement of a given output at minimum cost or as producing maximum output with a given expenditure. For both definitions the efficient combination of capital and labor can be determined with the aid of an isoquant map. Each isoquant shows the combinations of labor and capital that will yield a particular amount of product. To find the combination of resources that minimizes the cost of an output, it is necessary to find the point of tangency between the isoquant representing the amount desired and a relative price line for capital and labor. For example, if labor costs $2 per unit and capital $1 per unit, the relative price line would have a slope of 2. In Figure 5.3, several lines with slopes of 2 are superimposed onto the isoquant map. The combination of labor and capital that minimizes the cost of producing 283 units, for example, is shown by the tangency (*A*) of that isoquant with a price line (*bb*) which occurs at 4 units of capital and 2 units of labor (costing 4 × $1 for the capital + 2 × $2 for the labor = $8). All other combinations of capital and labor yielding 283 units of output will cost more; for

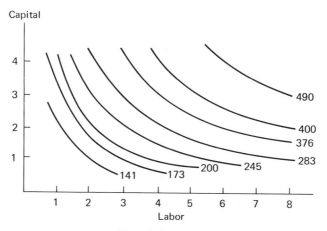

Figure 5.2   Isoquant Map

example, 2 capital and 4 labor costs 2 × $1 + 4 × $2 = $10, and 1 capital and 8 labor costs 1 × $1 + 8 × $2 = $17.

One can further determine the maximum output obtainable with a given budget by drawing a *budget line* on the isoquant map. The budget line is constructed by determining the maximum quantity of labor purchasable with the available money, given that no capital is bought and vice versa. A straight line drawn between these two points represents all combinations of labor and capital within the allotted budget. The maximum output given the budget constraint is represented by the isoquant tangent to the budget line. If the budget is $8, for example, the maximum output is 283 as seen by point *A* in Figure 5.3. With $8, the maximum labor purchasable at $2 per unit is 4 units and the maximum capital at $1 per unit is 8 units. Thus, relative price line *bb* is also the

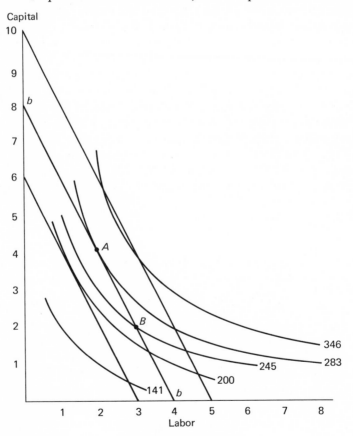

Figure 5.3   Efficiency

budget line for $8. Note that point B is also on the budget line and therefore represents a combination of labor and capital that can be purchased. But 2 units of capital together with 3 units of labor is on the isoquant representing 245 units of output. Therefore, if the $8 budget is utilized to purchase that combination of resources, output is not maximized. Indeed, 283 is the highest isoquant that the $8 budget line touches and is the maximum production obtainable with the $8.

Both of these illustrations demonstrate the utilization of isoquants in finding the optimum combination of factors of production to use. Of course, it is the relative prices of the factors of production (the price of capital relative to the price of labor)—geometrically represented by the budget line—that determines the optimal combination of factors.

FACTOR PAYMENTS

In our economic system the payments for the use of the factors of production determine the distribution of income among the population. Therefore, the determination of the payments made to the factor owners is vital to every individual. Basically, the interaction of supply and demand determine how much a factor of production is paid. However, a great deal lies behind that basic fact, and several qualifications to it are necessary.

The supply of each of the factors of production is of a different nature. The supply of land or more generally, natural resources, is in a sense fixed. That would suggest that the supply curve for, say, coal is a vertical line (as *ss* in Figure 5.4A): So much coal exists and that amount will be supplied, no more and no less, regardless of the price. In fact, however, the supply curve of many natural resources is of the normal kind sloping upward to the right (*ss* in Figure 5.4B). Owners of coal would rather hold it than sell at what they consider to be too low a price. For land itself, the perfectly inelastic supply curve is a good abstraction of the supply for rental purposes. There is just so much land available, and it will not be used up. Therefore, there is no incentive to withhold any from the rent market in the hope of a higher price in the next period. The essence of the difference between the two types of factors is that one is consumed in use and hence must be sold outright, whereas the other is not consumed in use and thus can also be rented.

Labor supply is more complex. Looking first at an individual's supply curve of labor (the offering of the services of a man's time), it

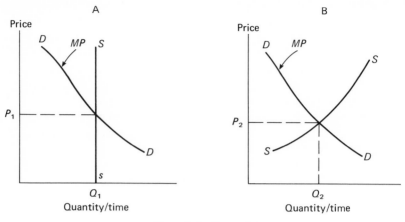

Figure 5.4   Factor Prices

is found that it begins at a positive price. Below some minimal wage more energy is expended in working than could be replaced by the purchase of food with the wage earned therefrom. At higher wage rates, the contour of the supply curve of labor is determined by the relative strength of the income effect and the substitution effect.

As the wage rate increases, an individual's income is increased. He will consequently be able to purchase more goods and services, leisure being one of them. However, the purchase of leisure is equivalent to working less. Thus, the income effect leads to less work as wages rise. The substitution effect of a rise in wages has the opposite effect. As wages increase, leisure becomes more expensive in terms of the earnings that are foregone in order to consume leisure. When one good becomes more expensive relative to others, one naturally tends to purchase less of it and more of the goods that have not increased in price. Therefore, the substitution effect of a wage rate increase leads to the purchase of less leisure, that is, to more work.

For the economy as a whole, the labor supply at any point in time is seen to be of the general shape of the supply curve in Figure 5.4B, that is, upward sloping to the right. Over time, the aggregate supply curve for any group is more like the shape of the curve *BD* seen in Figure 5.5, that is upward sloping to the *left*, reflecting a choice of less work as the wage rate increases.[12] Since the aggregate supply curve at any given time is a summation of each individual's supply curve, in addition to wages, demographic factors (size, age composition, and sex composition) strongly affect the aggregate supply of labor.

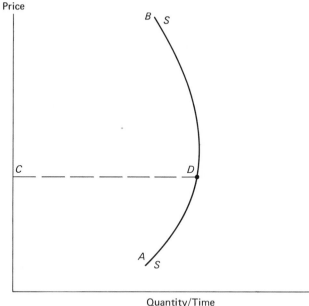

Figure 5.5   Backward Bending Supply of Labor

The more people of working age, for example, the greater the aggregate supply of labor at any given wage.

The supply of capital is different from either of the above. In the short run it is extremely inelastic much like land. A fixed amount of capital exists in a given year, and the owners will rent it out at the best price they can get. In the long run, however, the supply curve is of a rather normal shape, slanting upward to the right. The reason for this is that in the long run capital can be created or used up, and the rate at which this is done depends upon the rental price of capital.

Although the supply curves of the various factors of production differ markedly, the demand for those factors of production does not. The demand for any factor of production depends on its marginal productivity, the added output that is garnered from adding an additional unit of the factor to the productive process. This, as was mentioned above, is an idealization; other things do play a role, for example, desire for personal prestige, and in some cases, nepotism and discrimination. However, these other variables are generally of secondary importance to this rational, profit-maximizing criterion. The demand curve, which is the same as the curve of marginal productivity of a factor, decreases as more and more of the factor is added to production (the law of diminishing marginal productivity); since the marginal productivity decreases as the quantity increases, the curve slopes downward to the right. A business man would be willing to pay P_2 for Q_2 units of the factor of production being considered (see Figure 5.4B). He would not be willing to pay any more than that because the added output of the last unit hired is valued at only P_2, by definition of the marginal productivity curve. He does not want more than Q_2 at that price because, as can be seen in Figure 5.4B, the next unit of the factor adds less to the product than the value, P_2, which must be paid for it. It is, of course, the intersection of the supply and demand curves for each of the factors of production that determines its price at any given time. The price might be P_1 for labor, capital in the long run, or many natural resources, or P_1 for land in its narrow sense or capital in the short run.

If the world were static and perfect competition prevailed so that the economy was always in equilibrium, the tale of factor pricing would be finished. Since the world is not purely competitive and the economy is not in equilibrium at all times, several qualifications have to be made to the methods of establishing the price of a factor of production described above. This is not meant to suggest that the intersection of the supply and demand curves does not set the price and quantity. Rather, the supply and demand curves themselves are displaced. Examples are the minimum wage laws and unionization. Minimum wage laws dictate the shape of the supply curve of labor at its lower end. Instead of the supply curve shown as AB in Figure 5.5, it will be like CDB: perfectly elastic at the minimum wage up to a certain quantity at which point the normal supply curve takes over. Unionization can have a variety of effects on the supply curve of labor, depending on the type of union and its policies. Some unions set a wage for each job and allow as many workers to be hired as the industry desires (this would be depicted by a horizontal supply curve). Others limit the membership as well as stipulating a wage or a minimum wage (the supply curve then can be somewhat complicated but generally would have a vertical section). Similarly, if there are monopolies on the production side operating in the economy, monopoly profits will be earned which give latitude for a price to prevail other than the free market price for a factor of production. Monopolies, on the other hand, could give businesses the power to force sellers to accept less than the marginal product value of their factors. With monopoly profits businesses can afford to pay more than marginal product for a factor if they so desire. And with monopoly power in the hands of labor unions, they can demand a wage larger than the value of the marginal product of their labor. As a consequence of such elements in the economy, the demand and supply curves differ from their counterparts as seen under free market conditions. However, the free market is the ideal to which we can turn for a good first estimate, at the least, of factor price determination.

QUESTIONS FOR DISCUSSION

1. Discuss the construction of a production possibility frontier between the level of reading (or science) skills of slow learning and fast learning students in an elementary (or secondary) school (assume the class is split 50–50). At what point on this frontier would you choose to produce? How might you justify your choice on either moral or economic grounds?

2. What alternative methods of production are utilized in the institution in which you are studying? Why is the same combination of labor and capital not used in all cases?

3. Do you envisage any opportunities for economies of scale at your institution? Any diseconomies? Does either exist at the elementary or secondary school level?

4. What implications might be drawn from the theory of decreasing marginal returns to a factor when considering the best way of increasing the reading skills of urban elementary school children?

5. What determines how much a teacher is paid in a theoretical construct? What elements determine this in the real world? Do the latter elements imply that the theory is invalid?

PROBLEMS

1. For the following production function
$$Q = 6K + 3L^2$$
   (a) Calculate output, Q, when 5 units of capital and 2 units of labor are utilized.
   (b) Does this production function exhibit constant returns to scale?

2. Utilizing the data presented in Table 5.2, what is the marginal product of labor at the point where 5 units of labor and 1 unit of capital are being employed? What is the marginal product of capital at that point? What are the marginal products if labor is increased to 7 units? What is the explanation for these differences?

3. Referring to Figure 5.3, if the cost of labor were $1 per unit and capital $2 per unit, what would be the most efficient combination of labor and capital to use in producing 283 units of output? What would be the cost per unit?

Chapter 6 BASIC STUDIES IN EDUCATIONAL PRODUCTION

THE application of production theory to educational issues is one of the newer developments in educational research. Nevertheless, research on educational production functions and educational productivity has already highlighted some crucial issues in education: (a) the question of measuring educational output, costs, and ultimately productivity; (b) cost-effectiveness decisions in teacher recruitment and retention; and (c) economies of scale in school operation. Three articles are reproduced in this chapter, each dealing with at least one of the three issues enumerated above.

Woodhall and Blaug, in their article, "Productivity Trends in British University Education, 1938–62," analyze and discuss productivity trends specific to the British higher educational system. Their methodological approach has universal applicability. The authors preface their empirical research with a discussion of the conceptual problems encountered in quantifying educational output.[1] They construct three alternate measures of educational output based on "cultural," "educational," and "economic" criteria and note that the results from all three measures are roughly comparable. After constructing an input series and comparing changes in both educational inputs and outputs, Woodhall and Blaug conclude that productivity in British university education has delined from 1938 to 1962. This finding is in contrast to productivity advances in other sectors of the British economy. The authors note that this productivity decline

Notes to Chapter 6 will be found on pages 372–378.

is one of the forces contributing to the economic plight of British institutions of higher education—a predicament equally true of the United States educational scene.

The Woodhall and Blaug article refers to two theoretical concepts discussed in Chapter 5 and notes their use in production function research. The authors assume "constant educational returns over time," by which they mean that doubling the number of school *years* doubles the amount of education obtained; and the theory of factor payments is alluded to in calculating the lifetime earnings of university graduates. In addition the authors illustrate the statistical use of index numbers, both as measures of change and as tools to inflate or deflate monetary measures.

The Levin article, "A Cost-Effectiveness Analysis of Teacher Selection," develops a production function for analyzing pupil achievement scores on standardized verbal examinations. The effects of teachers' verbal ability and years of experience on student achievement are quantified utilizing data from large city elementary schools. The study applies the information on the effects of these two teacher attributes and their costs to determine optimum criteria for teacher selection. It further distinguishes between the pay-off of these teacher attributes on the achievement of white and Negro students. Thus, the study has important implications for education efforts directed at the needs of disadvantaged youngsters. Although Levin couches his study in the broad reference frame of a cost-benefit analysis—a technique we do not explore until the next chapter—the methodology and conclusions are easily understandable.

Attention is called to two methodological techniques in the Levin study: the utilization of the utility maximizing theorem—as discussed in Appendix A of Chapter 3—in the purchase of teaching skills [equation (3) in the article], and the use of regression analysis in determining the cost of various teacher characteristics.

Riew's article, "Economies of Scale in High School Operation," focuses on the question of whether economies of scale (size) exist in educational institutions. Drawing upon the theory of the firm, he postulates a parabolic (U-shaped) relationship between average cost and enrollment and utilizes the technique of regression analysis to develop a model for determining the existence of economies of scale.[2] The model is then tested on data for individual senior high schools in Wisconsin, and the theoretical hypothesis of economies of scale is validated.

The concept of economies of scale is applicable for many levels of aggregation. Although Riew tests for the existence of economies of scale at the level of individual schools, one could also test for their existence at the classroom or school district level. In addition similar studies could be undertaken for elementary and higher education.

In each of the three studies the authors indicate that their research is just one step in applying production theory to educational issues. Additional refinements and extensions will undoubtedly be introduced in this area of educational research. In the meantime a firm beginning has been made in generating economic data and testing hypotheses necessary for an overall evaluation of educational productivity.

PRODUCTIVITY TRENDS IN BRITISH UNIVERSITY EDUCATION, 1938–62

MAUREEN WOODHALL AND MARK BLAUG

Despite the current interest in productivity measurement, very little is known about the productivity of the educational system, one of the largest sectors of the modern economy. Yet the twin pressures which dominate education today—strong demand for increased output and serious scarcity of resources to produce additional output—suggest the need for an economic analysis of the relationship between inputs and output. In this paper, we make a preliminary attempt to meet this need through a study of productivity trends in British university education since 1938.

Productivity is usually defined quite simply as output per unit of input. Clearly, where there are different inputs, there will be different ways of measuring productivity. Most studies of industrial productivity have concentrated on the productivity of labor as indicated by the ratio of total output to the number of man-hours employed. Consequently, improvements in productivity caused by a change in the utilization of capital have gone unrecorded. To overcome this deficiency in the measurement of productivity trends, economists have advocated measuring the ratio of output to a composite index of all the inputs. In the case of education, it would be particularly misleading to concentrate on labor productivity

Reprinted from *Minerva* 3 (1965): 483–98. Copyright © 1965. (The authors have kindly furnished us with the correction of an error appearing in the original version, and the correction has been incorporated in this reprinting.—Eds.)

since most developed countries are now dedicated to the deliberate reduction of pupil-teacher ratios as a matter of educational policy. They are in fact committed to the planned diminution of labor productivity in education. For this reason, if for no other, we will measure university productivity by an index of output per unit of combined inputs or, in the economist's terminology, by an index of total-factor productivity.

The purpose of productivity measurement is to provide a yardstick of economic efficiency in different time-periods for individual firms within an industry, or for an industry considered as a whole. The same techniques are used in each case but, of course, the problems of measurement will vary. Similarly, a study of educational productivity could treat the entire educational system as one industry, or confine itself to examining the productivity of different levels, or even of different individual institutions. For the purposes of this article, the universities will be regarded as a single industry producing higher education and comparison will be made between the years 1938, 1952, and 1962. The sources of the data are the annual reports and returns of the University Grants Committee[3] and the report and appendices of the Robbins Committee on Higher Education.[4] Since some of the official figures are themselves only rough estimates, we do not claim a high degree of accuracy for our final index. Even a crude calculation, however, may clarify the nature of productivity trends in higher education. At least it demonstrates that productivity analysis need not be confined to industries producing commercial goods and services but can be extended to the social services.

We do not imply a rigid analogy between the university and the factory: we will in fact examine some of the ways in which the process of education differs from that of manufacturing. We are convinced, however, that the comparison as such is illuminating. Some educationists have argued that the economic criteria of productive efficiency are entirely inappropriate to schools and universities for the simple reason that these are not profit-maximizing institutions.[5] But the principle that scarce resources should be combined in such a way as to maximize the achievement of an objective, whatever its character, is surely as relevant to public, as to private activities. The inefficient use of government funds is as undesirable as the inefficient use of private resources. This is the chief justification for attempting to measure the productivity of higher education.

SOME CONCEPTUAL PROBLEMS

In order to calculate the total-factor-productivity of an industry, it is necessary (1) to define and measure all inputs and outputs in quantitative terms; (2) to isolate variations in the quality of both inputs and outputs and express them in terms of constant quality; (3) to combine the various inputs and outputs in some appropriate manner; and, of course, (4) to divide the former into the latter. The first problem in considering the education industry is to define output. What is the end-product of a period of schooling? One of the peculiar features of universities is that they represent a vast multiproduct industry, providing teaching and research in a wide range of subjects at many different levels. All these elements have to be combined and expressed in equivalent units. Furthermore, the final product is intangible and, at first sight, incapable of being quantified. When physical measures are not available, as in the case of all the service industries, the common procedure is to use money values adjusted by a price index as an estimate of quantity. But there is no market mechanism for universities and so no money valuation of output. It is true that fees are charged but these do not represent the true economic costs of different courses of study. When some measure of the value of educational output is needed for purposes of national income accounting, the standard approach is to use expenditures on inputs as a proxy measure of the value of output. Thus, in the national accounts education is valued by the costs of labor and materials.[6] But this solution is useless for an analysis of productivity, since it implicitly assumes that the ratio of inputs to output never changes. Some other estimate of the amount of education produced is our first requirement.

In the present analysis we must perforce limit ourselves to what can be readily quantified and measured. In the case of higher education the end-product is simply a degree. It is quite true that education consists of more than passing examinations but we do not yet have any quantitative data on intellectual insight and curiosity, social maturity, personal or cultural awareness, or the many other desirable by-products of higher education. Our measure of productivity is confined to what we can now measure; it is subject to alteration the moment other dimensions come to be quantified.

The definition of inputs involves fewer conceptual problems; inputs of universities include raw material (in the form of students), labor (of lecturers and administrative staff) and capital (in the form of buildings and equipment). The main difficulty is one of expressing each of these in real terms and combining them into a single index. The simple solution is to measure each input in terms of current money values corrected for changes in its own price[7]; but once again this is complicated by the absence of a market mechanism. Nevertheless, this is not an insuperable difficulty. For example, the market value of university buildings is difficult to calculate because they are not rented and have little second-hand value owing to their special features. But an imputed value can be calculated and this raises no new conceptual problems: imputed rents are a familiar feature of national income accounts.

Even when both inputs and outputs have been measured in real terms, there remains the question of quality changes. If, as some people believe, more education means worse education, a rise in output per unit of input may not indicate an increase in productivity. On the other hand, if it is true that to compare the educational system of the 1920s with that of the 1960s is "like identifying a crystal radio set with Telstar,"[8] then productivity must have risen astronomically. It all depends on what has happened to the quality of output and input. We lack really satisfactory measures of educational quality. But there are a number of factors which may be used as approximate indices of improvements in quality. Most previous studies of educational productivity have either ignored or made inadequate allowance for variations in quality, although the problem of quality is crucial to an analysis of productivity.[9]

PREVIOUS STUDIES OF EDUCATIONAL EFFICIENCY

While economists have been concerned with the yield of educational investment and with the question of the proper share of national resources which should be devoted to education, they have not been particularly concerned with the efficiency with which resources are allocated within the educational system. The problem of the productivity of education has been discussed very generally by such writers as John Vaizey and Seymour Harris.[10] Hector Correa made use of the concept of a production function for education in one of his works but failed to estimate it or to explore its implications for productivity analysis.[11]

Solomon Fabricant and H. D. Lytton have estimated the productivity of labor for the entire American government sector in recent years, including the productivity of teachers in schools.[12] They both concluded that increases in the quality of educational output compensated for the decline in output per teacher (measured by the pupil-teacher ratio); in consequence, no change took place in the productivity of education. The same conclusion was reached by W. Hirsch in a study of educational costs, unsupported, however, by adequate empirical data and in neglect of changes in quality.[13]

Other attempts in this country and in the United States to assess the efficiency of education have emphasized the influence of particular variables rather than the combined effect of all the inputs. One example of a full-scale multivariate analysis of the input-output relationship in education is an American study—"Project Talent"—based on a random sample of 1,000 secondary schools; output in this study is measured in terms of pupils' scores in specially administered achievement tests and variations in these scores are then analyzed in relation to a wide range of school and community characteristics.[14]

In the field of higher education there has been practically no analysis of input-output relationships. In America there are a few studies of costs per pupil and a number of controlled experiments on the efficiency of different teaching methods and various sizes of class. In Great Britain, even a general concern with internal economic efficiency is a novel idea in universities. The Hale Committee on University Teaching Methods, which reported last year, could find only two examples of controlled experiments in the efficiency of different methods of teaching.[15] Bruce Williams, who has frequently argued that universities should show more concern with efficiency, says that when the issue was once raised as to what universities were doing to increase their own productivity "the members of the conference thought the question strikingly funny."[16] This study of productivity trends in British universities is intended, therefore, to initiate a systematic analysis of the problem. The authors are aware of its crudities and hope that the present study will be used as a point of departure for further and more refined investigations.

THE OUTPUT OF UNIVERSITIES 1938–62

The basic unit for the index of output is a student completing a course. The number of annual degrees awarded is, therefore, our first estimate of output but this understates the actual outflow of students by the number who leave unqualified. Despite the pejorative implications of the term "wastage," even an incomplete education may be assumed to be better than none at all; hence, some allowance has been made for wastage. The Robbins Report shows that wastage among undergraduates entering in 1957 was 14 per cent, and that wastage rates have declined since the war.[17] There is little information about wastage among postgraduate students, but we have assumed that it is less than wastage for undergraduates but with a similar rate of decline for 1938–57. The number of graduating students, before and after allowance for wastage, is as given in Table 6.1.

These simple totals refer to university degrees in all subjects and at all levels. It is at this point that one of the important qualitative variables

Table 6.1

	1938	1952	1962
Degrees and diplomas awarded	15,909	26,429	37,619
Graduates plus unqualified students	18,337	29,957	42,006

should be taken into account. Obviously, there is no simple method of assessing the value of different courses of study. If the number of degrees is to be weighted to allow for quality differences, the system of weighting must depend on the standard by which the relative value of different kinds of education is assessed. One solution would be to distinguish between degrees requiring different lengths of study, but not between different subjects. If one ascribes great value to the cultural influence of education, greater weight might be given to degrees in the humanities and social studies than to those in science. Lastly, a strictly economic interpretation of this problem of quality-weights would weight different degrees by the "price" they command in the labor market, on the grounds that higher education is an investment in future earning potential. This last alternative most nearly resembles the usual solution in economic analysis of weighting different products by their market values.

In order to test the effect of each set of assumptions we have calculated an index using three weighting systems, which we have labelled respectively "the educational," "the cultural," and "the economic" index, as well as a simple, unweighted index. One of the most interesting findings of this study is that the choice of weights does not make a very significant difference to the final measure of productivity (the actual effects of adopting alternative weighting assumptions will be examined below). Other assumptions as to the relative value of different university courses could, of course, also be tested by using entirely different weighting systems. The most extreme view of all, namely that different types of education are completely incomparable, would imply that there is no way of combining different degrees into one index and that arts faculties and science faculties, for instance, must be regarded as entirely separate industries.

Our "educational index" therefore weights each degree by the average length of course leading to it, so that the greatest weight is given to postgraduates, less to those with first degrees, and least of all to those who leave before completing a course.[18] This weighting system implicitly assumes constant educational returns over time, which may be unrealistic for higher education, but for the present we have no evidence to support or reject this assumption. In order to assess the economic value of different subjects, we need to know the distribution of graduates with different subjects of study among different occupations and the relative lifetime incomes of each occupational group. Some information on both these points exists but unfortunately the data on graduate income differentials are very scanty.[19] A very rough system of weights has been constructed for broad groups of subjects by faculties. This economic assessment gives greater weight to science and technology graduates than to arts graduates because on average they have higher earnings. The actual weights used are based on the ratio of the average earnings of arts, or science, graduates to the average earnings of all graduates taken together. Of course, earnings differentials not only reflect an employer's evaluation of a degree but also individual differences in ability and background.[20] However, the "economic index" reflects approximately the relative value placed upon different kinds of higher education in the labor market and so measures the value of output under the assumption that one of the purposes of higher education is to prepare students for future careers. Finally, the "cultural index" rejects this vocational definition of education and reverses the economic weights by giving more weight to arts graduates than to scientists.[21] The actual weights used were in fact the reciprocals of the "economic" weights.

The effect of using each weighting system is as given in Table 6.2.

Table 6.2
Output of Universities 1938–62

	1938		1952		1962	
	No. of graduates	Index 1952 = 100	No. of graduates	Index 1952 = 100	No. of graduates	Index 1952 = 100
Unweighted Index	18,337	61	29,957	100	42,006	140
"Educational"	17,789	60	29,634	100	42,520	143
"Cultural"	18,045	60	29,892	100	42,543	142
"Economic"	17,513	60	29,157	100	41,887	144

While the actual quantity of output varies according to the weighting system used, the index is not very sensitive to different weighting assumptions. This is because the strongly rising trend in the number of students during this period overshadows the effects of different trends in the various faculties.

There is one important element of educational quality which has been ignored in this analysis, that is, variations in the class of degree, and in the standard required by different universities for the same degree. The Robbins Committee, for instance, observed that "there is the possibility that degree standards since the war have been higher than they were before the war."[22] This possibility makes it impossible to use class of degree alone as an indicator of quality. There would in any case be little value in adjusting the output index for changes in the proportion of first-class degrees, for example, without making a corresponding adjustment on the input side to allow for differences in the measured ability of students, which in turn creates additional unsolved difficulties. Students vary in native ability and home background, and also in formal qualifications on entry, but there is no reliable evidence of the ability of students on entry, since British universities do not give any form of intelligence tests; even the number of General Certificate of Education "Advanced Level" passes of the average entrant would be misleading, as an increase may simply reflect a tendency for pupils to sit for more subjects, rather than a genuine increase in ability. Our unit of output is not, therefore, of completely standard quality, since a degree in 1962 may have a higher educational value than one in 1938, due to advances in knowledge. On the other hand, it is perfectly conceivable that all the effects of advancing knowledge have merely raised the quality of entrants into higher education without altering the essential nature of the educational process at the university level. This problem cannot be conclusively solved in our present state of knowledge. An economist's answer would be to compare the relative earning capacity of a modern graduate with that of a graduate in 1938 but there is not sufficient historical data on the lifetime earnings of graduates to do this. However, our index of educational output does allow for all the other qualitative changes and so isolates changes in the educational value of a degree, together with changes in productivity.

AN INDEX OF INPUTS

We turn now to the input side of the educational process. Once again, the variables must be defined in real terms of constant quality. One problem of applying a productivity index to universities is that the student is both an input and an output of the system. Our measure of output is in fact an estimate of the "value added" by the process and some estimate has to be made of the input of students' time. Although this is a free input from the university's point of view, students' time has a high opportunity cost. If they were not studying, students would presumably be working and earning, so that the earnings they forego while at university represent the imputed money value of their time.[23] Estimates of earnings foregone by students have been used, based on the estimates made by the Robbins Committee,[24] and deflated by the average increase in juvenile wage rates between 1938 and 1962. This estimate of student input makes no allowance for variations in student quality, apart from allowing for the higher earnings foregone by postgraduate students (Table 6.3).

Table 6.3

Imputed Value of Students' Time in Real Terms (£m.)

1938	1952	1962
4.6	8.4	12.2

The number of teaching staff provides a first measure of the input of teachers' time but the number alone disguises important differences in quality. Despite many attempts to define high quality teaching, it remains a very elusive concept but two of the important factors appear to be qualifications and length of experience. Both of these are reflected by a teacher's grade, which in turn determines his salary, so that the number of teachers in each year has been weighted by their salaries. The money value of teachers' time must also be expressed in real terms and for this purpose an average index of university salaries has been used as a price deflator. In theory the academic salary structure does not take into account the relative scarcity of different subjects but W. G. Bowen has shown that teachers in science and technology faculties tend to be promoted to higher grades at an earlier age than arts staff, which has the effect of creating subject differentials.[25] The real value of teachers' salaries, therefore, provides an estimate of the input of teachers' time and any changes in the teachers' length of experience, qualifications or subject appear in the index as an increase in quality (Table 6.4).

Table 6.4

University Teachers' Salaries in Real Terms (£m.)

1938	1952	1962
6.3	13.2	24.2

The input of other goods and services, such as books and the time of administrative staff, can be estimated from the current expenditure of universities, making due allowance for price changes during the period. The University Grants Committee publishes, periodically, a specially constructed index of university costs.[26] And this index has been used to deflate current university expenditures; for the period 1938–52 the index was not calculated, so an index of retail prices was used as a rough approximation (Table 6.5).

Table 6.5

Universities' Current Expenditure in Real Terms (£m.)
(excluding Teachers' Salaries)

1938	1952	1962
7.7	15.2	30.5

Finally we have estimated the value of university capital, based on the Robbins Committee's calculations of imputed rent for 1962, which used current estimates of the capital cost of a new university place, and a depreciation rate of 6 per cent, spread over 60 years.[27] The Robbins Report figures do not allow for the increased quality of university buildings, about which there is no information, but an index of building costs has been used to allow for price changes. This calculation may well be the least reliable of our estimates but the value of capital has the smallest share of all the input factors, so that inaccuracies in this calculation do not have a significant effect on the final productivity index (Table 6.6).

Before these estimates can be combined into a total-factor index, some allowance has to be made for the fact that universities are a multiproduct

Table 6.6

Imputed Value of University Capital in Real Terms (£m.)

1938	1952	1962
5.2	9.2	13.0

industry producing teaching and research. These twin functions are clearly closely related and interdependent; to borrow C. F. Carter's phrase, "like mutton and wool, they are joint products of the academic sheep."[28] But although the allocation of resources between teaching and research is not clear-cut, it is obvious that some proportion of the inputs of staff time, buildings, equipment and materials is devoted solely to research and cannot, therefore, be included in an index of educational productivity. Both the Robbins Committee and the University Grants Committee have made rough estimates of the time and expenditure devoted to research, which suggest that in 1952 just over half the total (apart from student time) was allocated to teaching.[29] Since 1938 there has been an increase in research activity, due to the development of specialized research units in some universities, so we have assumed that the proportion of expenditure devoted to teaching has declined from 60 per cent in 1938 to 54 per cent in 1952 and 52 per cent in 1962.[30]

We can now compare the relative growth of each factor of input during this period (Table 6.7), and finally combine them into a single index.[31]

Table 6.7

Input of Universities, 1938–62
(Index 1952 = 100)

	1938	1952	1962
Teachers' Time	54	100	177
Other Expenditure	56	100	194
Capital	62	100	136
Students' Time	54	100	145

The inputs which have increased most rapidly during this period are teachers, educational materials and other services; these inputs have also increased their share of the total costs of education, while the other factors, capital and the value of students' time, have risen more slowly and their share in total costs has declined (Table 6.8).

The real values of each of the inputs, adjusted to allow for the proportions devoted to research, can now be combined to provide a composite index of all the factors for each of the three years. It is the ratio of output to

Table 6.8

**Relative Contribution of Input Factors
(Percentage of Total)**

	1938	1952	1962
Teachers	24	25	27
Goods and Services	28	29	33
Capital	19	17	14
Students	29	29	26

this composite input index which provides a measure of the productivity of universities.

EVIDENCE OF DECLINING PRODUCTIVITY

What does this tell us about trends in university productivity since 1938? Whatever set of educational assumptions is adopted, the increase in inputs has been greater than the increase in output, which means that the production of one graduate in 1962 needed more resources than in 1952 or in 1938: productivity has steadily declined. The extent of this fall in productivity depends on the weighting system used for output (Table 6.9).

Table 6.9

**Rates of Change in University Productivity, 1938–62
(Average Annual Percentage Change)**

	1938–52	1952–62	1938–62
Unweighted Output	−0.6	−1.7	−1.1
"Educational" Output Weights	−0.5	−1.5	−0.9
"Cultural" Output Weights	−0.6	−1.6	−1.0
"Economic" Output Weights	−0.5	−1.5	−0.9

When no allowance is made for changes in the quality of output, the fall in productivity appears greater than when the output of graduates is standardized for variations in the standard and subject of their degree. Other assumptions about the quality of output would, in turn, produce a different estimate of the fall in productivity. For instance, between 1952 and 1962 not only did the number of teachers in universities rise but their quality, as measured by their real salary, also increased; if this increase is assumed to have produced an equivalent increase in the quality of graduates, the rate of productivity decline is reduced to 1.2 per cent per annum between 1952 and 1962. Some people may wish to argue that we have still neglected increases in the educational value of a university degree and that the index provides evidence of rising quality, rather than falling productivity. This is a question which can only be settled by further attempts to find objective measures of educational quality. However, even under the most optimistic assumptions there is no evidence at all of any increase in productivity and the ratio of output to inputs has declined more rapidly in recent years.

To grasp the full implications of this conclusion, let us compare these trends with productivity trends in other service industries. In a study of trends in labor productivity between 1920 and 1962, C. H. Feinstein showed that output per man-hour has risen more rapidly in the postwar period than before 1938 and that this faster rate of increase has been almost entirely due to improvements in the productivity of the service industries.[32] His measure of productivity, however, ignores the contribution of factors other than labor. A more recent study of inter-sectoral productivity takes into account the contribution of capital, and shows that between 1948 and 1963 productivity in the goods sector rose by 2.79 per cent and in the service sector by 1.34 per cent a year.[33]

The trends in educational productivity, therefore, run directly counter to trends in the service sector as a whole. Productivity in universities has declined since 1938 and there has been a deterioration in recent years; in the service sector generally, productivity has been rising and at a steadily increasing rate. This means that the provision of university education is continually absorbing more of the country's resources, since the price of each factor and, even more important, the opportunity cost of each factor reflects the rising productivity of other industries. Although increased productivity in the industries producing educational materials will have the effect of lowering the relative cost of these inputs, the salaries of university staff tend to follow in the wake of the aggregate rate of change of labor productivity. If overall productivity is rising, while the productivity of higher education is falling, it follows that the faster the general pace of technical advance, the greater the upward pressure on the costs of universities. Faster technical change is a blessing as far as educational equipment and building materials are concerned but a curse from the point of view of hiring university staff.

CONCLUSIONS

There is no one simple explanation of the decline in productivity of universities, just as there is no single reason why productivity in other industries has risen. An improvement in productivity may be the result of a technological innovation which enables resources to be combined more efficiently; it may be the result of an increase in capital per worker, or an improvement in the quality of capital, or simply the result of economies of scale. Deakin and George, in their study of intersectoral productivity, ascribe 70 per cent of the increased productivity of both goods and service industries since 1948 to improved technical and organizational knowledge, and the remaining 30 per cent to increases in capital per head.[34] One of the outstanding differences between universities and conventional industries in the period under review is that in almost every industry new and more efficient methods of production have been introduced, while the technology of teaching has remained unchanged. It is still true to say that, in the field of education, the last dramatic innovation was the printed book.

Indeed, all the efforts of universities appear to be directed towards decreasing productivity rather than increasing it. A striking example is the constant pressure for smaller classes and higher staff-pupil ratios. Despite a considerable body of research, particularly in America, which has demonstrated that "class size in itself is a relatively minor factor in educational efficiency as measured in terms of student achievement or of any other measurable outcome,"[35] the smaller class remains one of the chief preoccupations of educational policy. Even though a small class may have important educational advantages in certain subjects and at certain age levels, it is extremely doubtful that it provides the ideal means of communicating all sorts of knowledge at every level; in a good many circumstances, particularly in higher education, it is simply an expensive luxury.[36]

Although there is now a serious shortage of well-qualified teachers, the possibilities of substituting capital for labor in education or economizing on the time of teachers are persistently ignored. Some universities have experimented with the use of educational television and recently there has been an upsurge of interest in techniques of programmed learning,[37] but compared with research into new industrial techniques such experiments in the technology of teaching are still on a very small scale.

In order to make more efficient use of capital, universities have been urged to introduce fourth terms, or "two-shift universities." One intriguing proposal is that efficiency would actually be improved by a slight increase in the ratio of vacations to terms, provided the organization of the academic year were changed, to encourage students to make better use of the long vacation. This sort of major reorganization would raise a great many problems and it may be true that the advantages of such changes have been exaggerated by some writers. On the other hand, many smaller changes and experiments could be introduced in universities without causing major disruptions.

The Hale Committee on University Teaching Methods, having noted an extraordinary lack of interest in the efficiency of teaching techniques on the part of many university staff, concluded: "If during the forthcoming period of expansion the standard of university education is to be maintained, and if at the same time no more than legitimate claims are to be made on the national revenue and pool of ability, then university building and plant and the time of university teachers will have to be better used."[38] Our picture of the trend in university productivity underlines the urgency of action along the lines of this declaration.

A COST-EFFECTIVENESS ANALYSIS OF TEACHER SELECTION

HENRY M. LEVIN

It has been widely recognized that the educational systems of the large cities have failed to effectively teach or significantly motivate large numbers of disadvantaged youngsters.[39] The recent public response to these failures has been to increase spending for the schools in order to compensate for disadvantages in the backgrounds of their students. Indeed, the Elementary and Secondary Education Act of 1965 alone has provided over $1 billion a year in additional school expenditures for students from low-income families. Given these infusions of dollars, school districts, state governments, and the U.S. Office of Education have been increasingly concerned about how to get the most impact out of the additional financial support. These governments have looked increasingly to cost-effectiveness analysts for the answers, and the response has been a profuse outpouring of cost-effectiveness studies.[40] Interestingly, each of these studies has examined the relationship between total costs and a hypothetical set of outcomes without examining the particular programs on which the money was spent. That is, the process by which education is produced has been ignored, and only a gross relation between dollar expenditures and outputs has been surveyed. The internal efficiency of different educational strategies has not been explored.

Yet the educational decision maker is faced with the problem of how to spend additional resources in the most effective way possible. In doing this he is handicapped by some formidable obstacles. First, there is little unanimity on what schooling output is or on how to measure a multidimensional array of outcomes. Second, there is almost no theory which describes the relations between schooling inputs, the educational process, and schooling outcomes. And third, there is even a great deal of vagueness on what should be considered as schooling inputs. For example, it has been suggested that students contribute to the education of fellow students and that teachers' attitudes may be more important than other teachers' characteristics. Finally, even student performance on standardized achievement tests is so confounded by the student's own social class, his abilities, and his general environmental milieu, that it has proven very difficult to measure school effects separately from those caused by other influences.[41]

The result of all this confusion is that additional expenditures for education have been spent in very traditional ways, most particularly on

Reprinted from the author's manuscript which subsequently appeared in the *Journal of Human Resources* 5 (1970): 24–33. Copyright © 1970 by the Regents of the University of Wisconsin.

reductions in class size and the addition of remedial specialists. This very unimaginative route is taken despite the plethora of alternatives that are available: new instructional technologies, radically different curricula, and different types of teachers represent possibilities that have been scarcely considered while schools do more of what they have always done with reduced class sizes and a few additional specialists. Unfortunately, the cost-effectiveness studies undertaken thus far have done little to delineate the most effective strategies for any particular objective (*e.g.*, raising reading scores). Indeed, one study has stated this shortcoming quite honestly: "A key part of this final analysis, which is missing completely from this study, is the analysis of how differences in program inputs can affect the direct measures of achievement."[42]

COST-EFFECTIVENESS AND TEACHER SELECTION

If one were to attempt to help the school decision-maker spend his money more efficiently, where would he start? An obvious place to begin would appear to be teacher selection, for teachers' salaries represent about 70 per cent of current operating expenditures for the elementary and secondary schools. Thus, we might want to ask two questions:

1. Which teachers' characteristics show a relation to a goal that most of us would accept for the schools, *i.e.*, student performance on a standardized test of verbal achievement?
2. What does it cost the schools to obtain teachers with different characteristics?

Given answers to these two questions, we wish to ascertain whether we can obtain teachers with more effectiveness per dollar of expenditure.

The first question might be answered if we were to estimate a production function of the form:

$$A = F(X, Y, Z_1, \ldots, Z_k) \tag{1}$$

Where A is the achievement score for an individual, X represents a vector of social class and background influences which affect achievement, Y represents a set of non-teacher characteristics for the schools, and $Z_1, \ldots, Z_k$ represents a set of teacher attributes. Ordinarily the assumption is made that F is convex to the origin and continuous throughout its domain[43] (and that the first order partial derivatives are positive and the second order partials are negative).

Corresponding to question (2) would be a budget constraint

$$B = (P_1 Z_1 + P_2 Z_2 + \cdots + P_k Z_k) \tag{2}$$

which in this case would apply only to the teachers' costs, where P_1, ..., P_k denote the prices of teacher characteristics Z_1, ..., Z_k respectively. Let us call this a teachers' quality budget constraint, since we are assuming that teacher-student ratios are constant, and that the question before us is that of obtaining teachers of a better quality for a given teachers' budget.[44] While we are using this example only for illustrative purposes, this approach does have the advantages of keeping the problem down to a manageable— but still meaningful—size.

Assume that we wish to maximize (1) subject to constraint (2). The solution to this problem would require obtaining each type of teachers' quality Z_i until its additional contribution to achievement $(\delta A/\delta Z_i)$ relative to its price (P_i) were equal for all Z_i $(i = 1, \ldots, k)$.[45] That is:

$$\frac{\delta A/\delta Z_1}{P_1} = \frac{\delta A/\delta Z_2}{P_2} = \cdots = \frac{\delta A/\delta Z_k}{P_k} \tag{3}$$

What if the school decision-maker has no knowledge of production relations (1) or the relative prices (P_i) in (2)? This is certainly likely to be the case in the present instance where the knowledge gap is so great. Yet, assume that the decision-maker does indeed wish to maximize (1). Then, as cost-effectiveness analysts, we would like to give him information as to which teacher characteristics represent "best buys" in improving achievement scores within the confines of a limited budget.[46]

PRODUCTION ESTIMATES

What follows are the results from admittedly early representations of (1) and (2) which I believe yield insights into the teacher selection problem. Eric Hanushek has estimated educational production functions for black and for white sixth graders in metropolitan schools.[47] Using standardized achievement scores as measures of output and other data on inputs from the Survey of Equal Opportunity data, Hanushek estimated relations similar to (1) for white in 471 elementary schools and for blacks in 242 elementary schools in the metropolitan North. Thus, the analyses were cross-sectional single equation estimates for 1965–66 done separately for black and for white students, where the school was the unit of analysis. That is, student and teacher data were averaged for each school. While Hanushek specified these functions using social class and other variables as arguments, we will discuss only the net estimated relationships between teacher characteristics and student verbal score.

In general, Hanushek found two teacher characteristics that were consistently related to the verbal scores of sixth graders. These two traits were the number of years of teacher experience and teacher's verbal score. The means and standard deviations for these variables are shown in Table 6.10 and the estimated payoffs to each characteristic are displayed in Table 6.11.[48]

Table 6.10

Means and Standard Deviations for Samples of Negro and White Sixth Graders

	Negro		White	
	Mean	St. Dev.	Mean	St. Dev.
Student Verbal Score	26.68	4.20	35.70	4.54
Teacher Verbal Score	23.98	1.80	24.77	1.43
Teacher Experience (Years)	11.29	4.00	11.88	4.56

Source: Eric Hanushek, *op. cit.*, p. 39 and p. 75.

Table 6.11

Output in Student Verbal Score for Each Additional Unit of Teacher Verbal Score and Experience

	Additional Points of Student Verbal Score	
	Negro	White
Each Additional Unit of Teacher Verbal Score	.175	.179
Each Additional Year of Teacher Experience	.108	.060

Source: Estimated from results on p. 37 and p. 73 in Eric Hanushek, *op. cit.*

Thus, for each additional point of teacher verbal score the Negro students showed an increment of .175 points and the white students an increment of .179 points in student verbal score. For each additional year of teacher experience, the test scores of Negro students were about .108 points higher and the test scores of white students were about .060 points higher.

TEACHER COSTS

The relative prices for teacher characteristics are taken from my estimates of earnings functions for teachers.[49] In this work I estimated the relationship between teachers' salaries and teachers' characteristics. The estimates were derived for four metropolitan regions considered as labor markets, and the data were derived from the same source as that used by Hanushek.

Table 6.12 shows the annual dollar return to teachers for specific characteristics within an eastern metropolitan region. While this result represents a linear function for an aggregate sample of teachers, results are available for non-linear forms of the equation and by sex and race of teacher analyzed separately. For illustrative purposes, however, this equation will suffice.

Among this large sample of almost 3,000 teachers, about $24 of annual salary was associated with each additional point of teacher's verbal score; males were receiving about $400 more than females; and each additional year of college training was worth almost $400 to a teacher. Teachers with non-academic majors were receiving about $160 more than were their

Table 6.12

Estimation of Earnings Functions for Eastmet Teachers

Teacher Characteristics	Slope Coefficient	t Statistics
Verbal score	$ 23.98	5.6
Female	−398.59	10.1
Years of schooling	396.04	17.8
Miscellaneous major	159.73	3.5
Graduate of teachers' college	−125.73	3.0
Years of experience	78.91	36.0
Certification level	564.09	23.1
Discrepancy on proportion white	18.27	2.3
Mean salary	7,084.56	
Standard deviation	1,679.76	
$\bar{R}$	.80	
R^2	.65	
Sample size	2921	

counterparts who majored in elementary education or academic subjects; graduates of teacher colleges were receiving less than graduates of other institutions. For each additional year of teaching experience, teachers were receiving about $79, and there were also higher returns to each successive certification level and to dissatisfaction with the racial composition of one's students ("discrepancy on proportion white").

What is of particular interest to us is that the approximate annual cost to the schools of obtaining a teacher with an additional year of experience was about $79 and that of obtaining a teacher with an additional point on the verbal scale was about $24, *ceteris paribus*. Combining these estimates with the results in Table 6.11, we obtain the approximate costs of raising student test scores with two strategies: recruiting and retaining teachers with more experience, and recruiting and retaining teachers with higher verbal scores.

SOME FINDINGS

Accordingly, Table 6.13 shows the relative costs of improving student performances under alternative recruitment strategies.[50] It is important to emphasize the relative costs of each strategy rather than the absolute ones.[51] In terms of relative costs, for a given test score gain for Negroes, it appears that obtaining teachers with higher verbal scores is about 1/5 as costly as obtaining more teacher experience; and the teachers' verbal score route is ten times as efficient as teacher's experience per dollar of expenditure for increasing the verbal scores of white students. The obvious policy implication is that school districts are obtaining too much experience as against verbal proficiency.[52] Accordingly, the schools should try to increase the recruitment and retention of verbally able teachers while paying somewhat less attention to experience. How much tradeoff should be made is not evident given our linear results.[53]

Table 6.13

Relative Costs of Increasing Student Verbal Achievement

Strategy	Approximate Cost for Increasing a Student's Verbal Score by One Point	
	Negro	White
Teacher's Verbal Score	$ 26	$ 26
Teacher Experience	$128	$253

Another interesting observation is that teacher experience appears to be twice as effective per dollar of expenditure for Negro students as it does for white ones. Giving equal weights to point gains for whites and Negroes, the schools might wish to assign their more experienced teachers to the schools attended by Negro students for higher total yields. What might explain this phenomenon? One possible interpretation is that a more experienced teaching staff and low teacher turnover show greater benefits to Negro than to white students because of the lesser stability of the Negro home. It is well-known that Negro students are far more likely to come from "broken homes" (ones where one or both parents are absent) than are white students. That is, stability and continuity of the school environment may have their greatest impact on those students characterized by the least stable home environments.[54]

The overriding implication of this analysis is that school salary policies should provide financial incentives that will attract and retain teachers with greater verbal skills, a policy that would represent a distinct break from tradition. On the other hand it is suggested that the schools grant too large a reward for experience. The result of reducing salary increments for experience and implementing them for verbal performance would appear to attract a more capable teaching staff with regard to the production of student achievement.

Of course, these two strategies could not be considered as true alternatives if the teachers with higher ability were also those with greater experience. In fact, this is not the case. The zero-order correlation between experience and verbal ability for the several thousand teachers in Eastmet was not significantly different from zero. There was a significant pattern among the newer teachers, however. That is, the teachers with the highest verbal facility were those with no teaching experience, the new entrants to the profession. Unfortunately, it appears that many of the most highly endowed of these individuals leave the schools within three years so that the stock of teachers with three years or more experience shows significantly lower test scores than those with less than three years' experience.[55] This finding is consistent with the fact that the schools do not reward such proficiencies while other employers do. It seems reasonable that this adverse retention could be reversed by a more competitive salary policy, one that did account for the teacher's verbal facility.

These findings are not the final answer by any means. They are meant to be illustrative rather than definitive. There are grounds for expecting specification biases on both the production and cost sides. Yet, it would take enormous biases—all in the same direction—to offset our finding that it appears far more efficient to improve student achievement by raising teachers' verbal score than by increasing teacher experience.

ECONOMIES OF SCALE IN HIGH SCHOOL OPERATION

JOHN RIEW

In the school year 1963–64, according to the National Education Association, the total expenditures to educate 41.7 million pupils of the Nations' public schools exceeded 21 billion dollars. This expenditure figure shows a significant increase from 15.6 billion dollars in 1959–60 and 5.8 billion dollars in 1949–50 which were spent, respectively, for 34.2 million and 24.1 million pupils. In view of the magnitude of the resources involved and the rapid growth of their amounts, inquiry into scale economies in public education has not received adequate treatment by researchers.

The main reasons for this seem to be (1) the difficulty of determining the quality of various schools, and (2) varying opinions regarding the importance of the implications of such a study. The cost per pupil may reflect differences in the quality of education among schools, unless this quality differential is somehow taken into account. Then, if a study indicates an economic advantage for large size schools, there is a question of how this fact should affect policy decisions when there are other factors to be considered.

The United States Office of Education, for many years, has been making surveys of public school costs in cities of varying sizes. Their results in general show higher per-pupil costs for schools in larger cities. In the year 1958–59, the cost per pupil in cities with a population of less than 10,000 was 312 dollars. The cost in cities with populations ranging from 10,000 to 24,999 was 305 dollars. In cities with populations from 25,000 to 99,999, it was 321 dollars, and in cities of over 100,000 people, 361 dollars.[56] In 1939–40, the equivalent figures were 80 dollars, 87 dollars, 102 dollars and 127 dollars, respectively.[57]

The surveys obviously were not intended for analysis of economies of scale in school operation. Although large schools are typically in large

Reprinted from the *Review of Economics and Statistics* 48 (1966): pp. 280–87. Copyright © 1966 by the President and Fellows of Harvard College.

cities and small ones in smaller cities, city population is hardly a suitable index of school size. Also these surveys do not account for differences in the quality of schools among size classes.

The first serious inquiry on the subject was made recently by Werner Z. Hirsch.[58] In his analysis, which employs multiple correlation and regression techniques and uses an elaborate device to distinguish quality differences among schools, he finds no significant economies of scale. He thus concludes that consolidation is unlikely to solve the fiscal problems of public schools. Hirsch uses a school district as the unit of observation. A study based on school districts undoubtedly has its merits, but schools, by and large, operate independently within a district. Thus, a more meaningful analysis of the size-cost relation, as Hirsch also implies, should be based on *individual schools*. Of the 27 St. Louis public school systems included in his study, all but six had enrollments of more than 1,500. To test the validity of a conjecture that significant scale economies exist over a relatively low size-range into which the nation's great majority of schools fall,[59] we need a sample with a larger number of smaller units.

Schmandt and Stephens, in a rank order correlation analysis, offer the conclusion that there is a significant negative relation between school size and per pupil current expenditures.[60] They too attempt to consider quality variation among schools, but for the measure of quality they use the number of subfunctions performed in each school. As the authors admit, this fails to differentiate the quality of each subfunction and gives equal weight to all such functions. Their study was based on 18 "school district areas" of Milwaukee County, the district areas again taken as the basis of analysis.[61]

In these previous studies,[62] elementary and secondary schools are combined into individual units. Elementary schools operate differently from secondary schools. Most important, the secondary schools call for a higher degree of specialization in the teaching staff and for more facilities than do the elementary schools. Thus, these two levels of public schools should be considered as two distinct industries, and a joint treatment results in mixing two possibly dissimilar tendencies.

THE APPROACH AND THE DATA

The present study, in analyzing the relationship between school size and cost, concentrates on public high school systems and approaches the subject on the basis of individual schools rather than school districts. This study deals exclusively with the senior high schools, comprising grades nine to 12 and ten to 12. Junior high and combined high schools of grades seven to 12 were not included because of the probable cost variation associated with the differences in organization.

Wisconsin high schools were chosen as the object of the study because the state offers unusually good sources of information for the purpose.

In Wisconsin, the State Department of Public Instruction, actively committed to aid for public education, secures quite a thorough annual report from each school district. The report contains a school census and detailed information on revenues and expenditures for all elementary schools and for all high schools in the district separately. However, neither the annual report nor the district files give separate accounts for individual schools. Thus, for this study, districts were selected which had only one high school. Many larger schools are in larger school districts and eliminating these districts which have more than one high school reduces the number of large schools in the sample. There is, however, a sufficient number of districts with one high school of larger size for the purposes of this study.

All told, there were 430 public senior high schools in the state in 1960–61. We observe in Table 6.14 that more than half of these schools had an enrollment of less than 300 and only about one-quater had an enrollment of more than 500.

Table 6.14

**Distribution by Enrollment—
Wisconsin Public High
Schools 1960–61**

Pupils in Average Daily Attendance	Number of Schools
200 or less	134
201–300	93
301–500	86
500 or more	117
Total	430

Source: Wisconsin Department of Public Instruction, *The Summary of High School Preliminary Reports* (1960–1961).

Undoubtedly, educational programs and qualities among these schools vary and it will be futile to attempt an inquiry into size-cost relations without taking into account these variations.

As a partial measure of quality for this analysis, a step was first taken to select only those schools which were accredited by the North-Central Association. In 1960–61, there were 152 accredited public high schools, of which 142 encompassed grades nine to 12 or ten to 12. The elimination of districts with more than one high school reduced the sample size by 26. To further narrow differences in standards, schools which appeared to rank considerably above the majority were excluded. This was done by eliminating schools where the 1960–61 average teacher salary exceeded $6,500. This produced an additional loss of seven schools (several schools paying high teacher salaries were already excluded when large districts with two or more high schools were left out).[63]

We have, thus, 109 schools (92 four-year and 17 three-year high schools) which survived the tests of accreditation and "non-exceptionality" and are by and large comparable in organization. In setting a floor based on the judgment of the North-Central Association and arbitrarily setting a ceiling based on average teacher salary, the intent was to reduce variations in the standard of schools and analyze the size-cost relation with minimum interference from these variations.

In Table 6.15, schools are grouped by size, and average per pupil expenditures are related to various size classes. Additional information is then provided for respective size classes concerning (1) average teacher's

Table 6.15

Averages of Operating Expenditures and Characteristics of Teachers in 109 Accredited High Schools of Wisconsin Grouped by Size, 1960–61

Number of Schools	Pupils in Average Daily Attendance	Operating[a] Expenditure Per Pupil	Average Teacher's Salary	Percentage Teachers Holding Master's Degree	Average[b] Years Taught	Pupil-[c] Teacher Ratio	Credit[d] Units Offered	Average[e] Course Load Per Teacher
6	143–200	$531.9	$5,305	18.1	6.3	17.3	34.7	3.8
12	201–300	480.8	5,187	15.1	6.1	18.2	36.9	2.9
19	301–400	446.3	5,265	18.8	6.3	20.0	39.6	2.5
17	401–500	426.9	5,401	18.5	7.4	20.9	44.0	2.3
14	501–600	442.6	5,574	23.5	7.5	20.7	46.5	1.9
13	601–700	413.1	5,411	22.5	6.8	20.9	45.3	1.7
9	701–900	374.3	5,543	22.3	7.1	24.1	46.4	1.8
6	901–1,100	433.2	5,939	34.0	7.3	21.4	57.7	1.6
6	1,101–1,600	407.3	5,976	36.5	11.9	24.4	63.4	1.6
7	1,601–2,400	405.6	6,230	54.5	11.2	24.2	80.3	1.6

[a] The figures represent the sum of current operating expenditures on administration, teacher's salaries, other instruction, operation, and maintenance. Expenditures on transportation, auxiliary services (school lunch, pupil recreation and health programs) and other minor items are not included.

[b] The mean of median years taught in individual schools within each size-class. (For other variables, the average was the mean of mean values for individual schools in each size-class.)

[c] Number of pupils in average daily attendance divided by number of teachers, the latter being the full-time equivalent of staff members devoted to teaching only.

[d] A two-semester course meeting five times weekly is counted as one credit unit. For smaller schools, the number of credit units relate to a two-year program because in these schools some courses are offered only in alternate years.

[e] Total credit units divided by number of teachers. In determining the number of teachers, multiple counting is avoided. If, for instance, because of large enrollment, several teachers teach the same course, they are counted as one. When a teacher devotes part of his time, say two-fifths, for a course taught by others, only that fraction is subtracted.

Sources: For information on accreditation, *The North Central Association Quarterly*, XXXVI (Summer 1961), 123–27; For teacher degrees, credit units, number of pupils and number of teachers, Wisconsin Department of Public Instruction, *High School Preliminary Report* (1960–1961); for operating expenditures, teacher's salaries, and years of teacher experience, Wisconsin Education Association, *Expenditures Per Pupil in City Schools* (1960–1961), *Expenditures Per Pupil in Village Schools* (1960–1961), *Salaries in City Schools* (1960–1961), and *Salaries in Schools Under Supervising Principles* (1960–1961). (The data in these Wisconsin Education Association bulletins are abstracted mostly from the Annual Report of School District and High School Preliminary Reports to the State Superintendent of Public Instruction.)

salary, (2) ratio of teachers holding a master's degree, (3) average years of teacher experiences, (4) average pupil-teacher ratio, (5) number of credit units offered, and (6) average number of courses taught by a teacher. The first three are assumed to reflect teacher qualifications, the fourth class size, the fifth breadth of school programs, and the last the degree of specialization in instruction. While the foregoing aspects are not all that may be relevant in judging a school they do constitute important ingredients of school qualities.[64] The size-cost relation, then, can be observed along with those measures which indicate the nature and direction of quality biases that may be associated with size.

The expenditure figures in Table 6.15 relate to operational items only; neither capital outlays nor debt services are included. Of the operational expenditures, those for transportation, auxiliary services, and other minor items are excluded. The per pupil costs of transportation often vary more with population density, and the distance a school bus has to travel, than with the size of a school, which may or may not reflect population density. As for auxiliary services, which include school lunch, pupil recreation and health programs, a comparison of costs is made difficult because some schools, especially larger ones, do not have lunch programs.

Thus, included in our analysis are outlays for *administration, teacher's salaries, other instruction* (salaries for clerical assistants to the teaching staff, text books, library books, and other instructional supplies), *operation* (salaries and wages of the custodial staff, fuel, utilities, etc.), and *maintenance* (staff salary, supplies, and contract services related to property mainte-nance). For high schools of Wisconsin as a whole, these items in 1960–61 comprised 92.1 per cent of total operating expenditures (the total excluding costs of transportation) and 63.0 per cent of all school expenditures.[65]

Table 6.15 provides a fairly comprehensive picture and may be con-sidered highly informative. We shall first examine the table and then, for further insights, we shall turn to a more rigorous statistical analysis.

FINDINGS AND EVALUATIONS

1. The per-pupil expenditures decline fairly steadily from $531 to $374 as enrollment rises from less than 200 to 701–900. Within the above range of enrollment, (a) smaller schools have lower average pupil-teacher ratios, (b) larger schools, on the other hand, have relatively more teachers with advanced degrees on their faculty, and, more important perhaps, (c) larger schools offer a broader curriculum and more specialized instruction.[66] The number of credit units, an indication of the breadth of curriculum (see note d to Table 6.15), ranges from 34.7 for schools with less than 200 pupils to 46.4 for those with 701–900 pupils. The average number of courses taught per teacher varies from 3.8 for the smallest schools to 1.8 for those with 701–900 pupils.[67]

2. The per pupil expenditures, after a fairly consistent fall, rise from $374 to $433 as enrollment increases from 701–900 to the next size-class of 901–1,100. However, this rise in expenditures accompanies a notable rise in the proportion of teachers with a master's degree and a considerable broadening of the school curriculum. It appears that, with enrollment in the vicinity of one thousand, the demand for advanced courses and for teachers with advanced training rises and becomes more effective.[68]

3. As enrollment rises from 901–1,100 to 1,101–1,600, the per pupil expenditures fall again, from $433 to $407. Then, with a further increase to 1,601–2,400, the expenditures remain stable while the ratio of master's degrees in the faculty and the number of credit units continue to rise.

The average pupil-teacher ratio varies rather moderately from 17 to one for schools with less than 200 pupils, 20 to one for those with 301–700 pupils, and about 24 to one for most of the larger schools. The pupil-teacher ratios for schools observed here are all relatively low and differences in pupil-teacher ratios do not seem crucial (none of the individual schools included in the present study had an average ratio of more than 27 to one).

The significance of the pupil-teacher ratio has been challenged for some time and more so recently. Past studies of class-size provide little evidence that large classes materially affect the academic efficiency of the class. After reviewing a great number of class-size studies conducted in the past, Otto and von Bergersrode conclude that "...mere size of class has little significant influence on educational efficiency as measured by achievement in the academic subjects...," and that "...although experimental evidence does not provide a clear-cut answer to the class-size issue, the general trend of the evidence places the burden of proof squarely upon the proponents of small classes."[69]

Within the range of enrollment of less than 200 to 701–900, then, advantages of a larger school may be considered overwhelming. A larger school not only spends considerably less per pupil but has decisive advantages in curriculum and in teacher specialization.

Whether schools with an enrollment of more than 701–900 provide additional economies depends on one's appraisal of the cost differential as against the differences in what the schools offer. With enrollment of 1,101–1,600 or 1,601–2,400, the per pupil expenditures are $407 or $406 as compared with $374 for schools with 701–900 pupils. However, these larger schools distinguish themselves with broader curricula (63.4 or 80.3 credit units against 46.4), higher proportions of faculty holding advanced degrees (36.5 or 54.5 per cent against 22.3) and teachers with more experience (11.9 or 11.3 years against 7.1). If one believes these improvements in standards more than compensate for the differences in expenditures this then may be construed as an economy.

One may make an evaluation by direct examination of Table 6.15 which provides comprehensive information on the subject. Judging school qualities involves subjective values. Given the size, the cost, and variables that are considered relevant to school qualities, one could make his own appraisal and final judgment.

Nevertheless, this approach leaves some important questions unanswered. If, for instance, we agree that there are economies of scale and that cost per pupil decreases with an increase in the size of enrollment, we would want to have estimations on such decreases in cost and on their statistical significance. It should be noted also that the figures shown in our table are average values for each size class and tend to conceal variations within classes.

In the estimation of possible cost savings, we seek to isolate the influence of size upon cost. For this we would need to consider other factors which are expected to affect the cost. Presumably, the most important of such factors is school quality. Regardless of the method of analysis, we must make certain assumptions as to what constitute school qualities and our conclusions necessarily must be evaluated with reference to the manner in which qualities are taken into account. Besides quality differences, there are other conditions to account for variations in input requirements and thus in average costs among schools.

The method employed here to approximate the net relationship between school size and per pupil cost is least-squares multiple regression analysis. The analysis is based on the 109 selected high schools which are included in Table 6.15. Using largely the factors already introduced in the table, our regression equation includes the following variables:

X_1—Operating expenditures per pupil in average daily attendance.
X_2—Enrollment (number of pupils in average daily attendance).
X_3—Average teacher's salary.
X_4—Number of credit units offered (a two-semester course meeting five times a week is counted as one unit).
X_5—Average number of courses taught per teacher.
X_6—Change in enrollment between 1957 and 1960 (the 1960 enrollment is taken as a percentage of the 1957 enrollment).
X_7—Percentage of classrooms built after 1950.

Used here as our quality variables are average teacher's salary (X_3), number of credit units offered (X_4), and average number of courses taught per teacher (X_5), which may be considered to represent, respectively, teacher qualifications, the breadth of curriculum, and the degree of specialization in instruction. The pupil-teacher ratio is left out in view of the controversies as to how the ratio is associated with classroom efficiency and of the fact that the pupil-teacher ratios observed in the present study are all relatively low. A preliminary result, furthermore, indicated high correlation between average teacher's salary and teacher status with respect to degree and experience; thus, these two were also eliminated.[70]

Changes in enrollment over a period of a few years (X_6) may indicate the pace at which demand for school services changed and thus possibly reflect some lagging adjustments in cost. The last variable, the proportion of new classrooms (X_7) was included because costs of maintenance and operation may vary by the ages of school properties.

In this statistical test, we assume a parabolic relationship between per pupil cost and enrollment. The relations between the cost and the other independent variables were all assumed to be linear. The following results are then obtained:

$$X_1 = 10.31 - \underset{(.063)}{.402X_2} + \underset{(.000023)}{.00012X_2{}^2} + \underset{(.013)}{.107X_3} + \underset{(.640)}{.985X_4}$$
$$- \underset{(11.95)}{15.62X_5} + \underset{(.189)}{.613X_6} - \underset{(.109)}{.102X_7}.$$

The figures in parentheses are standard errors of the net regression and the statistically significant coefficients (at a probability level of .01) are underlined. The coefficient of multiple determination adjusted for degrees of freedom lost, R^{*2}, is .557 and is highly significant at a probability level of .01.

Thus, about 56 per cent of the variation in average per pupil operating expenditures among the 109 high schools in 1960–61 was accounted for by the six independent variables of which average teacher's salary, enrollment, and changes in enrollment were statistically significant.[71] The partial correlation coefficients of these variables are:

$$r_{12.2{}^2 34567} = .539,$$
$$r_{12{}^2.234567} = .465,$$
$$r_{13.22{}^2 4567} = .648, \quad \text{and}$$
$$r_{16.22{}^2 3457} = .307.$$

When school enrollment (variables X_2 and X_2^2) is eliminated from our multiple regression analysis, R^{*2} is reduced from .557 to .374. Holding constant the effects of changes in the other five variables, then, 18.3 per cent of the variation in per pupil operating expenditures is explainable in terms of variation in enrollment.

Our regression equation suggests, further, that an enrollment increase of one pupil, holding the other variables constant, lowers average per pupil operating expenditures by $[40.2 - 2(.012X_2)]$ cents at X_2 level of enrollment until X_2 finally reaches 1,675.[72] Thus, a school with an enrollment of 200, for instance, if it behaves in "average fashion," will reduce its per pupil operating expenditures 35.4 cents by having one more pupil. For a school with 500 pupils, adding one pupil would reduce per pupil expenditures by 28.2 cents and for one with 1,000 pupils, by 15.8 cents. Increase in the enrollment of a school from 200 to 500, the other independent variables held constant, would thus mean a saving of $95.45 in average per pupil operating expenditures.[73] With an increase in enrollment of from 500 to 1,000 the expected saving in per pupil expenditure would be \$111.00 and from 1,000 to 1,675 the expected saving would be \$54.67.

These figures of course provide only approximations and are subject to error limitations. However, if we are concerned with an "average" school and our assumptions on school qualities are acceptable, they may be considered as meaningful estimates.[74] That the coefficient of X_6 (the change in enrollment) is significantly positive may deserve some attention. It suggests that under conditions of rapid expansion, the school operates on a short-run cost curve above the level that is achievable under a full long-run adjustment to increased enrollment levels.

A larger school may mean an added transportation cost, especially in a thinly populated area. This additional cost (and perhaps the nonmonetary costs of fatigue, time, parental concern, etc.) would have to be subtracted from the "saving" referred to above. This point, however, should not be overly stressed. There are indications that in the great majority of instances a small enrollment is simply a reflection of a small size of the school district rather than population sparsity. "In only 19 states," a C.E.D. study points out, "...is the average geographic area covered by a school system as much as 225 square miles—equivalent to an area 15 miles square. In 21 states it is less than 49 square miles."[75]

A recent study conducted by the Wisconsin Department of Public Instruction reveals, furthermore, that differences in average transportation costs between rural and urban areas and between districts covering large areas and those covering small areas are considerably less than commonly believed. In the 1961–62 academic year, the average of per pupil transportation expenditures in the most thickly populated counties of Milwaukee, Racine, Kenosha, and Winnebago (each with population density of more than 200 per square mile) was \$54.16 as compared with \$65.10 for the most thinly populated counties of Sawyer, Bayfield, Florence, and Forest (each with the density of less than ten per square mile) where school districts are much larger in area.[76] This may in part be accounted for by differences in service qualities. The better explanation, however, is that in school transportation the fixed costs (depreciation, driver salary, insurance, garage rental, etc.) comprise such an important part that differences in the mileage of operation, in many cases, affect the total transportation cost much less than is often anticipated.[77]

In the present analysis capital outlays are excluded as they generally fluctuate widely over time. When they are taken into account, greater variation in per pupil costs among size groups may be expected. Physical education programs and a library, for instance, require many provisions which a school of any size should not lack. For a satisfactory high school program, various equipment and provisions for science laboratories, language, music, and vocational training are basic and essential. For these items, smaller schools bear larger overhead costs. As general standards of high schools continue to improve with increasing investment in capital items, the issue will become even more important.

CONCLUSION

Differentiating educational qualities among individual schools is a difficult task, but based on what may be considered as reasonable assumptions, the study of Wisconsin high schools suggests that economies of scale at this level of public education are very significant.

Taking the high schools as a whole, capital outlays in recent years comprised roughly a quarter of the total expenditures. Their inclusion in the analysis would most likely have strengthened the present conclusion. This would have increased cost variation among schools, the higher overhead costs being expected to fall on smaller schools.

A sample with a larger number of schools, especially of the upper size classes, and with its size range extended beyond the present limit of 2,400 pupils would have been more informative. The virtue of "that little red schoolhouse" may be of more than an emotional nature. But whatever the merits, they ought to be considered negotiable. When better informed of the opportunity costs, one may wish to reexamine his traditional preference.

QUESTIONS FOR DISCUSSION

1. What measures of output would you propose for use in a study of productivity of elementary schools? How would you quantify them?

2. Which assumptions made by Woodhall and Blaug do you find most unrealistic? In what way might these assumptions be improved?

3. In what practical ways might a school administration or school board make use of Levin's findings? What factors tend to prevent any use of these findings? Do you feel that the findings are solid enough to act on? Why?

4. How might Levin's methodology be applied in your area of vocational interest?

5. Over what enrollment ranges does Riew find increasing returns to scale and decreasing returns to scale? What implications does this finding have for your state?

Chapter 7 ASPECTS OF INVESTMENT

EXPENDITURES on goods and services are undertaken with the objective of present or future satisfaction. Goods and services that yield immediate satisfaction are designated consumption goods. There are two types of consumption goods, non-durable and durable. The former yield immediate satisfaction, and the latter yield satisfaction in both the present and the future. Phonographs, automobiles, and refrigerators are examples of durable consumer goods whereas food, cleansers, and newspapers are non-durable consumer goods. Investment goods are ones to be used in the production of future goods. The difference between durable consumer goods and investment goods is that the latter yield satisfaction only through their ability to influence consumption in the future whereas the former also yield direct satisfaction.

Education has attributes that qualify its inclusion into both consumption and investment categories. Many would assert that the process of acquiring education is inherently pleasant and that once acquired, education enables one to achieve greater appreciation and enjoyment in such areas as art, literature, and music. These characteristics of education point to its inclusion in the consumption category. In addition to these benefits, there are definite financial payoffs to additional years of schooling and training. Thus, acquiring education (schooling and/or training) in the present increases one's ability to earn more and hence consume more in the future. The weight of research in the area of the economics of education deals with the investment aspects of education, and it is as an investment good that education will be analyzed in this chapter.

Notes to Chapter 7 will be found on page 379.

Investment and investment goods are extremely important aspects of the modern economy. It is through investment that indirect methods of production can be undertaken. And it is indirect production methods that lead to greater output for each man-hour of input.[1] It is a technological fact that more total output can be generated if part of the effort to be expended is first applied to the production of capital and then this capital is utilized together with the remaining effort, than if all the labor is applied directly to the task at hand. The use of capital, together with the division of labor (having each individual specialize in the performance of one task of production), has led to the present high productivity of American labor.

There are strong logical and causal relationships between investment and the interest rate. Therefore, the causes and functions of interest in the economy are investigated first in this chapter. Second, the role of interest in determining the value of things at different points in time is discussed. Next, methods of investment decision making are presented and compared. The concluding section discusses how these concepts were integrated and applied to education by Gary Becker in his theory of investment in human capital.[2] In the next chapter the tools developed here are utilized to evaluate empirically specific educational activities.

INTEREST

The theory of interest is a somewhat confusing area of economics. This is largely because there are two sides to the determination of the level of interest rates: In the first (the production side), the interest rate depends on the size of capital's contribution to output, and in the second (the monetary side), the interest rate depends on the supply and demand for loanable funds. The *interest rate* is the rental cost of money. An interest payment, then, is payment for using money for a period of time. The relationship between time and interest is an essential one because interest is defined in terms of a time unit. We begin with what is known as the pure theory of interest. Only after the case for the *existence* of an interest rate is established will the setting of the *level* of the interest rate first from the point of view of loanable funds and then from that of production be investigated.

The best way of introducing the concept of pure interest is to ask the question: Which is preferable, having $100 today or the absolute assurance of receiving $100 one year from now? The reasons for choosing the $100 today account for the existence of the pure rate of interest.

First, people tend to perceive present needs more acutely than future needs. Today's empty stomach or yearning to see a movie has stronger effects than the anticipation of either a year from now. If one gives up immediate satisfaction, such as that derivable from the $100, one then expects in the future, as compensation for waiting, greater satisfaction than that which has been foregone.

A less obvious rationale for pure interest is that the postponement of current consumption means that more can be produced in the future. The postponement of present consumption leads to greater consumption in the future, and the pure interest rate is a manifestation of this increment.

Those are the reasons for the existence of pure interest. But there are additional quite compelling reasons for interest. Loaning money has inherent risks such as those of inflation and non-payment. The risk from inflation is that $100 one year from now will not be able to buy as much as $100 today. If there is an annual 5 per cent price rise, one would have to charge 5 per cent interest simply to be able to purchase the same goods a year from now as could be bought now. The greater the expected price inflation, the higher the interest rate will have to be to cover that risk. The risk of non-repayment of a loan is determined by the characteristics of the promiser. Your confidence in repayment will be greater if the promiser is the federal government, less if it is General Motors (even G.M. could go broke), less yet if it is a friend, and even less if it is a casual acquaintance who you happen to know has not held a job for more than one month at a time and moved to your town only six months ago! The difference in interest rates owing to such uncertainties is called the *risk premium*. If one felt, for example, that there were only a 95 per cent chance that a loan would be repaid, a risk premium would have to be charged to compensate for the chance that the loan would never be collected. The risk premium is one important factor explaining why loans for consumer purchases tend to have such high interest rates.

Another factor determining interest level is the transaction cost of making a loan. The lender incurs the real costs both of estimating how reliable the borrower is and of going through the process of legally obligating the borrower to repay. Even when the borrower is the federal government, loaning money costs time and energy, since at the very least the resources have to be transferred. The cost to a loan company of investigating the transient acquaintance mentioned above is correspondingly higher, as is the consequent interest rate charged. There are great opportunities for economies of scale here.

The transaction costs are unlikely to be very different whether a loan is for $10 or $10,000. Therefore, this cost per dollar of loan is of the order of one thousandth as great for the latter as the former loan.[3]

Finally, charging interest derives from the inconvenience of not having the resources available if they should happen to be needed. If one retained his $100 rather than loaned it, it would be available in case of an emergency. Having assets (the $100 or an I.O.U. which replaced it is an asset) which are available for spending immediately gives one *financial liquidity*. Part of the interest rate is a premium for illiquidity. The liquidity of a debt instrument such as a bond is a function of the market for it. If there is a large market, one could easily sell his claim for future payment at short notice. This would be true for United States Treasury bonds for example. On the other hand, there is not a very large market for Jim Smith's I.O.U.; it is therefore much less liquid and Mr. Smith must pay a higher illiquidity premium than does the United States Treasury.

It is the summation of the pure interest rate, the risk premium, the transaction cost, and the illiquidity premium that make up the rate of interest on a loan. But even that is not the whole story. As can be seen in Figure 7.1, there are many different interest rates coexisting at any given time. One can also see that the rates for each of these securities fluctuate markedly over time. The differences seen in a particular year can be explained by differences in the risk, liquidity, and transaction costs of the different types of investments. But these do not explain the fluctuations over time for a given type of investment. Surely there have not been fluctuations of such magnitude in the risk or the transaction cost or even the liquidity of, for example, treasury bills (short term obligations of the government) over time, and inflation has not varied much except for the last several years. Why, then, the range of rates? The answer lies in the interaction between supply and demand.

The exact interest rate for any loan is a function of the demand and supply for loanable funds. The amount of funds available for loans is a function first of the income of individuals. When people have more income, they will have more funds left over after taking care of absolute essentials. Making loans directly, or indirectly through depositing money in a bank (banks utilize deposits for granting loans), competes with other uses of income. Just as more of all other goods (except inferior goods) are purchased when income increases, *ceteris paribus*, so too will the purchase of future income (that is, savings) increase. Indeed, savings, which leads to the acquisition of bonds,

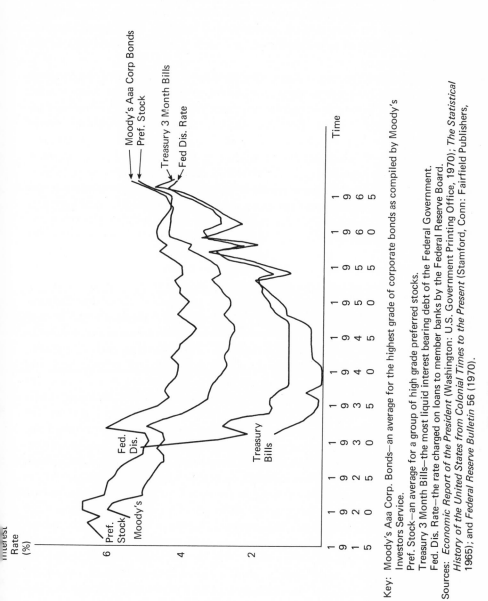

Key: Moody's Aaa Corp. Bonds—an average for the highest grade of corporate bonds as compiled by Moody's
     Investors Service.
     Pref. Stock—an average for a group of high grade preferred stocks.
     Treasury 3 Month Bills—the most liquid interest bearing debt of the Federal Government.
     Fed. Dis. Rate—the rate charged on loans to member banks by the Federal Reserve Board.

Sources: *Economic Report of the President* (Washington: U.S. Government Printing Office, 1970); *The Statistical
         History of the United States from Colonial Times to the Present* (Stamford, Conn: Fairfield Publishers,
         1965); and *Federal Reserve Bulletin* 56 (1970).

Figure 7.1   Coexisting Interest Rates

bills, or debt instruments of banks (if they are put in savings accounts), has an income elasticity greater than one. As income goes up, savings goes up by an even greater proportion. The effect of increased income on the supply of loanable funds is a shift upward to the right of the supply curve.

The other essential factor determining the amount of funds available for loans is the interest rate, which is the price that is offered for funds. The higher the interest rate, the more will the use of income for making loans win in the competition among all the possible uses of the income. One can think of a higher interest rate as meaning a lower cost of future goods relative to goods purchased in the present. At a 10 per cent interest rate it would cost $100 of present money to purchase $110 of future goods deliverable a year from now. If the interest rate were lower (say 1 per cent) the cost would be much greater ($108.91 to be exact).[4] Thus, as the interest rate goes up, the price of future goods goes down. As was discussed in Chapter 3, when the price of a good goes down, more is purchased. The effect of higher interest rates on the amount of loanable funds is seen as a movement *along* a given supply curve rather than a shift *of* the supply curve.

The size of the demand (that is, the position of the demand curve) for loanable funds is largely technologically determined. It will depend on just what opportunities for productive investment exist in the economy. For example, if there are slums to clear and mass transit to install—investments that require a great deal of capital and that will greatly increase productivity—there will be a great demand for loans. On the other hand, the demand is not solely technologically determined because of the human factor; technological possibilities are seen through human eyes. It is the human interpretation of the possibilities that determines how much demand there will be for investment and therefore for loans. Two men faced with the same data about a gold mine may come up with opposite answers to the question of what the productivity of the gold mine will be. Similarly, one person may see possibilities for great profit in a business that another man has given up as a lost cause. Again, given the shape of the demand curve, each interest rate or price of a loan will imply a different quantity actually demanded. Of course, it will be the point of the intersection of the demand curve and the supply curve that will finally determine the interest rate and the amount of loans that will clear the market. Any interest rate higher than that associated with the intersection of the two curves would imply a greater supply than demand, which would lead to price cuts on the part of the offerers of loanable funds.

An opposite adjustment would result if the initial interest rate were below the equilibrium value. Thus, the intersection price, which is the interest rate, and quantity will inevitably be established.

Just as with other goods in the economy, the market allocates the scarce resource, loanable funds, among competing uses through supply and demand determination of the price. If the market clearing interest rate is 8 per cent, all those projects that yield less than 8 per cent will not be undertaken and those that yield 8 per cent or more will be undertaken. If the potential investments yielding 8 per cent or more require more funds than there are loanable funds at that rate, the 8 per cent interest rate is not the market clearing interest rate. Demand being greater than supply, the interest rate will rise until the market does clear. This allocation function of interest rates is extremely important to the economy. Without interest rates the allocation of investment resources is extremely difficult.[5] Without interest how can one choose, for example, between building a railroad that follows the natural contours of the land (thereby having a low capital cost but high current operating costs because of the hills and curves that must be traversed) and one using bridges, tunnels, and other devices which cut the operating costs but greatly increase the capital cost? The inclusion of interest charges makes comparable the high present cost–low future cost and the low present cost–high future cost alternatives. Exactly how interest rates are in practice used in making these decisions is the topic of the next section.

PRESENT DISCOUNTED VALUE

How can one determine whether some future payment is worth foregoing the present consumption required to acquire it? More concretely, how is one to know whether he should be willing to give up $100 now for the promise of $110 next year? Alternatively, how much should he be willing to give up today for the promise of $110 one year from now? These are both aspects of the same question, and the answer is derived in both cases from the calculation of *present discounted value (PDV)*.[6] Put simply, PDV is the value today of payment(s) in the future. The interest rate determines what the PDV of a given future payment is. The easiest way of getting an understanding of PDV is through an example. If the interest rate is 10 per cent, $1,000 today will be worth $1,100 in one year Let us formally derive that result:

$$\$1,000 \times 10\% = \$1,000 \times .10 = \$100$$

which is the interest earned on the $1,000 principal loaned for one year. Adding this to the principal gives $1,000 + $100 = $1,100. Put into symbols:

$$PDV + r \cdot PDV = F$$
$$PDV(1 + r) = F$$
$$PDV = \frac{F}{(1 + r)} \tag{1}$$

where PDV = amount in the present,
r = interest rate,
and F = payment in the future.

If two of the three factors in equation (1) are known, the third can easily be derived. Going back to the two questions asked at the beginning of this section: Should we be willing to give up $100 now for the promise of $110 in a year? When these figures are inserted into equation (1), it can be solved for the interest rate which balances the present and the future payments:

$$\$100 = \frac{\$110}{(1 + r)}$$
$$\$100(1 + r) = \$110$$
$$\$100 + \$100r = \$110$$
$$\$100r = \$110 - \$100 = \$10$$
$$r = \frac{\$10}{\$100}$$
$$r = 10\%$$

If the interest rate for loans prevailing in the economy is 10 per cent, the $100 today and the $110 in a year are equivalent. If the interest rate in the economy (say, 9 per cent) is lower than the interest rate (10 per cent) calculated for the offer being considered, one should definitely take the offer because it yields more than can be earned elsewhere. If the general interest rate is higher, say 11 per cent, one should not take the offer.

The second question posed was: How much should one be willing to give up today for the promise of $110 next year? To answer this the rate of interest in the economy is needed. Say it is 10 per cent. In this case equation (1) is solved for PDV, since r and F are already known:

$$\text{PDV} = \frac{\$110}{1 + .10} = \frac{\$110}{1.10} = \$100$$

Thus, one should be willing to pay no more than $100 for the promise of $110 in one year. The final question that can be answered by the equation is: How much must I be promised one year from now for $100 today if the interest rate is 10 per cent? This is solved in the same manner as the other two and the answer is $110. (Try it!)

In general, as the reader may have already noticed or figured out, there is an inverse relationship between interest rate and present discounted value. Given a future payment, the higher (lower) the interest rate, the lower (higher) the PDV. It was already seen that the PDV for an F of $110 at 10 per cent is $100. If the r is 100 per cent and F is $110, the PDV is $55.[7] Also, for a zero per cent interest rate the PDV is $110.[8] If these three sets of value are plotted on a graph of PDV versus r, the inverse relationship is immediately obvious (see Figure 7.2). It is this inverse relationship that explains why the price of a bond (which is its PDV) goes down when the interest rate in the economy goes up and vice versa.

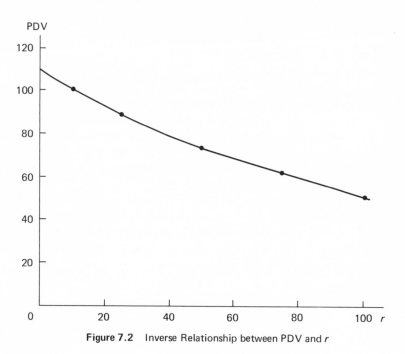

Figure 7.2   Inverse Relationship between PDV and r

So far the investigation of the relationship between PDV, interest rate, and future payments has been limited to one-year time periods. The technique is equally valuable (and almost equally as simple) for payments further in the future. What is the future payment that can be expected two years hence from a present value of $100 when the interest rate is 5 per cent? The answer can be found by breaking the problem into parts. At the end of the first year the value is $100(1 + .05) = $105. Taking this as the investment (or PDV) at the beginning of the second year, the final future payment, F, is $105(1 + .05) = $110.25. Putting this in the form of a formula we have:

$$PDV = \frac{F}{\dfrac{(1 + r)}{(1 + r)}} = \frac{F}{(1 + r)^2}$$

or

$$\frac{F}{\dfrac{(1 + .05)}{(1 + .05)}} = \$100$$

$$\frac{F}{(1 + .05)} = \$100(1 + .05) = \$100(1.05) = \$105$$

$$F = \$105(1 + .05)$$

$$F = \$110.25$$

Common knowledge will verify that $100 invested at 5 per cent for one year yields $105 and $105 invested for an additional year yields $110.25. In general, a payment t years in the future has a PDV of $F/(1 + r)^t$. Other things being equal, the further in the future a payment comes, the less is its PDV. This is seen by referring to the formula for PDV; because it is positive, the denominator, $(1 + r)^t$, becomes larger and larger as t becomes larger.

PDV of future payments one year and t years later have been dealt with. Most investments have many payments rather than just one. The methodology already developed is immediately generalizable to the multiple payment case. The PDV of a set of future payments is merely the summation of PDVs for each payment:

$$PDV = \frac{F_1}{(1 + r)^1} + \frac{F_2}{(1 + r)^2} + \cdots + \frac{F_t}{(1 + r)^t} \tag{2}$$

where t is the last time period.

For example, when the interest rate is 10 per cent, an investment with a payoff of $100 in each of the next three years has a PDV of:

$$\frac{\$100}{(1 + .10)^1} + \frac{\$100}{(1 + .10)^2} + \frac{\$100}{(1 + .10)^3} = \$90.91 + \$82.65 + \$75.19$$

$$= \$248.75$$

It must be kept in mind that the interest rate utilized in calculating PDV is crucial in determining its absolute and comparative value. For example, compare the PDVs of two packages, A and B. Package A consists of $100 today plus $500 in ten years whereas B consists of nothing today plus $1,000 in ten years. Table 7.1 shows the PDVs of A and B at 10 and 20 per cent and indicates that both A and B have higher PDVs at a 10 per cent than at a 20 per cent discount rate. In addition it can be seen that at a 20 per cent discount rate, A has the higher PDV and is thus the better package, but at a 10 per cent discount rate this is reversed (as shown in Table 7.1).

Table 7.1

PDV Comparison of Two Investments

	Payments		Present Discounted Value	
Investment	Today	In 10 years	At 20%	At 10%
A	$100	$500	$180	$293
B	0	$1,000	$162	$386

We now have the methodology for calculating the present discounted value of any investment. Certain assumptions have been implicit in all these calculations. First, it has been assumed that the interest rate is known not only now but in the future. This could be interpreted as assuming that the interest rate will not change. If the interest rate is expected to change, formula (2) would have to be altered by subscripting the rs as well as the Fs and substituting the appropriate interest rate for each year in the future.[9] Secondly, it has been assumed that the future payments are known with certainty. This can be alternately interpreted as implying that the future payments are the expected values of a set of possible payments.[10]

COST-BENEFIT ANALYSIS

Being able to calculate the PDV of a stream of returns enables one to choose between different investments. When considering investments of equal size, the one with the highest PDV net of costs is the best. There are two concepts employing PDV that are often used in discussions of investment decision making. These are the *benefit-cost ratio* and the *internal rate of return*.

The benefit-cost ratio is simply the PDV of the future benefits (F) divided by the PDV of the costs (C). Including costs in the form of a PDV makes the formulation general in that costs, like benefits, can occur over a protracted period of time. The benefit-cost ratio (B/C) is defined as:

$$B/C = \frac{\sum_{t=1}^{n} \frac{F_t}{(1 + r)^t}}{\sum_{t=1}^{n} \frac{C_t}{(1 + r)^t}} \tag{3}$$

where n is the last time period.[11]

A B/C value of 1 implies that the PDV of the benefits exactly equals the PDV of the costs. Therefore, the value of B/C has to be equal to or above 1 before the investment is worthwhile. The higher the B/C ratio, the better is the investment. Again, the interest rate utilized in calculating the B/C is very important. Typically, the lower the interest rate, the higher the B/C.[12]

Such benefit-cost ratio calculations have been employed since World War II in governmental decision making concerning the construction of dams and other water resource utilization projects. Many of the decisions made in the past have recently come under attack. The attacks have not been directed at the logic of cost-benefit analysis but rather at the choice of an interest rate for discounting costs and benefits. Those calculating the B/C for government investments have tended to use interest rates of the order of 2 to 4 per cent, the cost of government borrowing in the 1940s and 1950s. They argued that because that was the cost of borrowing for the government, it is the appropriate interest rate to charge. The attackers counter that government's borrowing costs are low because there is no risk to the loaner in lending to government. However, there is a risk in the projects undertaken by government and it is this risk that should be reflected in the interest rate charged.[13] They also argue that the market for loanable funds is not a perfect one, and the government has an unfair advantage in it, thereby taking funds away from highly productive private activities and putting them into government activities which are less productive.

The internal rate of return (i) has come into prominence partly because it eliminates investment decision making's crucial dependence on the interest rate used to discount the costs and benefits. The interest rate internal to the investment being considered is (i). It is defined in either of two equivalent forms—the interest rate which equates the PDV of the costs to the PDV of the benefits:

$$\sum_{t=1}^{n} \frac{F_t}{(1 + i)^t} = \sum_{t=1}^{n} \frac{C_t}{(1 + i)^t} \qquad (4a)$$

or the interest rate which makes the PDV of the benefits minus the costs equal to zero,

$$\sum_{t=1}^{n} \frac{F_t - C_t}{(1 + i)^t} = 0 \qquad (4b)$$

Put in terms of the benefit-cost ratio, the internal rate of return would be the interest rate for which $B/C = 1$. In the internal rate of return formula it is i which is solved for. No interest rate is assumed. Therefore, the difficult problem of deciding which interest rate to use for discounting among the many that coexist in the economy, given the subjective nature of time preference, is bypassed.

In practice the internal rate of return is found through either an iterative process or graphs. The equation for the internal rate of return is generally not algebraically solvable when there are costs or benefits in more than two years because it becomes an equation that involves powers of i greater than 2. The iterative process involves choosing an interest rate, calculating the net PDV,

$$\sum_{t=1}^{n} \frac{F_t - C_t}{(1 + i)^t}$$

and, if it is positive (negative), choosing a lower (higher) interest rate and recalculating. This is done repeatedly until a PDV of zero (approximately) is found. The interest rate that yielded the zero PDV is the internal rate of return.[14] Employing the graphic method, one plots the PDV of the costs and benefits at various interest rates. The interest rate at which the curve for costs intersects the curve for benefits is the internal rate of return (PDV of costs = PDV of benefits at that interest rate); for example, interest rate i_a in Figure 7.3A. Alternatively, the PDV of the *net* benefits can be plotted at various interest rates; the interest rate at which this curve cuts the x-axis (zero value of PDV) is the internal rate of return, for example, i_a in Figure 7.3B.

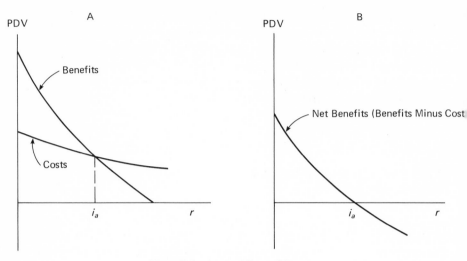

Figure 7.3   Internal Rate of Return

The use of internal rate of return implies a new rule for investment decision making: Choose the investment with the highest internal rate of return. However, this rule is also open to attack on several fronts. The first is a technical problem: There may be more than one value of i that will satisfy the equation. In other words, occasions occur when an investment has more than one internal rate of return. This is not usually a problem for educational investments because it can only happen when the pattern of costs and benefits is such that they are intermingled in time. If all the costs occur before the benefits begin, there is only one value of i that will solve the equation. Most, and perhaps all, educational investments follow a regular pattern of costs preceeding benefits.

The second difficulty is much weightier: Selecting the investment with the highest internal rate of return is not always optimal. There are two types of situations that can occur when comparing two investments:

1. One investment's PDV-r curve may be above the other at all interest rates (curve a is above curve b in Figure 7.4A).
2. The PDV-r curves may intersect (see Figure 7.4B).

In situations of the first type the criteria of the highest PDV and the highest i are clearly consistent because investment a in Figure 7.4A has a higher internal rate of return and a higher PDV than investment *b* at every interest rate. In the second case the discount rate at which the curves intersect is known as the *cross-over point*. At interest rates greater than that of the cross-over point, *C*, the two criteria agree again; investment *a* has both the higher internal rate of return and the higher PDV. It is at interest rates lower than that of the cross-over point that the two criteria conflict: As seen in Figure 7.4B, investment *a* has a higher *i* but a lower PDV than investment *b* at interest rates lower than *C*. When the two criteria conflict, the highest PDV should determine the investment chosen. The decision as to which investment to make, if either, depends on the market interest rate faced by the decision maker. Say *C* is 5 per cent and the decision maker can borrow or lend at 8 per cent. Then his situation is described by a point to the right of the cross-over point and he should choose investment *a* since *a* has a higher PDV than *b* to the right of *C*. If the relevant interest rate for the investment decision maker is 4 per cent, he should choose *b* because 4 per cent is to the left of *C* and *b* has a higher PDV there. Why not merely compare the PDVs of the two investments using the relevant interest rate for the investment decision maker? If one knew who that decision maker was and what he considered the relevant interest rate, one indeed should. The usefulness of the cross-over point analysis is that it presents sufficient information for

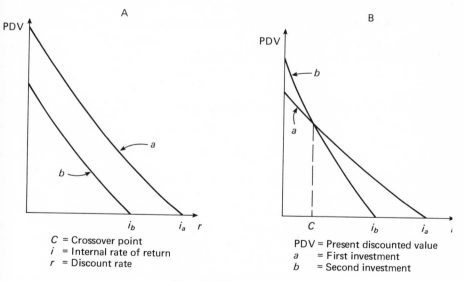

C = Crossover point
i = Internal rate of return
r = Discount rate

PDV = Present discounted value
a   = First investment
b   = Second investment

Figure 7.4 Investment Choice

anyone to make a decision, regardless of what he considers the relevant interest rate for him to be.

Why, then, is the internal rate of return so often employed? The answer is that the internal rate of return is a much overused decision-making criterion. Although in general the cross-over point is a preferable datum, many sets of educational investments fall into the category of not having a cross-over point owing to the time streams of costs and benefits of educational investments being so similar. In addition, because the cross-over interest rate can be referred to only when two alternate investments are being compared, it is more limited in its applicability than the internal rate of return statistic that can be quoted for any single investment. The best information about an investment upon which one would ideally make a decision is the full PDV-r graph such as those seen in Figures 7.3B and 7.4, and these are increasingly being utilized.

INVESTMENT IN HUMAN CAPITAL

All the elements discussed so far in this chapter—interest rates, present discounted value, investment, and investment decision making—can be brought together in the consideration of investment in human capital.[15] In this section we follow Gary Becker's presentation appearing in his book, *Human Capital*.

The methodology for cost-benefit analysis that was developed earlier can be applied to the questions of how much education (schooling and training) an individual should acquire and how it is to be paid for. In general each person can profitably acquire more education so long as the present discounted value of the benefits is equal to or exceeds that of the costs. That is so long as

$$\sum_{t=1}^{n} \frac{B_t}{(1 + r)^t} \geq \sum_{t=1}^{n} \frac{C_t}{(1 + r)^t}$$

it is worthwhile to continue investing in human capital.

The major economic benefit of education is the increased productivity of the person receiving it. If we accept the assumption that the wage a person is paid is equal to his marginal product (his contribution to output), then it follows that the increased productivity derived from investing in education will have a positive effect on his earnings.[16] The costs of such an investment are the resources utilized in acquiring it, including the student's time. The expenditure of these resources can therefore be treated as an investment yielding a stream of future benefits, the increased output and earnings of the workers.

As was noted in the introduction to this chapter, education has aspects of both consumption and investment. Because no method has yet been devised to divide the resources utilized for education into consumption and investment compartments in empirical work, the full cost of education is typically considered to be investment costs. To the extent that some of the expenditure on education is for current consumption, the costs of education are overestimated in empirical studies. In addition, the long-run consumption aspects of education— the enjoyment of reading, of having knowledge, and the like—are not accounted for in the benefits, again due to the difficulty of measurement. Because investment costs are overestimated and benefits are underestimated, educational benefit-cost ratios and internal rates of return are biased downward (underestimates). Therefore, an educational investment with a benefit-cost ratio of less than one or an internal rate of return lower than that which may be earned on other investments may still be worthwhile.

The discussion that follows concentrates on training. Becker makes a distinction between two types of on-the-job training to develop an understanding that is generalizable to the entire human capital field. This distinction assists in explaining the incidence of the costs and benefits of education.

Increased productivity derived from *general training* is characterized by being applicable in many firms. Examples of general training abound. On-the-job training in the skills of a carpenter, secretary, medical doctor, teacher, and meat carver are but a few. Once the individual has attained some general training, the firm employing him must increase his wage to correspond to his higher marginal productivity. Otherwise, the newly trained worker would move to a firm which would pay him the value of his enhanced marginal product. Since any gains the firm derives through increased worker productivity must be paid for in higher wages, the firm would not be willing to absorb any of the costs of general training. As the firm has no net gains, it cannot be responsible for any of the costs. From the worker's point of view, the situation can be described by Figure 7.5. While he is receiving general training, his net income $(a—b)$ is lower than it would otherwise be (W_o) because he must pay for the direct cost of his training and incurs indirect costs (opportunity costs) consisting of the use of his time in which paid employment could have been undertaken. Thus, the income in the years that a worker is acquiring general training is shown to be below that which it would be were he not being trained. Later, as his wages rise due to his increased productivity, his income (*b—c*) is greater than it would have otherwise been. The worker should, of course, continue to invest in general education so long as the discounted benefits are greater than the discounted costs.

Specific training is defined as on-the-job training useful only to the firm providing it. Examples of job categories for which the training is purely specific are harder to come by because most on-the-job training is a mixture of general and specific training. Missile operation, however, is one example. The development of specific skills, on the other hand, is widespread. The time taken to teach a secretary where the supplies are kept is an example of an investment in the development of a specific skill. That knowledge will not effect the secretary's productivity in any other firm. Similarly, a teacher's learning how attendance is kept and reported in a particular school system is the creation of a specific skill not transferable to any other firm.

In the case of specific training the employee would not be willing to bear any of the costs because the increased productivity is not salable elsewhere, and the employer will not have to increase the wage offered in order to keep the worker. The employer, on the other hand, is not willing to pay for the entire cost unless he can be assured that

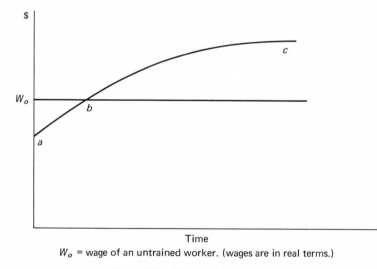

W_o = wage of an untrained worker. (wages are in real terms.)

Figure 7.5 Educational Investment

the trained worker will stay with his firm long enough to recoup these costs. Because lifetime employment contracts are illegal in most places (due to fears of creating slave-worker situations), it is difficult to assuage the firm's fears of a trainee leaving prematurely. Consequently, specific training typically falls somewhere in the middle—the employee bears some of the cost through lower wages while attaining the training and achieves some of the benefits through being paid more after attaining the skills. The relative proportions depend on the particular situation and bargaining powers of those concerned. Of course, the same cost-benefit calculus works here in evaluating the worth of a training effort as for the general training case.

Schools fit easily into the framework developed. As Becker puts it:

A school can be defined as an institution specializing in the production of training, as distinct from a firm that offers training in conjunction with the production of goods. Some schools, like those for barbers, specialize in one skill, while others, like universities, offer a large and diverse set. Schools and firms are often substitute sources of particular skills. This substitution is evidenced by the shift over time, for instance, in law from apprenticeships in law firms to law schools and in engineering from on-the-job experience to engineering schools.[17]

Whatever the mixture of on-the-job training and schooling, the costs and benefits can be analyzed with the technique provided. Putting the development of skills in this investment framework is a very useful way of looking at the world. It helps integrate education and educational institutions of all sorts into the general economic system. The next chapter presents some specific studies of education and training as investment activities.

QUESTIONS FOR DISCUSSION

1. What are some of the expenditures that your school makes which should be considered investment? What criteria did you use in categorizing the expenditures?

2. In what ways does the rate of interest prevailing in the economy affect the typical school district? Universities (private versus public, rich versus poor)?

3. What interest rate should be used in finding a benefit-cost ratio?

4. What types of applications of cost-benefit analysis could be made to the institution at which you are studying? How practical and how valuable do you think these might be?

5. Investment in physical capital (apartment buildings, factories, drill presses, and so forth) can be depreciated for tax purposes, thereby decreasing the net cost to the purchaser. Should the purchase of education be treated similarly, since there is an aspect of investment in human capital? What difficulties do you see in adopting such a practice?

PROBLEMS

1. What is the PDV of $500 payable two years in the future?

2. If the market rate of interest is 8 per cent and the cross-over rate for two investments is 10 per cent (investment A above investment B to the left of the cross-over and vice versa to the right), which investment is preferable?

3. What is the PDV of the following stream if the interest rate is 5 per cent?

end of year:	1	2	3	4	5
	−$200	−200	+400	+300	+100

4. What is the internal rate of return for the following investment stream?

end of year:	0	1	2
	−$450	−111	+665

Chapter 8 BASIC STUDIES IN EDUCATIONAL INVESTMENT

THE use of investment theory in educational decision making is one of the most extensively researched areas in the field of economics of education. Although most of the empirical research in this area has been conducted since the 1950s, studies quantifying the return to an investment in education appeared as early as 1935.[1] The macro-micro dichotomy can be employed to classify research in this area. Macro studies analyze the aggregate return to an educational investment on a national or regional level, whereas micro studies focus on particular educational decisions or projects. Both the macro and micro studies fall under the broad category of cost-benefit analyses, since in all cases costs and benefits are compared.

The most widely known studies in the area of educational investment are the macro ones analyzing the rate of return to investment in schooling. The first article reproduced in this chapter, "Total and Private Rates of Return to Investment in Schooling," by W. Lee Hansen, is illustrative of the methodology employed in educational investment studies. Utilizing 1950 Census of Population data, Hansen calculated social and private internal rates of return to elementary, secondary, and higher education in the United States. Social rates of return were calculated by including *all* costs and benefits attributable to obtaining an education, both those accruing to the individual and/or his family and to society at large, whereas private rate-of-return estimates include only the costs and benefits to a student and/or his family.

Hansen finds that as of 1949 private rates of return exceeded the social rates, a feature that is generally true in the United States because

Notes to Chapter 8 will be found on pages 380–384.

171

part of the costs of schooling are paid for by society at large. This situation, however, raises some interesting policy questions reflecting on the current arrangement for financing education. Are the large governmental subsidies justifiable? Should extensive loan programs be inaugurated to replace part of the governmental subsidy, at least on the higher education level?[2] Such a step would lower governmental costs and private benefits, thereby diminishing the differential between the social and private rates of return. These issues will undoubtedly become of more importance as the divergence between educational needs and governmental ability and willingness to meet these needs increases.

Private rate-of-return estimates are reported by Hansen on a pre- and posttax basis, indicating the effect of federal income tax on benefits from successive units of education. With two exceptions posttax private rates exceeded the social rates. Rate of return estimates— social, pretax private, and posttax private—are reported both for marginal units of schooling (for example, from 1–3 years of college to the fourth year of college) and for more extended periods of schooling (for example, high school and college). The average rates of return are the weighted average of the marginal rates that they encompass. Marginal-average comparisons indicate that the economic return to school dropouts is less than to graduates. The rate of return to students with only two years of high school or college, respectively, is less than to high school or college graduates. There appears to be an economic premium assigned to graduation above and beyond the return to additional years of schooling. Although Hansen does not explain this premium, economists generally attribute it to prevailing labor market conditions. Many employers prefer graduates to dropouts, believing that a graduate displays, among other characteristics, a greater degree of perseverance and hence will prove to be a better employee. Because this belief is usually backed up by a wage or salary higher than that offered dropouts, a premium to graduation exists.

The concluding section of Hansen's article contrasts his findings on the financial return to schooling based on a rate-of-return approach to previous research findings based on calculations of lifetime income or present value of lifetime income only. By omitting cost considerations and in some instances ignoring the "time shape" of returns, these studies give the erroneous impression that some levels of schooling are more profitable than they actually are. The rate-of-return approach incorporates both timing and cost considerations and readily permits comparisons of the net return to schooling with alternate returns in other sectors of the economy. On the basis of such comparisons, policy makers are better able to decide whether, from an economic point of view, investment in education (or any other enterprise) should be increased relative to other proposed expenditures.

Cost-benefit analyses are equally amenable to micro investigations and two such studies are reproduced in this chapter. The first study, "Education of New York City Public School Teachers: An Economic Analysis," by Clara H. Friedman, analyzes the financial implications of alternate means of acquiring thirty postbaccalaureate credits and consequently qualifying for a salary increase. Friedman focuses her study on the New York City elementary and secondary school system.

Three alternate methods of acquiring thirty postbaccalaureate credits are compared: full-time graduate study, part-time graduate study, and "in-service" courses. Appropriate cost estimates are attached to each of these educational choices and the benefits of a salary increase are contrasted with the three cost profiles. Friedman concludes that, based on the salary schedule existing in 1962, "it does not pay New York City public school teachers to secure education on a full time basis past the minimum entrance requirements into the profession." Part-time graduate training is also found to be a poor investment so long as the same salary differential can be obtained by taking "in-service" courses.

Aside from highlighting the basic shortcomings in teachers' salary plans, the methodology adopted by Friedman can be applied to analyzing decisions to enter the teaching profession, given its overall salary schedule, *vis-à-vis* other career choices, and can be applied to analyses of other salary differentials in teaching (post-Masters degree differentials). The technique is equally applicable to a host of compensatory education programs aimed either at a specific group of disadvanted youngsters or at any age group within the school-attending years.

A second illustration of a micro study utilizing a cost-benefit approach is David A. Page's "Retraining under the Manpower Development Act: A Cost-Benefit Analysis." Manpower training and retraining has been one of the major devices used during the 1960s to assist unemployed and untrained workers to overcome educational and personal deficiencies that can lead to employment difficulties. As such, it is an attempt to reduce unemployment stemming from a worker's lack of skills (structural unemployment), as opposed to unemployment due to an overall deficiency in the number of available jobs (insufficient aggregate demand). Page's research points to one way of evaluating such programs.

Page analyzes the labor market experience of 907 persons who enrolled in manpower training courses in Massachusetts during the period 1958 to 1961. An interesting methodological framework is devised to estimate improvements in a person's labor market earnings attributable solely to training, a framework applicable to many programs that are associated with the "War on Poverty." The study concludes with an enlightening discussion of the limits of cost-benefit studies in areas where not all costs, benefits, and exogeneous factors affecting costs and benefits are quantifiable—issues that should be kept in mind in all empirical research.

TOTAL AND PRIVATE RATES OF RETURN TO INVESTMENT IN SCHOOLING

W. LEE HANSEN

The costs of schooling and the money returns resulting from investment in schooling are currently receiving more and more attention by economists, not only because of their possible implications for economic growth, but also because they may help individuals to determine how much they should invest in the development of their own human capital. This note provides some further evidence on these two topics; it presents estimates of internal rates of return based on both total and private resource costs for various amounts of schooling, from elementary school through college.

The fragmentary treatment of both the costs of schooling and the money returns to schooling found in much of the recent literature provided the stimulus for preparing these internal rate-of-return estimates. For example, Miller calculates life-time income values by level of schooling,[3] Houthakker estimates, on the basis of alternative discount rates, the present value of income streams associated with different levels of schooling,[4] Schultz provides estimates of total resource costs of education by broad level of schooling,[5] and Becker and Schultz calculate for several levels of education the expected rates of return, sometimes on a total resource cost basis and at other times on a private resource cost basis.[6] Given this diversity of treatment, it is difficult to obtain an overall picture of the relationship among rates of return to different amounts of schooling or to see the nature

Reprinted from the *Journal of Political Economy* 71 (1963), 128–40. Copyright © 1963 by the University of Chicago.

of the differences between the rates of return as viewed by society and those viewed by individuals. Moreover, the relationship among the various methods of contrasting the economic gains from education—the lifetime income, the present value, and the rate of return comparisons—has been obscured.

It becomes important to understand what some of these relationships are when society and individuals allocate such a large portion of their resources to schooling. At the societal level, for example, we might be interested in determining whether to allocate more funds to reduce the number of dropouts from high school or to stimulate an increased flow of college graduates. As individuals, we would more likely be concerned with deciding whether to continue or to terminate our schooling, on the basis of the relative costs that will be incurred and the benefits that will accrue. To this end, the comprehensive sets of internal rates of return developed here should be useful as a first approximation in seeking answers to questions of this kind.

At the outset, it should be made clear that the measured rates of return are money rates of return; any other costs and benefits associated with schooling are excluded from consideration. In addition, there are problems of measurement, many of which have not been resolved, that make the estimation of even direct money rates of return difficult. Some of these difficulties are discussed in Part I, which outlines the methods and data employed. Part II presents evidence on rates of return to total and to private resource investment in schooling. Part III contrasts three different methods of measuring the economic gains to schooling, while Part IV offers some concluding comments.

I. ESTIMATION PROCEDURES

To estimate internal rates of return to investments in schooling, we require data on costs—total resource costs and private resource costs—for various levels of schooling as well as data on age-income patterns by each level of schooling. From these, life-cycle cost-income streams can be established that show for each level of schooling the flows of costs incurred during schooling and the subsequent flows of additional income that can be attributed to that schooling. The internal rate of return is then estimated by finding that rate of discount that equates the present value of the cost outlays with the present value of the additional income flows.

The basic source of income data is the *1950 Census of Population*,[7] which provides distributions of income for males by age and level of schooling in 1949. From these, average income figures can be calculated for each age-schooling category, as shown in Table 8.1. Although Houthakker had previously presented such figures, his method of estimation produces a rather peculiar bias.[8] In addition, Houthakker's data show mean incomes of

176   Basic Studies in Educational Investment

all males over age fourteen, whether they were receiving income or not. But to the extent that only income recipients are represented in the data shown here in Table 8.1, most of the males outside the labor force, either because of school attendance (younger males) or retirement (older males), are probably excluded. Exclusion of these groups seems likely to provide better estimates of the age-income profiles, particularly at their extremities.

In order to make the task of estimating the rates of return more manageable, the age-income profiles were assumed to commence at the "average" age of completion of each level of schooling.[9] For those with one to four years of schooling, the average amount of school completed was taken as two years; hence the age-income profile for this group was assumed to begin at age eight. For the next group, those with five to seven years of school, six years of schooling were assumed, so that its age-income profile begins at age twelve. The other level of education groups and the ages at which their age-income profiles were assumed to begin are as follows: eight years, age fourteen; one to three years of high school, age sixteen; four years of high school, age eighteen; one to three years of college, age twenty; and four years of college, age twenty-two. In fact, however, for age groups under fourteen the age-income profiles take values of zero, because no income data are collected for these groups.[10]

Table 8.1

Average Income by Age and Years of School Completed, Males, United States, 1949

| | | | | Years of School Completed | | | | |
| | | Elementary School | | | High School | | College | |
Age	0	1–4	5–7	8	1–3	4	1–3	4+
14–15	$ 610	$ 350	$ 365	$ 406	—	—	—	—
16–17	526	472	514	534	$ 429	—	—	—
18–19	684	713	885	1,069	941	$ 955	—	—
20–21	944	1,009	1,216	1,535	1,652	1,744	$1,066	—
22–24	1,093	1,227	1,562	1,931	2,191	2,363	1,784	$1,926
25–34	1,337	1,603	2,027	2,540	2,837	3,246	3,444	4,122
35–44	1,605	1,842	2,457	3,029	3,449	4,055	5,014	7,085
45–54	1,812	2,073	2,650	3,247	3,725	4,689	5,639	8,116
55–64	2,000	2,045	2,478	3,010	3,496	4,548	5,162	7,655
65 or more	1,140	1,189	1,560	1,898	2,379	3,155	3,435	5,421

Source: See nn. 5 and 6.

Two major cost variants are used in the calculations—one for total resource costs and the other for private resource costs. The rationale and procedures for estimating total resource costs have been set forth by Schultz.[11] Total resource costs include (1) school costs incurred by society, that is, teachers' salaries, supplies, interest and depreciation on capital, (2) opportunity costs incurred by individuals, namely, income foregone during school attendance, and (3) incidental school-related costs incurred by individuals, for example, books and travel. Private resource costs include the same three components except that in (1) above, tuition and fees paid by individuals are substituted for society's costs which are normally defrayed through taxation.

In developing the cost figures used in these estimates, whether on a total or a private resource basis, the opportunity costs were taken directly from the age-income profiles of the alternative level of schooling being used in the calculations. For example, at age eighteen the opportunity cost for the person undertaking four years of college is the income that the high-school graduate would obtain from ages eighteen to twenty-one. This procedure made it unnecessary to rely upon indirectly estimated opportunity cost figures and yielded at the same time a more detailed set of opportunity costs by age and level of schooling.[12] In completing the estimates of per student total resource cost, school costs paid by society and school-related expenditures incurred by individuals were derived from Schultz's results.[13] In completing the estimates of private resource costs, the amount of tuition and fees paid per student was obtained from already available estimates.[14] Again, the school-related costs from Schultz's work were used. While the latter costs have an arbitrary quality to them, they seem to be reasonable.[15] The cost figures, exclusive of opportunity costs, by age and grade are summarized in Table 8.2.

Lifetime cost-income streams were then constructed for each level of schooling with the help of the appropriate age-income profiles and the age-

Table 8.2

Average Annual Per Student Costs, Exclusive of Opportunity Costs, by Age and Grade, United States, 1949[a]

| | | Total Resource Costs | | | Private Resource Costs | | |
| | | School Costs | Other Costs | Total | Tuition and Fees | Other Costs | Total |
Age	School Level (1)	(2)	(3)	(4)	(5)	(6)	(7)
6–13	Elementary	$201	—	$201	—	—	—
14–17	High School	354	31	385	—	31	31
18–21	College	801	142	943	245	142	387

[a] Though these cost data are indicated as being for 1950 in Schultz, "Capital Formation by Education," *op. cit.*, they actually apply to the 1949–50 school year. Thus these data may overstate somewhat the costs of schooling relative to the income derived from that schooling.

Source: col. (2), *elementary school:* Schultz, "Capital Formation by Education," *op. cit.*, Table 3, col. (11), 1950 figure divided by number of elementary school students in 1950, from *Statistical Abstract*, 1955, Table 152; *high school:* Schultz, "Capital Formation by Education," *op. cit.*, Table 5, 1950, col. (4) divided by col. (1); *college: ibid.*, Table 6, 1950, col. (4) divided by col. (1).

Col. (3), *elementary school:* assumed to be zero; *high school: ibid.*, Table 5, 1950, col. (5) divided by col. (1); *college: ibid.*, Table 6, 1950, col. (4) divided by col. (1).

Col. (4), sum of cols. (2) and (3).

Col. (5), *elementary school and high school:* assumed to be zero; *college:* based on average tuition and fee charges, derived from *Biennial Survey of Education, 1955–56*, chaps. i and iv, after adjusting veteran charges for non-tuition items (see n. 13).

Col. (6), same as col. (3).

Col. (7), sum of cols. (5) and (6).

cost estimates. This was done by taking the difference between the cost-income profile for a given level of schooling and the income profile for the particular base level of schooling used in the comparison. For example, in the case of investment in four years of college, the income profile for the base group, high-school graduates, begins at age eighteen. The cost-income profile for the person who completes four years of college also begins at age eighteen; during the four years to age twenty-one it reflects both school and school-related costs and thereafter the somewhat higher income profile of the college graduate. The cost-income stream, the *difference* between these two profiles, reflects at ages eighteen to twenty-one both school and school-related costs as well as opportunity costs; at ages beyond twenty-one the difference reflects the net income stream resulting from four years of college. An additional adjustment is required to reflect the incidence of mortality; this involves adjusting the net cost-income stream downward to reflect the probabilities that at each age the costs or returns will not be incurred or received, respectively.[16] Finally, the internal rates of return must be estimated by finding that rate of discount which sets the present value of the cost stream equal to the present value of the net return stream.

When considering private rates of return, it is important to show them on both a before- and after-tax basis. Not only will all rates of return be lower after tax, but also the relative declines in the rates will differ, given the progressivity of tax rates and the positive association between income and educational levels. The differences among the before-tax and after-tax rates could be of considerable importance to individuals in the determination of their own investment planning.

To estimate the after-tax incomes and rates of return, the original income data in Table 8.1 were adjusted for federal income tax payments; while it probably would have been desirable to adjust for all types of taxes, this could not be done in view of the paucity of data. Subsequently, the rates of return were calculated in the same way as described for the before-tax data. The actual after-tax income figures were obtained by multiplying each income figure by the appropriate ratio of after- to before-tax income, derived from Houthakker.[17] These ratios prove to be almost identical to those that would have resulted had the marginal tax rates been applied to the distributions of income recipients in calculating after-tax income.[18]

As in most empirical studies the available data prove to be somewhat unlike those that we require, and so the rate of return estimates do not provide a full picture of the profitability of schooling.[19] Therefore, several features of the data and the nature of their effects on age-income profiles, and hence on rates of return, deserve mention before the results are discussed. First, since only income rather than earnings data are available, the income profiles used reflect in part receipts from other assets. On the assumption that the relative income from other assets is a positive function of the level of earnings itself, the impact of this would presumably be to raise the age-income profiles of the higher level of schooling groups. Second, certain problems of "mix" exist within the data. For example, among those with little schooling there may be heavy concentrations of certain minority groups, such as Negroes and Puerto Ricans. If they are effectively discriminated against, then the age-income profiles of the lower level of schooling groups would be depressed below their expected level. On the other hand, at higher levels of schooling the age-income profiles may be raised somewhat by reverse discrimination that favors sons, relatives, and others of higher social-economic status. Third, since those people who complete more schooling ordinarily possess greater intelligence, as measured by intelligence scores, some part of the differential income received might have accrued to them anyway. Although our present knowledge makes it difficult to separate the impact of intelligence and schooling, the observed income differences among the lower and higher levels of schooling undoubtedly overstate, and by increasing amounts, the differentials attributable to schooling.[20] Fourth, all cost elements were considered as investment even though some portions might better be regarded as consumption. To the extent that any of the cost is considered as consumption, the investment costs are overstated.[21] Fifth, all estimates rest on cross-section cost-income relationships and thereby ignore future shifts in the relationships of the cost-income streams. And finally, any number of other factors may impinge on the observed income differentials, in the form of education at home, on-the-job-training, and so forth.

While some would suggest that the presence of such problems seriously limits any conclusions concerning the empirical relationships between income and schooling, it nevertheless seems worthwhile to set forth the rate of return estimates in their crude form.[22] From them some preliminary conclusions about resource allocation can be drawn.

II. INTERNAL RATE OF RETURN ESTIMATES

The Return to Total Resource Investment

Internal rates of return to total resource investment in schooling appear in Table 8.3. The boxed figures in the diagonal to the right show the rates of return to each successive increment of schooling and can be interpreted as "marginal" rates of return. For example, the rate of return to the first two years of elementary school is 8.9 per cent, to the next four years of elementary school 14.5 per cent, and so on to the last two years of college 15.6 per cent. Although the marginals provide all of the necessary information, average rates of return to successively more years of schooling can be derived from the marginals; since the average rates are of some interest, they are also shown in the columns. For example, in column (1) we see that at age six the expected rate of return to investment in two years of elementary schooling is 8.9 per cent; the rate of return to investment in six years of elementary schooling (the weighted average of the two marginals) is 12.0 per cent, and so on to the investment in sixteen years of schooling, which yields a 12.1 per cent rate of return.

Several features of the configuration of rates of return deserve comment. First, the marginal rates rise over the first few years of schooling, reaching a peak with the completion of elementary schooling. This clearly suggests that rapidly increasing returns to schooling prevail over the early years and that a small initial amount of schooling, the first two years, has relatively little impact on earning power. Second, the trend in the rates is downward thereafter, though it is not smooth by any means. While the rate of return to the first two years of high school drops dramatically, it rises somewhat with the completion of high school. The rate drops once again for the first two years of college, and it then displays a significant rise with the completion of four years of college. At this point one can only speculate as to the reasons underlying these declines.

Evidence such as this on the marginal or incremental rates of return is ordinarily used in discussing resource allocation. If on the basis of these rates of return a given amount of resources were to be spent on schooling, the ranking of the marginals from high to low is as follows:

Grades 7–8, 15–16, 3–6, 11–12, 9–10, 0–2, and 13–14.[23] At an alternative rate of return to society of, say, 10 per cent, investment in all grade levels except the last three would be justified. Were the alternative rate, say, 7 per cent, only the last level would be excluded.

Viewing the matter in this fashion would be quite satisfactory if the rates of return declined steadily as we moved to successively higher increments of schooling, but because the marginal rates fluctuate some averaging is required. If we look at marginal rates for broader increments of schooling, for example, eight years of elementary school, four years of high school, and four years of college, then the rates of return to additional investment quite clearly decline, as shown by the respective figures: 15.0 per cent (col. [1], row [3]), 11.4 per cent (col. [4], row [5]), and 10.2 per cent (col. [6], row [7]). At an alternative rate of return of 10 per cent, investment in all levels of

Table 8.3 Internal Rates of Return to Total Resource Investment in Schooling, United States, Males, 1949[a]

	From:		(1)	(2)	(3)	(4)	(5)	(6)	(7)
To:	Age Grade		6 1	8 3	12 7	14 9	16 11	18 13	20 15
(1)	7	2	8.9	–	–	–	–	–	–
(2)	11	6	12.0	14.5	–	–	–	–	–
(3)	13	8	15.0	18.5	29.2	–	–	–	–
(4)	15	10	13.7	15.9	16.3	9.5	–	–	–
(5)	17	12	13.6	15.4	15.3	11.4	13.7	–	–
(6)	19	14	11.3	12.1	11.1	8.2	8.2	5.4	–
(7)	21	16	12.1	12.7	12.1	10.5	10.9	10.2	15.6

[a] All rate-of-return figures are subject to some error, since the estimation to one decimal place was made by interpolation between whole percentage figures.

schooling becomes profitable. But were the original rates considered independently of each other and an alternative rate of return of 10 per cent prevailed, it would not pay to permit any new enrollments, the schooling of those people in elementary school would be terminated at Grade 8, and of those people already in high school and college, only students in their last two years of each would be allowed to graduate. To allocate investment in schooling this way would obviously reflect a very short-run view of the implied economic opportunities.

However, it might be desirable to consider some longer time horizon instead, particularly if the alternative rate of return were expected to remain reasonably constant over time. Given an alternative rate of return of, say, 10 per cent, investment through the completion of college could easily be justified for each age group currently enrolled, since every rate of return figure in the bottom row (row [7]) of Table 8.3 exceeds 10 per cent. Understandably, this result is no different than that obtained earlier.

On the basis of even longer-run considerations only the rate of return to investment in the schooling of new school entrants may be relevant, especially if schooling is thought of as a good to be purchased in large, indivisible quantities, for example, schooling from Grade 1 through college, or schooling from Grade 1 through high school. In this case the rates of return shown in column (1) indicate yields of 13.6 and 12.1 per cent, respectively, and suggest the obvious advantages of seeing to it that everyone completes college or high school, as the case may be. In fact, this averaging of the marginal rates makes such investment attractive at an alternative rate as high as 12 per cent.

The Return to Private Resource Investment

Internal rates of return to total resource costs of schooling are of undeniable importance in assessing the efficiency with which an economy's resources are allocated, but for individuals and/or their parents the relevant rates of return are those based upon private resource costs. These private rates of return both before and after tax are shown in Tables 8.4 and 8.5, respectively; the tables are to be read in the same fashion as Table 8.3.

For all levels of schooling under eight years, private rates of return have no real meaning (they are infinitely large) since opportunity costs are assumed to be zero, school-related costs are negligible, and tuition and fees are not charged. Above Grade 8, however, all private rates of return before tax are higher than the total rates of return shown in Table 8.3, with the greatest disparities appearing at the younger ages and lower levels of schooling, where individuals pay smaller proportions of total resource costs; private rates of return after tax are also higher than total rates of return with but two exceptions. Otherwise, the general configuration in both the columns and the diagonals appears to be about the same for both total and private rates, whether before or after tax, though the levels do differ.

When individuals and/or their parents plan an investment program in schooling, the private rates of return justify securing more schooling than

Table 8.4 Internal Rates of Return to Private Resource Investment in Schooling, before Tax, United States, Males, 1949[a]

	From:		(1)	(2)	(3)	(4)	(5)	(6)	(7)
To:	Age	Grade	6 1	8 3	12 7	14 9	16 11	18 13	20 15
(1)	7	2	b	—	—	—	—	—	—
(2)	11	6	b	b	—	—	—	—	—
(3)	13	8	b	b	b	—	—	—	—
(4)	15	10	28.3	34.6	25.9	12.7	—	—	—
(5)	17	12	25.6	29.4	23.3	15.3	18.6	—	—
(6)	19	14	18.1	18.7	14.8	10.4	9.5	6.2	—
(7)	21	16	18.2	18.7	16.2	12.9	13.0	11.6	18.7

[a] All rate-of-return figures are subject to some error, since the estimation to one decimal place had to be made by interpolation between whole percentage figures.

[b] This indicates an infinite rate of return, given the assumption that education is costless to the individual to the completion of eighth grade.

Table 8.5 Internal Rates of Return to Private Resource Investment in Schooling, after Tax, United States, Males, 1949[a]

	From:		(1)	(2)	(3)	(4)	(5)	(6)	(7)
To:	Age	Grade	6 1	8 3	12 7	14 9	16 11	18 13	20 15
(1)	7	2	b	—	—	—	—	—	—
(2)	11	6	b	b	—	—	—	—	—
(3)	13	8	b	b	b	—	—	—	—
(4)	15	10	27.9	33.0	24.8	12.3	—	—	—
(5)	17	12	25.2	28.2	22.2	14.5	17.5	—	—
(6)	19	14	17.2	17.5	13.7	9.4	8.5	5.1	—
(7)	21	16	17.2	17.3	14.4	11.5	11.4	10.1	16.7

[a] All rate-of-return figures are subject to some error, since the estimation to one decimal place had to be made by interpolation between whole percentage figures.

[b] This indicates an infinite rate of return, given the assumption of costless education to the individual through the completion of eighth grade.

do the rates of return on total resource investment. For example, the marginal rates of return to elementary, high-school, and college schooling are infinite (col. [1], row [3]), 15.3 per cent (col. [4], row [5]), and 11.6 per cent (col. [6], row [7]), respectively. Thus, investment in schooling through college is still profitable even if the private alternative rate is as high as 11.5 per cent. But, on an after-tax basis, the alternative rate of 10 per cent just permits private investment at the college level (Table 8.5, col. [6], row [7]).

When schooling is viewed in large blocks, a somewhat different picture emerges. If the decision-making age is fourteen and the objective is to complete schooling through college, the alternative rate of return would have to exceed 12.9 per cent (col. [4], row [7]) on a before-tax basis and 11.5 per cent on an after-tax basis for the investment to be unprofitable. If the decision-making age is six and the objective is to complete schooling through college, the alternative rate would have to exceed 18.2 per cent (col. [1], row [7]) on a before-tax basis and 17.2 per cent on an after-tax basis, for the investment to be unprofitable.

A comparison of the total rates of return with the private rates of return after tax is of interest in suggesting the extent to which distortions in the private rates caused by federal income taxes are offset by the counter-distortion of subsidized schooling. An examination of the results in Tables 8.3 and 8.5 indicates that even though income taxes do substantially reduce the levels of private rates of return, public subsidization of schooling makes the private rates of return net of tax considerably more attractive than the rate of return earned on total resource investment. Only two exceptions appear (col. [6]); these suggest that the student pays more than his own way in securing schooling at the college level. This might indicate the need for a restudy of the assessment of the costs of college against the individual, unless the possible underinvestment in college training that would be produced is regarded as acceptable in some broader sense. But these exceptions aside, the fact that private rates of return after taxes exceed the total rates of return would, in the absence of restraints on sources of private financing, probably give rise to overinvestment in schooling by individuals. However, a fuller treatment of the effects of other forms of taxation and methods of financing schooling would be required before any definitive judgment could be reached.

III. ALTERNATIVE MEASURES OF PRIVATE ECONOMIC RETURNS FROM SCHOOLING

The economic returns to individuals from schooling can be observed from three different points of view: (1) the value of lifetime income as set forth by Miller,[24] (2) the present value of lifetime income as set forth by Houthakker,[25] and (3) the rate of return on investment in schooling as set forth here. While the lifetime income and present value of lifetime income methods, particularly the former, are rather widely used, they are not relevant to ranking the direct economic returns to schooling when schooling is treated as a type of investment expenditure. Both of these methods completely ignore the costs of schooling, while the lifetime income approach suffers from the further defect of ignoring the time shape of the returns. Because the rankings of the economic returns differ so substantially, it seems desirable to present all three measures of the returns and to discuss them briefly. To make the comparisons more manageable, we shall deal only with the additional returns to different amounts of schooling as seen at age fourteen. The before- and after-tax results appear in the upper and lower halves, respectively, of Table 8.6.

Table 8.6

Alternative Methods of Comparing Value of Private Economic Returns to Investment in Schooling, as Viewed at Age Fourteen, United States, Males, 1949

Schooling from Completion of Grade 8 to Completion of	Additional Lifetime Income (1)	Present Value of Additional Income at				Internal Rate of Return (Per Cent) (6)
		3 Per Cent (2)	6 Per Cent (3)	8 Per Cent (4)	10 Per Cent (5)	
			Before Tax			
2 years high school	$ 16,802	$ 7,756	$ 2,301	$1,190	$ 545	12.7
4 years high school	46,038	18,156	6,488	3,601	1,949	15.3
2 years college	66,763	23,800	7,352	3,215	996	10.4
4 years college	141,468	49,429	17,252	8,722	4,135	12.9
			After Tax			
2 years high school	$ 14,143	$ 5,081	$ 1,956	$ 996	$ 436	12.3
4 years high school	38,287	13,580	5,362	2,929	1,547	14.5
2 years college	52,485	17,000	5,364	2,084	336	9.4
4 years college	109,993	36,575	12,824	6,170	2,611	11.5

The value of additional lifetime income associated with higher levels of schooling is frequently cited as a justification for investment in schooling by the individual. Clearly, the values of additional lifetime income resulting from successively greater amounts of schooling (col. [1]), indicate that more schooling pays substantially larger dollar returns than less schooling.[26] But, since a portion of the costs of schooling is excluded from consideration,[27] the full extent to which these returns offset the costs of schooling is not at all clear. Even more important, the fact that the time flows of these returns also differ remains hidden in the calculation of the lifetime income values. By virtue of these omissions, the impression emerges that any and all amounts of schooling are worth obtaining.

Another method of measuring the economic returns to schooling involves comparing the present values of additional lifetime income, a various discount rates, to successively greater amounts of schooling. The values, at discount rates of 3, 6, 8, and 10 per cent appear in columns (2), (3), (4), and (5), respectively.[28] Again, schooling pays at any or all of the discount rates used, though the rankings do shift about as the discount rate is varied. For example, at 3 and 6 per cent the rankings coincide with those shown by the value of additional lifetime income, but at an 8 per cent discount rate schooling to the first two years of college becomes absolutely less attractive financially than schooling to high school, whether before or after tax. And at a 10 per cent discount rate the after-tax return to schooling to the first two years of college falls below that to the first two years of high school. Even though the present-value figures are quite sensitive to the discount rate used, once again all schooling pays. But the basic flaw in this method of calculation is the omission of some of the costs of education from the calculation; specifically, the method fails to subtract the present value of the non-opportunity costs from the present value of the additional income. Doing so would undoubtedly cause some additional changes in the rankings, particularly at the higher discount rates.

Finally, the rate-of-return approach remedies the defects inherent in the other two methods. The relevant data on internal rates of return from Tables 8.4 and 8.5 (see Table 8.6, col. [6]), reveal a much different ranking of the returns to schooling. On a before-tax basis, investment in schooling to completion of high school, with a 15.3 rate of return, yields by far the most attractive return, followed by schooling to college with 12.9 per cent, and schooling to the first two years of high school with 12.7 per cent; schooling to the first two years of college, with a 10.4 per cent return, lags far behind.

When we shift to rates of return on an after-tax basis, the rankings of the return on schooling to the completion of college and to the completion of the first two years of high school change. Since the marginal tax rates are a function of the amount of the income differential, the effect of the tax on the college rate of return is decidedly greater than its effect on the rate of return to the first two years of high school, for example. Given the fact that the original rates of return were almost identical, the after-tax return to completion of college now drops considerably below that to completion of two years of high school.

In conclusion, it appears that ranking of the returns to investment in schooling by the rate-of-return method is clearly superior to the methods employed in the work of both Miller and Houthakker. Whether the more general rate-of-return rule is in fact superior to the present-value rule (when properly used) still remains an unsettled issue that will not be discussed here.[29]

IV. CONCLUSION

Estimates of the internal money rates of return to both total and private resource investment in schooling have been presented to provide a more complete picture of the costs of and returns to schooling. While the rates of return to private resource investment obviously exceed those to total resource investment, we find that the rates of return to the various increments of schooling also differ and have somewhat different implications for resource allocation at both the societal and individual level. Basically, the marginal rates of return rise with more schooling up to the completion of Grade 8 and then gradually fall off to the completion of college. We also find that private rates of return after tax almost invariably exceed the total rates of return, a situation that could presumably induce private overinvestment in schooling. Finally, the rate of return provides a superior method of ranking the economic returns to investment in schooling than do the more conventional additional lifetime income or present value of additional lifetime income methods currently used.

Thus, one might conclude that the high rates of return to investment in schooling go a long way toward explaining, or justifying, this society's traditional faith in education, as well as the desire of individuals to take advantage of as much schooling as they can. But clearly we need to know much more about the relationship between income and ability, the importance of on-the-job training, the significance of education in the home, and so forth. My own suspicion is that full adjustment for these factors would have the effect of reducing the relative rates of return, especially at the higher levels of schooling.

In addition, we have barely begun to consider the possible disparity between the rate of return to total resource investment and the "social" rate of return to investment in schooling that takes additional account of those returns that are produced indirectly. Intuition as well as the little evidence available suggests that these returns may be considerable, but a full accounting of the economic value of schooling will have to await further work.[30]

EDUCATION OF NEW YORK CITY PUBLIC SCHOOL TEACHERS: AN ECONOMIC ANALYSIS

CLARA H. FRIEDMAN

Differences in the amount of time required for job training have long been recognized as requiring compensating differences in income. A few empirical studies have been undertaken of the relation between differences in education and income.[31] These have found that income differences reflect not alone differences in education, but more than compensate for the required investment. The costs of educational preparation for job training may thus be viewed as an investment in human capital.

Such an analysis yields entirely contrary results for New York City public school teachers. Greater rewards, in terms of lifetime earnings, do *not* accrue to the teachers with greater preparation. Nor do the same income rewards apply for the same amount of preparation. Teachers who acquire postbaccalaureate preparation through on-the-job training have an earnings advantage over teachers who acquire the same postgraduate preparation prior to entering the school system, without regard to the fact that certification requirements make postgraduate preparation a job prerequisite for many teachers. Paradoxically, these results obtain under a pay plan which bases salary differentiation on differences in teachers' educational preparation,[32] and has "equal pay for equal preparation" as its cornerstone.

Reprinted from the *Industrial and Labor Relations Review* 18 (1964), 20–31. Copyright © 1964 by Cornell University. All rights reserved.

The inequalities resulting from the defective relationship between investment and returns are not at all recondite. They are experienced, if not perceived, by the teachers in the New York City school system. This analysis suggests that these inequalities are the crux of the teacher salary differential problem.

The inequalities explain the bitter opposition to the preparation pay plan long expressed by many high school teachers. The inequalities explain the inability of the New York City school system to recruit highly trained teachers with postbaccalaureate attainment beyond minimum certification levels.

The findings add an interesting variant to empirical data on costs and returns of investment in human capital. It is hoped they will also provide new insight into the vexing problem of salary differentials for New York City teachers. Indeed the problem, as analyzed here, transcends the preparation pay plan. Under any pay plan, for any group of employees, income differences should compensate for differences in the costs of whatever training is required or desirable. It would be the greatest of ironies if that principle were to be set aside for teachers, at the very time that more and better training is urged universally for them.

THE TEACHERS' INVESTMENT IN HUMAN CAPITAL

How much investment in human capital have New York City teachers undertaken? What has prompted their investment?

The answer to the first question must be an estimate, in the absence of data on the actual educational preparation of teachers. Next, motivation underlying the preparation, although an elusive kind of information, can be fairly inferred from all the relevant factors: certification requirements, convenience of on-the-job training, return on the investment.

The key to the educational distribution is the salary distribution, but these are by no means identical. The large number of teachers receiving more than the basic salary schedule is not a measure of the number with postbaccalaureate preparation.

The salary distribution gives an exaggerated view of educational attainment, for two reasons. First, many pre-1947 appointees benefited from exceptions granted in 1957 to redress the intitial salary disadvantage inflicted upon them when the preparation pay plan was inaugurated. (A large proportion of the high school staff is still made up of pre-1947 appointees—almost half, as of 1960. The percentage in the present elementary staff is indeterminate, but is undoubtedly much less than for high school teachers, because of the higher turnover rate of elementary teachers.) The exceptions gave all pre-1947 high school teachers the $800 differential, even though they might have only five years or less of educational preparation. Some pre-1947 appointees in elementary and junior high schools

Table 8.7

Salary Distribution, N.Y.C. Teachers, 1960–61
School Year

		Per Cent of Teachers Receiving	
School Level	Basic Schedule	$400 above Basic	$800 above Basic
Elementary	29.7	45.4	24.9
Junior High	16.0	39.2	44.8
Academic High	2.5	19.2	78.3
Vocational High	3.1	21.5	75.4
Combined	20.4	38.0	41.7

Source: Data derived from Madeline Morrissey, *Teachers' Salaries, 1960–61*, Board of Education of City of New York, Bureau of Educational Program Research and Statistics, Pub. No. 163, P.N. S–208, January 1961, p. 15.

were granted the $400 or $800 differentials without the fifth or sixth years of preparation.

Second, there are still some teachers who were certified when less than the baccalaureate sufficed for elementary teachers, and less than the fifth year sufficed for secondary teachers.

Taking everything into consideration, it would appear that the salary data overstate the teachers' educational attainment considerably for high school teachers, less so for elementary and junior high teachers. The teachers' educational preparation is estimated to be as shown in Table 8.8.

Even thus deflated, the figures indicate a high level of investment in human capital. How significant is this? Does it attest to the effectiveness of the preparation pay plan in eliciting widespread investment in human capital? Is it prima facie evidence that the preparation differentials yield

Table 8.8

Estimated Educational Preparation, Post-High School, N.Y.C. Teachers, October 1960

	Per Cent of Teachers with		
School Level	Four Years	Five Years	Six Years
Elementary	42.8	37.2	20.0
Junior High	20.4	40.4	39.2
Academic High	26.5	42.0	31.5
Vocational High	41.3	36.3	22.4
Combined	34.4	39.0	26.6

Source: Estimates are based on all available data, including most recent date for which academic degrees were reported (December 1946) and distribution of high school teachers by date of appointment (pre- and post-1947). Friedman, "Economic Analysis of Preparation Pay Differentials," unpublished Ph.D. dissertation, Department of Economics, Columbia University, 1962, pp. 125–45.

an investment return great enough to compensate for the costs of such investment?

Before examining the actual evidence on the return from the teachers' investment in human capital, two factors influencing that level should be noted. The first of these is certification requirements.

If certification were to require a fifth year of preparation, teachers would have no choice as to the amount of investment in human capital they would make. That is, if they chose to become teachers, the fifth year of preparation would be mandated for them, whether or not the mandate were accompanied by a preparation pay differential.

The fifth year is, in fact, presently mandated for a majority of secondary teachers; for almost three decades it has been a certification requirement for junior high and high school teachers of academic subjects.[33] If all the authorized teaching positions in the secondary schools (as of October 31, 1959) had been filled by teachers meeting no more than minimum certification requirements, almost two-thirds of the secondary teachers would necessarily have had the fifth year of preparation and thus automatically qualified for the $400 differential.

The certification requirements explain why a large proportion of secondary teachers must invest in the fifth year of preparation. But why do almost as many invest in a sixth year of preparation? And why do more than half of all elementary teachers invest in a fifth or sixth year of preparation, when certification requires no more than a baccalaureate degree from them?

Investment beyond minimum certification requirements is almost exclusively an on-the-job phenomenon,[34] but the high incidence of on-the-job training is not attributable simply to the fact that it yields additional income, *i.e.*, the $400 or $800 differentials. What is of overriding importance is that the on-the-job training may be achieved on a tuition-free basis, without loss of earnings, by means of the Board of Education's In-Service Training Program.

The program was first offered in 1936, with courses approved by the New York State Department of Education, to satisfy requirements for in-service credit for salary increments. Certain in-service courses were designated as acceptable for the preparation differentials, when these became available. The peaks of teacher participation in the in-service program correspond with the proffer of the fifth-year differential in 1947 and of the sixth-year differential in 1957.[35]

Whether studies in the In-Service Program are equivalent in every respect with those in full-time postgraduate attendance is beyond the scope of this analysis.[36] Nevertheless, it should be noted that a distinction is made, for teacher certification: the fifth year of preparation is not acceptable through on-the-job training for secondary teachers of academic subjects. In salary terms, no distinction is made: the same preparation differentials apply, whether the course credits are acquired on the job or prior to beginning teaching service.

In income terms, a distinction does exist, as will be shown. Teachers whose postbaccalaureate preparation is acquired on the job have significantly higher lifetime earnings than those who acquired the same educational preparation on a full-time basis.

RETURNS FROM THE TEACHERS' INVESTMENT IN HUMAN CAPITAL

Why Misconceptions Exist

The calculation is essentially a simple one, taking into account the costs of the investment and the value of income from the preparation differentials. The fact that it has not been made heretofore is perhaps attributable to the common misconception of regarding the income from preparation differentials only as a plus and gross amount, in excess of income from the basic salary schedule, without regard to its net value or present value.[37]

The misconception has been compounded by the unverified assumption that the income return from the preparation differential is greater than the salary loss which may be involved in its acquisition. The highest administrators in the Board of Education put forth this view:

Those who decided to remain at college to earn a fifth year of professional and/or academic preparation before entering teaching as a career do not start service as a regular teacher on a higher salary step because of the advanced preparation but do receive a salary differential grant of $400 for each year during their entire teaching career in the New York City school system. In financial returns the additional year of college preparation is much larger than one year of salary credit.[38]

The facts are otherwise. It will be shown that the financial returns are not much larger; and among teachers receiving the same differentials, it will be shown that differences nevertheless exist in their incomes. This is because income differences among individuals arise in part from differences in the individuals' earning lifetimes—which are intrinsically governed by the training time preceding paid employment. As Mincer states:

Occupations differ...in the amount of training they require. Training takes time, and each additional year of it postpones the individuals' earnings for another year, generally reducing the span of his earning life.[39]

The difference in training time has several effects on income. First, it results in foregone earnings, by shortening the period during which income would otherwise be earned. Second, it may involve costs for educational training and supplies. Third, it results in postponement of earnings.

How do these circumstances apply to New York City teachers? For them, the difference in earning lifetimes is inevitably one year, comparing most secondary teachers (for whom the fifth year of preparation is mandated) with elementary teachers and all others. It may, however, be one or two years, for any teacher voluntarily choosing to acquire the fifth or sixth year of preparation before accepting a teaching post which requires only the baccalaureate degree or the fifth year of preparation.

As to costs for educational training, this factor is negligible for most New York City teachers, because of the widespread utilization of tuition-free facilities in the City colleges, as well as in the Board's In-Service Training Program. As to postponement of earnings, this is unavoidable for teachers whose postgraduate preparation precedes their teaching employment. Such teachers receive each annual instalment of income (referring only to basic salary here, apart from the preparation differential) one year later than if they had begun teaching with the baccalaureate.

Taking note of all these circumstances we can make earnings comparisons among teachers in terms of the present values of life earnings. The latter is standard treatment for future income, in economic theory and practice. The concept is expressed by Clark:

A sum received early in life will have a large present value. A sum received later a small present value. This is a proper rating of likely future salaries because the portion of an early received salary saved will have a longer period to earn interest than that of a salary received later....

The principle of this calculation is similar to that of banking practice. A man enters a bank and wishes to borrow $5,000 for five years, agreeing to pay 6 per cent interest per annum. At the end of five years he will have to pay the bank a total of $6,691 in principal and interest to discharge the loan; so that we may say the present value of $6,691 due in five years is now $5,000. Similarly, if a man's salary five years from now will be $6,691, its present value at 6 per cent discount is just $5,000. Five thousand dollars is the amount of money a bank would pay now theoretically for a salary of $6,691 to be earned five years from now.[40]

HOW PRESENT VALUE IS CALCULATED

The annual instalments in the teacher's income stream are known, salary progress being strictly in accord with the formal salary schedule. For the first fourteen years, Salary Steps 1 through 14 govern seriatim; thereafter, the maximum salary (Step 14) continues in effect until cessation of employment.

The model developed for the present value calculation in this study uses the salary schedules which became effective September 1, 1961.[41] All assumptions in the model derive from widespread practices in the New York City school system and relate to the realistic choices available to an entering teacher.

The lifetime teaching period, comprising the total number of annual instalments in the income stream, is 38 years in the model. This accords with all available information on career spans in the New York City school system.[42] Service retirement is the most common type of cessation. Retirement is permitted after thirty years service at age 55. Teaching service past retirement age is usual.

The 38-year career span applies, in the model, to the teacher who begins teaching immediately after receiving the baccalaureate degree. This category, one of three used in the model, corresponds with the large number of teachers (chiefly elementary) for whom the baccalaureate alone is the certification requirement.

For the second category, the career or earning span is reduced to 37 years, because the teacher enters the school system one year later, with the fifth year of preparation. This category fits many secondary teachers (of academic subjects), for whom the fifth year is a certification requirement.

For the third category, the earning span is reduced to 36 years, because the teacher enters the school system two years later, with the sixth year of preparation. No teaching posts require so much preparation for certification, but the category is included because it is the highest level of educational preparation for which there is salary recognition.

The three categories actually represent the three choices available to a college graduate resolved upon a teaching career.[43] Additional investment shortens the teacher's active working life, but does not affect the duration of his active life. The college graduate, age 22, who becomes a teacher and retires at age 60, will have 38 years of employment if he begins teaching immediately, but only 37 years (or 36) if he postpones his employment until he acquires thirty postgraduate credits (or sixty).

The high incidence of on-the-job training is represented in the model by three situations:

1. The baccalaureate teacher qualifying for the $400 differential at Salary Step 4.
2. The same teacher going on to qualify for the $800 differential at Salary Step 7.
3. The teacher entering the school system already qualified for the $400 differential, who goes on to qualify for the $800 differential at Step 4.

These three-year time allowances assume optimum celerity in acquiring additional preparation. As noted earlier, this conforms with the opportunity available to all teachers, and occurs among large numbers of teachers.

As to direct cash outlays for on-the-job preparation, none is assumed in the model, due to widespread utilization of tuition-free facilities.

The model assumes that foregone earnings are not involved for teachers undertaking after-school programs of study. There is, in fact, no earnings loss, based on the teacher's primary responsibility as a full-time day school teacher. There could be a loss in "moonlighting" earnings, but it may not even be necessary to forego a multiple job while enrolled in a limited study program. The teacher in the after-school study program certainly foregoes leisure time which may well have psychic value—but this is not calculable, and allowances can not be made for it in this context.

In discounting future earnings, the model uses two interest rates. The 5 per cent rate is probably quite acceptable at the present time, as a "risk-less" interest rate consonant with generally available investment opportunities. The 10 per cent rate is used as an upper limit for more uncertain, yet possible, rates of return. Use of more than one interest rate illustrates that the rate selected for discounting will in itself affect the results.

The actual formula for calculating the total lifetime earnings is derived from the present value equation, with each year's salary being discounted at the 5 per cent interest rate (for one series, and at the 10 per cent interest rate for the other series), according to the date at which it becomes available in the future.

The formulae for teachers entering with fixed preparation levels are as follows:

$$V(4) = \frac{Y_1}{1.05} + \frac{Y_2}{(1.05)^2} + \frac{Y_3}{(1.05)^3} \cdots + \frac{Y_{38}}{(1.05)^{38}}$$

$$V(5) = 0 + \frac{Y_1 + \$400}{(1.05)^2} + \frac{Y_2 + \$400}{(1.05)^3} \cdots + \frac{Y_{37} + \$400}{(1.05)^{38}}$$

$$V(6) = 0 + 0 + \frac{Y_1 + \$800}{(1.05)^3} \cdots + \frac{Y_{36} + \$800}{(1.05)^{38}}$$

Symbols: V represents the sum of present values, for teachers beginning with various years of educational preparation (4, 5, or 6).
Y refers to the basic salary, $+\$400$ to the differential for fifth-year preparation, $+\$800$ to the differential for sixth-year preparation. The subscript refers to the applicable salary step (and/or year of teaching service).
1.05 is the compound amount of 1, and the 5 per cent interest rate, n being 1.

The formulae for teachers acquiring additional preparation on the job are adapted from the basic formulae. For example, in the case of the baccalaureate teacher acquiring fifth-year preparation at Salary Step 4, the formula would become at that point:

$$\frac{Y_4 + \$400,}{(1.05)^4} \quad \text{instead of} \quad \frac{Y_4}{(1.05)^4}$$

Table 8.9 summarizes the results of the calculation.

Table 8.9

Present Value of Lifetime Earnings (38-Year Career Span) of Teachers with Different Educational Preparation (based on N.Y.C. Teacher Salary Schedules of September 1961)

Educational Preparation (1)	Total Earnings, Present Value In Dollars, Discounted at		Index of Earnings[a]	
	5 Per Cent (2)	10 Per Cent (3)	(4)	(5)
Baccalaureate	$122,800.92	$65,439.09	100.0	100.0
Teacher entering with 5th year	$122,029.32	$62,809.24	99.4	96.0
Teacher entering with 6th year	$120,872.01	$60,078.63	98.4	91.8
Baccalaureate qualifying for 5th year at Step 4	$128,458.77	$68,337.91	104.6	104.4
Baccalaureate qualifying for 5th year at Step 4, 6th year at Step 7	$133,175.65	$72,541.33	108.5	110.9
Teacher entering with 5th year, qualifying for 6th year at Step 4	$127,358.09	$65,434.75	103.7	100.0

a Index in Column 4 is derived from "Earnings" in Column 2. Index in Column 5 is derived from "Earnings" in Column 3.

THE RETURNS

The most striking feature of the salary relationships disclosed by the present value calculations is that the higher the level of educational preparation at which the teacher enters the school system, the lower is the value of total earnings.

Before in-service preparation becomes a factor, the differences are very small, less than 2 per cent, but they are in the wrong direction. For example, without in-service preparation, the difference in life earnings is about $2,000 (discounted at the 5 per cent rate), between the teacher entering with the sixth year of preparation, and the teacher entering with the baccalaureate—$2,000 more going to the latter.[44]

More striking is the fact that the salary disadvantage is enlarged to a significant percentage when in-service study equalizes preparation. Consider the total earnings of two teachers, each with the fifth year of preparation. The one who began teaching with that much preparation earns about 5 per cent less than the one who began teaching with the baccalaureate degree and subsequently acquired the one year of postgraduate preparation during a three-year in-service period. (Discounted at the 10 per cent rate, the earnings deficiency would be almost 9 per cent.) And the higher level of initial preparation, the greater the earnings deficiency becomes.[45]

Perhaps the most significant comparison encompasses the typical situation in the New York City school system: teachers entering with the minimum preparation required for certification at their school level, and thereafter enrolling in the in-service program to qualify for the highest preparation differential available in the salary plan. Consider the teacher who must have the fifth year of preparation in order to begin secondary school teaching, and then acquires the sixth year during a three-year in-service period.

His total earnings do not exceed or even equal earnings of the teacher who could begin teaching with the baccalaureate and thereafter acquire the fifth and sixth years of preparation during an in-service period of six years. The earnings deficiency, for the teacher initially having the fifth year of preparation, is almost 5 per cent (or, discounted at the 10 per cent interest rate, almost 11 per cent).

These results flout the principles of the preparation pay plan. Instead of providing equal compensation for equal preparation, the plan in effect penalizes the teachers who enter the school system with the highest level of educational preparation. The penalties are even greater if the career period is less than the 38 years used in the model, and if there are educational expenses for pre-service preparation.

In broader terms, how do these results relate to general expectations and experience on income returns for additional capital investment? The economic reasonableness and necessity of income differences compensating for required differences in the amount of training are widely asserted. Friedman and Kuznets found, as did Walsh in an earlier study, that "returns in the professions exceed returns in other pursuits by an amount considerably in excess of the extra cost involved." Similar results obtained when the extra costs consisted almost entirely of interprofessional differences in training periods.[46]

The teachers' situation is just the reverse. The $400 and $800 differentials do not overcome the one-year and two-year differences in periods of training. In fact since the differentials are extensively achieved under the In-Service Program, the positions which require or offer one- or two-year differences in training are the least attractive, financially.

THE RESULTS

The ambivalence of the returns from the teachers' investment in human capital explains why some investments are made extensively, and others sparingly or involuntarily.

Ordinarily, additional preparation should and would result in compensatory differences in earnings. If it did not, more advantageous choices would presumably be made.

The additional preparation does yield much more than compensatory differences in earnings, where the investment is on the job, tuition free, and without loss of earnings. This explains the widespread on-the-job investment in human capital. Conversely, the additional investment does not yield compensatory differences in earnings, but results in an earnings loss, where the investment involves foregone earnings of one year. The loss is still greater if the investment includes two years of foregone earnings.

Nevertheless, such investments are made. Why do individuals fail to make more advantageous choices?

Chiefly because advantageous choice is limited for some individuals. The prospective teacher who prefers secondary to elementary teaching, or is more suited to it, has no choice as to the method of achieving postgraduate preparation. Certification requirements mandate the fifth year of preparation, prior to entering teaching service, for secondary teachers of academic subjects. The certification requirements create a captive supply of teachers who forego one year's earnings to invest in human capital.

Has the captive supply maintained an adequate supply of secondary teachers? The greatest imbalance of teacher supply and demand in New York City is at the secondary level, but the imbalance clusters around a few subject areas, especially mathematics and science.[47] Individuals qualified in these areas would not be likely to choose teaching over other occupations if they made a simple calculation of economic returns in public school teaching, as compared with returns in other fields requiring their subject mastery. Reenforcing that decision, though not solely determining it, would be the economic disadvantage accruing to fulltime graduate attainment in the public school system.

Where individuals can make a choice, they generally make it advantageously, even in the New York City school system. We noted earlier that hardly any teachers enter the school system with more than the required years of preparation. Virtually all choose to acquire the additional preparation while they are fully employed, and do not make investments involving one or two years of foregone earnings.

It is not suggested that present or prospective teachers in the New York City schools have actually calculated the financial disadvantages the pay plan imposes upon teachers entering with postbaccalaureate preparation, or, if they did, that the net income effect of the preparation differentials would be *the* critical element in their career choice. Many reasons influence career choice. Nevertheless, the net income effect must be a negative consideration for an individual deciding between a career in teaching or in some other profession which values graduate attainment.

The present value calculation has not been made heretofore for New York City teachers, and an analysis along these lines has never been presented in the teacher salary situation. The fact is, however, that the deficiencies are at least dimly seen. Witness the paucity of teachers entering with more than minimum certification requirements, and also the persistent dissatisfaction which secondary teachers have evinced since the establishment of the preparation pay plan. Discontent was climaxed in 1950 by the extracurricular stoppage in the high schools, and in 1962 by the one-day strike throughout the school system. It beclouded agreement on the 1963–64 salary schedule, a strike again being threatened by the United Federation of Teachers.

The dimensions of the inequalities in investment returns, as shown by the present value calculation, do more than discourage accessions to the teaching force of highly trained individuals. The calculation also makes clear the economic basis for the salary grievances of secondary teachers, *but only to the extent that the fifth year of preparation is mandated for them.* In this respect their difficulties, as well as their complaints, indeed date back to the establishment of the single salary or preparation pay plan in 1947.[48] Under the former position differentials, the hierarchical salary standing of secondary teachers was not reversed, despite the element of foregone earnings. Under the preparation differentials, the salary equality promised to secondary teachers in lieu of salary superiority became, in fact, salary inequality, as the present value analysis discloses.

THE EFFECTS OF RECENT CERTIFICATION AND SALARY CHANGES

This analysis, made in 1962, was based on the certification requirements and salary schedules then in effect. Are the conclusions altered by the certification changes and salary changes which have occurred subsequently?

The certification changes add still greater weight to the analysis. The changes will become effective September 1, 1966. The fifth year of preparation will be mandated for all teachers, regardless of school level or subject, but the mandate will not apply in the same way to all. Secondary teachers of academic subjects must still complete the fifth year of preparation prior to beginning teaching service, *i.e.,* their investment in human capital must include one year's foregone earnings. All others may complete their one postbaccalaureate year within a five-year in-service period. The choice between acquiring postbaccalaureate preparation through in-service or pre-service training is a choice between investing for a gain or investing for a loss. Can there be any doubt as to the choice which will overwhelmingly be made?

If all teachers had to enter the school system with equal preparation, then equal educational attainment and investment would be achieved, and equality in income streams would be assured. The new certification requirements, however, maintain the present system.

As to the post-1962 salary changes, have they invalidated the statistics or the sense of this analysis? The statistics are obviously affected by selective or general increases in the salary schedule. The various earnings deficiencies and advantages shown in Table 8.9 are based on the September 1961 salary schedules. On July 1, 1962, these were changed, increases of about $500 being granted.[49] Further increases in the salary schedule will take place in 1964, under terms of the 1963 settlement between the Board of Education and the Federation of Teachers.[50]

Accordingly, dollar amounts in present value comparisons would change. The percentages or the salary relationships would remain essentially the same, because the new and higher salaries are still being applied to all teachers under the same circumstances (foregone earnings for some, on-the-job training for others, and so forth).

In addition, the July 1, 1962, salary changes provided a so-called "promotional differential" of $475 (which will be raised to $725 on January 1, 1965, pursuant to the 1963 settlement). The promotional differential will affect, but only temporarily and not entirely, the salary relationships between teachers with in-service training and those with pre-service training. Eligibility requirements are such that this new differential is almost in the nature of a general increase, albeit deferred for many elementary teachers in view of their certification changes not becoming effective until 1966.[51]

The post-1962 salary changes have not eliminated from the teachers' salary plan its basic shortcomings, in terms of returns for investment in human capital. The relevance of the present value analysis, which illumines the shortcomings in teachers' compensation, is not limited to this particular salary system. Under any kind of plan it would be economically indefensible to impose a salary disadvantage upon those with more educational preparation, or more intensive preparation—especially in a field which holds more education to be a great good, and in a milieu which increasingly rewards investment in education.

RETRAINING UNDER THE MANPOWER DEVELOPMENT ACT: A COST-BENEFIT ANALYSIS

DAVID A. PAGE

The need for training of the structurally unemployed has become widely recognized and publicized. Virtually every comprehensive study of the unemployment problem conducted in recent years has identified training, or retraining, as a partial remedy. These studies range from reports of the Joint Economic Committee and The Committee for Economic Development in its report on Depressed Areas in 1961, to general articles in newspapers and magazines.

In recent years, Congress has enacted several laws designed to provide workers with new skills, including the Free Trade Act, the Area Redevelopment Act, and the Manpower Development Act. It is against the backdrop of general recognition of widespread need that Congress has given nearly unanimous, bipartisan support to these programs.

The purpose of this paper is to analyze the attempt to maintain a higher level of employment in the United States by retraining those who,

Reprinted from John D. Montgomery and Arthur Smithies, eds., *Public Policy*, volume 13 (1964), pp. 257–67. Copyright © 1964 by the President and Fellows of Harvard University.

for whatever reasons, have become unemployed. Data for the analysis were drawn from a statistical summary of a population of 907 retrainees assisted in Massachusetts between 1958 and 1961.[52] The population was comprised of 618 men and 289 women from all areas of Massachusetts, who sought retraining as a means of improving the steadiness of their employment, and increasing their weekly salary. The program took place under Massachusetts law, but an economic analysis of this experience should provide insight into the costs and benefits likely to occur under the Manpower Development Act.

OBJECTIVES OF THE MANPOWER DEVELOPMENT ACT

The Manpower Development Act (MDA) has as its general objective the retraining of underemployed and unemployed workers for necessary skills, so that they may be more gainfully employed citizens and make a greater contribution to the national economy.[53] In economic parlance this would normally be called an "efficiency" objective.[54]

The Act is based on the assumption that there are large numbers of jobs waiting to be filled if workers with obsolete skills can somehow be retrained to qualify for them. It implies that vocational training for unemployed workers is a more satisfactory way to meet one aspect of the unemployment problem on a long range basis than simply providing relief in the form of unemployment compensation and welfare payments.

Writers of the Act suggest that the more rapidly our economy advances the more rapidly skills become obsolete. Despite the fact that training is already being carried on by public educational authorities assisted by the federal government's vocational education program and by private schools, in the minds of the legislators it was clear that

combined federal, state, local and private efforts fall far short of the total need, and that without an intensive, nationwide program to provide opportunities for retraining tens of thousands of worthy men and women will never be able to obtain the skills which will enable them to be self-supporting and to make their maximum contribution to the nation's productivity.[55]

The MDA established a program to fill this need. It directed the Secretary of Labor to take the initiative in determining the training needs of the nation in consultation with local authorities, and it provided funds for establishing training programs primarily through existing public educational authorities. It also authorized the payment of subsistence allowances to trainees. In the interests of public information it requires the Secretary of Labor to report annually on the nation's manpower requirements and resources, and the President to report annually to the Congress.

COSTS AND BENEFITS OF RETRAINING

In order to have some sense of what may be expected of the Manpower Development Act and its implementation, it should prove useful to examine the costs incurred and benefits derived from retraining the 907 men and women involved in the case study. Taking as the objective economic efficiency, the net benefits accruing to society may be measured in terms of this objective.

Capital costs for retraining under the MDA will tend to be negligible, since the Act requires the Secretary of Health, Education and Welfare to provide training facilities through agreements with the states and states' vocational agencies. The states in turn are to provide for such training through existing public education agencies or institutions. If state facilities are inadequate or inappropriate to this purpose arrangements may be made with private educational and training organizations. Funds are, at the present time, intended only to make minor repairs deemed necessary for adequate training. In the Massachusetts case no capital costs were incurred that were attributable to the training program.

Costs of operations and maintenance can conveniently be divided into three classifications: (1) costs of education; (2) costs of subsistence allowances, including transportation during retraining; and (3) costs of supervision. Costs of supervision have to be estimated since the Act is to be administered through existing structures of government. Except where additional governmental expenses have been incurred as a result of the training program, the administrative opportunity cost may be considered negligible.

Cost of education, or "tuition" includes such items as rental on equipment and facilities and instruction. There are few economic questions involved here, the main problem being simply one of measurement. Since tuition was actually charged the Massachusetts trainees, real values may be used in the analysis.

Subsistence costs represent a somewhat more complex problem. The MDA provides for subsistence allowances for trainees and their families totaling not more than the amount qualified for under the respective state unemployment compensation allowances. Moreover, these allowances are provided only if funds are not available through unemployment compensation. Therefore, only the differential amount should be charged to the retraining program, since presumably this cost would be incurred regardless of the existence of a training program. In the Massachusetts case, subsistence chargeable to retraining amounted to approximately 83 per cent of total subsistence during the training period. The Act provides for subsistence for a period not to exceed 52 weeks. Anyone undergoing training in excess of one year would be forced to procure funds from other sources.

Both types of costs may be incurred in on-the-job training. The Act provides for supplementary education as well as differential subsistence payments to on-the-job trainees.

Since all costs may be expected to accrue during the training period, there is no need to reduce them to present value, and the total cost equation may be written as

$$C_t = C_e + C_m + C_k + C_s$$

where:

C_t = total costs

C_e = educational costs

C_m = subsistence costs

C_k = capital costs

C_s = supervision

Using the costs incurred in the present case, total costs of retraining may be computed for the group.

Gross benefits to be derived from retraining in terms of our efficiency

Exhibit I

Costs of Retraining

Tuition	$	567.10 (average)
Subsistence during Retraining		143,000.00 (total)
1959 Employment Compensation		24,000.00
Net Subsistence during Retraining		119,000.00
Supervisory		a
Travel		b
Number Trained		907

$$C_t = C_e + C_m + C_k + C_s$$
$$= 907(\$567.10) + \$119{,}000 + 0 + 0$$
$$= \$633{,}359.00$$

a Supervisory expenses were of course not zero but the program was administered through regular machinery and no estimates were available.
b Travel allowances were negligible in this case study.

objective may be measured as the change in individual income streams. Denoting b_i as the benefit of the ith individual, y_1 as the income of the ith individual with retraining, and y_{0_i} as the income of the ith individual without retraining we may write

$$\Delta b_i = y_{1_i} - y_{0_i},$$

and summing over the group of all retrainees, we obtain

$$\sum_{i=1}^{n} \Delta b_i = \sum_{i=1}^{n} (y_{1_i} - y_{0_i}).$$

Since the average group income with and without retraining will be used rather than individual gains (or losses), the benefit equation may be rewritten as

$$B = N(\bar{y}_1 - \bar{y}_0)$$

where B is total benefit for the group, and N is the number of retrainees. Or, for the sake of simplicity

$$B = Y_1 - Y_0$$

where the Y's denote total group income with and without retraining.

In this regard, three refinements must be made. First, an individual's income with and without retraining may include transfer payments from unemployment compensation and welfare. Since only earned income may be taken as a measure of productivity, transfer payments should be deducted from total income to determine net gains to an efficiency objective.[56] Denoting total income with and without retraining as Y_{t_1} and Y_{t_0}, and total transfer payments with and without retraining as Y_{p_1} and Y_{p_0}, the benefit equation may be rewritten as

$$B = (Y_{t_1} - Y_{p_1}) - (Y_{t_0} - Y_{p_0}).$$

And, using the statistical summaries of the information supplied by the trainees, the gross benefits may be calculated.

Exhibit II

Gross Benefits to Retraining

Gross Benefits	
Total income with retraining	$ 3,823 (average)
Total income without retraining	2,847
Increase	976
Per cent increase	34.2%
Transfer payments without retraining	24,000 (total)
Transfer payments with retraining	8,000
Decrease	16,000
Per cent decrease	66.7%
Number of trainees who found jobs using training skills	438

$$B = (Y_{t_1} - Y_{p_1}) - (Y_{t_0} - Y_{p_0})$$
$$B = [(3823)(438) - 8000] - [(2847)(438) - 24,000]$$
$$= 443,488$$

Five hundred and eighty-two of the original 907 trainees completed the approved training courses and found employment. But only 438 were employed in the field for which they were trained at the time the survey was taken. The primary reason (33 per cent) given by the trainees for not finding a job related to their training was the absence of vacancies, as evidenced by unsuccessful applications to different firms. Eighteen per cent had discontinued training. Thirteen per cent had become pregnant or ill, 10.8 per cent had found new jobs not related to training, 7.9 per cent had returned to their fomer employment, and others (1.9 per cent) had just finished training and were still looking.

Second, allowances must be made for cyclical changes in the economy. If improvement in income could be attributed to improvement in the overall economy as, for example, between a prewar and wartime economy, benefits cannot reasonably be attributed solely to retraining. Similarly, if there has been a downturn in the economy this too must be taken into account in evaluating benefits to retraining. To do so we will let ϕ represent the per cent of income attributable to retraining after allowing for changes in the economy. To determine ϕ, the net change in income during the training period of a control group was measured. The group was comprised of a random sample of individuals in the central claims file of the Bureau of Employment Security having six characteristics similar to those of the trainees.[57]

There are two significant factors to be considered in determining the ϕ factor for the benefit equation: (1) the change in income of the control groups, and (2) the nature of the increase, whether earned or transfer payments. Denoting Y_{ct_1} and Y_{ct_0} as the change in total income and $Y_{ct_1} - Y_{ct_0}$ as the change in transfer payments of the control group during the training period, the general economy factor expressed as a per cent may be written as

$$\phi = 100 - 100\left[\frac{(Y_{ct_1} - Y_{cp_1}) - (Y_{ct_0} - Y_{cp_0})}{Y_{ct_0} - Y_{cp_0}}\right]$$

and the benefit equation now reads

$$B = \phi[(Y_{t_1} - Y_{p_1}) - (Y_{t_0} - Y_{p_0})]$$

Exhibit III

Control Group Experience

Total income after the training period	\$ 3,854 (average)
Total income before the training period	3,489 (average)
Transfer payments after the training period	26,000 (total)
Transfer payments before the training period	20,000 (total)
Number in Control Group 104	

$$\phi = 100 - 100\left[\frac{(Y_{ct_1} - Y_{cp_1}) - (Y_{ct_0} - Y_{cp_0})}{Y_{ct_0} - Y_{cp_0}}\right]$$

$$= 100 - 100\left\{\frac{[104(3,854) - 26,000] - [104(3,489) - 20,000]}{104(3,489) - 20,000}\right\}$$

$$= 100 - 100\left\{\frac{30,000}{344,000}\right\}$$

$$= 100 - 8.7$$

$$\phi = 91.3$$

Third, gross benefits accruing in future time periods must be reduced to present value to be compared with costs occurring at present. To do so a time period must be selected which reflects the remaining working life of the trainee. In the case study the average age of the trainees was 30 years. It is assumed that they would be eligible for retirement at the age of 65, and that therefore the average remaining working life (time period for the present value factor) would be 35 years.

More difficult is the problem of choosing an interest rate to be used in discounting future benefits. The tendency here should be to select a reasonably high rate of interest since, in such cases, one is concerned more with immediate payoff rather than long-term benefits accruing to future generations. Furthermore, as an employee increases in age, the greater the likelihood that: (1) he will be eligible for early retirement, and (2) he will have fewer financial responsibilities. In evaluating the case study future benefits were discounted at a rate of 10 per cent.

Exhibit IV

Present Value Factor

Average working life of trainees	65 years
Average age of trainees	30
Time period for present value factor	35
Rate of interest to discount future income to present value	10%
Present value factor (PV)[58]	9.644

Other benefits to efficiency would be the difference between consumption of public goods and services and the amounts paid in taxes for goods and services with and without retraining. For example, an individual may be consuming public medical care without payment while unemployed; whereas with retraining the amount of taxes paid by the trainee should correspond roughly to public services consumed if placement is successful. These benefits, although important, will not be considered here because of the difficulty of measuring them, but they do exist and should be kept in mind.

Net benefits resulting from retraining may then be written as

$$N = PV(\phi B) - C$$

and using the gross benefit and total cost calculations from exhibits I, II, III, and IV

$$
\begin{aligned}
N &= PV(\phi B) - C \\
&= 9.644(91.3)(443,488) - 633,359 \\
&= 3,900,000 - 633,359 \\
&= 3,266,641 \\
N &= 3,300,000 \text{ (approximately)}
\end{aligned}
$$

and net benefits occurring as a result of retraining in this instance amount to approximately $3,300,000.

This figure is, of course, based upon several major assumptions. First is that the incomes of the retrainees remain relatively constant throughout the remainder of their working lives. One would expect the incomes of those who remain employed to increase and the effect would be simply to increase net benefits. Similarly, it is assumed that without training the incomes of the trainees would have, on the average, remained constant. To the extent that the earned income of the trainees would have increased (or decreased), benefits are again overstated (or understated). But major changes in income, taking the group as a whole, would appear unlikely in the absence of significant changes in the economy. Moreover, the more remote the change the less would be the impact since gains or losses must be reduced to present value.

Second, it is assumed that all of those who found jobs would remain employed throughout the remainder of the period used in discounting gross benefits. This is unlikely since some skills will no doubt again become obsolete, some will not live to the end of the period, and there will be attrition due to health and sundry other factors. To the extent that there is attrition net benefits will be reduced. Factors such as careful screening, aptitude testing for jobs, and careful selection of new skills should act to keep this to a minimum.

A third assumption, and the one most difficult to assay, is related to displacement. To the extent that retraining of workers and placement in the work force redistributes existing work or displaces other workers and does not generate new income for previous labor voids in the economy, benefits accruing to the efficiency objective are overstated. It has been assumed in the analysis that there would be no displacement of workers as a result of retraining.

The displacement problem is a complex one. Its analysis requires distinction between zero displacement, partial displacement, and total displacement. Obviously, zero displacement involves no loss of worktime and income by those already in the labor market. Partial displacement would result in either a loss in worktime, income, or both to those in the labor market. Total displacement would result in a replacement, one for one, of those in the labor market, or about to enter the labor market, by retrained workers.

Generally speaking, in a competitive economy such as that of the United States, it can be assumed that there is little partial displacement or spreading of the work as a result of retrained workers' entering of the labor force, since employers are not likely to hire unnecessary workers if such a practice is avoidable. Total displacement and the question of whether others, particularly younger workers coming into the labor force, have been deprived of potential employment opportunities as a result of this and other retraining, may be another matter. Over 50 per cent of the trainees were enrolled in schools for barbers and beauticians; while 18.5 per cent were being trained as draftsmen, technicians, office machine operators and mechanics; 4.4 per cent as secretaries, stenographers, and typists; and 4.6 per cent as practical nurses. The demand for these occupations in the New England area appears to be far in excess of supply, and one would expect little total displacement of workers as a result of the impact of the retrained workers on the labor force. But the amount of displacement from retraining is a matter of judgment, as is the question of whether this is desirable.

Finally, it has been assumed in the study that administrative costs were negligible. Under the federal program administrative costs would be incurred, and should be attributed to the costs of retraining. This cost might be expected to reduce somewhat the economic benefits of the program. However, a relatively high rate of interest (10%) has been used to discount future benefits. Experience will probably indicate that a lower rate of interest should be used in the analysis of retraining. In light of the opportunity costs of public funds a 5 per cent (or lower) rate of interest would probably be more appropriate. A lower interest rate would increase the value of gross benefits, and should more than compensate for increases in training costs due to the inclusion of administrative expenses.

CONCLUSIONS

It is readily apparent that under the circumstances and assumptions of this case study, retraining is worthwhile. Benefits to the efficiency objective from training the 907 Massachusetts workers amount to approximately $3,300,000 over the working life of the retrainees. Moreover, the analysis has not taken into account the increased utility to the worker resulting from the opportunity to reexpress his preference as to his field of endeavor. In addition, if redistribution of income is taken as an objective, benefits are again understated. The additional income in the form of subsistence allowances during retraining amounts to an extension of unemployment compensation. To those who are unemployed and to the nation as a whole this may be considered a real gain.

On the national scale similar results may be expected from the MDA program providing its administrators determine what jobs are reasonably certain to be available, and then select individuals for retraining who are unemployed or underemployed, and are willing, and potentially well qualified, to hold these positions. This procedure would simply be one which meets the requirements of the MDA. Properly administered, the federal program should produce national economic and social gains, and help reduce the functional and structural segment of "normal" unemployment.

QUESTIONS FOR DISCUSSION

1. How and why do the social and private rates of return to education differ, as found in the Hansen study?

2. What do you expect has happened to the relative rates of return for various levels of education in the last decade? Why?

3. How does Friedman handle foregone earnings? Is this formulation appropriate for teachers?

4. Discuss Page's conceptualization of the benefits of retraining.

5. What effect would a recession (or strong upturn) have on the benefit-cost ratio for a training program such as the one discussed by Page?

Chapter 9 ECONOMIC GROWTH AND PLANNING

MANY objectives of economic policy coexist in every country. Price stability, low unemployment, equitable income distribution, economic growth, and minimization of environmental pollution are but a few. The growth objective is one which, if realized, eases the achievement of many others. When there is economic growth, more resources are made available for increasing employment, for decreasing pollution, for raising the income of the lowest economic stratum, and so forth.

Education is one of the many elements which influence economic growth, and it does so in several ways. The first route by which education affects development is in providing people with specific skills useful in productive processes. Skills such as typing, accounting, and chemical engineering are developed by education and markedly increase the capacity of those individuals possessing them to contribute to the production of goods or services.

Second, education provides general knowledge and methods of problem solving that the individual can apply to the work in which he is engaged. Knowledge and methods of problem solving are two factors that can contribute to the most important aspects of economic growth—innovation, adaptation, and entrepreneurship. With simple or even complex skills, one can continue the work of the past, but the milieu for growth is created by new methods and ideas.

Third, education can contribute to development by providing or developing attitudes amicable to production. One of the most important changes for less developed countries is the change in people's attitudes toward work from those of traditional societies (children expecting to do the same work as their parents did, with the work pattern being erratic and at a pace of one's own choice) to those

Notes to Chapter 9 will be found on pages 384–385.

observed in modern societies (great occupational mobility with closely prescribed work conditions). Schooling, by its structure, is a process that develops attitudes conducive to the modern work rhythm.

Finally, education may serve development by providing a screening system that assures that the most able individuals reach the highest positions in the most economic fashion. There is a significant cost of identifying talent, and the great use of educational attainment as a criterion for selecting among job applicants indicates that education is used by producers for this purpose.

The first section of this chapter begins with a definition and history of economic growth. It ends with two models of economic growth, the neoclassical and the labor surplus. The second section goes on to discuss economic planning and educational planning and their role in promoting growth, especially in less developed countries (LDCs).

ECONOMIC GROWTH

Economic growth is the increase in some measure of the economy over time. It can be specified in terms of the change in any of the national income concepts, but GNP, the total of all final goods and services produced in a year, is most commonly used. For example, because the real GNP in the United States in 1967 (in 1958 dollars) was $673 billion and in 1968 was $707 billion, the real growth over the year was $34 billion. This can be alternately presented as a growth rate for GNP:

$$\frac{\$34 \text{ billion}}{\$673 \text{ billion}}$$

or 5 per cent.

There are two factors that could account for a situation in which there was positive growth that did not improve the well-being of the average man. First, in the United States where the GNP per capita is about $4,500, an increase of $18 billion in one year would not mean any increase in GNP per capita if the population increased by 4 million (from 200 to 204 million) in that year. Although the growth of GNP is 2 per cent, the increase in GNP per capita is zero, thereby leaving the people, on average, no better off. Second, the effect of growth of income on any individual is dependent on the distribution of that income increment. If the United States GNP per capita grew at a 2 per cent rate during the year so that it increased by, say, $24 billion and the entire $24 billion's worth of resources went to the five owners of the New York Jets football team or any other small group, the average person would observe no improvement in his economic well-being. Such a situation could be contrasted, for example, to one in which the same increase in GNP was distributed among the 20 million people with the lowest income, thereby increasing their income by $1,200 each.

Because national income accounts statistics are utilized in measuring economic growth and those statistics have many conceptual and statistical problems built into them, one might be tempted to assert that growth statistics are very unreliable. Actually, they are much more accurate than most others. A growth figure is derived from the comparison of two stock or level figures each of which is imprecise in the same manner. So long as the GNP figures are derived in a consistent manner and the economy does not undergo radical institutional change, the effect of the many arbitrary decisions will not be felt. If GNP is underestimated by the same proportion in, for example, each of two years, the measured growth rate will not be affected at all, as is seen in Table 9.1. For developed countries, the caveat of no

Table 9.1
Actual and Measured Growth

Year	1	2	Growth
Actual	100	110	10%
Measured (incorrect by 10%)	90	99	10%

major institutional changes is likely to be fulfilled. For LDCs this is less likely, but growth statistics are nevertheless undoubtedly more reliable than statistics on absolute levels of economic activity, even in LDCs.

Before looking at theories of economic growth, it is useful to put economic growth into perspective. Economic growth has been rare in the history of mankind. Most of the economic and political history consists of events designed to shift the apportionment of the world pie in one direction or another. It is only in the last few centuries in a few countries that the pie has been expanding steadily, although slowly, bringing a new factor into the picture. Indeed, today about half the world's population is still living at a subsistence level, that is, a level of income just sufficient to acquire enough food, clothing, and shelter to maintain life.

The industrial revolution, the watershed that marks the beginning of the story of sustained growth, as distinguished from short periods of rising income per capita, began in the eighteenth century in Great Britain. The simultaneous occurrence of several inventions and new power sources, together with a large export market due to colonialism and free trade, new supplies of labor that had been freed from agriculture, new monetary institutions and the like brought about a revolution: steadily increasing income per capita. The manufacturers who sprang up in response to the new circumstances typically reinvested their substantial profits into their firms creating more and more capital. Thus the key to the continuance of the steady growth was the savings and investment by the owners of capital.

The description of the industrial revolution just depicted was what did happen and not a theory or model of *how* or *why* it happened. In order to guide policy, it is necessary to understand the processes that underlie and tie together events. The lessons of the past can be applied to the future only with a theory and model thereof, that is, some systemization and understanding of causality. We now briefly develop two models of economic growth: the neoclassical and the labor surplus.

The Neoclassical Model

In the neoclassical model, growth results from increases in any of the factors of production. We demonstrate the development of the model by beginning with a two factor production function:

$$Y = f(K, L) \qquad (1)$$

where Y is output, K is capital, and L is labor.

Growth in production could then be represented by:

$$\Delta Y = f(\Delta K, \Delta L) \qquad (2)$$

Division of (1) by (2) yields:

$$\frac{\Delta Y}{Y} = f\left(\frac{\Delta K}{K}, \frac{\Delta L}{L}\right) \qquad (3)$$

Since the change in anything divided by its original amount is by definition its rate of growth, (3) can be transformed into:

$$G_Y = f(G_K, G_L) \qquad (4)$$

where G is a symbol representing the growth rate.

The growth of output in the neoclassical model is thus dependent on the growth of capital and labor—the factors of production. But how and why do capital and labor grow? Capital grows through net investment, that is, investment over and above that which is necessary to replace depleted capital. In all modern industrial economies, net investment is taking place because the people prefer to increase their future consumption at the expense of present consumption. So long as essential present consumption needs can be met without exhausting the produce of an economy, and opportunities for profitable investment exist, the supply of capital will continue to grow.

The growth of labor is a net result of several elements. First is the rate of population increase. The raw material for labor is population. But as has been shown earlier, the supply of labor is a complex thing. As a nation becomes richer, there is a tendency for fewer hours of labor to be offered per capita. Over time, labor force participation rates for different groups change. In the United States the proportion of women working has steadily increased while the proportion of teenagers and elderly males has decreased. The increase in labor is, therefore, a result of the balancing of these several factors.

Equation (4) can be changed from a functional to a specific form as follows:

$$G_Y = aG_K + bG_L \qquad (5)$$

where a is labor's share in total output and b is the share of capital in total output.[1]

Thus, the growth of output is equal to the growth of capital times capital's share of total output plus the growth of labor times labor's share of total output. In this formulation capital and labor independently contribute to output. Since this is a two-factor model with only capital and labor affecting output and a and b are the shares of those two factors in total output, $a + b$ must equal 1 if the entire growth of output is to be accounted for.

As was suggested earlier, the objective of economic growth generally is not merely to increase the output of the economy but rather to increase the standard of living of the population. That is, what is important is the growth of income per capita, not merely income. Equation (5) can be simply manipulated to show the rate of growth of income per capita. Since $a + b = 1$, $a = 1 - b$, so that $1 - b$ can be substituted for a in equation (4) to yield:

$$G_Y = (1 - b)G_K + bG_L \qquad (6)$$

Subtracting the growth rate of labor from both sides (with the assumption that the growth rate of labor and of population are the same) results in:

$$G_Y - G_L = (1 - b)G_K + bG_L - G_L \qquad (7)$$

A rearrangement yields:

$$G_Y - G_L = (1 - b)(G_K - G_L) \qquad (8)$$

Since $G_Y - G_L$ is the growth rate of income per capita, this shows that the lower the growth rate of labor, the greater will be the growth rate of income per capita for a given growth of capital.[2]

For the neoclassical model a representation of the production function would look like the isoquant map shown in Figure 9.1. Such isoquants represent a production function that allows for substitutability between capital and labor. With L_a labor and K_a capital, production would be at the level represented by isoquant X. An increase of labor to L_c with no change in capital would increase output to the level represented by isoquant Y. Similarly, if only capital had been increased, to level K_b for example, production also would have been increased to the level of isoquant Y. If both labor and capital are increased, to L_c and K_b, output would be increased even more, to isoquant Z. Thus, the neoclassical model recognizes that added capital is a possible substitute for added labor and vice versa and that increases in either result in economic growth.

When the growth equation of the neoclassical model is tested against the actual data for the United States, one observes that something is amiss. Historically, the value of the share of capital in national income (a) has been about one-quarter and the share of labor (b) about three-quarters. Capital has been growing at about 3 per cent per year and labor by about 1 per cent per year. Thus, the neoclassical growth model would predict that the growth of income would have been at the rate of about 1.5 per cent:

$$
\begin{aligned}
G_Y &= aG_K + bG_L \\
&= .25 \cdot 3\% + .75 \cdot 1\% \\
&= 1.5\%
\end{aligned}
$$

Actually, the United States economy has been growing at about 3 per cent per annum. Hence, there is a discrepancy of 1.5 percentage points between the actual growth rate and that which the model attributes to the growth of labor and capital.[3] This discrepancy has become known as the "residual factor" controversy. One way of looking at it is to assume that some factor or factors of production were left out of the production function and that these account for the 1.5 percentage points of growth that are otherwise unaccounted for. Some commentators suggest that this residual factor is simply a mea-

Capital

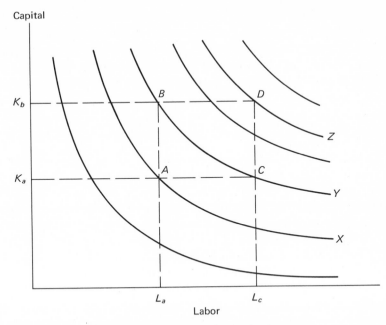

Figure 9.1   Neoclassical Production Isoquants

sure of our ignorance: It includes not only other uncounted factors of production but also any errors in the measurement of the amount of growth of the relative shares in the output of labor and capital. Another view is that the residual 1.5 percentage points are accounted for by technological progress.

Technological progress is a term that is utilized to describe the fact that the inputs into the production process and/or the production process itself have improved over time so that the same nominal quantity of inputs yield more output in succeeding time periods.

Technological progress has been divided into two sorts for analytical purposes: disembodied and embodied. *Disembodied technological progress* can be defined as technological progress that is not embodied in some factor of production. That is, its occurrence is entirely independent of the factors of production. Examples of disembodied technological progress include the idea of interchangeable parts, time-motion study improvements, and discovery of better travel routes. Each of these leads to greater output from the existing factors of production and requires no new capital, labor, nor any other factor of production. Education is probably a key factor in the creation of disembodied technological progress. It is through education and knowledge and their application to practical problems that disembodied technological progress is achieved. Disembodied technological progress could be entered into the neoclassical growth model, equation (5), by simply adding a *parameter*, γ, representing disembodied technological progress:

$$G_Y = aG_L + bG_K + \gamma \qquad (9)$$

A value of 1.5 per cent for γ would bring the growth equation up to the required equality.

Embodied technological progress can be defined as improvements in the quality of the factors of production that lead to their having greater productivity. These improvements are inexorably tied to the factors of production. Without the factors of production, embodied technological progress could not exist. Examples are myriad. Better educated, better trained, and healthier labor are examples of what might be considered technological progress embodied in labor. Examples of embodied technological progress in capital include any new machine that does the same job costing less or a larger job costing the same: electric typewriters, the newest movie projectors, automatic telephone switching systems, and "jumbo" jets. These also can be integrated into the basic neoclassical model:

$$G_Y = aG_N + bG_J \qquad (10)$$

N is "effective" labor and $G_N = f(G_L, \phi_1)$, where ϕ_1 is the rate of embodied technological progress of labor. J is "effective" capital and $G_J = f(G_K, \phi_2)$, where ϕ_2 is the rate of embodied technological progress of capital.

Thus, the effect of increasing the amount of education, be it in school or on the job, received by new entrants into the labor force or members of the existing labor force is brought into the production function through ϕ_1.

Such embodied technological progress is embodied not only in those new factors of production representing an increase in the total stock, but also in those replacing the factors being retired from production each year. That is, additional labor and capital that both replace retiring labor and capital and represent increases in the total of those factors of production are more productive due to improved technology embodied in them—increased education and new machines, for example.

The methods employed to date for attempting to measure the values of ϕ_1 and ϕ_2, the rates of embodied technological progress in capital and labor, have utilized the growth of education and expenditures on research and development, respectively. No one has yet succeeded in attributing all of the growth of output to specific changes in the economy. Edward Denison's attempt has come closest, but he still ends up with a residual, which he attributes to changes in knowledge but which is nevertheless a residual, of .53 per cent out of 2.93 per cent or 18 per cent of the total growth of output for the period he was studying. (A chapter from his work is presented in the next chapter of this book.)

The Labor Surplus Economy Model

In the neoclassical model increases in capital and labor are both treated as factors that lead to increased growth of output. The reader with even a casual knowledge of less developed countries (LDCs) may have been uneasy about the contention that increased labor will always lead to increased economic growth. Is there not, in fact, vast unemployment in many LDCs and would not an increase in the LDCs labor supply merely mean more unemployment?

The difficulty is that the neoclassical model assumes full employment of resources whereas that is one of the ends toward which most LDCs are still striving. The labor surplus economy model was developed to try to explain this process of attaining full employment from the present position of excess labor supply in which many LDCs find themselves.

The labor surplus economy model, first delineated by W. Arthur Lewis and elaborated by Gustav Ranis and John Fei,[4] suggests the road for development that may be followed by countries with labor surpluses. The hallmark of a labor surplus economy is that the work being done could be accomplished by fewer workers. For example, in the agricultural sector there may not be enough land for labor to be fully utilized. Therefore, the work is spread over the existing labor force with the result that many people work to less than their capacity. Similarly, in urban areas petty traders, for example, are so numerous that none are fully employed and many actually *work* only a small fraction of the day even though they are *at their place of work* the full day.

The model posits a dual economy. Part of the economy is the traditional sector where labor surplus is the norm and methods do not change. The other part of the economy is modern, using capital and new techniques and only as many workers as needed. (For the modern sector, the neoclassical model might indeed apply.) The development consists of movement of labor from the traditional sector to the modern one. The labor surplus economy model describes the economic results of this labor movement.

All the labor in the modern sector is paid labor's marginal product, which is the output of the last worker.[5] This means that there is a surplus above wage payments because the output of the earlier workers was greater than their marginal product (law of decreasing returns to a factor). The curve AB in Figure 9.2 shows the marginal product of labor. With wages at the level W_0 and OC labor employed, a surplus equal to the area W_0AB is available for the employer. If this surplus is invested in more capital, the marginal product of labor curve will move up to DE since each worker now has more capital to work with. But the employer can still hire labor at W_0, where W_0 is a higher real wage than that earned in the subsistence sector, since there is an unlimited supply of labor that can be brought in from the traditional sector of the economy. Hence, an even greater surplus is earned (W_0DE) and more capital created, moving the marginal product of labor curve upward again. This process continuously repeats itself until the unlimited supply runs out, at which point (F) all labor is fully utilized and productive and the supply curve of labor turns up, that is, more labor may be had only at a higher price. Once this has

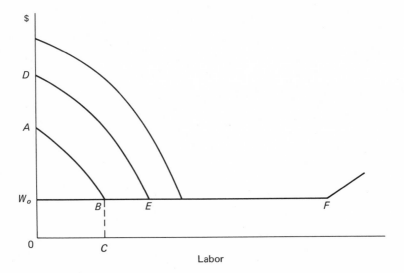

Figure 9.2   Growth in a Labor Surplus Economy

been attained, the economy has passed from the less developed to the developed category where sustained economic growth is the norm.

There are many problems that tend to prevent development from proceeding along these lines. First, wages must be kept down so that profits increase. This is difficult in poor countries, especially when government is a large employer. Second, capitalists must invest in productive domestic enterprises and not put their money into Swiss bank accounts or Riviera hotels. Finally, the food that was feeding the people who move from the traditional to the modern sector must still somehow be made available to feed them. This must be accomplished in the face of the desires of those growing the food to increase their standard of living by consuming more of it.

PLANNING

One way of trying to insure growth is through the utilization of economic planning. Planning is a particularly important tool for LDCs. For several reasons LDCs do not seem to be able to rely on the market to produce sustained growth to the extent countries that developed in the past did. Of the two most important reasons, the first is the growth rate of population, which is at an unprecedented height in most LDCs. Due to the advancement of science, death rates have fallen dramatically and birth rates have not followed suit. No country that is now highly developed accomplished its development while its population was growing rapidly. The second factor is that the LDCs are in a world that includes highly developed countries. Competition from developed countries cuts off for the LDCs the very same routes the now highly developed countries followed in their successful attempts at development. In addition developed countries provide patterns of high consumption which, when copied by poor countries, leave little for investment purposes. Finally, most LDCs have a large government sector, a sector that does not have the full range of market forces affecting it. It is because of these difficulties that economic planning has been accepted as a rational supplement to the free market in most LDCs. Although we could discuss planning in terms of the mathematical models employed in the planning process,[6] we instead present a descriptive discussion of the several types of planning and their advantages and disadvantages.

In education, planning also has a significant role in developed and less developed countries. As was discussed in Chapter 1, education is for the most part a public good so that market forces are not completely free to determine the quantity and price of education that would be optimum. In addition for education there is a long time span between its beginning and the time the individual acquiring it tries to sell his skills in the market place. This long lead time (as much as ten years after secondary school for a physician, for example) makes it difficult for the consumer to evaluate its worth. If a surplus or a dearth of some type of skill develops, it takes a long time before the reactions of the market in terms of a decrease or an increase of salary will create the required adjustment of fewer or more people acquiring that skill. For both these reasons planning is very useful as a device for filling the market void in determining the optimum size and nature of the educational system.

Planning can be defined as the process of specifying policy within the framework of a model with the objective of attaining some goal or goals at the lowest possible cost. This is a definition of formal planning; *de facto* planning of various degrees of sophistication is continuously undertaken in an economy. Examples of informal planning include the vice president of a company calling his sales managers together to plot out the sales campaign for the coming season or the school principals meeting with the superintendent of schools to discuss the type and number of teachers to be hired for the coming year. Indeed, all activities implicitly have a planning element. Even when there are no changes, an implicit decision of no change is made.

To be most effective planning needs to involve, in the drafting process, all the agencies and individuals to be affected by the plan. There is a significant history of economic and educational plans being completely sterile documents; lack of involvement of the operational agencies is often one reason for this. Not having been privy to the formulation of the plan, they have no direct interest in seeing it fulfilled. A second reason could be lack of machinery for following up the plan. To expect fundamental or even lesser changes in a large bureaucracy to develop from the mere publication of a document is unrealistic. A third reason could be that it may have been a purely political document to begin with, drafted with no expectation of implementation. With this overview of planning as background, a closer view of the benefits and costs of the process is in order.

The benefits derived from planning are several. First, there is the expectation of consistency. Without planning, there is every probability that the set of policies adopted will be such that they conflict or overlap in some vital way. That is, the policies and goals may be such that the policies cannot achieve the goals due to internal contradictions.

An example of an inconsistency is a set of policies such as the following: teacher-student ratio (T/S) is to remain constant; enrollment (S) is to increase by 10 per cent; teacher (T) numbers are to remain constant. This is a very obvious case of an inconsistency.

$$T/S = b;\ S \text{ increases};\ T = k$$

where b and k are constants. Given the size and complexity of an educational system or an economy, there can be inconsistencies in programs that are not obvious. Such inconsistencies can lead to very costly errors.

Consistency is a problem in any given year and also over time. Consistency over time is perhaps even more important than in any given year because of the greater chance of error. Usually it is not too difficult to see how pieces fit together in a given year. But over time there is much less probability of a fit without a *formal* apparatus designed to assure a fit. How can we assure that the number of classrooms (which take, say, one-and-a-half years to build), the number of teachers (which take, say, one to three years of training, depending on the type and place), and the number of students at each of several levels of education will match without a plan in which to check the consistency of the policies regarding each of these items? Thus consistency, which may seem so obvious as to be trivial but is far from trivial in its importance, is one benefit of planning.

A second benefit derived from planning is the specification and clarification of objectives and priorities. The process of planning for a period of one or several years necessitates the spelling out of ideas and desires on the part of both civil servants and politicians (in the case of government programs). Such exercises cannot help but improve the ideas and the will and ability to carry them out. The process of transforming an inconsistent plan into a consistent one ideally utilizes priorities, although it does not have to. *De facto* priorities are always in effect in that certain things are done before others. The planning process implies *specifying the objectives* and *weighing them against one another*, thereby imposing a rational priority system on them rather than allowing a nonrational (i.e., a thoughtless) priority system to prevail. "Let's cut the number of students to make it consistent" is one way of approaching the consistency problem above. But a decision on which is most important—(1) more students, (2) constant teacher/student ratio, or (3) no extra teachers—is a better approach to the problem.

Closely allied with this second sort of benefit is the disclosure of what information is needed to operate the system rationally. In the setting of objectives and priorities, certain sorts of information which are not available become obviously necessary or useful. Therefore, the planning process creates as a spin-off information on what sorts of data need to be gathered. The amount of data possible to collect is infinite. Because data collection has a positive time and resource cost, it is a real service to determine which sorts of data are needed and will be useful.

Third, planning leaves one with a structure in which evaluation can be systematically undertaken. With a plan, specified objectives, and policies, the actual events that occur can be juxtaposed against the plan to determine whether policies were the right ones for meeting the objectives, what should be considered that was not considered, what need not be considered, and so forth. All of these will, or can, lead to better plans in the future. Without a plan, evaluation can still take place, but it is much more difficult and less likely to occur. Planning does not assure evaluation—bureaucrats and politicians seldom feel they have time for such action. However, planning does ease the task of evaluation if there is an inclination to do it. It is the absence of evaluation procedures that many decry as one of the larger failings of many actions of the poverty program in the United States.

The fourth benefit from planning is a psychological one. There are two aspects of this benefit, one general and one rather narrow. Generally, the specification of objectives can have a psychological effect on the people affected by the plan, an effect that helps lead to the fulfillment of those objectives. The setting of goals can lead to the striving to meet them. More narrowly, for economic or educational planning in LDCs, there is a greater likelihood of foreign aid coming in to assist planned than unplanned growth. Planning may be evil or good in general but in any case, it has been shown that it can bring in additional resources, and this is a positive benefit derived from planning.

The first cost of planning is the resources used in the process. A tremendous amount of manpower can be taken up in the planning process. Manpower is not required only in a planning office but in all areas and at all levels of the system since people need to communicate and be communicated to.

A second cost (or is it a benefit?) of planning is that it necessitates centralization. Centralization is a cost in that policy makers and planners are, by their nature, not involved with the day-to-day minutia of economic or educational production. They cannot know the problems peculiar to each town and hamlet, school, and product. Therefore, centralization can lead to abstractions that are not workable when the actual forms of the problems are confronted. On the other hand, decentralized decision making can also be ineffective. How is the young man to know whether atomic physics or mechanical engineering has the best future in his country? These are things much better seen from an aggregate or centralized viewpoint. Thus, arguments exist on both sides of the question of the costs of centralization.

Another cost of planning is political. The publication of a plan means that the priorities of the policy makers are opened to attack. Any action that even seems to be inconsistent with the plan is likely to be political fodder for the opposition. Stated objectives not met are even more explosive political tinder.

A final cost to be mentioned here is the effect of a large scale planner making a mistake. If an individual producer or school principal attempts something new and it is a disaster, the cost is limited because the weight of one project in the nation is slight. However, if a planner errs, there can be a great loss due to the wide scope of the plan.

Two comments about planning in general are in order here. The idea of a rolling plan is the first. A *rolling plan* is one that is specified for a given number of years, say five, and periodically reevaluated and revised. For example, a five year plan for 1971–75 would be revised in 1971 and changed to a five year plan for 1972–76. The next year it could be changed to a 1973–77 five year plan, and so on; each year a new five year plan based on the last would be promulgated. Such a system has the advantage of keeping the goals realistic and relevant and of bringing new conditions into the plan. On the other hand, it has the disadvantage of being even more costly in terms of the resources necessary to make the plan. There is a real danger with a rolling plan of a planning office spending all of its time repeatedly rewriting the plan rather than seeing that it is carried out. Generally, a plan that is rolled annually is not so efficient as one that is rolled every two or three years.

Second, it should be noted that it is possible to have both micro and macro planning in the sense of either geography or size. One can have planning on any geographic basis: neighborhood, city, sub-national region, nation, international region, world. Planning can also be on a project or subject basis either by an individual firm or a government agency. Micro educational planning is discussed in

Chapter 11. We now turn to a detailed discussion of one type of macro planning—educational planning.

EDUCATIONAL PLANNING

Three approaches to educational planning have been charted and, to varying extents, tried: (1) the demand-for-education approach, (2) the rate-of-return approach, and (3) the manpower-requirements approach. Each of these approaches will now be described.

The *demand-for-education approach* to educational planning is quite simple: School places are provided for everyone who wants to go to school. Although this rule is simple on the surface, it becomes much less clear after digging into it a bit. First, since this is planning, it is necessary to know how many will want various types of education in the future. Projections have to be made. Population projections are the basic data for this task. However, a problem still remains in that the amount of education and type desired both depend on the cost of education, income of families, job expectations, and possibly other factors. The simplest method of dealing with these problems is to ignore them. One method of ignoring them is to assume implicitly that the population growth rate will be the growth rate for all levels and types of education. If population grows by X per cent, college education, elementary education, and all other levels and types grow at X per cent. Ignoring problems has obvious costs.

For the most part this has been the only type of educational planning used in the United States and many other countries. Many states' higher educational programs are based on requests to the legislature from the state university for funds to expand at the same rate as demand for places. Of course, education below that level is, effectively, compulsory in the United States. Because education is not free to the individual student even if no tuition is charged (foregone earnings are a cost), the demand is far from universal. The legislatures or the voters modify the planning by refusing at times to finance the expansions requested.

In some less developed countries this type of educational planning exists at least at lower levels. Some less developed countries do indeed have universal primary education, which amounts to planning in the form of meeting the demand for education. The so-called demand for education also influences the size and expansion of secondary and higher education in many countries. This is really political and not economic demand. Economic demand means that there are means to pay for it, which is not completely meaningful in a no-tuition school system.

The faults of the demand-for-education approach are primarily two. First, it specifies no priorities. When insufficient resources are available to meet all the demand for education, it does not suggest the best road to follow. Second, it is difficult to determine the actual demand for education when education is subsidized, because the public is not faced with the true price of education.

The second approach to educational planning is the *rate-of-return approach*. This approach has not been used as an exclusive methodology for the planning of any entire educational system. However, it has been applied to subsectors of the system and as a supplementary tool in social demand and manpower planning approaches. The rate-of-return approach to educational planning suggests that various educational programs be ranked according to their rates of return. (The methodology for this and empirical examples of it are the substance of Chapters 7 and 8.) The programs giving the highest returns, assuming they are greater than the return on other investments in the economy, should be increased relative to other programs. For example, Hansen found the following social internal rates of return to three levels of education in the United States: primary education—15.0 per cent; secondary education—11.4 per cent; and higher education—10.2 per cent.[7] These results suggest that either primary or primary and secondary education be increased relative to higher education.

The first criticism of this approach is that it is based on a concept dealing with averages, and what is really needed is one dealing with marginals. That is, the rate of return is the average earned by all those with a given amount of education. The real question is: What did the last man earn, not the average man? If we were to expand a certain type of education, we would not add average men but additional, or marginal, men. If average earnings are different from marginal earnings, as they undoubtedly are, decisions based on the average could easily be incorrect. Unfortunately, there is no way of specifying who the marginal man is; therefore, the marginal rate of return cannot, at present, be found. Second, future rather than past rates of return are what are needed for planning. Third, the assumption that the wage equals the marginal product of labor is often not a realistic one. We have already discussed the possibility of favoritism or nepotism making these unequal. In addition educated people might be hired at wages above their marginal product for the prestige of having college graduates or doctorates working for the firm. In the context of LDCs, the extended family system can affect the relationship between work and payments (food or cash).[8] Finally, the rate-of-return analysis does not give any quantitative answers for planning. It suggests which direction to move in but not how far. For example, if the rate to university education is 10 per cent and the rate to secondary school is 8 per cent, planning on the basis of rate-of-return analysis would prescribe an increase in university education, but it cannot specify the size of the increase.

The final approach to educational planning and the one explicitly used most often is the *manpower-planning approach*. Many countries, especially LDCs, utilize manpower planning to assist in educational and overall economic planning. The general methodology employed is fairly uniform. Unfortunately, the difficulties are just as uniform.

The basic goal of manpower planning is the determination of how many people possessing each skill level will be needed at some future date for the economy to run smoothly, given its expected size and nature at that time. The educational system is then geared to produce the required number of individuals with the necessary skills. Thus, the size and nature of the required educational system is determined.

The first step in formulating a manpower plan is to acquire projections for aggregate output (GNP) and sectoral output (GNP_s, where s is agriculture, industry, mining, and the like) in some target year. Such projections may already be available, as in cases where a national or regional development plan exists, or may have to be developed. These yield a target GNP and set of projected ratios of GNP_s/GNP. These may be further broken down into projections of the growth of particular industries, GNP_i, within each sector, such as coffee, cotton, rice, and bananas within the agricultural sector, yielding a set of GNP_i/GNP_s ratios. Next, a projection of the productivity of labor in each industry is made (L_i/GNP_i). Then a projection of the occupational distribution in each industry's labor force is undertaken (L_o/L_i), that is the proportion of the total labor in an industry which is in each of the various possible occupations. Finally, a projection of the educational distribution of each occupational group (L_e/L_o) is made so that the number of graduates of different types of education in each occupation in each industry is available. Put all together, they yield the amount of labor with each amount of education needed in the target year if the target growth is to be achieved.

$$\text{GNP} \cdot \frac{\text{GNP}_s}{\text{GNP}} \cdot \frac{\text{GNP}_i}{\text{GNP}_s} \cdot \frac{L_i}{\text{GNP}_i} \cdot \frac{L_o}{L_i} \cdot \frac{L_e}{L_o} = L_e$$

Normally these projections are made on the basis of data about the economy in the recent past or in the present. For example, look at the last item, L_e/L_o. This might be estimated on the basis of a labor force survey that yielded a set of proportions of those with each educational level in each occupation of the type shown below.

Table 9.2

Percentage of Labor Force in Each Occupation Which Has Each Educational Level[a]

Educational Level		E_1	E_2	E_3	E_4	E_5	E_6	E_7
Occupation	O_1	5	15	57	20	2	1	0
	O_2	27	35	21	9	6	1	1
	O_3	2	1	4	6	8	15	64
	O_4	3	8	47	40	2	0	0
	$\vdots$	$\vdots$	$\vdots$	$\vdots$	$\vdots$	$\vdots$	$\vdots$	$\vdots$
	O_z	6	5	20	23	27	11	8

[a] Where the E_i's ($i = 1, 7$) are levels of education and the O_i's ($i = 1, Z$) are occupations.

On the basis of such a set of proportions, one projects future educational needs for each occupation. One problem with such a procedure is that it is necessary to be very familiar with the peculiarities of every occupation and the economy in general. Otherwise you can have cases such as have been seen in India where it would appear that secretaries need master's degrees. In India there is so much competition for the few scarce jobs and so much fear of the use of subjective criteria (such as family, caste, or religion) in making a selection that jobs are often allocated on the very objective standard of education. Thus, when 100 people apply for a secretary's job, the one with the most education gets it. As a result in this analysis it appears that secretaries need extremely high educational requirements.

However, that is not all. Subtractions from and additions to the existing stock of employed labor also have to be estimated. Subtractions (wastage) are a result of deaths, retirements, changes in status, and emigration. Additions result from the output of the education system, movements into the labor force of those not previously in it (for example, unemployed women or immigrants), and changes in status due to on-the-job or other training outside the formal education system. When all these have been evaluated, the major portion of the task of matching educational output and manpower requirements is completed. The next step is to make any alterations in the original estimate of the manpower requirements for the educational system itself on the basis of the projections of the amount of manpower the schools need to supply to the rest of the economy.

It is in making all these projections that the art of manpower planning comes in. For LDCs especially (but not only) there are typically very few data to go on. The statistical series are usually short-lived, even in countries that have been independent a hundred years as in Latin America and some African and Asian countries. Second, many LDCs have recently gone through dramatic structural changes due to the advent of independence, and simple projections by their nature assume continuity in structure, not radical change. Finally, the name of the game is change. Even if there were long historical data series to project and no radical changes occurred in the structure of the economy, it would not be desirable to project past trends because the stagnation of the past is not what is wanted in the future. The object is to change the dynamics of the economies to situations of sustained growth.

For example, in many LDCs the manpower structure has been top-heavy. There have been too many professional and managerial personnel relative to the number of supervisors and technicians and skilled and semiskilled workers. Because of this imbalance, doctors often do work that nurses are perfectly capable of doing by their training; architects do work that draftsmen can do equally as well; and so forth. Even if the architect is a better draftsman than the draftsman, it is still wasteful for him to do drafting because he has a relative or *comparative advantage* in doing architectural work. That is, his advantage in doing architectural work is greater than his advantage in drafting.[9] The case of Uganda affords an example of this problem. Uganda was found to have a ratio of about $1:2.5$ for the numbers of highest level to medium-level manpower. To project on that basis would be to maintain past problems in the future since something like a $1:4$ ratio is, it appears, much better.

The indefiniteness of that last statement points up one of the largest problems of manpower forecasting and planning. There is really very little evidence existent and very little research going on into what that ratio should indeed be. The same is true of many other parameters necessary for manpower planning. The correct ratio between high- and medium-level manpower could be derived by specifying the individual production function so that the trade-off between different types of labor could be found. With that information and knowledge of the costs of labor with different amounts of education, the optimum mix of labor could be determined.

Another extremely difficult problem to handle is that of experience. So far we have been talking about educational requirements as if they were the only dimension of manpower quality, as if a new graduate of the university and one with 15 years' experience were substitutable on a one-to-one basis. Of course, this is a simplistic view of reality. One manner of bringing experience into the manpower calculus is as follows: the age (a proxy for experience) distribution of the existing labor force in a given occupation is surveyed. If the age distribution of the labor force implied by the plan is markedly different in the target year, some sort of adjustment may have to be made. This could take the form of adjusting the educational requirement for a portion of the group—for instance, requiring more education for some to try to compensate for the lack of experience.

A final problem, which is also an example of how government policy can affect the manpower and educational situations, is the effect on wastage of retirement and "citizenization" policies.[10] The retirement age suggested and/or enforced by government greatly affects the retirement age in the economy as a whole. The effect of citizenization programs on the wastage is obvious.

In addition to the practical difficulties already mentioned in carrying out the manpower planning procedure, theoretical questions also exist. First, manpower planning ignores the cost of education. Second, it neglects low-skill labor entirely. Although a concentration of efforts on relatively scarce high-level manpower is not an unreasonable procedure, it is quite clear that bottlenecks at lower levels can and often do develop. Trying to bring low-level manpower into the analysis would complicate it greatly in that the numbers involved are very large. Next, manpower planning makes the implicit assumption that the educational requirements for each job are rigid when in fact a range of educational backgrounds is typically seen for almost every job. Finally, it is not always possible to evaluate the quality of the planning in terms of the economic results in the country. If the GNP and manpower targets are both met, one could assume that the plan was correct. However, in any of the other three cases (GNP target missed and manpower target hit; GNP hit and manpower missed; and both missed), it is not clear whether the manpower plan was correct or not. Because of this, it is difficult to improve upon the planning that has taken place in the past.

All three types of educational planning are lacking in two regards. First, they all deal with quantity and not quality. None of them are concerned with the quality of education and what different quality could mean to development, nor the trade-off between additional quality and additional quantity. Probably the main reason for this is the lack of knowledge about such trade-offs or how even to measure quality of education. Is quality measured by the education of the teachers, the expenditure per pupil, the students per teacher, the curriculum, the examination results, the pass or graduation rates, or what?

The second is the general failure to take non-system education into account. Many kinds of non-system education exist: private correspondence courses, on-the-job training, reading, apprenticeships, literacy campaigns, and night schools. These are typically not integrated into any of the three planning approaches to education. This is not to say that they could not be handled. Indeed, some countries, like Norway and Sweden, have rather comprehensive plans and programs in these areas. The United States is moving in that direction, as can be seen in all of the training programs recently implemented. Rate-of-return analyses have been undertaken on some of these types of education, and they could be integrated into any planning undertaken on that principle.

At the beginning of this section it was asserted that the market does not provide the necessary signals in the case of education owing to its being a public good and its long gestation period. The description of the various approaches to educational planning followed, and it was seen that their shortcomings are many. What, then, should be done?

The answer is two-fold. First, although educational planning of all types has many practical and theoretical problems, quite successful educational planning is taking place. Therefore, in spite of its shortcomings, educational planning has made a positive contribution to greater efficiency in this sector of the economy.

The second facet of the answer is the undertaking of new research to eliminate the shortcomings of educational planning.[11] Taking the manpower planning approach as an example, more information on the methodology, assumptions, and assumed parameters must be included in the plans if they are to be of benefit in improving the multinational effort towards effective manpower planning. Specifically, a range of educational targets should be specified depending on the meeting of general economic targets. Then, at the end of the plan it will be possible to see whether the methodology was correct or not. Also, attention must be paid to the state of the labor market when drawing up the plan. Existing unemployment must be taken into account. Hiring practices must be considered; that is, the ratio of substitution between labor with different amounts of education in the performance of various functions. For example, how many clerks are necessary to replace the efforts of one secretary? How many untrained technicians for one trained technician, if any? If it can be derived through interviews and direct observation or in any other way, such information would suggest the kind of trade-offs that should be considered in order to determine which is the optimum educational package. Through research and experience the planning that is taking place will undoubtedly continue to be improved, and planning will play a larger and larger role in education.

QUESTIONS FOR DISCUSSION

1. Are the rate-of-return studies of greater use in micro or macro educational planning? Why?

2. Does the school you are attending utilize planning? How might it be extended (or instituted)?

3. What kind(s) of national educational planning is there in the United States? How effective and important is it?

4. What problems do you see in any attempt to apply the neoclassical model to less developed countries (in particular, focusing on the way education is dealt with in the model)?

5. In what ways is the use of aggregate number of years of education possessed by the members of the labor force an unsatisfactory measure of the input of education into production?

PROBLEMS

1. What is the growth rate of an economy if the GNP is $20 billion in 1969 and $21 billion in 1970? If it is $19 billion in 1968 and $21 billion in 1970?

2. If GNP is growing at 2 per cent per year, what is the rate of growth of GNP per capita if population is growing at 1 per cent per year? If population is growing at 3 per cent per year?

3. You are given the following facts about an economy:

Government Expenditure	$ 60	Output	250
Consumption	150	Capital Stock	500
Investment	40	Population Growth Rate	2%
Savings	40	Labor's Share	3/4
Exports	50	Capital's Share	1/4
Imports	50		

What is the rate of growth of output as defined by a simple neoclassical model?

Chapter **10** **BASIC STUDIES IN EDUCATION AND ECONOMIC GROWTH AND PLANNING**

THE literature on the relationship between education and economic growth and planning is extensive. In many countries education is considered one of the main roads to the achievement of economic and political growth and development. For both developed and less developed countries, the policy implications of research in these areas are potentially great. Yet relatively little substantive research has been undertaken showing the nature of the relationship between education and growth, and research on educational planning is in a similar state of development.

There are several approaches to the problem of determining the relationship between education and economic growth. One approach utilizes the calculation of rates of return to educational investments as described in Chapter 9. The rates found are then applied to the total investment in education to determine the size of the annual output attributable to the educational investment. A second approach is to correlate some measure of education with some measure of economic well-being, interpreting a high correlation as meaning that education is important to economic development. The best known attempt to do this is that of Harbison and Myers.[1] They correlated GNP per capita with an index of secondary and higher education enrollment rates for seventy-five nations and found a very high correlation ($r = .88$). Unfortunately, this approach is helpful neither in predicting the future nor in suggesting policy actions since it contains no model to show whether education causes growth or growth causes education. The high correlation could just as easily be used to justify the latter hypothesis as the former because as a country grows it becomes richer, and it can therefore afford more education.

Notes to Chapter 10 will be found on pages 385–390.

A third approach is utilized by Edward Denison who attempts to quantify all the factors that contribute to economic growth in his pathbreaking book *The Sources of Economic Growth in the United States and the Alternatives Before Us.* Denison analyzes the economic growth of the United States during the twentieth century and shows how growth may be increased in the future. He employs a neoclassical growth model as a framework for his calculations. Utilizing a wide and imaginative set of data, he calculates the rate of growth of the various factors of production and the share that each factor contributes to output. With this data Denison specifies the sources of the growth in GNP in the United States.

In Denison's formulation the major and explicit effect of education is its influence on labor's productivity as discussed in "Education and Growth" (Chapter VII of Denison's book) which, together with some additional tables, constitutes the first selection in this chapter. He determines education's contribution to growth by calculating the increase in effective labor to which it has led. The increase in the amount of education embodied in the labor force is used to inflate the figures for the quantity of labor entering into production by a factor accounting for labor's increased productivity due to its greater education. In terms of the neoclassical growth model presented in Chapter 9, Denison is using a growth formula as follows:

$$G_Y = aG_J + bG_N + cG_R$$

where Y is GNP; a, b, and c are the shares of capital, labor, and land; J is effective capital; N is effective labor; and R is land.

Denison also asserts that education has an effect on growth through a second route: the increase of knowledge. The distinction between education and knowledge is similar to that between embodied and disembodied technological change. Education is embodied in a factor of production, labor, whereas knowledge is not. Denison does not directly estimate the contribution of increased knowledge. Rather, he assumes it to be the explanation for the "residual" growth in the economy, that is, the difference between the actual total growth and the portion of growth that he succeeds in explaining by changes of the amount and quality of land, labor, and capital. Attributing the residual to growth in knowledge is, of course, only one of many possible explanations.

Denison discusses the potential for increasing growth through increased investment in education. He notes that the potential in the

United States for the period 1960–80 is less than for the preceding years (1929–57) due to the great improvements in the educational level of the labor force in the past. On the other hand, he points out that investment in education is not wholly at the expense of other investment. Rather, some is at the expense of current consumption so that even in the United States it is quite worthwhile to increase educational investment in the quest for growth.

To put the education chapter of Denison's book in perspective, summary tables of the full results of the study are also reproduced. The range of inputs into production considered by Denison and their respective rates of growth are given in Table 10.4, both absolutely and per employed person. Table 10.5 itemizes the portion of the growth of output attributable to the growth of each of the inputs.

Two selections from actual plans are the next readings in this chapter. The first is one full Part (part II) of *The Regents Statewide Plan for the Expansion and Development of Higher Education, 1964*. This plan was the beginning of a series of plans for higher education in New York State as mandated by the New York State Legislature. Many other states have adopted such a system (indeed, New York was not the first), and others are moving in that direction.[2]

The basic approach to educational planning behind this plan is the social-demand approach. The first part of this selection discusses the methodology and data utilized in projecting the forthcoming demand for higher education in New York. However, the planners felt that the manpower-planning approach to educational planning also had something to contribute in the context of higher educational planning in New York State. Therefore, they discuss the general employment trends by occupational grouping and, in some instances, by individual occupations. In particular, the outlook for those occupations utilized by the higher education industry and some of those prepared for by higher education are emphasized.

The rest of the plan, which is not reproduced here because of its length, discusses in detail the nature of the educational system that will be needed to meet the needs earlier enumerated. Plans for specific two-year colleges, colleges of arts and sciences, universities, and specialized institutions of higher education are detailed. These are costed out in both capital and recurrent cost terms.

The second planning document is a volume from the *Tanzania Second Five-Year Plan for Economic and Social Development 1st July, 1969– 30th June, 1974: the Survey of the High and Middle Level Manpower Requirements and Resources*. Tanzania, an extremely poor country

(1970 average annual income per capita is about $75) located in East Africa, is about the size of Texas and New Mexico combined and has a population of thirteen million people. It is poor not only in natural resources but also in education.

The Tanzanian educational system follows the British model. Elementary school consists of seven years (Standards 1–7).[3] Secondary school has two parts, the first being four years (Forms 1–4), capped by the Cambridge School Certificate Examination (CSC) and the second being two years (Forms 5 and 6), capped by the Higher School Certificate Examination (HSC). The university course is typically three years and there are teacher-training options open at several levels. Even now, only about half the children enter primary school, and there are large scale cutoffs after four years, at the end of elementary school (87 per cent of elementary school graduates in 1967 did not go on to secondary school), and after the first four years of secondary school (78 per cent did not continue to the last two-year cycle of secondary school in 1966). In 1962 only 10 per cent of those over the age of fifteen were literate. In spite of or perhaps because of its poverty, Tanzania has one of the most active and successful planning systems in the less developed part of the world. This is particularly true of its educational planning.

Tanzania has taken the manpower-requirements approach in its educational planning. The size and structure of its educational system are molded to fulfill the demands for manpower made by the overall and the manpower development plans. The document reproduced below demonstrates the detail that is necessary for manpower planning. In it are comparisons of the projections made at the beginning of the first five year plan and the reality at its end. As is pointed out in the plan, one of the most important things to remember when considering the success of the projections of the first plan is that the government did everything it could to insure the realization of the projections. That is an essential part of planning.

Together, these two educational planning documents show that macro planning is widely applicable in education. The success that both New York State and Tanzania, as well as many others, have already had with educational planning demonstrates that, although there is vast room for improvement, planning does have a positive contribution to make to education.

EDUCATION AND GROWTH

EDWARD DENISON

This chapter considers the contribution that increased education of the labor force has made to past growth and is likely to make to future growth, together with the possibilites for altering future growth through the education route. It can deal only with changes in the *amount* of *formal* education received by members of the labor force. It cannot take into account changes (presumably improvements) in the quality of a day's schooling.

The fact that human knowledge has increased, providing more or better information to be imparted in school, is viewed as part of the effect of the "advance of knowledge" on growth rather than of increased education. Conversely, the beneficial effect of a better-educated population on the rate at which knowledge advances will be classified as a contribution of the "advance of knowledge" rather than allocated back to education.[4]

THE EFFECT OF ADDITIONAL EDUCATION ON THE QUALITY OF THE LABOR FORCE

It is evident that additional education increases an individual's ability to contribute to production and his earnings. We need first to quantify this relationship. Data on the 1949 money income of males 25 years of age or more, classified by their age and number of years of school completed, can be obtained from the 1950 Census of Population.[5] Typical differentials by level of education for males of the same age are about as shown in the first column of Table 10.1, although there are considerable differences among different age groups. These differentials represent the combined effect of additional education and the fact that, at the same age, individuals with more education have less work experience; they reflect the net benefit to earnings of additional education over the additional experience foregone for additional schooling.

Reliance, for broad groups, on the marginal productivity explanation of the distribution of income permits us to treat differentials in average earnings among these groups as a measure of differentials in the average contribution to production made by the individuals comprising them. However, the difference in education received and the associated loss of experience are not the only characteristics that distinguish the groups, so that the differences in average earnings cannot be used without adjustment to measure earnings

Table 10.1

Years of School Completed	(1) Mean Income as Per Cent of Mean Income of Eighth Grade Graduates	(2) Mean Income Differentials Used to Represent Effect of Education (Per Cent of Income of Eighth Grade Graduates)
None	50	70
Elementary School:		
1 to 4 years	65	79
5 to 7 years	80	88
8 years	100	100
High School:		
1 to 3 years	115	109
4 years	140	124
College:		
1 to 3 years	165	139
4 years or more	235	181

differences that are *due to* differences in education and associated loss of experience—the information that our investigation requires.

Clearly, the reported income differentials overstate these differences. Individuals of greater ability are more likely to continue their education. Wolfle states that most of those who do not enter high school come from the lower half of the ability distribution. The average score on the Army General Classification Test of those who enter high school is 105, of those who graduate from high school 110, of those who enter college 115, of those who graduate from college 121, and of those who receive the Ph.D. degree 130; however, there is a wide dispersion at each level.[6] Among individuals with similar AGCT scores, those with better school grades are more likely to continue their schooling.[7] Insofar as this may reflect greater energy, application or motivation that carries over into later life, the income differentials shown reflect these attributes as well as differences in length of education as such.[8]

Too much should not be made of these points, however. Even if the association between natural ability or energy and amount of education were very close, the earnings differentials would have to be ascribed in large part to the acquisition of education. In fact, the association is far from complete. Wolfle notes that intelligence seems to be less important than other factors in determining which high school graduates do and which do not go on to college. Even among recent students, education of parents and family income, as distinguished from attributes of the student, are major determinants of the amount of education received.[9] Parents' occupation, age at marriage, and many other influences are also at work.[10] The association between ability and education must have been much smaller for the 1950 labor force, upon which Table 10.1 is based, than for recent students, who are usually expected to complete high school, or at least to continue school until age 16, if of average ability or better. Every group in the 1950 labor force, classified by years of school completed, included individuals with a wide range of natural ability and school grades. The number who attended college was much too small to include most of those with exceptional ability. Most had not completed high school.

It is likely that the larger portion of reported income differentials for the 1950 labor force in fact reflects the effect of additional education. I shall make the explicit assumption that, on the scale used in Table 10.1, three-fifths of the reported income differentials represent differences in incomes from work *due to* differences in education as distinguished from associated characteristics; these adjusted differentials are shown in column 2 of Table 10.1.[11] This three-fifths assumption is one of three major assumptions in this study that importantly affect the results at which I shall ultimately arrive for the sources of past growth, and that do not flow arithmetically from any data that can be adduced.[12] (The others concern the relationship between hours and output and the importance of economies of scale.) I claim no more than that this is a plausible assumption. Later in this chapter I show how different assumption would affect my results.

This assumption makes possible a calculation of the effects of increased education on past growth. For each year for which I could derive a distribution of individuals by number of years of school completed, I have calculated what the average earnings of males over 25 would have been if the earnings at each educational level were a constant fraction (that given in the second column of Table 10.1) of *actual* 1949 earnings of eighth grade graduates. The differences from period to period in average earnings so computed can be used to isolate the effect of changes in the length of schooling, measured in years, on average income. An adjustment is then possible to take account of changes in the number of days of school attendance during the year.[13]

Distributions of males 25 and over by years of school completed are provided for 1940 and 1950 by the Census of Population. The Census Bureau has projected the distribution forward to 1960, 1970, and 1980 by the "cohort" method. This assumes, for example, that the 1950 distribution for those 25 to 29 years of age will be applicable to those 35 to 39 in 1960, those 45 to 49 in 1970, and those 55 to 59 in 1980. Distributions for the younger age groups are estimated by extrapolating recent trends.[14] By a similar technique, I have constructed rough distributions for 1910, 1920, and 1930 by working backward from 1940.

Although these distributions require estimates for the older age groups in the years prior to 1940 and the younger age groups in future years, as well as some obvious assumptions about the distribution of deaths, any resulting errors are unlikely to impair our results much if the Census data for 1940 and 1950 are themselves accurate. However, there are indications that these data are biased. Although reporting by the youngest age class appears approximately correct, for older age groups there is evidently overstatement of educational achievement and this overstatement increases with age.[15] The effect on projections made by the cohort method, if no adjustment were made, would be to understate the improvement in educational attainment over time, and hence the contribution of education to growth.

Use of distributions taken directly from the 1940 and 1950 Censuses, in implementation of the technique described above, indicates that the upward movement in the distribution of males by years of school completed would have raised average earnings by 4.44 per cent over that ten-year period. A similar computation that uses a 1940 distribution derived by working backward from the 1950 Census (a procedure comparable to that followed in other periods) yields only 3.63 per cent. The difference, .81 percentage points in a decade, is taken as a measure of the bias in the projection procedure, and calculated increases in every other decade have been adjusted by that amount.[16] The results are shown in column 1 of Table 10.2. Column 2 of the same table shows percentage changes in the average (arithmetic mean) number of years of school completed by males over 25.[17]

Not only the number of years of education but the number of days spent in school per year have greatly increased. By estimating for each Census year (from Office of Education data) the number of days per year spent in school at the time each age group was attending school, I compute the average number of school days represented by each year of school attended. The percentage increases calculated from these estimates are shown in column 3

Table 10.2

Calculation of the Effect of Longer Education on Labor Earnings Per Man[a]

Period	(1) Labor output per man considering only years of education	(2) Average number of years of school completed	(3) Average number of days of school attended per year of school completed	(4) Average total number of days of school attended	(5) Labor output per man based on total days of education	(6) Labor output per man based on total days of education
			Per Cent Change			*Annual Rate of Change (per cent)*
1910 to 1920	2.7	9.0	6.7	16.3	4.9	0.48
1920 to 1930	3.3	8.9	8.8	18.4	6.9	0.67
1930 to 1940	4.1	10.2	10.8	22.0	8.8	0.85
1940 to 1950	4.4	10.4	10.9	22.4	10.4	1.00
1950 to 1960	5.1	9.8	9.3	20.0	10.3	0.99
1960 to 1970	4.7	8.8	8.1	17.6	9.4	0.90
1970 to 1980	4.8	8.2	7.0	15.7	9.1	0.88
1910 to 1930	6.1	18.6	16.1	37.8	12.1	0.57
1930 to 1960	14.2	33.6	34.2	79.3	32.6	0.94
1960 to 1980	9.7	17.6	15.6	36.0	19.4	0.89
1910 to 1960	21.2	58.5	55.8	147.0	48.6	0.79
1910 to 1980	32.0	86.5	80.1	236.0	77.4	0.82

a Based on males 25 years of age or older.

Table 10.3

Component Indexes for Labor Input and Index of Labor Input Fully Adjusted for Quality Change (1929 = 100)

Year	(1) Index of labor input adjusted for hours	(2) Index of quality as affected by education	(3) Index of quality as affected by age-sex compo- sition and quali- fications of women	(4) Final index of labor input fully adjusted for quality change
1909	72.5	89.4	97.8	63.4
1910	74.6	89.8	98.0	65.7
1911	76.2	90.2	98.1	67.5
1912	78.8	90.6	98.2	70.1
1913	79.6	91.1	98.2	71.2
1914	78.4	91.5	98.3	70.5
1915	78.1	92.0	98.4	70.7
1916	83.8	92.4	98.5	76.3
1917	87.0	92.8	98.6	79.7
1918	90.6	93.3	98.6	83.3
1919	85.6	93.7	98.7	79.2
1920	85.4	94.2	98.8	79.5
1921	77.6	94.8	98.9	72.7
1922	83.5	95.4	99.1	79.0
1923	90.4	96.1	99.2	86.2
1924	88.9	96.7	99.3	85.4
1925	92.6	97.4	99.5	89.7
1926	96.2	98.0	99.6	94.0
1927	96.3	98.7	99.7	94.7
1928	97.6	99.3	99.8	96.8
1929	100.0	100.0	100.0	100.0
1930	93.9	100.7	100.1	94.6
1931	86.3	101.5	100.2	87.8
1932	79.0	102.4	100.3	81.1
1933	77.4	103.3	100.4	80.2
1934	78.9	104.1	100.5	82.5
1935	84.3	105.0	100.5	89.0
1936	93.9	105.9	100.6	100.0
1937	98.9	106.8	100.7	106.4
1938	92.9	107.7	100.8	100.9
1939	97.8	108.6	100.9	107.2
1940	102.8	109.6	101.0	113.8
1941	114.3	110.7	101.2	128.0
1942	127.7	111.8	101.5	144.9
1943	144.9	112.1	101.7	166.4
1944	148.8	114.0	102.0	173.0
1945	140.1	115.1	102.2	164.8
1946	122.5	116.3	102.5	146.0
1947	121.8	117.4	102.7	146.8
1948	122.8	118.6	103.0	150.0
1949	119.0	119.8	103.2	147.0
1950	121.2	121.0	103.5	151.8
1951	129.1	122.2	103.6	163.4

Table 10.3—*continued*

Year	(1) *Index of labor input adjusted for hours*	(2) *Index of quality as affected by education*	(3) *Index of quality as affected by age-sex composition and qualifications of women*	(4) *Final index of labor input fully adjusted for quality change*
1952	131.9	123.4	103.7	168.8
1953	133.2	124.6	103.9	172.4
1954	128.6	125.8	104.0	168.2
1955	133.2	127.1	104.1	176.2
1956	136.1	128.3	104.1	181.7
1957	135.0	129.6	104.1	182.1
1958	131.4	130.8	104.0	178.8
	Projected (high employment)			
1960	139.3	133.4	104.0	193.3
1965	147.7	139.6	103.4	213.2
1970	158.2	146.0	104.1	240.3
1975	168.4	152.5	105.1	269.9
1980	179.3	159.3	106.4	304.0

of Table 10.2.[18] The increases in days per year are of roughly the same magnitude as those in years of school completed.

The product of indexes of the averages number of years of school completed and of the average number of days attended per year provides an index of the average total number of days of school attended by males over 25. Percentage changes based on such indexes are shown in column 4.

It is reasonable to suppose that increasing the number of days spent in school per year raises a man's contribution to production just as much as will an equal percentage increase in the number of years spent in school. In each decade, therefore, I multiply the percentage increase in labor earnings per man ascribed to increases in the number of years spent in school (column 1 of Table 10.1) by the ratio of the percentage increase in the average total number of days spent in school (column 4) to that in the average number of years spent in school (column 2) to obtain the full contribution of the increase in the amount of education to labor output per worker. The results are shown in column 5.

The meaning of the numbers given in this column, for example the 10.3 per cent increase shown from 1950 to 1960, is this. Provided males over 25 are typical, I estimate that, all other things being equal, if the labor force in 1950 had been as well educated as that of 1960, it would have contributed 10.3 per cent more to production than it actually did. Since labor represented about 75 per cent of the national income at that time, the national income would have been larger by 7.7 per cent. (Or, alternatively, if the 1960 labor force had been only as well educated as the 1950 labor force, it would have contributed 9.9 per cent[19] less to production than it did, and so on.)

I use the estimates given in column 5 of Table 10.2, with interpolation for intervening years, to construct an index of the average quality of labor as it is affected by changes in the amount of education received by the labor force. This index is shown in column 2 of Table 10.3.

The computations made, it will be noted, refer to males 25 and over, but in appraising the contribution of education to growth I shall use them as if they referred to the entire labor force. This is unlikely to introduce any appreciable error.[20] Further refinement would require data (particularly income differentials) that are largely unavailable.

THE CONTRIBUTION OF INCREASED EDUCATION TO PAST GROWTH

The education that the United States labor force has received has increased at a rate that can only be described as phenomenal. Its average member in 1960 had spent four-fifths again as many days in school as his counterpart in 1930, and two and one-half times as many as his 1910 counterpart.

With such enormous advances, it is not surprising to find that improved education has made a major contribution to economic growth. By my calculations, from 1929 to 1957 it raised the average quality of labor by 29.6 per cent, or at an average annual rate of .93 per cent. (This is practically the same rate as that given in Table 10.2 for the 1930–60 period.) The contribution was equivalent to an increase of the same amount in the quantity of work done, and the procedure used in that connection may be followed to estimate its contribution to the growth of national product. Multiplication of .93 by 73 per cent, the average share of labor in the national income over this period, yields .68 percentage points, or 23 per cent, of the 2.93 percentage point growth rate of national product as the direct contribution of more education. (After further adjustments, my final estimate remains 23 per cent.)

When related to the growth of national product per person employed the contribution of additional education appears still more impressive. My final estimate is that education contributed 42 per cent of the 1.60 percentage point growth rate in product per person employed.

The main specific assumption underlying these results is that differentials in labor earnings *due to* differences in education equal three-fifths of observed differentials in money income among adult males of the same age classified by years of education. The effect of alternative assumptions can be easily approximated by multiplying my results by the ratio of the desired percentage to 60 per cent.

For example, if a figure of 50 per cent were substituted for 60, we would credit five-sixths of 23 per cent, or 19 per cent, of the growth of total product to education. Substitution of 67 per cent would ascribe to education 26 per cent of total growth.[21]

My calculation of the contribution of more education to past growth does not take account of the fact that, had schooling not been extended, many of the children who would not have been in school would have been working so that the labor force would have increased more rapidly. However, the labor of a child worker should be counted as much less than that of an adult male. The effect of this loss of labor on the 1929–57 growth rate is estimated at less than 0.1 percentage points.

THE CONTRIBUTION OF INCREASED EDUCATION TO FUTURE GROWTH

The rate at which increased education was improving the average quality of the labor force more than doubled from the 1910–20 decade to the 1940–60 period. According to the projections shown in columns 5 and 6 of Table 10.2, 1940–60 is a peak; the rate of improvement will be moderately lower in the next 20 years than in the past 20 years. In the seventies the prospective shift of the age composition of the labor force toward the younger, better educated groups masks what would otherwise be a much larger decline.

The projection is mildly optimistic, since it stems from the higher of two Census Bureau projections.[22]

When the 1957–80 period is compared with 1929–57 as a whole, the computed decline in the rate of improvement of labor force quality due to education is only from .93 to .90, so that for this time comparison it offsets only a little of the rise in the rate of increase of employment, adjusted for hours, that was projected earlier.

STIMULATING THE CONTRIBUTION OF EDUCATION TO GROWTH

Increased education is not only one of the largest sources of past and prospective economic growth. It also is among the elements most subject to conscious social decision. The laws governing school attendance and child labor have a pervasive effect, and schools are largely publicly operated and financed.

However, the influence of education on output is dispersed over a very long period. The changes in the educational background of the labor force measured in Table 10.2 reflect mainly improvements in schooling that were achieved many years earlier.

The median age of all persons in the labor force is 40 years. Only improvements in education achieved by about 1925 affected as many as half

able 10.4[a]

rowth Rates for Real National Income and Underlying Series, Total and Per
erson Employed (Per cent per annum)

	Total			Per Person Employed		
	1909–29	1929–57	1960–80	1909–29	1929–57	1960–80
eal national income	2.82	2.93	3.33	1.22	1.60	1.62
crease in total inputs, adjusted	2.24	1.99	2.16	.65	.67	.47
djustment	−.09	−.11	−.11	−.09	−.11	−.11
crease in total inputs, unadjusted	2.33	2.10	2.27	.74	.78	.58
Labor, adjusted for quality change	2.30	2.16	2.29	.71	.84	.60
Employment and hours	1.62	1.08	1.27	—	—	—
Employment	1.58	1.31	1.68	—	—	—
Quality of a man-year's work due to shorter hours	.03	−.23	−.41	.03	−.23	−.41
Annual hours	−.34	−.73	−.53	−.34	−.73	−.53
Quality of a man-hour's work due to shorter hours	.38	.50	.12	.38	.50	.12
Education	.56	.93	.89	.56	.93	.89
Increased experience and better utilization of women workers	.10	.15	.12	.10	.15	.12
Changes in age-sex composition of labor force	.01	−.01	−.01	.01	−.01	−.01
_and	.00	.00	.00	−1.58	−1.32	−1.65
Capital	3.16	1.88	2.50	1.55	.56	.81
Nonfarm residential structures	3.49	1.46	NA	1.87	.13	NA
Other structures and equipment	2.93	1.85	NA	1.33	.52	NA
Inventories	3.31	1.90	NA	1.70	.58	NA
U.S.-owned assets abroad	4.20	1.97	NA	2.58	.64	NA
Foreign assets in U.S. (an offset)	−1.85	1.37	NA	−3.46	.06	NA
rease in output per unit of nput, adjusted	.56	.92	1.14	.56	.92	1.14

[a] Tables 10.4 and 10.5 are Denison's summary tables listing all the factors of production he analyzed and their tribution to growth.—Eds.
[b] Growth rates based on high-employment projection.
NA — not available.

of the members of the 1960 labor force throughout their schooling. The education provided before World War I was still of importance. Even radical extensions of schooling for children now in school would change the average educational background of the labor force only moderately from that already in sight in the next decade or two.

This observation is in no sense intended to discount the importance to

Table 10.5

Allocation of Growth Rate of Total Real National Income Among the Sources of Growth

	Percentage Points in Growth Rate			Per Cent of Growth Rate			
	1909–29[a] (Commerce)	1929–57	1960–80[b]	1909–29[a] (Commerce)	1909–29[a] (Kendrick-Kuznets)	1929–57	1960–80[b]
Real National Income	2.82	2.93	3.33	100	100	100	100
Increase in total inputs	2.26	2.00	2.19	80	71	68	66
Labor, adjusted for quality change	1.53	1.57	1.70	54	48	54	51
Employment and hours	1.11	.80	.98	39	35	27	29
Employment	1.11	1.00	1.33	39	35	34	40
Effect of shorter hours on quality of a man-year's work	.00	−.20	−.35	0	0	−7	−11
Annual hours	−.23	−.53	−.42	−8	−7	−18	−13
Effect of shorter hours on quality of a man-hour's work	.23	.33	.07	8	7	11	2
Education	.35	.67	.64	12	11	23	19
Increased experience and better utilization of women workers	.06	.11	.09	2	2	4	3
Changes in age-sex composition of labor force	.01	−.01	−.01	0	0	0	0
Land	.00	.00	.00	0	0	0	0
Capital	.73	.43	.49	26	23	15	15
Nonfarm residential structures	.13	.05	NA	5	4	2	NA
Other structures and equipment	.41	.28	NA	15	13	10	NA
Inventories	.16	.08	NA	6	5	3	NA
U.S.-owned assets abroad	.02	.02	NA	1	1	1	NA
Foreign assets in U.S.	.01	.00	NA	0	0	0	NA
Increase in output per unit of input	.56	.93	1.14	20	29	32	34
Restrictions against optimum use of resources	NA	−.07	.00	NA	NA	−2	0
Reduced waste of labor in agriculture	NA	.02	.02	NA	NA	1	1
Industry shift from agriculture	NA	.05	.01	NA	NA	2	0
Advance of knowledge	NA	.58	.75	NA	NA	20	23
Change in lag in application of knowledge	NA	.01	.03	NA	NA	0	1
Economies of scale—independent growth of local markets	NA	.07	.05	NA	NA	2	2
Economies of scale—growth of national market	.28	.27	.28	10	10	9	8

[a] "Commerce" and "Kendrick-Kuznets" headings refer only to the growth rate of total product. Contributions in percentage points under the Kendrick-Kuznets heading would be identical with those shown under the Commerce heading except for "real national income," 3.17; "output per unit of input," .91, and "economies of scale—growth of national market," .32.

[b] Growth rate based on high-employment projection.

NA: Not available.

Note: Contributions in percentage points are adjusted so that the sum of appropriate details equals totals. Per cents of the growth rate have not been so

growth of decisions affecting education. We should take the long view. But it is only realistic to stress that for the near-term the educational background of the labor force has already been largely determined.

The following crude calculations illustrate the point. Suppose that, starting with those who would otherwise complete school in 1962 and continuing indefinitely, some action were taken that resulted in everyone remaining in school one year longer than he otherwise would. Suppose further, as would be in rough accord at prospective educational levels with the differentials given in Table 10.1, that the additional year raised the ability of these individuals to contribute to production by 7.5 per cent.[23]

By 1970 only about 15 per cent of the labor force would have benefited by extra education, and the average quality of the entire labor force would therefore be raised by 1.1 per cent. But loss of those in school instead of at work in 1970 would cost us about 2.6 per cent of the labor force. If these young workers are counted as of half the quality of the *average* worker, this would mean an offsetting loss of 1.3 per cent of labor input.[24] On balance, total labor input, adjusted for quality, would be reduced .2 per cent.

By 1980 we would be ahead. Almost 40 per cent of the labor force would have received the extra education, so average quality would be 3.0 per cent higher than otherwise. The cost would still be 1.3 per cent, so that total labor input, adjusted for quality, would be increased 1.7 per cent and national product 1.4 per cent. This would raise the growth rate of the national product, computed from 1960 to 1980, by .07 percentage points.

Ultimately, sometime around the year 2010, the quality of the entire labor force would be raised by 7.5 per cent, while the cost in labor lost that year would still be around 1.3 per cent. Labor input would be larger by 6.2 per cent and national product by 5.2 per cent. Over the entire 50-year period from 1960 to 2010 we should have raised the average annual growth rate of national product by .10 percentage points.

Provision of an additional year's education would require the continuing use of .3 or .4 per cent of the national product, leaving that much less for other uses. So far as output available for noneducational purposes is concerned, this would deduct the equivalent of .02 percentage points from the growth rate over a 20-year period but less than .01 over 50 years.

Aside from its noneconomic benefits, the net effect of the additional year's education would thus be to add .09 percentage points to the growth rate of output available for uses other than education over the next 50 years.[25]

To add a full year's schooling, over and above the considerable increase in education already in prospect, would be a large step, and the addition of .1 percentage points to the growth rate for 50 years would be a large result. However, it may surprise the reader that the effect would not be even larger in view of the importance of education to past growth. The reconciliation lies in the huge amount by which education has been extended in the past.

To consider growth over the long-run future, we must ask what changes in education are likely or possible. In practice, the amount of education received by young people cannot increase in the future at the rate that it has in the past.

The past great increase in schooling has been stimulated by the geographic expansion of 12-year public school facilities to cover the nation, the prohibition of child labor, and compulsory school attendance laws, as well as the decline in agriculture and such continuing influences as rising income. Though still exerting a strong delayed impact upon the educational level of the labor force, the effect of these great reforms on school attendance is running out. The remaining possibilities for increasing education through the high school years, though important in absolute terms and especially so in the South, are slight compared with past achievements. The average number of *days* a year that students spend in elementary and secondary schools is twice that of 1870. But in recent years it has been almost stationary. Indeed, except for some possible further reduction in absenteeism, to double it again would require the schools to remain open for all students 365 days a year. There is discussion of lengthening the school day, but little agreement as to the benefits this may be expected to bring.

A large further expansion in the proportion of young people attending college may be confidently anticipated. Moreover, if the income differential shown in Table 10.1 are near the truth, an additional year of education at the upper grades (and especially if college is completed) adds more to earnings than an additional year in the lower grades.[26]

But what is required to maintain the contribution of more education to the growth *rate* is maintenance of the *percentage* increase in the amount of education received, adjusted for the greater importance of the upper grades. For the long pull, this seems simply unattainable.

This prospect makes it all the more important to seek improvement in the quality of education, so as to offset the slackening of the increase in its quantity. But we should not be overly sanguine about this. Such objective evidence as is available suggests that the quality of a day's schooling has been improving for many years, even though my estimates cannot measure it. What is needed to prevent the contribution of education to growth from falling very sharply before the end of this century is a great *acceleration* in the rate of increase in quality.

This chapter has focused on education of the young, which comprises the great bulk of all formal education. Adult education, formal or informal, also affects the quality of the labor force, and more quickly. Its expansion could also help to maintain the contribution of education to growth.

The calculations in this chapter do not cover on-the-job training (unless provided by schools and colleges). This is undoubtedly a very important form of training but I do not know whether or not it has increased or decreased in amount per worker. Its omission involves the implicit assumption, so far as the past is concerned, that it has not changed in importance. In considering possibilities of stimulating future growth, more or better on-the-job training, as well as other forms of adult education, should not be overlooked.

"INVESTMENT" IN EDUCATION VS INVESTMENT IN CAPITAL GOODS

In the measurement of national income or product, expenditures for education, like those for food, housing, health and other commodities necessary to sustain an effective labor force, are considered outlays for final products, not intermediate products like the consumption of capital goods. Hence, in assigning a share of the growth of the observed national income to education no deduction was made for the costs of education. Moreover, and more basic, I think that the national income treatment is correct. Education directly benefits individual welfare and improves the individual's ability to participate wisely in social decisions, and these are probably even more important than its effect in raising income, large though this may be.

However, in considering the costs of stimulating education in order to accelerate growth, we must remember that individuals attending schools are ordinarily lost (or largely lost) to the labor force. As education is pushed to more advanced grades, the value of a year of this lost labor increases. The costs of providing schools must also be considered. The preceding section examined these costs. From this examination, I conclude that there can be no real doubt that, within the context in which actual decisions will be made, additional provisions for education will make a significant net contribution to long-term economic growth.

This conclusion must still deal with the contention that to devote more resources to education may not make a net contribution to growth because use of the same resources for capital investment might contribute as much or more. This argument can be dismissed rather easily, given the way decisions governing educational and investment expenditures are actually made in the United States.

Gary S. Becker has compared the additional lifetime income earned by the average student as a result of going to college with the total cost of providing a college education, including both the student's sacrifice of earnings while in school (about half the total cost) and the cost to him and to the college, regardless of the source of its funds, of providing his education. He finds the rate of return to be about the same as that on private capital investment.[27] If this is so, college education for more students could fail to make a net contribution to economic growth only if it replaced investment in capital goods by an amount equal to its full cost (including the value of the work not performed by the additional college students).

But to suppose it would do so is absurd, even if it is postulated that the growth of the capital stock is limited by saving propensities rather than by investment opportunities.[28] Insofar as the costs of higher education are publicly financed through taxation, this supposition requires that one believe additional taxes do not reduce consumption at all, but come entirely out of private saving. Insofar as the costs (including foregone earnings) are borne by the student and his family, it requires that over their lifetimes they spend no more for consumption, other than college expenses, than they would spend if they received the additional earnings that the student has foregone by attending college and if they did not incur expenditures for attending college.

I think it reasonable to suppose that the great bulk of the full cost of attending college replaces other consumption rather than saving, so that additional college enrollments would make a net contribution to growth even if the rate of return on a college education were only a small fraction of that on capital investment in "things."[29]

All this is not to deny, of course, that there may be *some* immediate offset in a lower rate of capital formation. But in the long-run the indirect effect of more education on the growth of the capital stock is more likely to be favorable than adverse, simply because the larger national income it will create will add to investment opportunities and to saving.

What is true of college education applies with even greater force to education in the lower grades, where both the earnings foregone and per pupil costs are much smaller.

NEW YORK STATE'S NEEDS IN HIGHER EDUCATION

UNIVERSITY OF THE STATE OF NEW YORK

More people, higher aspirations, more demanding job requirements—these are forcing every state in the Union to increase greatly the resources devoted to higher education. To do this will require mobilization of present resources in higher education for more efficient use and the addition of new resources as necessary, if a state is to meet the needs of the individual and also of the economy and the society. New York State must not only provide enough places for students; it must also develop the high quality and variety of educational programs required to prepare citizens adequately for this revolutionary century and beyond. Excellence is necessary in every category of education from technician training to postdoctoral research and from regular programs to single refresher courses. In addition to providing instruction, our colleges and universities must also increase research and community services to discharge their full responsibility to the people.

From The University of the State of New York, *The Regents Statewide Plan for the Expansion and Development of Higher Education, 1964* (Albany, New York: The State Education Department, 1965), pp. 9–27.

1. NEEDS OF THE INDIVIDUAL

Reduced to simplest terms, the needs of New York State for more higher educational opportunities are best expressed by estimating the number of persons who must be served, for their good and for the good of the State. Such an estimate must take into consideration two basic questions: (1) How many persons in New York State will there be in the foreseeable future who can successfully complete an education beyond the high school and by doing so be more productive and effective citizens? (2) How does this total reservoir of human talent compare in size with the actual enrollment of students likely to develop in New York State colleges and universities in the same period of time? As long as there is a difference in the size of the total reservoir of college-able persons and the actual enrollment, whatever the reasons may be to explain it, the Regents feel that the State's achievement in higher education is not at the level it should be.

To differentiate between these two groups, this Regents Plan terms the total reservoir of human talent capable of success in college study as "college-going potential" and designates the enrollment that is predicted as likely to

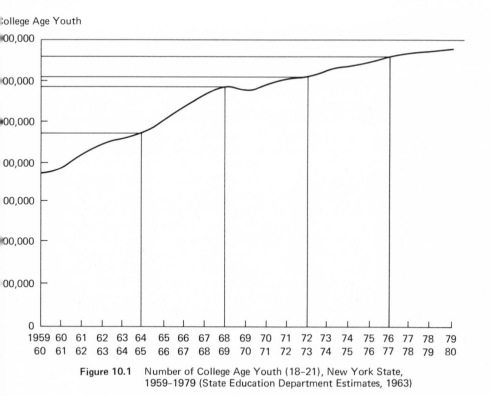

Figure 10.1   Number of College Age Youth (18–21), New York State,
1959–1979 (State Education Department Estimates, 1963)

High School Graduates

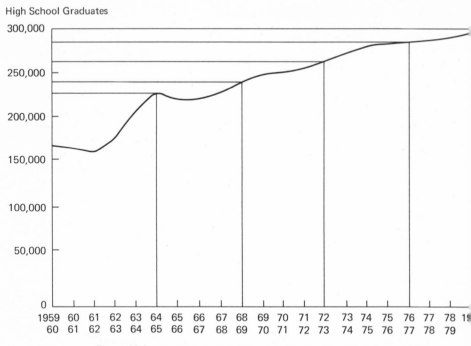

Figure 10.2 Number of High School Graduates, New York State, 1959–
1979 (State Education Department Estimates, 1963)

develop in higher educational institutions in the State as "probable college
enrollment." Attention now turns to the answers to the two basic questions
just stated and to the interrelated implications of the answers to these
questions.

The rising numbers of college-age youth and of high school graduates expected in New York State are shown in Figures 10.1 and 10.2. The increases
of about 50 per cent from 1959–60 to 1969–70 and of about 80 percent from
1959–60 to 1979–80 are impressive in themselves. Yet they do not tell the
whole story. The magnitude of the task and of the opportunity ahead is not
reflected fully in these larger numbers but rather in the higher aspirations
of students and their families throughout the State and the nation.

College attendance and a college degree are as necessary today as high
school attendance and a high school diploma were in the past. The economic, social, and cultural forces in our society are all pushing in this direction.
People are looking to higher education as an appropriate means to satisfying
and productive lives. Rising aspirations make education beyond high school
conceivable for many and rising incomes make it possible.

Beyond having to serve a rapidly growing population and its rising
aspirations for education, higher education must meet the steadily increasing

demands for greater knowledge and a higher level of skills. A heavy responsibility for developing a thinking public and for building the necessary skills rests on the colleges. College enrollment, therefore, has been rising in recent years even when the number of high school graduates remained almost constant.

Potential for College Attendance

How many people should attend college or other postsecondary institutions? The answer to this question is, ideally, all who have the capacity and the desire to benefit from postsecondary instruction of any kind. Otherwise human resources are wasted and consequences develop for both the individual and the society which are costly beyond measure. Postponement of an all-out effort for higher education postpones the bill; but eventually when the bill has to be paid, it will have increased by a staggering amount.

The proportion of a population that has the ability and desire to benefit from postsecondary education cannot be determined precisely. Views on the subject vary widely. The Regents base their estimates on two approaches. One widely acknowledged measure is the conclusion reached by the President's Commission on Higher Education in 1947. After analyzing results of an extensive testing program, the Commission held that at least 49 per cent of our population had the ability to complete two years of post high school general and vocational studies and 32 per cent were capable of completing an advanced liberal or specialized professional education.[30] The 1947 Commission also concluded that these were conservative estimates. The second measure used by the Regents is the relationship between scores achieved by New York State high school seniors on the Regents Scholarship Examinations and their success in collegiate programs. The Regents Scholarship Examinations are the nearest approach to a statewide testing program now available in the State. This measure establishes an even higher potentiality than that resulting from application of the standards of the President's Commission on Higher Education.

The estimates of undergraduate college-going *potential* of 18–21-year-olds within the New York State population based on these two measures are designated in this Plan as Potential A and Potential B. If the first measure (Potential A) turns out to be the correct one, some 480,000 persons could be in college on a full-time basis by 1970 and 547,000 by 1980; if the higher potential (Potential B) were to be reached, these figures would become 612,000 and 708,000.

Probable College Attendance

But what will actual college enrollments in the State likely be? How will these compare with the suggested "potential" or "ideal"? Actual undergraduate enrollment in New York State has fallen far short of the "potential" based on even the lower of the two measures described. In 1963–64, enrollment of full-time undergraduate students was nearly 150,000 under the estimate based on an application of the 1947 Presidential Commission standard of college potential to New York State population. The addition of part-time enrollment to full-time enrollment still leaves a gap of approximately 65,000, and further adjustments for migration of students in and out of the State does not reduce the gap substantially.

To project actual college enrollment is difficult because of the number, variety, and uncertainty of the variables which may affect the demand for college places. In order to test the consequences of alternative assumptions, two projections were made. One was based on the average trend of actual enrollments over the past five years, and the second was based on the more rapidly accelerating rates of the last two years and on optimistic assumptions of capability of the State's colleges and universities to expand to handle students as rapidly as they may demand admission to college. The result of applying these two projection techniques to full-time undergraduate enrollment and to full-time enrollment of all students is shown in Figure 10.3. By the end of the decade, the State can expect between 431,000 and 445,000 full-time students in college. This represents an increase of between 43 and 50 per cent over the fall of 1964.

The two estimates of undergraduate "probable enrollment" are related to the two estimates of "college-going potential" as shown in Figure 10.4. The implication of this comparison for the effort the people of the State

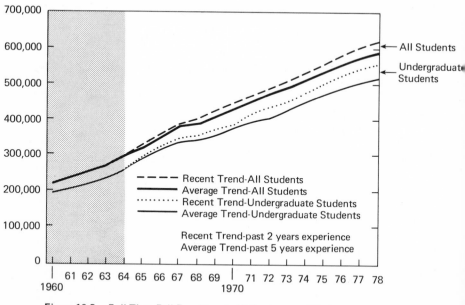

Figure 10.3   Full-Time Fall Enrollment, All Students and Undergraduate Students, in New York State Institutions 1960-64 Actual; 1965-78 Projected

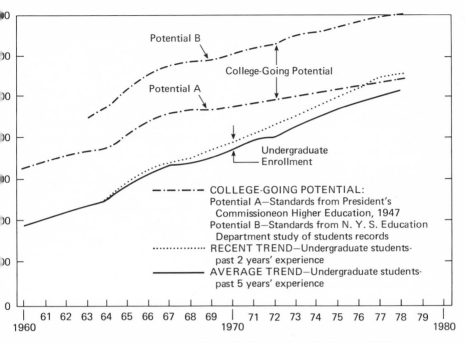

Figure 10.4   Estimates of College-going Potential and Probable Full-Time
Undergraduate Enrollment New York State

should make in higher education is striking. There is a dual job ahead—
formidable in both of its aspects. One is actually to enable the colleges to
accomplish their planned enrollment objectives and thus bring the estimates
of "probable enrollment" to fruition; the second is to enlarge the "probable
enrollment" as much and as fast as possible in order to come close to the
"ideal" as expressed by "college-going potential" in the State.

Probable Enrollments, by Classifications of Institutions

The projections of probable statewide enrollment were carefully made
and give a realistic figure of the total full-time enrollment that can be expected. However, there is still another question: What portion of this
statewide enrollment is to be accommodated by different institutions and
categories of institutions in New York State? Estimates of full-time enrollment to be expected in the several New York State categories of institutions
from 1964 to 1970 which can be used with reasonable confidence as a basis
for planning are summarized and presented graphically in Figures 10.5 to
10.7. These estimates were made by extrapolating recent enrollment trends
by categories of institutions, adjusting these trends for probably changes, and

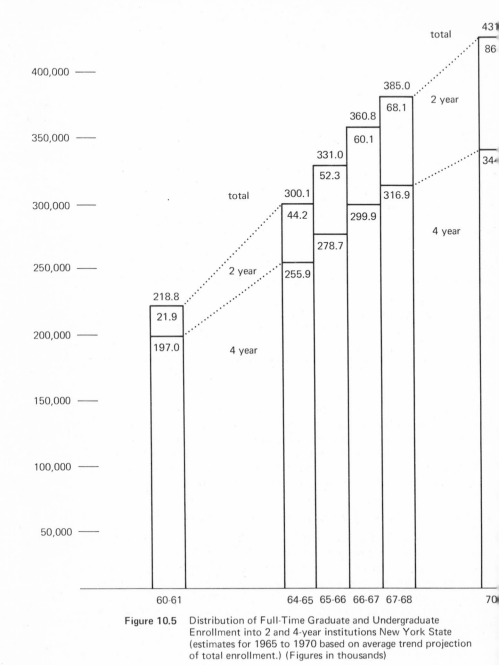

Figure 10.5   Distribution of Full-Time Graduate and Undergraduate
Enrollment into 2 and 4-year institutions New York State
(estimates for 1965 to 1970 based on average trend projection
of total enrollment.) (Figures in thousands)

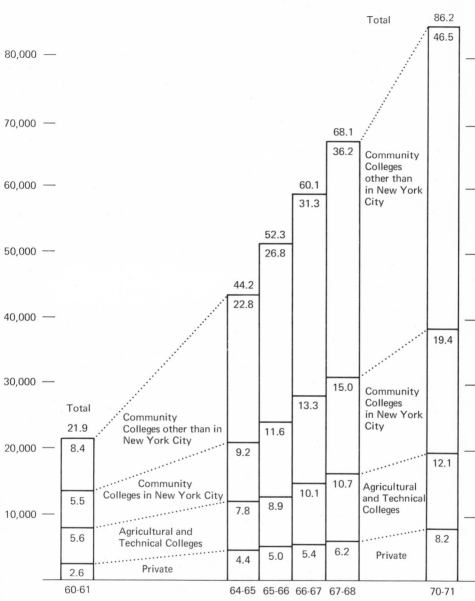

Figure 10.6   Distribution of Full-Time Undergraduate Enrollment in 2-year
Institutions, New York State (Estimates for 1965 to 1970
based on average trend projection of total enrollment.) (Figures
in thousands)

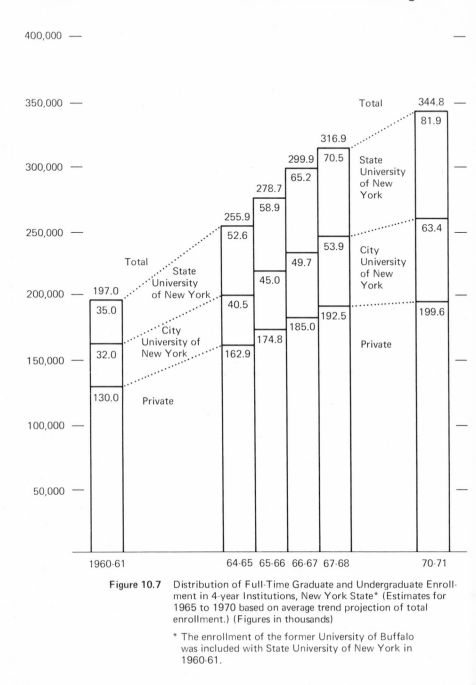

Figure 10.7   Distribution of Full-Time Graduate and Undergraduate Enrollment in 4-year Institutions, New York State* (Estimates for
1965 to 1970 based on average trend projection of total
enrollment.) (Figures in thousands)

* The enrollment of the former University of Buffalo
was included with State University of New York in
1960-61.

applying the resulting shares of full-time enrollment to the average trend projection of statewide enrollment discussed above.

The magnitude of the task just ahead and the increasing role expected of the two-year institutions are shown graphically in Figure 10.5. Total full-time enrollment will increase nearly 45 per cent between 1964 and 1970. That in two-year colleges will jump almost 100 per cent. Figure 10.6 graphically presents enrollment as it is likely to be distributed among different groups of two-year institutions, while Figure 10.7 shows how enrollment in four-year institutions is expected to be distributed among the privately controlled institutions, City University, and State University.

Some Regional Variations

New York State is a composite of social, economic, and geographic regions, each with a different pattern of likely future development. This fact was recently described in vivid fashion by the Governor's Regional Planning Commission.[31] Higher education in New York State must be prepared to cope with wide variations in the number of students residing in different regions, as well as with other differences among the regions. Variation is striking among the regions, for example, in the numbers of residents of the different regions who are attending college anywhere (in the State or outside); in this report the number of such students for a given region is called "enrollment originated." The New York Metropolitan Area, which was the residence of nearly 100,000 full-time undergraduate college students in 1963, is at the top of the list in student members, while the Northern Region, with fewer than 5,000 students residing in its boundaries, is at the bottom. As already stated, these students may seek college attendance at colleges within the region, in other regions within the State, or indeed, outside the State entirely. The amount of "enrollment originated" is important for evaluating regional needs for expansion in higher education in each region, and for recognizing the implications of differential rates of growth. Table 10.6 presents data for the twelve regions into which the State has been divided for higher education planning purposes, and makes clear the regional pattern of the demand for higher education as measured by the residence of the student.

Migration of students to attend college within the State and outside is very large. It reflects students' preferences for institutions, programs, and geographical locations, as well as relative costs of attendance, the pressure to gain acceptance at a particular institution, and institutional choices. The needs of individuals can be served most economically when students are not forced by program or space limitations to migrate across the State or across the nation to find an institution which can supply the education desired. More detailed discussion of the migration patterns of New York State college students will be presented in Part V (not included here—Eds.).

The salient points of the foregoing discussion of statistics on college

Table 10.6

Estimated Undergraduate Enrollment Originated in New York State by Economic Regions

Region	Estimated Enrollment			Increase	
	1962	1965	1970	1962–65	1965–70
Binghamton	5,325	6,406	7,851	1,081	1,445
Buffalo	21,934	25,756	34,603	3,822	8,847
Capital District	11,866	13,840	17,316	1,974	3,476
Elmira	5,513	6,434	8,028	921	1,594
Mid-Hudson	9,734	11,701	15,384	1,967	3,683
Mohawk Valley	5,915	7,115	8,854	1,200	1,739
New York Metropolitan	157,929	186,577	236,868	28,648	50,291
New York City	(99,842)	(112,859)	(133,654)	(13,017)	(20,795)
Long Island	(39,980)	(52,151)	(74,197)	(12,171)	(22,046)
Rockland-Westchester	(18,107)	(21,567)	(29,017)	(3,460)	(7,450)
Northern	4,836	5,613	7,016	777	1,403
Rochester	11,713	14,276	18,465	2,563	4,189
Syracuse	10,147	11,915	16,131	1,768	4,216
State Total	244,912	289,633	370,516	44,721	80,883

enrollment and college places in New York State can be summarized as follows. By 1970 it is expected that the number of college-age youth (18–21-year-olds) will total 1,200,000. In that year the number of high school graduates will almost be 250,000, or for four years aggregated, nearly 1,000,000. From this basic population group, it is estimated that there is a college-going potential of between 480,000 and 612,000 persons. Not all of these potential college students will enroll, however, unless there are changes in attitudes toward college attendance held by the general public, or more importantly, by certain sub-groups within the general society; in present practices in college admissions; and in character of programs of post-secondary school education available. At the same time, it should be observed that some persons beyond typical college age will enroll in college. Taking all this into account, it is estimated that by the end of the decade, between 431,000 and 445,000 full-time students will be in college. Thus the gap between potential and probable in 1970 will range between 49,000 and 181,000. Plans currently reported by private higher educational institutions, State University of New York (including the community colleges), and City University of New York, if implemented fully, indicate that places enough to accommodate the higher of the projected probable enrollments will be available in 1970. The approximate percentage of the total enrollments expected in 1970 is estimated for each major segment of higher education as follows: private colleges and universities, 48 per cent; State University of New York four-years units, 19 per cent; City University of New York four-year units, 15 per cent; and the public two-year colleges, 18 per cent. If this enrollment is reached, significant progress toward moving the probable toward the potential college enrollment will have been achieved.

2. NEEDS OF THE ECONOMY AND OF SOCIETY

There is another way to describe the needs for higher education. This is to point out the needs of the economy and society for trained manpower to fill its many jobs. In the broadest sense, the task of the educational institu-

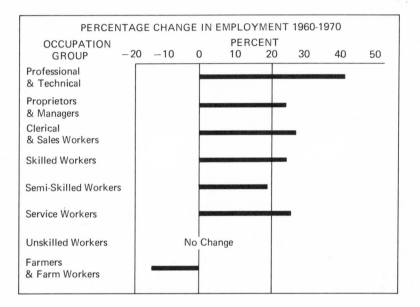

Average years of school completed
of those working in 1959

Occupation Group	Years
Professional & technical	16.2
Proprietors & managers	12.4
Clerical & sales	12.5
Skilled	11.0
Semi-skilled	9.9
Service	9.7
Unskilled	8.6
Farmers & farm workers	8.6

Source: U.S. Department of Labor

Figure 10.8   Growth of Occupational Groups, 1960-70, and Years of Education Completed.

tions will be to fit a growing and changing labor force into the growing and changing kinds of occupational positions. Beyond this, it is to identify and train leaders for society's future. This Plan is not the place, even if space permitted, to engage in a detailed analysis of the trends in the composition of the labor force and in manpower requirements which are placing new demands upon institutions of higher education. Analyses of this kind are well publicized in such reports as *Jobs 1960–70: The Changing Pattern*, published by the New York State Department of Labor, the various studies and reports of the U.S. Department of Labor, and special studies by interested groups.

The results of these various analyses are in general agreement and the trend can be summarized as follows: The kinds of occupations which will experience the most rapid expansion are those in the professional, higher level managerial and technical areas, and these in turn call most heavily on the institutions of education beyond the high school. Figure 10.8 shows graphically the future look for occupational change and the growing stress on manpower with advanced training. Also, at least for the remainder of this decade, the changes in the labor force will result in a relative scarcity of men and women in the prime working ages. The manpower development task of the educational institutions, therefore, will be to fill this gap by expanding their ability to prepare four groups of people to hold productive and responsible positions at higher levels in the job scale: the youth, the older worker, the non-white worker, and the woman who seeks a return to remunerative employment.

Specialized Manpower Needed

The most rapidly growing category of occupations is the technical and professional. Entry into these occupations places the greatest demand on college and university facilities. The preparation needed is specialized, complex, and frequently lengthy.

Most rapidly growing occupations will be in the areas of college faculty, engineering, physical and biological sciences, and interdisciplinary scientific positions. These occupations will also place the heaviest pressures on advanced training facilities for work at the doctoral level and beyond.

The health professions will experience nearly as large an expansion, and, if the best of available medical care is to be extended to a larger proportion of the growing and aging population, a much greater expansion will be needed.

The professional opportunities in law, accounting, library science, and social science will increase somewhat less rapidly than those listed above, but at a rate well above that of the general expansion of employment and, likewise, will require vigorously expanded undergraduate, graduate, and professional educational facilities.

Table 10.7 indicates the relationship between the estimated annual need of selected professional occupations and the number of first degrees awarded in 1962. Even if all recipients of first degrees in these selected fields enter employment in this State (an expectation that cannot realistically be held), they will by no means meet our needs. An expansion, in some cases reaching very high proportions, must be undertaken. The need for accountants and auditors, for example, is triple the number of degrees awarded.

Table 10.7

Estimated Annual Needs in Selected Professional Occupations and Degree Production in Related Academic Fields in New York State

Occupation	Estimated Annual Need	No. of 1st Degrees Awarded, 1962	Per Cent Increase Needed
Accountants & Auditors	4,900	1,651	197
Architects	270	146	85
Dietitians	350	19[a]	1,742
Engineers	8,650	3,010	187
Health Sciences			
Dentists	570	236	142
Nurses	4,900	3,482[b]	41
Pharmacists	540	455	19
Physicians	1,425	947	50
Lawyers	2,140	1,314	63
Librarians	561	325	73

[a] Refers to degrees in Food and Nutrition in Home Economics programs.
[b] Graduates of Diploma, Associate Degree and Baccalaureate Degree programs for the year ending June 30, 1962.

Table 10.8

Employment in Technical Occupations New York State, 1962

Occupation	Number	Per Cent
Draftsmen	20,972	14.1
Structural Design Technicians	2,516	1.7
Electronic or Electrical Engineering Technicians	19,585	13.2
Mechanical or Electro-Mechanical Technicians	22,446	15.1
Mathematics Technicians	831	0.6
Physical Science Technicians	8,969	6.0
Biological, Medical, Dental, and Related Science Technicians	25,445	17.1
Industrial Engineering Technicians	6,901	4.7
Civil Engineering and Construction Technicians and Specialists	13,464	9.1
Sales and Service Technicians	1,932	1.3
Technical Writing and Illustration Specialists	3,034	2.0
Safety and Sanitation Inspectors and Related Specialists	4,084	2.7
Product Testing and Inspection Specialists	8,059	5.4
Data Processing Systems Analysis and Programming Specialists	6,153	4.1
Airway Tower Specialists and Flight Dispatchers	1,373	0.9
Broadcasting, Motion Picture and Recording Studio Specialists	2,920	2.0
	148,684	100.2

Source: Forthcoming publication of New York State Department of Labor, *Technical Manpower in New York State*, Vol. 1, Chapter II, Table D.

The technical or semiprofessional occupations also will be expanding at very high but not uniform rates. It is difficult to draw a clear line of distinction between these occupations and those of the engineer or scientist at one extreme, and the semiskilled or craft occupations, at the other. These occupations are closely related to the engineering and scientific occupations, since the technicians both assist and, in some cases, replace higher-level technical employees. However, under careful and rigid definitions recent studies indicate that nearly 150,000 people are employed in technical occupations in New York State. Recent evidence indicates that employers were actively seeking to recruit nearly 5,000 technical and semiprofessional workers, which is a measure of the presently unfilled need.[32] This demand will further increase with the overall expansion of technical and professional employment in the State. Table 10.8 indicates some of the areas of high-level employment.

College Faculty—A Special Case

Faculty is the key to quality as well as quantity of opportunity in higher education. Colleges and universities in New York State historically have been able to attract able and dedicated teachers, scholars, and researchers. That they will continue to be able to do this depends much on the steps taken now with an eye to the future needs of the State.

That the need for more college faculty is outstripping the supply is generally recognized as a nationwide problem.[33] Concern about a concomitant decline in quality of faculties has increased in recent years. More and more, colleges and universities are having to hire persons with lower qualifications for academic work. The National Education Association's latest nationwide study of this matter found, for example, that whereas in 1953–54 some 31 per cent of new college teachers in institutions with programs of four years or more had earned doctor's degrees, the proportion had decreased in recent years to approximately 25 per cent; the percentage of new teachers having no formal education beyond the master's degree, on the other hand, has jumped from 32 per cent in 1953–54 to 40 per cent in 1961–63.

Comparisons of faculty in New York State colleges and universities with those of institutions included in the National Education Association nationwide study were made possible by cooperation of the national association. The eighty-five New York State institutions participating in the nationwide study indicated that colleges in this State, in comparison to like colleges nationwide, have been generally successful in recruiting competent and qualified staff through the fall of 1962 (the latest year of available statistical data for this comparison). In the fall of 1962, approximately 57 per cent of the faculty in private four-year colleges in New York State had the doctorate as the highest earned degree, 62 per cent of those in City University of New York four-year units, 50 per cent in State Uni-

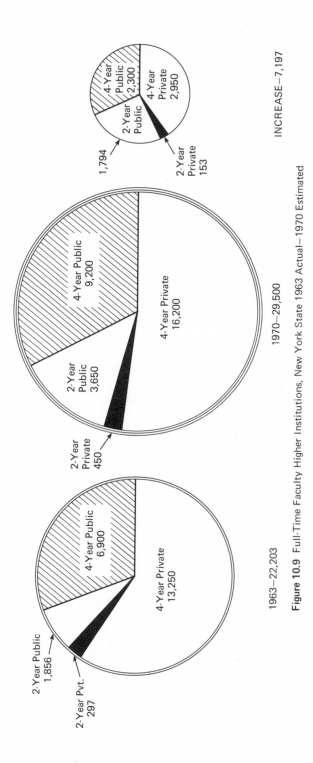

1963—22,203

2-Year Public
1,856

2-Year Pvt.
297

4-Year Public
6,900

4-Year Private
13,250

2-Year
Private
450

2-Year
Public
3,650

4-Year Public
9,200

4-Year Private
16,200

1970—29,500

1,794

2-Year
Public

4-Year
Public
2,300

4-Year
Private
2,950

2-Year
Private
153

INCREASE—7,197

Figure 10.9 Full-Time Faculty Higher Institutions, New York State 1963 Actual—1970 Estimated

versity of New York four-year units outside of the contract colleges, 14 per cent of the private two-year colleges, and 12 per cent of those under public auspices. These statistics compare quite favorably with national statistics for similar categories of institutions.

Examination of some trends in recruitment of *new faculty* in New York State institutions in comparison again with like institutions in the nation-wide study brings out some warning signals. The private universities, for example, in 1961–62 and 1962–63 employed a smaller percentage of new faculty with earned doctorates than their counterparts on the national scene. Consequently they employed proportionately more persons whose highest earned degree was the master's. The four-year units of State University of New York also followed this pattern with even larger differences seen between these colleges and state colleges in the nationwide study.

A comparison of New York State's recruitment of faculty in various subject matter fields and the national pattern shows the task ahead. Out of a total of 23 groupings of academic fields, the ten demanding the greatest numbers of new faculty by 1970 will be the biological sciences, business and commerce, education, engineering, English, fine arts, foreign language, mathematics, physical sciences, and the social sciences. This does not mean that these are all areas of present or projected shortage. It does indicate, however, that graduate education should give additional emphasis to these areas if faculty supply is to maintain or improve present levels of professional competence. Critical fields of shortage, both for the nation and for colleges in New York State, exist in the biological sciences, English, foreign languages, mathematics, physical sciences, and some fields in the social sciences, such as economics and sociology.

Within the group of community colleges and technical institutes a special area of critical shortage exists: instructors in fields which train technicians and semi-professional personnel. The public two-year institutions are recognized as the chief source of supply for these kinds of workers, but the sources of supply of instructional personnel to staff the programs are woefully few and weak.

The big push for new faculty members in New York State colleges and universities is just ahead. It will occur in the period of 1964–68 during which the large jumps in enrollment already reported will occur. The dimensions of the increase expected between 1963 and 1970 are shown in Figure 10.9. By the end of the decade, the State will need almost a third more full-time faculty in its higher educational institutions than it had in 1962.

Full Use of Human Resources

No examination of the needs of the economy and of society would be complete without reference to potential waste of human resources through lack of training for special segments of our population.

The U.S. Department of Labor estimates that between 1960 and 1970 women in the labor force will increase at a rate almost double the rate for men. Many of these potential workers will be women returning to the labor market after careers as homemakers. In these cases the training and experience of ten to twenty years before will need marked updating, perhaps on a part-time basis, so that the skills can be put to current use.

A more basic need is to prepare the coed of today so that fifteen or twenty years hence she will be able to return effectively to the labor market with a minimum of additional training. For these, no less than for the "career" woman, the need is to plan in college for a career rather than a job, to maintain high-level academic performance, and to continue into specialized training at the graduate level whenever possible.

The greatest waste of human resources in society today occurs in the non-white, minority, and culturally deprived groups, for whom education represents almost the only peaceful means of breaking out of the deprivation in which they live. The New York State Department of Labor has estimated that by 1970, nonwhites will constitute 12 per cent of the labor force of the State, as compared to 10 per cent in 1960. Recognition and development of the abilities available in the nonwhite and other minority groups to fill the kinds of positions most needed in our economy is a task and a challenge to all the people of the State. Leaders in higher education have a particular responsibility here. Although the State as a whole is concerned, the most acute need for action is local and regional, necessarily centering in the large cities. The problem in the elementary and secondary schools has been placed dramatically before us in recent years, but it is no less important for technical, general, and professional programs beyond the high school.

Maintenance of Skills and Abilities

Education is now a continuing task for most people. Today's most effective undergraduate, graduate, and professional education programs prepare the student to prepare himself. Educational institutions must, therefore, be alert to assist in the continuing self-education needed by individuals in a dynamic society. The needs of unemployed workers already "automated" out of their positions have to be met as well as the needs of a host of additional workers whose present type of employment will eventually disappear. Today's professional, technical, and managerial personnel face particularly acute requirements in this area of continuing education because new knowledge and new techniques are emerging at a rapid pace in every field. The need for conferences, institutes, workshops, independent study with guidance, and regular classwork for credit or without credit, will bulk large in the years ahead if our colleges and our universities are to discharge their obligations to individuals and to society.

3. CONCLUSION

To provide the quality and quantity of higher education which the citizens expect and society requires will tax both the private and public facilities now in existence and planned to 1970. All types of postsecondary institutions and most types of programs will be under continuous pressure to accommodate the numbers of youth arising from the post-World War II population increase. Adding to the demand will be the growing proportion of the population, youths and adults, seeking further education both as an end in itself and as a means for achieving or holding a position in a competitive society.

By 1970, it is expected that full-time enrollment will reach 431,000, which is an increase of nearly 100 per cent over 1960 and more than 40 per cent over 1964. The rise of part-time enrollment is expected to be almost as great, so that by 1970, New York State colleges will be expected to accommodate about 800,000 full- and part-time students. Full-time undergraduate enrollment, high as it promises to be, still will not include about 20 per cent of the persons who could complete a college program. A continuation of recent trends will not bring a closing of the gap between estimated full-time undergraduate enrollment and a conservative estimate of college potential until late in the 1970s.

The importance of graduate education, including doctoral and postdoctoral study, will continue to be critical. Graduate education not only supplies the high-level technical and professional personnel increasingly in demand by business, industry, and government, but also supplies the faculty in all fields of the arts, sciences, and humanities required to maintain, expand, and improve all of education.

SURVEY OF THE HIGH AND MIDDLE LEVEL MANPOWER REQUIREMENTS AND RESOURCES

UNITED REPUBLIC OF TANZANIA

I. TANZANIA'S MANPOWER POLICIES AND GOALS

It is (and has been since 1963) the policy of the Government of The United Republic of Tanzania:

a. To achieve essentially full self-sufficiency at all skill levels in the economy by 1980.

b. To give every Tanzanian child a basic (Primary) education as soon as the financial resources of Government permit, which is presently planned to be achieved by 1989.

From The United Republic of Tanzania, "Survey of the High and Middle Level Manpower Requirements and Resources," Volume IV of *Tanzania Second Five-Year Plan for Economic and Social Development 1st July, 1969–30th June, 1974* (Dar es Salaam: Government Printer, 1969).

c. To provide additional or further education (Secondary, Technical, University), *only* to the extent justified by the manpower requirements of the economy for development; further, to support students by bursaries only in post-Secondary courses which will produce the specific skills needed for development (almost all post-Primary students are financed by Government bursaries). This policy implies no disapproval of post-Primary education as a consumer good. It is simply based on a lack of resources and the existence of a large number of essential, urgent and competing demands for the very limited funds which are available.

In order to estimate the manpower requirements of the economy as a guide to Government investment in post-Primary educational and training institutions, a survey of middle and high level manpower requirements is carried out for each five year economic and social development plan period and it reflects the supply of skills needed to carry out the Plan as well as progress on the 1980 manpower self-sufficiency target. This is the second such manpower survey since Tanzania has undertaken formal economic development planning in 1963. The first survey, completed in 1964,[34] covered the five years of the First Plan (1964/65–1968/69), and this survey covers the second five years (1969/70–1973/74).

Based on the 1964–65 manpower survey, extrapolations were made estimating the total requirements for middle/high level manpower (jobs requiring a base of Secondary education or higher) all the way to 1980. This was essential because of the long lead-times and the tight interlocking relationship between Forms 1–4, 5 and 6 and the University which is inherent in the process of educational and training planning. Occupations requiring a University education (Category A) were extended to 1980 on a specific occupational basis (*e.g.*, physicians, engineers, agronomists, etc.). Sub-professional (Category B) and Category C occupations, direct employment of secondary school leavers, were estimated only by broad category. Plans for investment in educational and training institutions were made accordingly.

This second manpower survey, in addition to providing specific occupational requirements for all middle/high level skills for the next five years, has also made it possible to modify where necessary the 1980 manpower requirement targets—previously extrapolated from the 1964/65 survey. These modifications are discussed in Section V at the end of this survey report. (They are not major changes.)

II. EMPLOYMENT AND OCCUPATIONAL COVERAGE OF THE SURVEY

The Manpower Survey included 235 private and parastatal enterprises plus central and local Government. For the most part only employers of 100 or more workers were included (*no* establishment over 100 was omitted). However, exceptions were made in smaller firms offering specialized services such as chartered accountants, engineering advisory services, firms of architects, etc., because of the high concentration of scarce skills in them. While employment in the establishments surveyed is 73.8 per cent of all non-agricultural wage/salary employment in Tanzania the proportion of the nation's middle/high level manpower in the covered establishments is much higher than 73.8 per cent owing to the heavy concentration of such skills in Government, parastatals, large private firms, and the East African Community services, which were also included.[35]

Table 10.9

Occupational Sector and Employment Coverage of the 1968 Manpower Survey

Occupational Sector	Estimated Total Wage/ Salary Employment Base Year 1968/1969	Employment in Establishments Surveyed	Per Cent Surveyed of Total
Mining and Quarrying	6,000	4,464	75.0
Manufacturing	36,000	24,276	67.5
Construction	49,000	39,906	81.6
Utilities	10,000	10,000	79.0
Commerce	25,000	6,143	25.0
Transport/Communications	32,000	24,785	77.5
Services—Non-Government	28,000	13,020	46.4
Government[a]	64,000	64,000	100.0
Total	250,000	184,494	73.8

[a] The industrial activities of Government (*e.g.*, construction, etc.), are included in the appropriate industry sectors above. This figure represents residual Government employment, primarily basic administration. This method differs from the one used in the 1964 manpower survey where *all* Government employment was included in just one figure.

All of the surveyed establishments were visited by trained interviewers (university graduates with a minimum of three years work experience) from the staff of the Manpower Planning Division of the Ministry of Economic Affairs and Development Planning. Occupational terminology was reasonably well standardized by use of the International Labor Orginization's International Standard Classification of Occupations.

At first glance is may seem odd to omit most of the agricultural sector from the survey in a country where about 95 per cent of the population lives and works in the land. There are several good reasons for this which warrant some explanation. The great majority (95 per cent) of the peasant population are primarily self-employed subsistence farmers who raise a limited amount of cash crops also. On the average their productivity is not high and a majority are illiterate. Almost all individuals working in the agricultural sector who have the middle/high level educational base and skills to which this survey is directed are employed by establishments visited by the survey interviewers. All agricultural and veterinary extension workers are included, all agronomists, agricultural research scientists and silviculturists; salesmen of fertilizer and farm equipment companies; all middle and higher level skills in all Co-operatives (Primary Societies, Unions and the Central Organization) are in the survey including qualified cotton gin repair mechanics, and clerks and credit officers; all skilled manual workers from the Ministry of Lands, Settlements, and Water Development and the Ministry of Communications and Works who work in rural as well as urban areas; all primary school teachers, etc. The few large (non-sisal) plantations with industrial adjuncts (e.g., sugar mills) have been included, and also all dairies and state farms. Sisal plantations were covered only partly through the Tanzania Sisal Corporation. The coverage that was made suggested that not a great number of middle/high level manpower was omitted because of the limited sisal coverage.

Other than this the only parts of the agricultural sector not covered by the interviewers were the peasant smallholders themselves and the not-too-numerous large farms owned by self-employed farmers who employ a limited number of agricultural laborers.

The fact that the manpower survey does not attempt to enumerate the estimated 2.5 million peasant farmers does not indicate a lack of Government interest and concern with the improvement of their income and the quality of their lives. Quite the contrary. This has the top, number one priority in Tanzania's development plans. A vast expansion in agricultural extension workers is planned which will provide one "teacher-in-the-fields" to every 500 farm families by 1979. The present ratio is 1:5,000. Credit facilities will be greatly expanded; a net-work of consolidated rural training centres will be established; universal primary education will be achieved by 1989 with major changes in the nature of primary education to make it heavily oriented to rural life, in accordance with the policy of Education for Self-Reliance.[36] The nation-wide net-work of cooperatives is being strengthened and expanded. The second development plan provides for substantial expansion of farm-to-market roads, irrigation schemes, expanded rural health facilities, etc. All of these have their impact on middle/high level manpower requirements and are reflected in the Manpower Survey as noted previously.

The occupational coverage of the Manpower Survey is as follows:

    a. Top level posts in administration and management including senior officers, heads of principal departments and key staff specialists such as qualified accountants, personnel directors et al., and who normally, for the successful performance of their duty, are equipped with a twelve-year education or better plus a minimum of five years of progressively difficult assignments (and a proportion of whom require university level preparation).

b. Professional occupations such as those which often require degrees and certificates or licences to practice (doctors, lawyers, engineers *et al.*), and a minimum of five or more years of eduation/training above Form 4 specifically for the occupation held.

c. Technical occupations which are filled by sub-professional workers who work in direct support of and under the immediate supervision of professional persons. They usually require three years of progressive supervised training (post-secondary) in the given technical field or a combination of formal training in a technical college plus supervised experience (*e.g.*, engineering technicians, draughtsmen, laboratory technicians, etc.)

d. Highly skilled manual occupations, which are those in which incumbents must have had two to three years or more of combined training and experience in the specific duties of the job held. (The survey concentrated principally on the so-called "modern crafts" which involve metal working, precision measurements, electricity and electrical machinery, and require a much more substantial educational base than many of the traditional craft occupations such as shoemaker, tailor, stone mason, tile setter, painter, etc.)

e. Skilled office and clerical occupations which are those in which incumbents usually require a Form 4 education as a foundation plus at least six months of supervised training in a specific office skill, *e.g.*, personal secretaries, stenographers, speed typists, bookkeepers, cashiers, bank tellers, office machine operators (bookkeeping machines, calculators, tabulating machines, keypunch operators), switchboard operators, statistical clerks, cost clerks, payroll clerks and other specialized clerks.

To facilitate the planning of education and training institutions, demand and supply information on all of the occupations in the 1968/69 Manpower Survey were grouped into three broad categories (see Tables 10.13–10.15).

Category A—Jobs normally requiring a University degree.

Category B—Jobs which normally require from one to three years formal post-secondary (Form 4) education/training.

Category C—Jobs which normally require a secondary school education for standard performance of the full array of tasks involved in the occupation. This category includes the skilled office workers and the skilled manual workers in the "modern crafts."

(*A Category D* has been included to round out the picture of the skilled manual workers. These require a fairly high degree of manual skill, but do not require the more extensive educational base called for by the "modern crafts." They have not therefore been shown as a charge against secondary school outputs.)

III. METHODS FOR MAKING ESTIMATES OF FUTURE MANPOWER REQUIREMENTS

(a) General

Basically this type of manpower survey is a census of the (wage) employed skilled labor force taken at the place of employment instead of at the household as in a population census. Since, in a developing country high/middle level manpower is in short supply persons possessing these skills generally are fully employed. Therefore an establishment survey of this kind (conducted solely by personal interviews by trained personnel with top management) provides a fairly accurate picture of the stock of high/middle level manpower currently in the country. With this as a base it is possible to make reasonably sound estimates of future requirements. This is particularly true of the newly independent countries of Africa where it is possible to identify the expatriates or non-citizens who typically occupy the preponderance of high/middle level manpower posts at the time of independence. In fact the replacement of these with citizens within the first 15 to 20 years (or less if possible) after independence represents a major element of the total future manpower requirements. This element (localization) and the other elements making up the estimates of future manpower requirements are described below.

(b) Requirements for Replacement of Wastage and Localization

(1) *Localization Target.* Government's goal is to be essentially self-sufficient at all skill levels by 1980. The First Five-Year Plan period (1964/65–1968/69) was predominantly a period of institution building. Only toward the end of the period did outputs begin to take on substantial dimensions. This process of institution building will still go on at a reduced rate in the Second Plan period (a new Faculty of Agriculture at Morogoro for the University of Tanzania, a new Agricultural Diploma School in western Tanzania, etc.), but the base built in Plan One will make it possible to produce far greater numbers in Plan Two than in the Plan One period, and by the end of Plan Three (1979/80) the cumulative outputs should assure achievement of the self-sufficiency targets *providing* one serious flaw or weakness in Forms 5–6 education can be rectified. (See Footnote 39, Section IV.)

There are two five-year periods before the 1980 target. It is estimated there will be sufficient output in Plan Two to cover a number equivalent to 40 per cent of the existing stock of non-citizens now employed (with the two exceptions noted in Section V(c)). Thus in estimating total manpower requirements in the survey we have included a figure equal to 40 per cent of the existing non-citizen stock of expatriates (see column 8 in Tables 10.13, 10.14, and 10.15—Categories A, B, and C). During Plan Three with the slightly larger outputs which will come into being, a number equivalent to 60 per cent of the remaining 1968/69 stock of expatriates should be trained.

It would probably be useful here to point out that the manpower self-sufficiency goal means that for all practical purposes Tanzania will have trained by 1980 the required *number* of Tanzanians with the necessary educational base equal to the number of every middle/high level post in the country. There will of necessity be something of an overlap into the early 1980s since the young people emerging from the universities in the last several years of Plan Three will need to acquire some practical experience before taking over full command of the posts for which they were educated or trained. For example, the engineers coming out of university in 1979 will not be professionally qualified before their two years of "pupilage" are completed in 1981. A graduate in business administration in 1980 will not be in a position to take over the managership of a large industrial enterprise prior to gaining experience and knowledge of the operation.

Nevertheless this period of overlap for the graduates, in 1978, 1979 and 1980 is expected to be much shorter than is the normal situation in economically developed countries. In such countries young men often take 20 to 25 years to reach top posts. Much of that time, however, is not required to learn the job, but is mainly waiting for the incumbents ahead to die or retire. This will not be the case here, since replacement can be effected as soon as the trainee is ready.

(2) *Replacement of Citizen Wastage: (Citizens leaving the Labor Market for reasons of death and retirement).* Reliable data on mortality and rates of withdrawal from the labor market because of retirement is quite hard to come by in most African countries. By dint of considerable research Mr. George Tobias who made the first manpower survey here in 1962 (before Tanzania began development planning) derived an estimated rate of 4 per cent per year for the whole African population.[37]

Because of the work pressures of the preparation of the First Plan and the parallel manpower survey of 1964, the Manpower Planning Division used this same 4 per cent annual rate, or 20 per cent for the five First Plan years.

Time has permitted more opportunity to look into the problem in respect of this 1968/69 Manpower Survey. Considerable research has been undertaken in Government records and in those of a few parastatal enterprises as well as the Ministry of Health and Social Welfare. From this, two conclusions have emerged:

    i. The 4 per cent annual rate is still probably approximately correct for Tanzania's *population as a whole*.

    ii. The rate for the small (46,000 out of 12.6 million people) highly select group covered by this middle/high level manpower survey is far lower than that of the total population.

Insofar as the death rate is concerned these persons by and large live in environments roughly comparable to their counterparts in developed countries and have comparable death rates. They are relatively well paid; they can afford adequate and proper nutrition, they mainly live and work in urban areas with proper housing, sanitary facilities, clean water and adequate medical services available. Thus, their mortality rate can be expected, age group for age group, to be dramatically lower than that of the average subsistence peasant whose diet is often defective, housing poor, water polluted, and who is subject to infestation by parasites, malaria and other life-shortening and debilitating diseases. He typically does not have adequate medical services available for either preventative or curative purposes (one doctor to 50,000 population).

As indicated above, given a living environment comparable to those of developed countries, the middle/high level manpower cadre appears to have somewhat the same death rate at comparable age levels. The Tanzanian incumbents in the select categories of occupations covered by the Manpower Survey are predominantly quite young. Almost all are fairly recent entries to these posts, which prior to independence were largely held by non-citizens. Few Tanzanian Africans were able to obtain the secondary education base which these occupations normally require, so these jobs are mainly filled by Tanzanians who came out of school in 1961 or thereafter. Because of their relative youth, this manpower cadre has practically no losses from death. Similarly, very few of them can be expected to retire from the labor market for the next 20 years (not very many are over the 30–35 age bracket).

Based on Government and parastatal personnel records mentioned earlier, it would appear that over the past five years the death rate of individuals in the category of jobs covered by this survey has been only .5385 per cent for the total 5 years. The 5 years consolidated retirement rate was only 1.29 per cent making a combined loss rate from death/retirement for the five years of 1.8285 per cent.

This rate was used in this survey. The rate was not applied to individual occupations since the requirement so derived would have been fractional in the majority of occupations. For categories B and C it was applied to the total column 10 figure and added to it. The number derived for category A was too small to be significant.

(c) Requirements to Meet Net-Increase-in-Posts during the Second Plan

(1) *Government.* Circumstances make it possible to obtain more reliable estimates as to future increases in manpower requirements from Government than for the enterprise sector. This is especially true where the Manpower

Survey is undertaken as an integral part of a development plan as this one was.

Ministries of Government worked closely and intensively with the Ministry of Economic Affairs and Development Planning for the best part of a year during 1968/69. At the time estimated manpower requirements for net-increase-in-posts were obtained for this survey from the senior officers of the several ministries, each ministry knew approximately what its responsibilities, new projects, capital and recurrent funds were likely to be during the Second Plan (the draft plan had been approved in principle by the Cabinet). Under these circumstances it is not too difficult for knowledgeable senior officers to make fairly sound estimates of the net increase in the posts or occupations which will be required.

(2) *Enterprise Sector.* This sector includes both parastatals and private enterprises. Estimating for the net-increase-in-posts portion of total requirements in this sector is much more difficult and much less reliable than in Government. Individual enterprises are sensitive both to market forces and competition which managers find most difficult to anticipate at all, or to anticipate with any degree of accuracy. So we did not ask the managers of existing establishments for their estimates (and of course there are no managers at all to ask in respect of new enterprises coming into existence in the future). The method adopted proceeded in two stages. The first involved making an estimate of the increase to 1973/74 in total employment in each of the broad industrial divisions covered in the Manpower Survey (see Table 10.9). A factor of the current amount of GDP[38] per employed worker was computed for each industry division, applied to the increased target levels of GDP contained in the Plan for 1974 to produce a future gross employment total for each industry division. An estimated factor per year increase in productivity, compounded, was applied by sector to these gross employment increases. The modified figure in each case represented the total employment level estimated for the industry division in 1973/74, in the fifth year of Plan Two.

The second stage involved the construction of an occupational matrix (*i.e.,* the occupational composition pattern) for each broad industry division as it existed in 1968/69—the base year. The matrix involved computing the per cent of total employment represented by each high level occupation in the industry. For example, in "Manufacturing and Processing," Division 2–3:

Table 10.10

	Total Employment 1968/69	Per Cent of Total Employment in the Industry
Mechanical Engineers	60	0.18%
Motor Vehicle Repairmen	603	1.80

These percentages were then applied to the new employment totals for the same industry division as estimated for 1973/74. The difference between the 1968/69 employment in the occupation and the 1973/74 estimated employment in the same occupation was used for the "net increase" portion of the total requirements figure. (If it had been feasible it would have been much better to apply this approach to the "major groups," *i.e.*, narrower breakdowns within the eight divisions of the U.N.'s Standard Classification of Industrial Activities. Unfortunately in Tanzania's present stage of development there are many major groups within the divisions in which there are no establishments at all and many others with only one or two (for example, there is only one tobacco factory, one plastics factory, two meat packing factories, etc.).

This method used for making the estimates of the "net increase" part of the total requirements in the enterprise sector has two weaknesses. First, reliable productivity figures are difficult to obtain. The ones used in this survey are much better than in 1964 when no data at all was available.

Table 10.11

Estimated Employment Increases—Second Plan to 1973/74—Based on GDP Targets

Industry Sector	GDP 1968/69 Base Year (Shs. Million)	Estimated Employ-ment 1968/69[a]	GDP 1973/74 Second Plan Targets (Shs. Million)	Annual Rate of GDP Increase Per Cent	Estimated Employ-ment 1973/74[b]	Estimated Annual Increase in Produc-tivity[c]
Agriculture	1,480	[d]	2,085	7.1	—	—
Mining/Quarrying	155	6,000	122	3.0	6,000	(−)5.0
Manufacturing	384	36,000	707	13.0	57,000	3.0
Construction	278	49,000	512	13.0	71,000	2.0
Utilities	62	10,000	109	12.0	18,000	0.0
Commerce	830	25,000	1,220	8.0	37,000	0.0
Transport/Communications	316	32,000	486	9.0	42,000	2.6
Services—Non-Government	218	28,000	268.9	4.0	36,000	—
Government[b]	500	64,000	606.1	4.0	81,000	—
Total	4,223	250,000	6,116	—	348,000	—

[a] The 1968/69 employment is estimated from the Central Statistical Bureau's Annual Enumeration of Employment trends over the past several years.

[b] The industrial activities of Government (*e.g.*, Construction, etc.) are included in the appropriate sectors above. This figure represents the residual, and is primarily basic administration and security.

[c] The 1973/74 employment projections for the various industrial sectors (except Government and Services) have been modified by the application of estimated annual increases in productivity. These were derived from Tanzania's experience in the first four years of the First Five-Year Plan. No productivity rate was estimated for Government or Services for technical reasons. GDP for Government and Services is primarily the wage bill and is not, as in the other sectors, an evaluation, in money, of physical outputs or services rendered.

[d] There is no total of agricultural workers available in Tanzania, but only on agricultural *wage* employees (109,700). Since most of the GDP is produced by self-employed farmers no purpose would be served in attempting to corrolate the GDP by *all* farmers with the tiny number of agricultural wage employees.

Limited data was available this time. The creation of the National Institute for Productivity has stimulated interest in information of this kind. The other weakness involves the assumption that the occupational pattern existing in the broad industry divisions will not change so much by 1974 as to invalidate the "net increase" portions of the estimated total requirements for each occupation. Unfortunately information is not at hand to gauge with any degree of accuracy the extent of the shifts which may take place in the "major group" mix within the several industry divisions. This is primarily a problem in the Manufacturing Division and is not too serious a problem in Construction, Mining, Commerce, Transport, or Utilities.

With full awareness of the two main weaknesses the method was adopted as being the best available at the time the Manpower Survey was made.

(d) Requirements for Filling Vacancies Carried into the Second Plan

Vacancies identified in the course of the Survey are considered as un-met requirements and are carried forward as an element of total manpower requirements for the Second Plan. Considerable care is taken at the time of the employer interview to make sure vacancies cited really are valid current requirements for which the employer is actively recruiting.

IV. ESTIMATES OF SUPPLY

Under Tanzania's Manpower Policy the supply of high/middle level manpower (secondary and post-secondary education/training) is determined by the requirements for such skills in the economy. Assuming that the planned plant expansions at all secondary and post-secondary levels are carried out, and the necessary Science/Arts mix is achieved,[39] Tanzania's supply of middle/high level manpower will be sufficient by 1980 to achieve the goal of self-sufficiency at all skill levels. For the Second Five-Year Plan, which covers the first five of the 10 years to 1979/80, there will be shortfalls. These will almost all be in Category A and B occupations. There are a number of institutions to be built in Plan Two which will only come on-stream in the last year or two of the Second Plan, and will not be sufficient to meet a full one-half of such ten year targets as Agriculture's for certificated and diploma extension workers. In this case, the Second Plan shortfall will be made up in the Third Plan period (*e.g.*, by the new diploma school probably near Mbeya and several new schools for certificated extension workers). The same is true in respect of the planned expansion in 1971 of the Faculty of Medicine of the University of Tanzania, by raising their intake from 25 per year to between 100 and 130. There are a number of other similar cases.

The estimates of supply made in the various tables below also assume continuation of offering bursaries to the University of East Africa and elsewhere only where they will meet the particular skills required, and similar continuation of acceptance of donor scholarships only when they meet known skill needs. Continuation of the practice of "tying" bursary recipients is also assumed. It also assumes that the Ministry of National Education will either substantially improve the H.S.C. (Science) pass rate or increase Form 5–6 enrolments to yield the required number of qualifiers.

There is a special problem in respect of estimating supply outputs in most of the jobs in Category C, in contrast with the occupations in Categories A and B. Categories A and B jobs require a very substantial amount of formal education and/or training. Because it is formal and largely institutional the source, volume and timing of the supply are relatively easy to identify.

In Category C on the other hand the great majority of individuals master these skills by wholly informal means and do not undergo formal courses or pass through formal in-plant training schemes. This is true even in those craft occupations which have for generations been termed "apprenticeable." It is even more true in most of the new "industrial" skilled manual occupations which have emerged after the Industrial Revolution. These latter skills cannot normally be gained away from or outside the employing establishment because of the nature of the operation, or the special machinery and equipment involved, or the working environment itself. Examples of these are Rolling Mill Operators, Metal Furnacemen (Blast Furnace, Open Hearths *et al.*), Railway Engine Drivers, Linemen, Petroleum Stillmen, Alumina Plant operators, large scale excavating shovel and dragline operators, Rotary Pressmen, loom fixers, *et al.*

In other instances skills are acquired by means of a promotion ladder, where the individual masters a series of increasingly difficult posts prior to entering the final post. This is characteristic of Managers, "Inspectors and Supervisors, Transport," Traffic Controllers and Dispatchers, and many others.

The majority of training and skill acquisition occurs on-the-job and by informal means (which usually involves some instruction from a supervisor, watching coworkers, and obtaining help and advice from other workers in the occupation). However, such individuals normally enter the field equipped with all or a good part of a secondary school education.

There is no known technique for measuring the number of individuals who acquire competence in a Category C occupation each year through wholly informal means. Nevertheless it is certain that most of the demand is met in this way. It may be argued that the demand would be better met if more formal training means were employed, but this has never been conclusively established for most of the occupations in Category C.

By and large employers tend to do whatever they have to do in building up or attracting a skilled labor supply. They must in order to stay in business. The methods they pursue and the motivations they employ are both numerous and varied, but in one way or other they generally succeed in developing or attracting the skills they need. (As the supply of secondary school output available to employers for Category C occupations increases, the process of imparting specific job skills to such individuals will make the informal process both easier and more effective.)

Because of the dominating characteristic of informal skill acquisition in Category C jobs, no attempt was made to estimate a shortfall in Table 10.15, Column 12. Entries which are found in the "Supply" (Column no. 11) represent only the output of specific formal in-plant training schemes or apprenticeships identified in the course of the Survey and are of interest primarily in indicating the amount of such formal training which exists in the country in respect of the several occupations. As may be seen, it is quite small. As the newly inaugurated National Industrial and Apprenticeship Training Scheme (1968/69) becomes fully operative better data and increased identifiable supply should result.

It would be a mistake, however, to conclude that a small supply figure, or none at all in Table 10.15, Column 11, means that the requirements will not be met. There is every reason to believe that in one way or another, mainly through informal means, enough of the requirement will be met to enable the employing establishments to carry on. This currently is the situation insofar as the majority of employers is concerned and has been for some time. From questions asked in the course of the survey it would appear that many, if not a majority of employers (Government as well as private) have in the past been content with matters as they are and with the products of the existing system (or lack of one). There is, however, considerable evidence that a large body of employers who take this view have been in the past enabled to get by, and maintain their outputs of goods and services because of the presence of a "skeleton" supporting structure of highly skilled, well trained non-citizen supervisors, foremen or lead-men.

This situation has been changing rather substantially since Government issued its Policy on Employment of Non-Citizens in Tanzania[40] in mid-1966 and will change even more sharply during Plan Two. The employer is now required as a condition of the work or entry permit to satisfy the Labor Division (Ministry of Communication and Works) officials that he is training a Tanzanian (or seeking a qualified Tanzanian trainee) who will replace the non-citizen within a specified period, depending on the occupation involved. It is becoming evident that quite a few larger employers now look to this source of supply (Secondary leavers) to meet their training needs in the "modern crafts." Individuals having substantially less education find it difficult to cope with the complexity of these "modern" skills involving as they do the use of maths, reading of blue-prints, precision measurement, electrical theory, operating complex machinery and instruments, and maintenance of shop, cost and often inventory records. This trend is expected to accelerate during the Second Plan and provision is made for it in making the Category C requirements a charge against secondary school outputs.

V. GENERAL APPRAISAL OF THE DEMAND—SUPPLY OUTLOOK FOR THE SECOND PLAN

(a) Secondary School (Form 4) Outputs in Relation to Demand

The output of the secondary school system is the key to the problem of bringing into being the number and kinds of high/middle level manpower sufficient to meet the estimated requirements during the process of development.

The following Table 10.12 indicates the requirements estimated, based on the Manpower Survey, for each of the three categories of middle/high level occupations, and the Form 4 outputs planned to meet them.

Table 10.12

Manpower Demand and Supply: 1969/70–1973/74

Item	Demand (Estimated Require-ment)	Supply Form 4 Output Planned to meet Demand
Category A Occupations	3,849	—
Category B Occupations	12,333	—
Category C Occupations	13,109	—
Safety Margin (including provision for wastage from Form 5 through to University Graduation and from Category B Training Schools) (21.6 per cent)	8,050	—
Form 4 Output:		
Government Financed Schools	—	33,844
Private Secondary Schools	—	3,497
Total	37,341	37,341

(b) Outlook for the Individual Occupational Categories (A–B–C)

Lest the above balance of demand and supply (Table 10.12) look a bit too neat, it should be pointed out that while the Form 4 supply will cover all input needs, the time lags inherent in the five-year run through university (from Form 4) or eight years in the case of Medicine will result in part of the demand being met by this output early in Plan Three rather than in Plan Two, in the same way some of Plan One period demands were met by supply (university outputs) which went into the pipeline before 1964/65. In the case of Category B, unavoidable delay in obtaining funds and building new certificate and diploma institutions for Agriculture will delay the satisfaction of the demand by the Form 4 supply until the early/middle years of Plan Three. The new capacities for this and the expansions planned in certain university faculties are such that all shortfalls shown below in Categories A and B should be covered by 1979/80 (provided of course that the ominous development described in the footnote to Section IV—see bottom of page 389—can be corrected very soon).

DEMAND AND SUPPLY: 1969/70—1973/74
CATEGORY A OCCUPATIONS

	Five Year Require-ment	Estimated Outputs	Shortfall
Science/Maths based occupations (Engineers, Agronomists, Doctors, etc.)	2,233	1,459	−774
All Arts based occupations	1,560	1,268	−292
TOTAL	3,849	2,751	−1,066

CATEGORY B OCCUPATIONS

Five Year Require-ment	Estimated Outputs	Shortfall
12,333	10,227	−2,106

The relatively small shortfall in Arts is mainly in three specialized occupations (Economists at M.A. level, Auditors and Accountants). As noted before, major expansions in the faculties of Engineering, Agriculture and Medicine will permit substantial rises from present level of *inputs* in the early 1970s. In 1971 input capacity in Medicine will rise from 25 per year to over 100. The new Faculty of Agriculture opening with an intake of 30 in 1969 will expand to 80 in 1971. The new Faculty of Engineering opening with an intake of 30 in 1971 will rise to 80 in 1972. The bulk of the greatly expanded inputs will come out in the early years of Plan Three.

(c) Bridging the Gap

The shortfall in science based University level occupations of −774 or a figure equal to 34 per cent of the Plan Two requirements figure will have to be met by either recruiting and "renting" expatriate skills from overseas or by modifying the Plan Two 40 per cent localization target substantially, or both. Since there are currently some 1,436 non-citizens now occupying such jobs it would seem much more logical and more economical to retain a sufficient number of these highly trained people during this period than to bring in another batch of new non-citizens to replace them.

The shortfall in Category B cannot be met in the same way since it is concentrated in a very few occupations (*e.g.*, certificate level Agricultural and Veterinary extension workers), and in these occupations there is only a small number of employed non-citizens. Overseas recruitment for these kinds of posts is very unlikely to be productive, since fluency in Kiswahili

Table 10.13[a]

Category A Occupations (University Level)

I.S.C.O. Code (1)	Occupation (2)	Total Employment (3)	Employed Citizens (4)	Employed Non-Citizens (5)	Existing Vacancies (6)	Net Increase in Employment to 1973/74 (7)	Localization Target (8)	Basic Requirements (Col. 6+7) (9)	Total Requirements 1969/70–1973/74 (Col. 8+9)[b] (10)	Estimated Supply to 1973/74 (11)	Shortfall or Surplus (12)
	Science/Maths:										
0–01.20	Architect, Buildings	30	11	19	6	6	8	12	21	25	+ 4
0–01.30	Town Planner	11	4	7	0	10	3	10	14	5	– 9
0–01.40	Quantity Surveyor	15	2	13	7	2	5	9	15	4	–11
0–02.02	Civil Engineer, General	244	39	205	31	79	82	110	202	299 }	–191
0–02.18	Civil Engineer (Hydraulic)	1	—	1	5	28	1	33	36		
0–02.20	Civil Engineer (Soil Mechanic)	7	—	7	2	1	3	3	6		
0–02.24	Electrical Engineer, General	42	8	34	15	29	13	44	60		
0–02.38	Mechanical Engineer, General	138	19	119	19	93	48	112	168		
0–02.57	Mechanical Engineer (Textile)	24	4	20	4	5	8	9	18		
0–02.26	Electronic Engineer	5	3	2	2	0	0	2	2	0	– 2
0–02.34	Telecommunication Engineer	17	7	10	11	3	4	14	19	15	– 4
0–02.60	Chemical Engineer, General	5	0	5	0	1	2	1	3	6	+ 3
0–02.66	Metallurgist (Extractive)	9	5	4	3	0	2	3	5	5	0
0–02.70	Ceramic and Glass Engineer	1	—	1	0	0	0	0	0	0	0
0–02.74	Mining Engineer, General	14	3	11	3	0	4	3	7	7	0
0–02.84	Industrial Efficiency Engineer	5	2	3	1	5	1	6	7	0	– 7
0–02.88	Agricultural Engineer	6	0	6	2	3	2	5	7	5	– 2
0–03.10	Surveyor, General	76	23	53	12	52	21	64	89	21	–68
0–11.10	Chemist, General	41	11	30	7	18	12	25	39	39	0
0–19.30	Geologist, General	14	2	12	1	5	5	6	12	12	0
0–21.10	Veterinarian, General	65	26	39	11	63	16	74	94	77	–17
0–22.10	Biologist, General	6	2	4	0	0	2	0	2	2	0
0–22.24	Botanist	1	0	1	0	0	0	0	0	0	0
0–22.30	Zoologist	11	1	10	3	0	4	3	7	7	0
0–22.90	Biologist and Animal Scientists N.E.C.[c]	44	13	31	23	32	12	55	70	50	–20
0–23.20	Agronomist	122	53	69	43	189	30	232	275	231	–44

283

Table 10.13—continued

I.S.C.O. Code (1)	Occupation (2)	Total Employment (3)	Employed Citizens (4)	Employed Non-Citizens (5)	Existing Vacancies (6)	Net Increase in Employment to 1973/74 (7)	Localization Target (8)	Basic Requirements (Col. 6+7) (9)	Total Requirements 1969/70-1973/74 (Col. 8+9)^b (10)	Estimated Supply to 1973/74 (11)	Shortfall or Surplus (12)
	Science/Maths—continued										
0-23.30	Horticulturalist	3	2	1	0	5	0	5	5	0	- 5
0-23.40	Silviculturist	32	15	17	14	22	7	36	45	12	- 33
0-23.50	Soil Scientist	2	0	2	1	3	1	4	5	0	- 5
0-31.10	Physician, General Practice	441	65	376	58	272	93	330	444	201	- 243
0-32.10	Dentist	19	5	14	1	2	2	3	5	10	- 5
0-51.10	Pharmacist	50	15	35	1	25	14	26	42	12	- 30
0-59.40	Dietician	4	0	4	—	2	2	2	4	0	- 4
0-61.20	University Teacher (Sciences)	57	14	43	7	76	17	83	105	I.N.A.[1]	I.N.A.
0-69.40	Graduates Teacher (Secondary School), Science/Maths	375	92	283	33	84	283	117	400	414	+14
	Sub-Total: Science/Maths Based Occupations	1,937	446	1,491	326	1,115	707	1,441	2,233	1,459	-774
	Arts:										
0-61.20	University Teacher (Arts)	63	16	47	9	8	20	17	37	I.N.A.	I.N.A.
0-69.40	Graduates Teacher (Secondary School), Arts	307	76	231	27	56	231[d]	83	314	314	0
0-69.42	Graduate Teacher (Technical Training College)	65	25	40	0	0	40[d]	—	40	42	+ 2
0-69.90	Teachers, N.E.C.	44	25	19	15	5	8	20	20	I.N.A.	I.N.A.
0-81.10	Lawyer, Government	77	47	30	32	73[f]	12	105	123	140	0
0-81.10	Lawyer, Non-Government,[g] including Self-Employed	140	25	115	—	17	0	17	17		
0-92.90	Authors, Journalists and Related Writers	31	22	9	9	0	4	9	13	13	0
0-Y1.10	Accountant, Professional	169	36	133	14	95	53	109	170	45	- 125
0-Y1.10	Auditor, Professional	40	23	17	3	20	7	23	31	0	- 31
0-Y2.10	Social Worker, Professional	10	3	7	0	32	3	32	36	19	- 17
0-Y3.10	Librarian	30	10	20	3	16	8	19	28	20	- 8

Code	Occupation										
0—Y4.20	Economist	86	37	49	12	65[e]	20	77	97	59	−18
0—Y4.40	Statistician, Professional	16	6	10	15	19	4	34	40	25	−15
0—Y9.20	Sociologist	2	0	2	1	—	—	1	1	1	−1
0—Y9.41	Personnel Specialist, Industrial	88	74	14	4	41	6	45	51	49	−2
0—Y9.47	Occupational Analyst	2	0	2	2	0	0	2	2	2	0
0—Y9.53	Translator	5	4	1	2	0	0	2	2	2	0
1—01.50	Administrators (Government)	426	375	51	114	59	20	173	183	183	0
1—11	Directors, Managers[h] and Working Proprietors	542	162	380	25	200	150	225	355	355	0
	Sub-Total: Arts Based Occupations	2,143	966	1,177	287	706	586	993	1,560	1,268	−292
	Grand Total: Category A	4,076	1,403	2,673	613	1,821	1,293	2,434	3,849	2,704	−1,066

a The data in columns 3 through 10 in all categories of occupations in Tables 10.13, 10.14 and 10.15 represents 100 per cent for each such occupation in Tanzania's economy. As indicated in Table 10.5, the establishments visited in this survey accounted for 73.8 per cent of the total non-agricultural wage employment in the country. These figures are blown up by industry sector, in the amount necessary to represent 100 per cent. For ease in representation a number of related occupations (3 digit minor groups of the International Standard Classification of Occupations) have been listed as one group; for example, in Category A occupations, code 1–11 (Directors, Managers and Working Proprietors); in Category B, code 6–01 (Deck Officers, and Pilots, Ship); and in Category C, code 7–53 (Mechanics-Repairmen). Nevertheless, information was gathered and processed for every specific five digit occupation and the data is on file in the Ministry of Economic Affairs and Development Planning.

b Column 10 is not exactly the sum of columns 8 and 9 in all instances. A factor of 5 per cent has been added to each Science/Maths based occupations in Category A, and to the highly specialized Arts based ones (professional Accountants, Lawyers, etc.). This is to take into account losses from moves out of the occupation after graduation. (This is based on information from a study of University of East African Science graduates from 1962 to 1966, done for the Manpower Planning Division by Mr. James A. Johnson in 1967.) A compensating reduction of 5 per cent has been made in requirements of certain Arts based occupations in Category A (Government Administrators, Managers, Directors, etc.), to which the 1967 study indicated these science based individuals moved. Adjustment in Column 10 was made, of course, only when the application of the 5 per cent factor yielded a whole number.

c "N.E.C." means "not elsewhere classified."

d By reason of a special Government priority, 100 per cent of non-citizens graduate secondary school teachers are scheduled for localization during the Second Plan. For all other occupations the localization target by 1973/74 is 40 per cent of the existing non-citizen stock. (In some cases, mainly in the Science based Category A occupations, this target will not be met. See section IV of the text.)

e All of the net increase figure is to be met at M.A. or Ph.D. level.

f This portion of total requirements for additional lawyers takes into account the need for lawyers in types of posts which have, as a stop-gap, been filled by laymen.

g There are a few lawyers who work for salaries in the private/parastatal sector. The majority of the group, however, are in private practice.

h The total requirements for Directors, Managers, and Working Proprietors (includes senior managerial staff as well as the managers themselves) is estimated at about 1,260. Based on information obtained in this survey on educational backgrounds of such individuals in 1967, it is believed that 25 per cent of such posts (315) will call for university degrees. This is considerably higher than the proportion of the existing managerial stock holding degrees. Only about 15 per cent of present managers hold degrees. The considerably higher figure of 25 per cent has been used here since the pace of localization will not permit the very long periods of on-job experience which has been typical of existing expatriate incumbents, and a higher level of education should make possible shorter training periods.

i The entry I.N.A. means "Information Not Available."

Table 10.14

**Category B Occupations
(Sub Professional)**

I.S.C.O. Code (1)	Occupation (2)	Total Employment (3)	Employed Citizens (4)	Employed Non-Citizens (5)	Existing Vacancies (6)	Net Increase in Employment to 1973/74 (7)	Localization Target (8)	Basic Requirements (Col. 6 + 7) (9)	Total Requirements 1969/70–1973/74 (Col. 8 + 9)b (10)	Estimated Supply to 1973/74 (11)	Shortfall or Surplus (12)
0-41.10	Nurses	2,155	1,754	401	169	986	119	1,155	1,274	1,274	0
0-53.20	Physiotherapist	6	0	6	0	2	2	2	4	2	2
0-53.40	X-Ray Operator, Medical	14	6	8	4	1	3	5	8	3	-5
0-53.90	Medical Technicians, Other	325	319	6	46	17	2	63	65	67	C
0-59.91	Assistant Medical Officer	83	78	5	26	0	0	26	26	0	Course Discontinued
0-69.30	Teacher (Primary School—Grade "A")a	2,009	1,881	128	0	4,923	51	4,923	4,974	4,974	0
0-69.33	Teacher (Primary School—E.O. III)	136	136	0	I.N.A.h	I.N.A.	0	I.N.A.	I.N.A.	I.N.A.	I.N.A.
0-69.41	Teacher (Sec. School—Non-Graduates)	675	350	325	0	143	325	143	468	468	
0-69.43	Teacher Trainers (Non-Graduate)	138	98	40	39	I.N.A.	I.N.A.	I.N.A.	I.N.A.	I.N.A.	
0-X1.10	Draughtsmen (General)	172	94	78	39	44	31	83	114	60	-54
0-X9.20	Engineering Technician (General)	1,095	659	436	174	435	175	609	784	528b	-256
0-X9.21	Engineering Technician (Textile)	79	18	61	9	25	24	34	58	62	+4
0-X9.22	Engineering Technician (Petrol)	15	9	6	1	7	2	8	10	4	-6
0-X9.30	Research Laboratory Technician	51	38	13	6	12	5	18	23	I.N.A.e	I.N.A.
0-X9.40	Industrial Laboratory Technician	84	65	19	4	47	8	51	59	I.N.A.e	I.N.A.
0-X.50	Agric./Vet./Forest/Fish/Game Extension Worker (Certificate Level)	2,411	2,323	88	48	2,738	35	2,786	2,821	1,550c	-1,271
0-X9.51	Agric. Extension Worker (Diploma Level)	321	200	121	17	584	48	601	649 }	524d	
0-X9.52	Veterinary Extension Worker (Diploma)	115	103	12	0	82	5	82	87 }		
0-X9.53	Forestry Extension Worker (Diploma)	56	50	6	0	40	2	40	42	42	0
0-X9.54	Fisheries Extension Worker (Diploma)	12	11	1	0	39	0	39	39	39	0
0-X9.55	Game Extension Worker (Diploma)	19	17	2	0	25	0	25	25	25	0
0-X1.45	Cartographer	7	7	0	1	5		6	6	I.N.A.	I.N.A.

Code	Occupation										
0–Y9.62	Designer (Industrial and Commercial Products)	4	0	4	0	1	2	1	3	I.N.A.	I.N.A.
0–91.25	Commercial Artist	3	1	2	0	0	1	0	1	I.N.A.	I.N.A.
0–Y1.10	Accountants (Non-Certified)	744	453	291	85	307	116	392	508	I.N.A.	I.N.A.
6–01	Deck Officers and Pilots, Ship	30	4	26	0	15	10	15	25	I.N.A.	I.N.A.
6–21	Air Pilots, Navigators and Flight Engineers	22	1	21	5	3	8	8	16	I.N.A.	I.N.A.
6–72	Radio—Communication Operators	30	20	10	19	10	4	29	33	33	0
9–02	Senior Police Officers	132	102	30	15	24	12	39	51	51	0
	Total Category B	10,943	8,797	2,146	668	10,515[g]	990	11,183	12,333[f]	9,706	1,592

[a] Only Grade A (and E.O. III) Primary School Teachers meet the criteria for inclusion in Category B Occupations (1–3 years formal training post-secondary). There are two other classes of Primary School Teachers (Grades B and C) who receive two years of post-primary training. The total employment of each is: Grade B—1,858; and Grade C—11,746. These totals will rise to 3,564 and 12,281, respectively, by 1974.

[b] This assumes that the Dar es Salaam Technical College can produce at its rate and capacity of 100 per year plus 28 currently in Training Overseas.

[c] The maximum output during the five Plan Years from existing institutions is 220 per year (totalling 1,100), plus one year's output (1973/74) of 450 from a new institution.

[d] The maximum output of existing facilities for five years is 340; plus an output of one year of 184 from the new agriculture and veterinary diploma level institution (opening in 1973).

[e] These Category B occupations normally are learned in-plant and on-the-job and are similar to Category C posts in this respect except in in-plant training is likely to be much more intensive and formalized.

[f] 1.89 per cent wastage of the citizen stock (158) has been added to the other 12,175 requirements listed above in column 10 to account for estimated deaths and retirements.

[g] This exceptionally large net increase estimated for Category B occupations is caused mainly by two large-scale crash programmes beginning in Plan Two: (a) a drive to achieve Universal Primary Education by 1989; and (b) a big expansion in the Agricultural Extension Service targeted for completion in 1979.

[h] The entry I.N.A. means "Information Not Available."

Table 10.15

Category C Occupations

Skilled Office Workers and Skilled Manual Workers in Occupations Requiring a Secondary School Education for Adequate Performance of the Full Array of Tasks Involved in the Occupation

I.S.C.O. Code (1)	Occupation (2)	Total Employment (3)	Employed Citizens (4)	Employed Non-Citizens (5)	Existing Vacancies (6)	Net Increase in Employment to 1973/74 (7)	Localization Target (8)	Basic Requirements (Col. 6 + 7) (9)	Total Requirements 1969/70– 1973/74 (Col. 8 + 9)[b] (10)	Estimated Supply[a] to 1973/74 (11)	Shortfall or Surplus (12)
1–01.60	Executive Officer, Government	1,683	1,513	170	446	286	68	732	800	800	0
1–11	Directors, Managers and Working Proprietors	1,636	982	654	45	600	260	645	905	70	0
2–01 & 2–91	Bookkeepers, and Cashiers and Office-Machine Operators	2,248	1,996	252	34	915	101	949	1,050	—	—
2–11	Stenographers and Typists	2,377	2,007	370	595	923	148	1,518	1,666	—	—
2–99	Clerical Workers, N.E.C.	11,802	11,087	715	1,289	2,216	286	3,505	3,791	—	—
3–31.20	Salesmen (Wholesale)	584	489	95	6	322	38	328	366	—	—
	Sub-Total: Skilled Office Workers	20,330	18,074	2,256	2,415	5,262	901	7,677	8,578	870	—
6–31.15	Driver, Railway Engine (Steam)	165	119	46	3	59	18	62	80	80	—
6–61.15	Transport Service Inspector (Railway)	358	252	106	11	123	42	134	176	—	—
6–62	Traffic Controllers and Dispatchers, Transport	104	62	42	0	136	17	136	153	10	—
6–71	Telephone and Telegraph Operators	622	595	27	20	210	11	230	241	—	—
7–15	Patternmakers, Markers and Cutters	23	17	6	1	11	2	12	14	—	—
7–33.50	Cold-Rolling-Mill Operator, Metal	50	50	0	0	30	0	30	30	—	—
7–42	Jewellers, Goldsmiths and Silversmiths	14	5	9	3	0	4	3	7	6	—
7–50	Fitter-Machinists, Toolmakers and Machine-Tool Setters	437	342	95	14	183	38	197	235	26	—
7–52.10	Fitter-Assembler, Metal Products, General	25	8	17	3	12	7	15	22	1	—
7–53	Mechanics-Repairmen (Textile Machinery)	1,172	848	324	10	510	130	520	650	37	—
7–53.35	Mechanics-Repairmen (Except Motor Vehicles and Textiles)	509	498	11	42	40	4	82	86	—	—

Code	Occupation									
7–53.75	Mechanic-Repairman (Motor Vehicles)	2,060	1,843	217	36	779	87	815	902	73	—
7–54.10	Sheet-Metal Worker	177	156	21	2	94	8	96	104	4	—
7–55.10	Plumber, General	472	470	2	2	111	0	113	113	3	—
7–55.40	Pipe Fitter	213	145	68	2	75	27	77	104	2	—
7–56.10	Welder, Gas and Electric	459	426	33	1	201	15	202	217	25	—
7–61	Electricians	859	723	136	19	352	54	371	425	4	—
7–61.55	Electrical Switchboard Operator, Power Station	26	19	7	0	19	3	19	22	11	—
7–62	Electrical and Electronics Fitters	29	14	15	1	15	6	16	22	4	—
7–63.10	Mechanic-Repairman, Radio	16	16	0	4	10	0	14	14	—	—
7–65	Lineman and Cable Joiners	457	429	28	0	168	11	168	179	33	—
8–01	Compositors and Typesetters	134	112	22	0	63	9	63	72	6	—
8–02	Pressmen (Printing)	73	54	19	0	32	8	32	40	6	—
8–03.20	Stereotyper	11	7	4	0	8	2	8	10	—	—
8–04.20	Engraver, Hand (Printing)	34	26	8	0	21	3	21	24	15	—
8–05.10	Photo-Engraver	13	6	7	0	3	3	3	6	—	—
8–06.20	Bookbinder, Hand	85	79	6	0	36	2	36	38	11	—
8–13.90	Furnacemen and Kilnman, Glass and Ceramics, Other	10	0	10	0	4	4	4	8	4	—
8–21.20	Miller (Grain)	37	31	6	0	3	2	3	5	25	—
8–24.15	Brewmaster	17	4	13	0	8	5	8	13	—	—
8–32	Cookers, Roasters and Other Heat Treaters, Chemical and Related Processes	14	11	3	0	7	1	7	8	1	—
9–01	Senior Fire Fighters	39	33	6	14	4	2	18	20	—	—
9–12.20	Chef and Head Cook	29	4	25	1	13	10	14	24	3	—
9–71	Photographers and Related Camera Operators (Professional)	10	8	2	3	1	—	4	4	—	—
	Sub-Total: Skilled Manual Workers	8,753	7,412	1,341	192	3,341	535	3,533	4,068		
	Grand Total—Category C	29,083	25,486	3,597	2,607	8,603	1,436	11,210	13,109		

[a] Only the products of organized training schemes have been entered in this column (supply from identifiable in-plant training schemes, apprenticeships, etc.). It is important to point out that a very substantial portion of the people in these occupations acquire their skills by wholly informal means, on-the-job in respect of which no records are kept, and hence no information was available to survey interviewers. The real supply, if it could be estimated, would surely be far larger than the output of the organized schemes which are recorded in Column 11.

[b] A 1.89 per cent wastage factor for death and retirement of existing citizens stock has been added to the 12,646 total of the items shown in Column 10.

289

Table 10.16

Category D Occupations

I.S.C.O. Code (1)	Occupation (2)	Total Employ-ment (3)	Em-ployed Citizens (4)	Em-ployed Non-Citizens (5)	Existing Vacan-cies (6)	Net Increase in Em-ploy-ment to 1973/74 (7)	Local-ization Target (8)	Basic Require-ments (Col. 6 + 7) (9)	Total Require-ments 1969/70–1973/74 (Col. 8 + 9) (10)	Esti-mated Supply to 1973/74 (11)	Shortfall or Surplus (12)
7–03	Weavers, Loom Fixers and Loom Preparers	292	282	10	12	157	4	169	173		
7–11	Tailors, Dressmakers and Garment Makers	41	41	0	0	24	0	24	24		
7–14.20	Upholsterer (Furniture)	22	14	8	0	8	3	8	11		
7–34.20	Blacksmith	169	145	24	1	45	10	46	56		
7–59.60	Saw Repairmen and Sharpeners	19	12	7	1	12	3	13	16		
7–71	Carpenters and Joiners	1,631	1,538	93	5	703	36	708	744	20	
7–81	Painters and Paperhangers, Construction and Maintenance	693	686	7	0	186	3	186	189	5	
7–91	Bricklayers, Stonemasons and Tile Setters	1,284	1,270	14	3	405	6	408	414		
7–92–7–93	Plasterers, Cement Finishers and Terrazzo Workers	105	105	0	0	72	0	72	72		
7–99.45	Building Maintenance Man	74	54	20	8	32	8	40	48		
8–26	Butchers and Meat Cutters	50	49	1	0	29	0	29	29		
8–27.90	Dairy Workers, Other	22	22	0	0	12	0	12	12		
8–72.20	Crane Operators (Bridge or Gantry)	237	173	64	0	14	27	14	41		
8–74.30	Dragline Operator	24	18	6	0	18	2	18	20		
9–11.20	Hotel Housekeeper/Steward	18	12	6	0	25	2	25	27		
	Grand Total	4,681	4,421	260	30	1,742	104	1,772	1,876		

is a "must." The shortfall therefore will not be met in Plan Two but should be mainly overtaken in the early years of Plan Three.

Category C Occupations

Since there are no institution building problems for these direct employment occupations, Form 4 supply will be equal in number to the total requirements. It must be borne in mind, however, that for a few occupations in Category C the learning period on-the-job may exceed the five year period of the Second Plan. This is mainly true in upper management posts.

VI. COMPARISONS WITH THE 1964 MANPOWER SURVEY

(a) Growth of High/Middle Level Manpower in Relation to Growth of Total Non-Agricultural Wage Employment

Total non-agricultural employment increased about 20 per cent. High/middle level employment increased about 49 per cent, or over twice the rate of total employment.

Table 10.17

	1964/65	1968/69 (Base Year– Plan Two)	Difference
Category A	2,801	4,076	
Category B	5,778	10,943	
Category C	20,910	29,083	
Total	29,489	44,102	(+14,613)
Total Non-Agricultural Employment	191,329	237,598	(+46,269)

(b) Estimated and Actual Form 4 Outputs: 1964/65–1968/69

1964 Manpower Survey (planned) Target	25,000
Five Year actual output	23,715
Shortfall	−1,285

(c) Where Did the Secondary School (Form 4) Outputs Go?

Form 4 output for the five years was 23,715. Employment of high/middle level manpower increased by only 14,607. What happened to the rest of the 23,715 Form 4 people? As of 1968/69 they were in the pipeline of various post-Form 4 education and training institutions as follows:

Approximately	1,260	in Teachers Training College
	2,400	in Forms 5 and 6
	1,490	in the University of East Africa

	2,892	in universities and training programmes over-seas (heavy non-degree element—Nurses, Technicians, etc., but all post-Form 4)
	740	in Agricultural Diploma and Extension Schools and Certificate Schools
	250	in the Dar es Salaam Technical College
Total	9,032	in post-Form 4 institutions
Add	14,607	Net Increase in High/Middle level Employment
	23,639	Total Accounted for
	23,715	Form 4 Outputs Total
	−76	Unaccounted for

(d) Notes on Individual Occupations

(1) ELECTRICAL ENGINEERS

$$1964 = 80 \text{ EMPLOYED}$$
$$1968/69 = 42 \text{ EMPLOYED}$$

In the course of the 1968/69 Manpower Survey the new figure which emerged for electrical engineers was so far below the reported stock of 1964 as to merit special investigation. Comparison of the 1964/65 establishment schedule of the major user (Tanzania Electric Supply Company Limited) with the 1968/69 schedule showed the difference could be accounted for in this one establishment. Consultation with TANESCO officials indicated that the personnel director of 1964 (since departed) had improperly counted as engineers a number of senior technicians. The actual increase of bona fide electrical engineers over the five years was relatively small.

(2) PHYSICIANS

$$1964/65 = 434 \text{ EMPLOYED}$$
$$1968/69 = 411 \text{ EMPLOYED}$$

The lack of movement here reflects the long lead-time for this profession: the course is five years post-Form 6. Thus the (small) *outputs* in the five years 1964/65 through 1968/69 reflected the equally small number which went into the pipeline in the five years previous to 1964. Only one class, which entered 1964/65, came out in the First Plan period. An additional drain on the supply which came on-stream during the First Plan period (about 37 graduates from the University of East Africa and an estimated 45 from overseas schools) was a decline in the number of expatriate doctors working in the Ministry of Health and the voluntary agencies. As a result, no meaningful increase took place in this important occupation. However, the number in the pipelines was substantially increased during the First Plan period. A total of 152 went into the University of East Africa during this period.

Beginning in 1970 inputs to the University of East Africa will rise from 50 to 100 per year with an additional 30 going overseas or possibly into a further expansion of the Faculty of Medicine at Dar es Salaam. This rate of input will by 1979/80 achieve the self sufficiency target of 800. (*Note:* only employed physicians are included in the 1980 demand figure of 800 and represent the "economic demand" which will exist in 1980 which is the number it is estimated to be needed to carry out Plan Two programmes and which the Government and voluntary agency resources will be able to finance. No self-employed doctors are included in these figures. Self-employed physicians are, however, included in the existing stock in columns 3, 4 and 5 of Table 10.15.)

(3) Secondary School Teachers (Graduates)

In 1964 only about 78 of the 563 Secondary School Teachers were citizens (38 African Tanzanians and 40 citizen Asians). By 1968/69 the citizen total rose to 168 out of a total employment of 682. This relatively modest increase does not properly reflect the attention and priority directed to this occupation in the 1964/65–1968/69 period. As in the case of other university produced skills only three output years (the last three) during the First Plan were subject to the planner's manipulation.

Beginning in 1965/66 inputs were raised from the previous year's 42 to 122, and the next year (1966/67) to 161. (These did not graduate until April, 1969 and are not included in the employment figure of 682.) By 1967/68 inputs were raised by 180 and will continue at that level through 1971. By 1973 it is anticipated that all but a very few of the graduate secondary school teachers will be citizens. This will be the first substantial professional occupation to be 100 per cent localized, and a number of years before the 1980 target.

This high priority for this occupation was adopted because Government decided that with 84 per cent of the secondary school system (the key to Tanzania's high and middle Manpower Target) staffed by expatriates the system was too vulnerable. In the event of any disruption in the relations of Tanzania with just two countries (U.S.A. and U.K. from which most of the expatriate teachers came), a possible withdrawal of the expatriate teachers would just about have closed down Tanzania's secondary schools. Government decided to remove this risk at the earliest possible date.

(4) University Teachers

The increase in the occupation from 31 in 1964/65 to 120 in 1968/69 reflects the development of the University of Tanzania. Total requirements for the Second Plan will total 142, mainly in Science, reflecting expansion of the Faculty of Medicine, the opening of the Faculty of Agriculture in 1969/70 and establishment of a new Faculty of Engineering in 1971 or 1972.

(e) **Accuracy of 1964 Manpower Survey Estimates of Net Increases in High and Middle Level Manpower Categories to 1968/69**

Category A:

Employment in 1964	2,801	
Net Increase forecast in 1964	1,323	
Total 1964 Survey Employment forecast for 1968/69	4,124	
Actual Category A Employment in 1968/69	4,076	Difference −48

Category B:

Employment in 1964	5,778	
Net Increase forecast in 1964	3,285	
Total 1964 Survey Employment forecast for 1968/69	9,063	
Actual Category B Employment in 1968/69	10,943	Difference +1,880

Category C:

Employment in 1964	20,910	
Net Increase forecast in 1964	10,020	
Total 1964 Survey Employment forecast for 1968/69	30,930	
Actual Category C Employment in 1968/69	29,083	Difference −1,847

Considering the relatively crude state of development of the "art" of high/middle level manpower forecasting and the many unpredictable variables, the estimates of the 1964 Manpower Survey were remarkably accurate. When the estimates for all three categories are aggregated the 1964 estimate of 1968/69 employment levels was almost 100 per cent accurate.

1964 Forecast   44,117 (Categories A-B-C totaled)
1968/69 Actual   44,102 (Categories A-B-C totaled)

One reason for the closeness of these "estimates" is that they are not really forecasts of what "may" happen, as would be the case in an unplanned economy. They are in fact *targets* and much of the machinery of Government is geared to the achievement of the targets set in the Manpower Survey (which in itself was an integral part of the 1964/65–1968/69 Five-Year Plan for Economic and Social Development). Conversely the targets themselves take into account some of the limitations and constraints on the ability of the nation to produce this category of skilled manpower. For example, because of the known lead times in the education/training process it was realized that planning could affect only the last several years outputs during the First Plan period in respect of university level output. The rest of the prospective outputs were already in the pipeline prior to the first year of Plan One. Because of this constraint the 1964 forecasts included a very low localization factor for expatriates (3 per cent per year in Government and 2 per cent in the private sector). The 1968/69 Manpower Survey has as its localization target 40 per cent of existing non-citizen stock by 1973/74. This takes into account the effect of planned institution building accomplished during the First Plan period, the outputs of which will come on-stream in Plan Two. Even then, because it has the longest lead time it is unlikely that the Category A—university level—localization targets, mainly in Science based occupations for Plan Two will be fully met by 1973/74. (See Table 10.13.)

Table 10.18

University Output Requirement Targets by 1980: Comparison of 1964 and 1968 Manpower Survey Estimates

Occupation	1980 Requirement Targets as extrapolated from the 1964 Survey	1980 Requirement revised on basis of the 1968 Survey
Science:		
Engineering	821	879
Medicine	700	800
Education	750	714
Science, General (B.Sc.)	205	184
Veterinarian	148	180
Architect	64	40
Geologist	27	24
Pharmacist	97	90
Agronomist	690	509
Town Planner	18	28
Forester	86	80
Dentist	68	20
Surveyor	90	170
All other Science based occupations such as miscellaneous Engineers (apart from civil, mechanical and electrical engineers), biologists, chemists, meteorologists, etc.	24	110
Total Science	3,788	3,828
Arts:		
Administration/Management	1,058	1,058
Education/Secondary Teachers	740	800
Lawyers, Accountants (professional, including Auditors)	309	300
Economists (At M.A. or Ph.D. level; also B.A.'s included in Administration/Management)	—	192
All other Arts based occupations (University Teachers, Librarians, Personnel Specialists, etc.)	268	421
Total Arts	2,375	2,771

(f) Modifications of 1980 University Level Output Requirement Targets

From the manpower requirements established in the 1964 Manpower Survey for the First Plan, the Manpower Planning Division extrapolated the estimated requirements for the self sufficiency targets of 1980. These requirement targets are used by the Ministry of National Education to plan the annual inputs needed to meet these 1980 targets and to make the annual offer of bursaries in the numbers needed to obtain these inputs. Extrapolations of this kind over such a long period are dicey things indeed. Unforeseen changes in the economy, and major shifts in Government programmes are only a few of the hazards.

The manpower requirements established for Plan Two (to 1973/74) provided an opportunity for modifying the original demand extrapolations in accordance with the economic forecasts and development programmes adopted for Plan Two. As we move closer to the 1980 target the estimated target figure becomes increasingly accurate.

All in all the overall modifications arising from the Second Plan Manpower Survey of requirements have not been of very great magnitude. It is important to note that while there are a few rather sharp changes in individual occupations in the two streams (Science and Arts), there is only a relatively small change in stream totals. This is reassuring since if the stream total is reasonably accurate, adjustment of the output in individual occupations within each stream can be made within three years from Form 6 for all

Table 10.19

Estimated University Output 1968/69–1973/74: Science-Based Occupations

Occupation or Faculty	Output University of E.A.	Output Overseas Universities	Total Output
B.Sc. (General)	61	37	98
B.Sc. (Education)	405	9	414
Medicine	126	75	201
Agriculture	206	25	231
Engineering (Civil, Mechanical, Electrical)	182	117	299
Veterinary Science	70	7	77
Architecture	19	6	25
Surveying	20	6	26
Geology	10	2	12
Dentistry	—	10	10
Pharmacy	—	12	12
Forestry	—	12	12
Town Planning	—	5	5
Miscellaneous other science-based occupations such as miscellaneous other engineers (*e.g.*, in mining, telecommunications), metallurgists, chemists, biologists	—	41	41
Total	1,099	364	1,463

occupations. This can be accomplished by simply altering the bursary offers in the (university level) occupations to be adjusted. The same option will be available to cope with future individual occupational shifts in demand which may develop over the years up to 1980.

Table 10.20

Estimated University Output 1968/69–1973/74: Arts-Based Occupations

Occupation or Faculty	Output University of E.A.	Output Overseas Universities	Total Output
Administration and Management[a]	356	—	356
B.A. (Education)	344	12	356
B.A. (Other)	151	18	169
Business Administration and Commerce (University College, Nairobi, and overseas)[b]	99	31	130
Accountancy (Professional)	—	45	45
Economics[c]	—	27	27
Law	131	9	140
Librarianship	—	20	20
Statistics (Professional)	—	25	25
Total	1,081	187	1,268

[a] In combination with Economics (in all cases), Statistics, Geography, Political Science or Sociology (at the University of Tanzania only).

[b] Commerce and Administration/Management outputs can be allocated to either Government Administrative posts or to the enterprise sector as supply. (See Table 10.13.)

[c] Undergraduates taking Economics courses are included in Administration and Management at the University of Tanzania. The 27 overseas are all in postgraduate courses.

QUESTIONS FOR DISCUSSION

1. How does Denison quantify the amount of education in the labor force? What problems do you see in utilizing that measure? Would correction of these problems lead to a larger figure at either end of the time span studied?

2. Why does Denison only include 60 per cent of the earnings differential between average individuals with different amounts of education? Does his assumption seem reasonable?

3. How could considerations of economic efficiency be incorporated into a state plan for higher education?

4. What changes would be necessary to adapt the New York Plan to lower levels of education?

5. How does the Tanzania Manpower Plan treat the following tradeoffs:
   (a) quantity versus quality
   (b) experience versus additional years of formal education
   (c) formal versus informal schooling.
   What effect does the Plan's treatment of these tradeoffs have on its conclusions?

Chapter 11 MAJOR ISSUES FOR THE SEVENTIES

AMONG the many issues that will dominate the educational scene in the next decade, three will be receiving special attention from economists. They are the financing of schools, both private and public, on all educational levels; the internal efficiency of the educational system; and the degree of competition within the educational sphere. An additional major issue is the purpose and function of education within society. The existing structure of the educational system is increasingly under attack for fostering conformity, suppressing initiative, and promoting the concept of learning as consisting of memorization rather than personal development. Although this issue has economic overtones, because it is argued that the economic system imposes these confining tasks on the educational enterprise, its roots appear to lie in the political, social, and philosophical rather than the economic realm.

The functioning of any mass educational system in the United States is heavily dependent on the policies established to deal with the issues of financing, efficiency, and competition. In this chapter attention is focused on exploring the extent of these three problems, the underlying economic causes giving rise to them, and possible economic solutions. As educational financing appears to be the most pressing of the three issues, the chapter begins with its analysis. The realization that financing problems differ in higher education *vis-à-vis* primary and secondary education dictates that these sectors be analyzed separately. It should be noted at this point that the financing problem is not independent of issues of efficiency and competitiveness. Part of the financing problem stems from lack of efficiency, which in turn

Notes to Chapter 11 will be found on pages 390–391.

stems in part from the absence of a competitive atmosphere in the educational realm, therefore we do not elaborate on this point.

FINANCING: ELEMENTARY AND SECONDARY SCHOOLS

The extent and severity of the financing problem was highlighted in an article appearing in the December 1968 issue of *U.S. News and World Report* entitled, "No Money, No Classes—Growing Problem in Some States," which reported that

For some 32,500 pupils in the public schools of three districts in Ohio, school has closed early this year. The money to pay teachers and keep classrooms open has run out....

Biggest city affected is Youngstown, with about 28,000 students. One reporter described the situation this way:

"Broke, without credit and almost without hope, Youngstown's 45 schools will close their doors...."

The troubles are typified by what happened in Youngstown. Five years ago, the city had one of the State's finest school systems. But tax revenues have not kept pace with expenses. As the city's industrial base grew, school tax rates remained static. Six new levies have been rejected at the polls over the past five years.

Since August, banks in Youngstown have loaned the schools 1.5 million dollars. Outlook for further loans is dim. School officials learned they had only $6,000 to meet a 1 million dollar payroll for December. They then decided to close the schools. All the closed districts have plans to reopen after the New Year—if the money is then available....

While Ohio provided the most dramatic example, some districts in other states were experiencing similar difficulties.

The near-bankrupt systems in Philadelphia and Pittsburgh were reported more than a year behind in payments to the State pension fund for retired school teachers. The total owed: more than 11 million dollars....

In Chicago, public schools are described as in a new financial crisis. Superintendent James F. Redmond predicted the system will fall at least 29 million dollars short of just standing still in its educational program—without considering any pay raise for teachers....[1]

Abstracting from what may be journalistic zeal, the fact still remains that the financing problem is real and crucial. Although the majority of the United States school systems are probably nowhere near being in the abysmal predicament of Youngstown, many share the budgetary problems of Chicago's schools. Unless the overall trend is reversed, the number of school systems finding themselves in the "Youngstown camp" may increase rapidly.

The underlying economic causes of this problem are of a dual nature: costs that are rising rapidly and tax revenues that are not. We shall discuss the revenue problem first, prefacing it with a brief overview of the United States tax system.

The aggregate United States tax structure parallels the nation's political structure. Taxes are levied by all three levels of government: federal, state, and local. Different levels of government have traditionally adopted different tax sources as their primary revenue base. Since the turn of the century, personal and corporate income taxes have been the prime revenue raisers on the federal level.[2] As the revenue needs of the federal government fluctuated, tax rates were adjusted to match the needs. Thus, tax rates rose during World War I, World War II, and the Korean War and were reduced in the periods succeeding each of these.

Prior to the twentieth century, the general property tax was the primary levy at the state level. But as revenue requirements and state responsibility for broad welfare services began to soar, corporation, license, and gasoline taxes moved to the fore as revenue sources. During the 1920s and 1930s there was widespread enactment by individual states of personal income taxes, retail sales taxes, and payroll taxes. Local tax revenues are drawn primarily from property taxes, permits, and fees. There has been a growing tendency since World War II for the localities to levy payroll, income, and sales taxes in an attempt to equilibrate revenue with markedly increased expenditure.

All tax sources are not equivalent in their revenue-raising capacity, as can be seen by utilizing elasticity measures. One can define tax elasticities as follows:

Nature of Tax	*Attributes of Tax*
Elastic	Tax revenue increases proportionately more than the tax base.
Unitary Elasticity	Tax revenue increases proportionately with the tax base.
Inelastic	Tax revenue increases less than proportionately with the tax base.

The *tax base* is the universe being taxed: income, purchases, property, inheritance. The tax base must be differentiated from the *tax rate*, which is the rate applied to the designated base. A 6 per cent sales tax is a tax whose base is sales and whose rate is 6 per cent.

In the public finance literature an alternate trichotomy exists for classifying different taxes. Under this scheme taxes are categorized as either progressive, proportional, or regressive. Although there is no theoretical correspondence between this trichotomy and the elasticity schema, in the United States economy progressive taxes are usually revenue elastic, proportional taxes usually display unitary revenue elasticity, and regressive taxes are usually revenue inelastic.

An example of an income (GNP) elastic tax is the personal income tax as levied on the federal level. As national income increases by 1 per cent, tax revenue increases by more than 1 per cent because as people earn additional income they move into tax brackets in which the tax rate is higher. State income taxes and some forms of sales taxes approach the unitary elasticity level. State income taxes are not as progressive as the federal income tax—they have fewer tax brackets, the tax rate does not increase as steeply between brackets, and the maximum tax rate is reached at lower income levels. A general tax on all sales could also fall into the unitary elasticity category.

Sales taxes based on staples, rather than luxuries, and property taxes are income inelastic. As income increases, the amount spent on such items does not increase as fast and only one tax rate applies. Property values are reassessed intermittently (often only at the time of resale). Because assessment partially determines the tax payment and reassessments occur rather infrequently, property tax revenues may not increase as rapidly as increases in income and property values. Compounding the revenue inelasticity of the property tax is the fact that property tax rates, in contrast to rates on other tax sources, are locally determined and susceptible to a high degree of voter leverage. Although tax rates are seldom central issues in state elections and almost never in national elections, they are quite often the determining factor in local contests, thereby deterring many politicians from supporting or initiating necessary tax increases.

The different revenue elasticities of the major tax sources is a clear indicator of their revenue-raising potential. The major revenue raisers are the personal and corporate income taxes, and these sources are by convention federal taxes. States and localities have typically depended on selected sales and property taxes, two of the smaller revenue raisers. Although states and localities levy income taxes, the revenue yielded by this tax is relatively small owing to the low tax rates and limited progressivity. The data presented in Table 11.1 on the sources of governmental revenue illustrate these points. Just as revenue sources are unequally distributed among the three levels of government, responsibility for providing public services is also un-equally distributed. The data presented in Table 11.2 indicate that education is a small item in the federal expenditure budget and the largest in the state and local budget. To compound the problem, the unequal distribution of tax revenue is not only a present phenomenon, but the relevant revenue elasticities of the respective tax sources prompt the prediction that the inequality may widen with time.

In a nutshell, the problem is that states, and especially localities, have utilized tax sources that are neither responsive nor adequate to the rising needs of these areas. The levying of additional taxes by the states and localities has not yielded sufficient revenue to overcome budgetary deficits.

Table 11.1

Governmental Revenue, by Level of Government, 1967 (in millions of dollars)

Revenue Source	All Governments	Federal	State	Local
TAXES	$176,121	$115,121	$31,926	$29,074
Property	26,047	n.a.	862	25,186
Personal Income	67,352	61,526	4,909	916
Corporate Income	36,198	33,971	2,227	(a)
Sales and Gross Receipts	36,336	15,806	18,575	1,956
Motor Vehicle and Operators' Licenses	2,454	n.a.	2,311	143
Death and Gift	3,773	2,978	795	(b)
All Other	3,961	840	2,248	873
	Percentage Distribution			
TAXES	100.0	65.4	18.1	16.5
Property	100.0	n.a.	3.3	96.7
Personal Income	100.0	91.3	7.3	1.4
Corporate Income	100.0	93.8	6.2	(a)
Sales and Gross Receipts	100.0	43.5	51.1	5.4
Motor Vehicle and Operators' Licenses	100.0	n.a.	94.1	5.9
Death and Gift	100.0	78.9	21.1	(b)
All Other	100.0	21.2	56.8	22.0

Notes: n.a. = not applicable to that level of government.
  (a) = minor amount of corporation taxes included in personal income tax figures.
  (b) = minor amount of death and gift taxes included in "all other" taxes.

Source: U.S. Bureau of the Census, *Statistical Abstract of the United States, 1969.* 90th Edition (Washington, D.C.: U.S. Government Printing Office, 1969), p. 408.

Table 11.2

**Government Expenditure by Type of Function, 1967
(in millions of dollars)**

Item	Federal	State and Local
National Defense	$74,515	$ 447
Space Research and Technology	4,856	0
General Government	14,791	10,059
International Affairs	2,871	0
Education	3,897	39,530
Health, Labor, Welfare	40,642	25,477
Veterans' Services	7,142	25
Commerce, Transportation, and Housing	8,256	16,114
Agriculture	4,169	1,020
Natural Resources	2,626	2,318
Total:	163,765	94,990

Education as a Per Cent of Total Government Expenditure, 1967

Government Level	Per Cent
Federal	2.4
State and Local	41.6

Source: *Survey of Current Business* 49 (1969): 33–34.

A second dimension of the problem relates to greater cost increases in education relative to both revenue sources and cost increases in other sectors of the economy. This dimension of the financing problem is equally applicable to private schools and accounts, in large part, for their deteriorating financial status. Although private schools do not raise any of their revenue from governmental tax sources, their tuition and donation revenues have not kept pace with the required expenditures as the total educational burden has increased. The relative cost disadvantage of the educational enterprise is due in part to the fact that the production of education is extremely labor-intensive. It is doubtful if one can find many other secors of the economy that are as labor-intensive as education. Not only is education highly labor-intensive, but the rate of mechanization (the rate of substitution of capital for labor) is probably lower than in any other sector of the economy.

Productivity increases in education *vis-à-vis* other sectors of the economy, and the service sector in particular, have been small. Education is produced today largely along the lines that it was produced for our grandparents. The basic combination of teacher, students, and elementary visual aids has hardly changed. The lack of change is especially unusual when viewed in relation to production changes elsewhere. The economic problem associated with labor-intensive production and low productivity are compounded by the major increases in teachers' salaries secured during the 1960s. Data on salary increases for various occupational groups whose educational attainment is comparable to that of teachers are presented in Table 11.3. It is clearly seen that teacher salary increases exceeded increases in each of a cross section of comparable professional occupations.[3]

Table 11.3

Percentage Increase in Average Salaries for Selected Occupations: 1961–68

Occupational Group[a]	Per Cent Increase
Accountants	31.2
Auditors	32.5
Chief Accountants	33.2
Attorneys	32.3
Managers, Office Services	32.0
Job Analysts	31.9
Directors of Personnel	32.2
Chemists	34.5
Engineers	31.0
Teachers	41.5

[a] With the exception of teachers, salary data is based on private industry figures.

Source: Teachers: National Educational Association—Research Division, *Economic Status of the Teaching Profession, 1968–69* (Washington, D.C.: National Education Association, 1969), p. 9. All other occupations: U.S. Bureau of the Census, *Statistical Abstract of the United States: 1969*, 90th ed. (Washington, D.C.: U.S. Government Printing Office, 1969), p. 231.

Because the problem of educational financing stems in large part from the institutional and legal framework surrounding the aggregate United States tax system, a large part of the solution depends upon tax restructuring and sharing. Tax restructuring can proceed along two lines. Changes can be made in both the tax base and the tax rate. Traditionally, the tax base (for the income tax) has been defined as all earnings and income minus certain predetermined exemptions and deductions. Examples of exemptions and deductions are the $650 exemption per dependent, deductions for medical and charitable expenditures, and exemptions on part of corporate dividends received. However, the United States tax laws are extremely complicated, and the number of actual exemptions, deductions, and areas of preferential treatment far exceed the knowledge of the average citizen.

The greater the number of exemptions permitted and the larger the deductions allowed, the narrower the aggregate tax base becomes. Given a set tax rate, the narrower the tax base, the lower the total tax revenue. Although there were, and may still be, valid reasons for permitting exemptions, deductions, and preferential treatment, these reasons are rarely reviewed. We find ourselves adding new tax loopholes without at the same time plugging up those that have existed for years. Thus, a first line of attack in obtaining additional revenue for such vital services as education appears to be tax revision aimed at widening rather than narrowing the tax base.[4]

In the absence of major tax revisions, or possibly in conjunction with such revisions, tax (revenue) sharing could also be instituted. The need for tax sharing stems from the fact that the federal government controls the most elastic source of revenue whereas the states and localities are assuming greater and greater roles in providing basic public services. One alternative to this development is that the federal government undertake a larger role in the provision of these public services. To an extent this is already happening in the areas of education and social welfare. However, if state and local autonomy are desirable features and if the growth of federal power is to be checked, tax (revenue) sharing is an appealing option. It entails a commitment on the part of the federal government to return a set amount of tax money each year to the state and local governments to use as supplements to their tax sources and is an attempt to redistribute tax income to coincide with the responsibility for providing public services.

One revenue sharing system, known as grants-in-aid, has developed in several forms: flat grants, equilization grants, and incentive grants. Flat grants are usually based on some absolute criterion such as population size or, in education, the number of students in average daily attendance (ADA).[5] Equalization grants can be viewed as attempts to compensate for inequality among areas by providing an amount to each area inversely related to its expenditures. Incentive grants attempt to encourage specific expenditures and are devised so as to elicit a greater financial effort than would otherwise be forthcoming. One formula upon which incentive grants can be based is a state's or locality's ranking on an effort/ability scale. The discussion in Chapter 2 indicates one way of constructing such an index. Although all grants-in-aid attempt to recreate a balance between means and needs, economists, by and large, favor the incentive grants-in-aid.

Incentive grants leave room for more versatility than flat or equalizing grants and do not suffer from the drawbacks of these other types of grant. Flat grants do not adjust for need; consequently, an area with a large population or number of students in ADA may receive more money than other areas having greater need. Equalization grants are deemed to be deficient in that they may discourage states or localities from appropriating funds up to the limit of their ability in some areas because of the knowledge that the federal or state government will compensate for their low appropriation.

A third solution is the institution of a state lottery whose proceeds are earmarked either exclusively or in large part for financing educational needs. Three states have already adopted such lotteries—New Hampshire, New York, and New Jersey—although the lottery proceeds have fallen short of initial expectations. A fourth solution to the financial crunch facing education lies in an attempt to achieve higher levels of efficiency in the production and distribution of education. Efficiency will be discussed in greater depth in a subsequent section of this chapter.

FINANCING: HIGHER EDUCATION

Almost all the issues raised and solutions offered in the previous section dealing with elementary and secondary education apply with equal validity and urgency to the field of higher education. Only issues and considerations exclusively applicable to higher education will be discussed here. The discussion focuses around two distinctive features of higher education: the role of government and proposals to ease the immediate burden of high tuition through a system of loans. By law the government has undertaken to provide each youngster a place in an elementary and secondary school system. Although many youngsters are schooled in private elementary and secondary educational institutions, they are guaranteed a spot in the public school system if they desire one; but this is not true for higher education. In many respects the economic pressure facing private universities is similar to the economic pressure confronting private primary and secondary schools.

Additional factors, however, add to the problem on the higher education level. Universities have been tending to (a) embrace new fields and new technologies, (b) accept broader responsibilities in the world at large, (c) educate more graduate students relative to undergraduates,[6] and (d) do more research. Furthermore, whereas tuitions have risen in recent years much faster than the prices of most other things, this rate of increase cannot be continued. A desire on the part of private universities to attract students from all socioeconomic levels and competition from low-tuition state universities limit the extent of future tuition increases.

One solution is a transfer of students from private universities to public universities. The rapid growth of state universities in the last few decades indicates that such a shift of the overall burden has indeed taken place. But all that is accomplished by such a development is a transfer of responsibility from the private to the public sector. Since public education on the elementary and secondary level is already suffering from a deficiency of funds, the addition of the financial burdens of private higher education onto the state and local budget would be ill conceived from a financial point of view.

Thinking has recently shifted to an alternate solution that falls under the broad title of federal loan programs. Noting the sizable returns to an investment in higher education, many policy makers argue that additional costs should be borne directly by the student body rather than society at large. To avoid a situation where only the affluent can afford a higher education, a system of loans is proposed.

Many loans proposals have been advanced in the last few years. We focus attention on two major types that, with minor variations, seem to predominate in the educational literature. A panel on educational innovation studying this question suggested the

establishment of a bank, which might be called the Educational Opportunity Bank, as an agency of the Federal Government. In order to obtain funds, the bank should be authorized to borrow money at going Government rates. It should be authorized to lend money to postsecondary students, regardless of the student's resources. A student should be able to borrow enough money to cover his tuition, costs, and subsistence at whatever college, university, or other postsecondary institution he is admitted to. The Bank would recoup these loans through annual payments collected in conjunction with the borrower's future income tax. At the time a loan was granted, the borrower would pledge a percentage of his future income for a fixed number of years after graduation. The Panel recommends that the number of years for repayment be 30, or perhaps 40, years. This period would be a fixed term for all borrowers. The percentage of income pledged would be proportional to the amount borrowed. Preliminary estimates are that the Bank could be self-sustaining if it charged borrowers 1% of gross income over 30 years for each $3,000 borrowed.[7]

A major attraction of this program is that it does not influence a student's career choice. If a fixed repayment fee is required, as most education loans today do require, many students in the humanities and the arts may feel that their future earnings prospects neither justify nor enable them to take such a loan. However, if a percentage of income is pledged, the projected financial burden of a loan is greatly diminished for those who expect relatively low incomes.

Howard R. Bowen has proposed an alternative scheme whereby the financial burden of higher education is partially removed from both the student's and university's shoulders. Bowen's plan consists of three parts:

1. Students would be financed partly by grants based on the difference between a minimal college-going budget and the financial ability of parents and students as determined by a means test. These grants would be available to all *bona fide* students from the freshman year to the Ph.D. on a showing of need.
2. In addition, students would have access to loans, without a means test, to take care of 'extras' over and above the minima provided in the grants or the amounts supplied by parents. Both grants and loans would be provided through federal programs but might be administered by the colleges and universities.
3. Institutions would receive unrestricted grants by which the federal government would share in future increases in costs per student and in number of students.[8]

Bowen's plan differs significantly from that of the panel on educational innovation. Grants rather than loans are given to the student, and grants are also given to the educational institution proper. In addition, equality of opportunity would be a greater reality under this system in that grants would be given to all needy students to acquire a minimal quality higher education. If the student wishes to attend a more expensive university, he can do so by borrowing the additional money required.

Whatever the actual system adopted, it appears that the federal government will, as in the case of elementary and secondary education, have to shoulder much of the burden of future higher education. Considering the high social rates of return to educational investments, this does not appear to be at all unreasonable.

EFFICIENCY

Efficiency,[9] defined in layman's terms, is "the ability to produce the desired effect with a minimum of effort, expense, or waste."[10]

Efficiency is desirable in its own right as a means of maximizing want fulfillment given limited resources, but it becomes even more compelling when the disparity between wants and needs is projected to widen, as it is in the field of education. The concept of efficiency is closely connected to that of productivity, for it is through maximized productivity that maximum efficiency is achieved. There are two aspects to the maximization of productivity. First, any given set of inputs should be utilized so as to produce the largest value of output; and second, for a specified output and quality level, inputs should be chosen and utilized so as to minimize production costs.

In attempting to apply efficiency and productivity concepts to education, one is immediately confronted by the problem of defining educational output. Although attempts have already been made in this area, as the Woodhall and Blaug article appearing in Chapter 6 indicates, there is still room for improving and extending the coverage of any productivity measure. Even in the absence of hard and fast productivity figures, steps can be taken to increase the internal efficiency of educational institutions and the distribution of the educational product.

One of the many inputs in the production of education is that of skilled labor—teachers. Because teachers account for an overwhelmingly large proportion of factor inputs into education, any improvements that can be made in teacher utilization will contribute to greater efficiency in education. Following patterns established throughout the economy, the division of labor is one factor that usually leads to enhanced productivity and efficiency. Division of labor already exists in higher education and in most secondary school systems. Its introduction into the elementary schools might be a positive contribution to overall efficiency. Although most teachers are not equally gifted or suited in all curriculum areas, the single teacher per grade must cover the entire curriculum range. Specialization within certain confines could improve the overall curriculum offering. Utilizing specialized teachers in reading and other subjects is one step in this direction; team teaching is another. In many instances it is more efficient to have team teaching, with curriculum areas divided according to a given teacher's specific expertise, than a system of parallel classes.

A second step that can increase efficiency in the production of education is the utilization and maximization of economies of scale (size) while avoiding diseconomies of scale. Greater size allows the distribution of certain fixed costs such as libraries, gymnasiums, language and speech laboratories, administration, and purchasing facilities among larger numbers of students, thus reducing the cost per student of these items. Many suburban and rural complexes have discovered that economies of size stem from school consolidations.

In some instances, however, school system size has exceeded the point where economies of scale can be reaped, and diseconomies of scale may appear. Many large urban school complexes have reached this point, and solutions involving school board decentralization have been suggested. A prime benefit of decentralization is the increased efficiency of school administration because the sheer size of the school district that must be administered decreases. Decentralization encourages selective experimentation that may lead to educational breakthroughs. A further benefit stemming from smaller size is increased parental influence and interest in areas such as curriculum and administration. Although this latter benefit may be more political than economic, it is nevertheless an important factor in the production of education.[11]

Efficiency can also be increased in the distribution of education. The school year normally runs from September to June on the elementary and secondary levels and is about a month shorter on the college and university level. The reasons for the summer vacation are traditionally given as stemming from the mores of an agricultural society and more recently of giving students a vacation during the hottest period of the year, when learning would be hampered by high temperatures. Our aggregate economic structure has since shifted in favor of industry and services and away from agriculture. Air conditioning mitigates the effects of high temperatures and in many instances makes the school a more comfortable place to be during the summer months than either a child's home or neighborhood streets.

There is no economic reason why a school's physical facilities should not remain in use during the summer session or during certain evening hours in the course of the school year. While the cost of such additional use must be weighted against the educational return, there are clear indications that the benefits exceed the costs. On the college and university level, this lesson has been learned by many, as extensive summer sessions and thriving evening divisions attest. Secondary school systems have adopted such programs to a lesser degree; elementary schools are barely moving in this direction. Although the age of the students is a deterring factor on the elementary school level, the organization of the school year along current lines has no particular economic justification. Not only could existing school facilities accommodate more pupils if more flexible scheduling were adopted, thereby reducing fixed costs per student enrolled, but the students' own time would also be economized. Remembering the high foregone earnings component of high school, college, and graduate schooling costs, the students' time should by no means be considered to be a free good. It is scarce, like any other input in the educational process, and should be considered as such.

Looking further at education from a micro viewpoint, many areas can be seen where potential for increased efficiency exists. Whether or not this potential will actually be realized is a matter yet to be determined. In most cases material is presented without evaluation because insufficient information is available for that purpose. Three interrelated areas, which deal with new methods in or new applications to the educational field and are discussed below, are planning and accounting techniques, capital goods for teaching, and research and development.

Several new planning and accounting techniques have been and are being applied to education with varying degrees of success in terms of increased efficiency. The most important of these are cost-benefit analysis, simulation, and program planning and budgeting. In Chapters 7 and 8 considerable attention was devoted to the cost-benefit methodology and its application to education. It was seen that this technique assists educational administrators in choosing the most efficient of alternative approaches to a given objective by providing a framework in which to compare the costs to the benefits of each contemplated approach. The versatility of this technique for handling diverse items of both costs and benefits was noted. Cost-benefit analysis is a necessary component of evaluation for each of the techniques discussed below because it is efficiency that is the objective of these innovations. None of these innovations should be adopted if they fail the cost-benefit test.

A second technique useful to educational administrators is that of *simulation*. Models of educational systems, when combined with modern high speed computers, can be utilized to determine the many ramifications of alternate policy actions before they are undertaken. This is accomplished by entering the change of policy being considered into the model of the school, university, or school system and then tracing (simulating) with the computer the hypothetical development of the system over many years. All too often decisions are made with only the effects in the following year in mind. Although such a decision may seem efficient, or even be efficient, for the time horizon of one year, it may be extremely inefficient over longer periods of time. It is only with the development of high speed computers that the simulation technique has become practical for analyzing complex problems involving hundreds of thousands of calculations. With simulation, the development associated with each of a large number of policy choices over long periods of time is made available for evaluation. Simulation models have been successfully utilized in planning for the University of Toronto and elsewhere.

The following illustration of the application of a simulation model to a problem in higher education demonstrates its usefulness:

Assume that [total university] enrollment forecasts exist for the coming decade....

Problem: What are the resource implications of the enrollment forecasts? How many teachers of various qualifications will be required? What physical facilities will be needed? What quantity of money will be called for?

How sensitive to errors in the forecasts are the answers to these questions? Do they depend crucially upon an assumed pattern of course enrollment?...

Taking the forecasted enrollments as data, the model would compute the quantities of staff, money, and facilities required to handle the load. For each year of the simulation, the computer would present (the) results...the established total dollar magnitude of the departmental budgets are shown together with the needs for staff and physical facilities....

The computations would be repeated with alternative assumptions about key factors such as the pattern of change in staff salaries, the distribution of students among the various faculties and courses, class sizes, rates of utilization of classrooms, etc. University operations would be simulated for the decade with a range of possible enrollment projections; this would illuminate the sensitivity of the results to errors in the projections....

Assisted by the simulation results for the coming decade, university planners and administrators should be able to make their decisions in cognizance of more and better information than is now possible.[12]

A third technique in this area is called *program planning and budgeting* (PPB). PPB is an approach to planning that emphasizes the ultimate objectives of the educational system or unit. These objectives are specified and an attempt is then made to fulfill them in the least expensive manner, *i.e.*, most efficiently. PPB generally encourages the systematic consideration of alternate approaches to given objectives and the periodic review of the performance of the unit in comparison to these objectives. The accounting system is revamped to reflect total expenditures toward overall objectives rather than expenditures on factors of production such as teachers, materials, and buildings.

A program budget for a graduate teachers college, for example, might itemize expenditures for such objectives as training teachers, training administrators, research toward the advancement of knowledge, and public service. These can be compared to a traditional budget so organized as to itemize expenditures by academic departments (curriculum and teaching, psychology, guidance, and so on), the administration, and the physical maintenance division. As Harry Hartley puts it, the program structure "makes the outputs of a school district visible and identifies the resources required to yield these outputs." [13]

Several school systems have adopted this approach including, for example, Baltimore, Chicago, Memphis, and Seattle. There are many schools and school systems undoubtedly too small for such activities to be profitable. As is true of many of the possibilities for increasing efficiency in education presented in this section, it remains to be seen how widely applicable and viable this technique will prove to be in the educational institutional environment.

Cost-benefit analysis, simulation techniques, and program planning and budgeting are potentially complementary rather than competitive methods of increasing educational productivity and hence efficiency. Similarly, all three are, or can be, utilized in the evaluation of new capital goods designed for the improvement of the educational experience.

The number of capital goods that have been introduced each year in the educational field has been growing steadily, and improvements on existing goods are also common. Many of these devices, such as video-taped lectures combined with closed circuit television, are labor-replacing or labor-saving. Others, such as activities utilizing electron microscopes and nuclear accelerators, allow things to be done which were formerly impossible. It is the former group which is most interesting from the point of view of efficiency since it involves alternate means of achieving the same end.

Although many have asserted that computers, teaching machines, video-tape, and other inventions have revolutionized the field of education, few institutions utilize these technologies. One area of economic growth theory deals with the speed and extent of diffusion of new technologies, and one of its basic hypotheses is that the greater the education level of those who will potentially use an innovation, the faster will be its spread. Because the average educational level of teachers and educational administrators has been increasing over time and innovations spread in their use with the passage of time, one can expect that these innovations will be utilized to a greater and greater extent in the future. Of course, the viability of such devices must always be of primary concern. However, as time passes, improvements are made and experience in the utilization of these machines is garnered, both leading to greater efficiency.

The amount of labor that may be saved is stupendous. Computer aided instruction, for example, can set up a program of study for each student based on his performance on every question on every quiz over a whole year. Depending on his performance on frequent quizzes, some questions and/or material will be repeated, some questions will be asked in different forms, and some potential questions will be skipped over in his program of instruction. For a teacher to make up an individual program for just one school day for each student based on a thorough analysis of each student's past examination performance would take days. This is but one example.[14] The number of such technologies is growing rapidly and with it the potential for new levels of efficiency.

We now turn to the area that creates and improves these devices and techniques: research and development. Expenditures on research and development have been shown to be extremely profitable in most sectors of the economy. Many large corporations—RCA, Kodak, Harper and Row, IBM, Random House, 3M, and CBS, to name a few—have recently begun programs of educational research and development in devising, for example, new visual aids, curriculum packages, and teaching machines. Education, after all, is one of the largest industries in the United States, ranking second only to defense. In addition, a new effort has been undertaken in the form of a network of federally supported regional educational laboratories of which over twenty are already in existence.

With increased expenditure on research in educational techniques, one can expect many new and improved methods and capital goods to be developed. One can also expect new commercial efforts toward having these adopted. Specifically, advertisements and demonstrations of newly developed methods will undoubtedly be increased dramatically as the commercial investment in this area increases. The fact that rapidly increasing efforts are going into educational research and development and many new techniques and machines have already been developed brings a ray of hope into the otherwise rather depressing outlook for the economic future of American education.

COMPETITION

It was noted in Chapter 1 that from the point of view of maximizing social and private output within a constraint of limited resources, competition yielded the optimum output level. It is by no means a coincidence that output is maximized under competition, for by its very nature competition forces producers to optimality as a means of guaranteeing survival. Although cutthroat competition may be nobody's ideal, economists believe that a feeling of competitiveness instills a real motive for optimum productivity and efficiency.

Public education on the primary and secondary level approximates a monopolistic rather than a competitive market. Although all eligible students are guaranteed a place in the school system, their choice is narrowly circumscribed by legal and institutional arrangements. It is true that a substitute for public education is available in the form of private and parochial school systems, but the degree of substitutability is far from perfect. Many families cannot afford the costs of private education; others are opposed to private education on social and egalitarian grounds. It should be intuitively obvious that two competing services, one requiring no direct outlay and the other requiring an outlay often in excess of $1,000 a year are far from perfect substitutes.

As a quasi-monopolist insulated against competitive forces by legal and institutional barriers, the United States educational system —especially on the elementary and secondary levels—is protected from competitive pressures that could stimulate efficient behavior. Economists realize that there are certain educational values and traditions that must be sheltered from competitive forces lest we risk compromising or sacrificing these principles.[15] Without tampering with these principles a fair degree of competition can still be instilled within the educational system.

Milton Friedman is widely regarded as the chief proponent of competition within the educational system.[16] Friedman's views are shared by many prominent educators who view competition as one step in an overall plan of educational reform. We illustrate the role assigned to increased competition in two of the most sensitive and compelling educational issues on the contemporary scene: school decentralization and student unrest.

Theodore Sizer, Dean of the Graduate School of Education at Harvard University, addressing himself to the issue of education in the urban ghetto, asserts that

...the 'consumer' should have some influence over the school he attends, enough to shape it in appropriate ways, but not enough to terrorize it. In a field where values are paramount—schools are places designed to *influence* children and as such are supremely moral enterprises—no group, students, parents, teachers or government, should have total control. There should be a balance. Many of today's school systems do not permit sufficient diversity among individual students and individual schools. In doing so, they foster a dull conformity. Competition among schools must be added to the balance.
Despite evidence to the contrary..., a change in control *can* lead to a change in the quality of children's learning.[17]

Focusing on the problem of education in the ghetto, Sizer reviews four schemes to increase competition. The first would entail drastic and total decentralization as an effort to give power and control over a school or school system to those in the immediate community served by that school. A second, more radical, plan would employ government funds to create separate, private school systems for minorities. Under this scheme voluntary decentralization rather than geographic decentralization would exist. In conjunction with the public, private, and parochial systems that now exist one would find additional private schools organized along ethnic lines, all financed to a degree by public funds. A third competitive scheme would entail subcontracting out certain areas of the curriculum, such as reading or arithmetic, to private educational companies who guarantee a specified result. Competition would then ensue among the private contractors, each one of whom would attempt to provide the educational service at the lowest cost. A fourth plan would give money directly to each parent for the education of their children and allow the parents to choose from among a spectrum of accredited educational institutions.[18] Institutions would then compete for the favor of the parents, offering competing or similar educational packages to various ethnic or socio-economic groups. To insure that any preexisting economic inequality did not lead to a neglect of the poor pupil under this voucher scheme, the value of a student's voucher could be inversely related to family wealth, thus making the poorer students the more attractive ones from a school's revenue maximizing viewpoint.
Sizer himself appears to reject the first two competitive schemes

in favor of a broad plan of educational reform containing elements of the voucher and subcontracting proposals. Fully realizing the missionary task involved in advocating greater competitiveness in education, Sizer summarizes his feelings as

...The public school is Mom and apple pie. The fact that it is a monopoly and that all children with few exceptions are *forced* to submit to *communal* schooling rarely dissuade July Fourth orators. The notion of deliberately creating entities to compete with Mom is jarring indeed, and will be lost on more than a few Washington lobbyists.

However, in context and as part of a large, careful scheme for the reform of American education, one or more schemes to abet competition among schools have considerable promise. Perhaps American educators and politicians are mature enough to see the promise as well as the problems.[19]

A greater degree of competitiveness is also being proposed at the college and university level, in this instance as a response to student unrest. Alan Peacock and Anthony Culyer have written an interesting article in this area which focuses on British higher education. With few exceptions, their observations are equally applicable to the United States scene. They suggest that since the allocation of scarce resources among competing uses is the heart of economics, economics is useful in investigating the tensions between students and university authorities over the use of educational resources. Because the normal allocative device of supply and demand clearing the market via an equilibrium price does not operate in education, producers (universities) are freed to ration out places on any criteria they desire. It is their preferences rather than those of the student consumers that count. Students therefore buy a product that their preferences have little power to effect, thereby creating tensions. In addition, as Peacock and Culyer point out

...Since universities are not required by statute or market to make profits, the costs to university men of increasing their 'utility' at work in a whole variety of ways are much lower than they would otherwise be. This results in an increase in their consumption of 'on-the-job' sources of satisfaction, and accounts for faculty tenure, magnificent gardens, and minimal inconvenience from customers (who have limited opportunities for 'shopping around' once they are admitted); research may take priority over teaching; student-staff contact hours are minimal; and the use of ancillary university facilities is 'awarded' on a hierarchical principle, which means that students may be denied the use of the more convenient parking spaces, lifts, common rooms, lavatories, and so on.

This monopoly organisation, as it often does in industry, has also led to the use of 'tie-ins': techniques for increasing monopoly profits by taking advantage of consumer dependence. In our universities their function is similar. The universities are not concerned with increasing profit, but they are maximising other objectives. By tying-in subsidised residences for students, the producers in universities are able to derive an additional source of satisfaction from enforcement of rules of conduct. Formal dinners with academic dress, ladies (or men) out by 10:30 p.m., and so on, are conducive to satisfaction of the benevolent wishes of universities' staffs, though often irritating to the students; but the students are bribed to accept these conditions by compensation in the form of residence at less than market-clearing price, and sometimes at a price less than the cost of provision. At some universities, residence is simply compulsory. At others, private flats are prohibited, at least until a student is twenty-one....

...Insecurity derived from such dependence on the supplier builds up tension. It is no longer even possible to control personal consumption (and investment) by 'voting with one's feet', or by having the right to a second chance, for suppliers can deny a customer supply, safe in the knowledge that there are many others to take his place....[20]

Peacock and Culyer's analysis suggests that the environment can be changed by action, coming either from above or within the universities, that would affect the administrators. Such changes could come in the area of university finance and the political control associated with it or could work within the university environment through the building up of countervailing power. It is the latter road that has been followed in Great Britain (and the United States). The rise of the cry for student power can be partly explained by the fact that the road to increased control is less costly for students because sit-ins and demonstrations have low opportunity costs.

Peacock and Culyer proceed to suggest the following threefold reform. First, universities should rely for the major source of their revenue on the purchasing power of students rather than on the financial support of a governmental agency. Students should be provided with adequate loan funds and/or subsidies to enable them to pay for the entire cost of their education. Second, greater freedom of entry into universities and greater diversity of universities or university programs should exist to broaden the realm of consumer choice. Third, the educational experience should be restructured to enable a greater degree of shopping around among competing educational institutions.

The advocates of increased competition in education are all attempting through their various proposals to increase the quality of schooling and to broaden the range of educational experiences open to all students. We applaud these approaches, for we firmly believe that it is through increased competition that the education industry can increase its efficiency and productivity.

QUESTIONS FOR DISCUSSION

1. How do population trends (natural increase and migration) affect the tax base for supporting public education?

2. What steps might be taken by a school board or a group of concerned citizens to counteract the deteriorating financial position many school systems are in? In what ways would each of your suggestions affect the financial situation?

3. What technological developments now extant do you think will most likely be widely adopted in schools in the 1970s? What are their economic aspects?

4. In what ways might competition be introduced into elementary school education (either between schools or within schools)?

Mathematics[1]

MODELS AND THEIR COMPONENTS

Mathematics is generally utilized in economics in the processes of building, testing, and quantifying models. *A model is an abstraction of a real situation.* It is the quality and relevance of the abstracting that determines the usefulness of the model. Reality is often too complex and includes too much data to be easily manipulated and studied. Models can be either dynamic or static. That is, they can be concerned with change over time or a description of something at a point in time. In this appendix we shall attempt to present the various definitions, tools, concepts, and techniques necessary to understand the models and mathematics utilized in this book.

Equations, Constants, Parameters, and Variables

A mathematical model consists of a system of one or more equations and/or functions. The model can be used to predict, project, or evaluate some thing or things. Before investigating the workings of models, we shall define and discuss equations and functions.

Relationships between two or more things can be expressed as equations or inequalities. An *equation expresses an equality* such as:

$$10 = 6 + 4$$

whereas an inequality expresses unequal relationships such as:

$$10 > 6 \quad \text{or} \quad 6 < 10.$$

the symbols $>$ and $<$ are representative of "greater than" and "less than," respectively.

Equations are of three types: identity, technological, and behavioral. An *identity* equation specifies a definitional relationship such as gross national product equals consumption plus government expenditure plus investment $(\text{GNP} = C + I + G)$ or the student-teacher ratio, R, equals the number of students divided by the number of teachers $(R = S/T)$. *Technological equations* describe technological facts: 8 hours of labor combined with a \$1,000 machine produces one desk

Notes to Appendix I will be found on pages 391–392.

($8L + 1,000K = 1D$). A *behavioral equation*, on the other hand, describes human behavior. For instance, the equation for a demand curve (as price, P, increases, the amount demanded, Q, decreases: $Q = -aP + b$, where a and b are constants) is a behavioral equation because it describes how people react to price, rather than a technological relationship. Equations may contain constants and/or variables. *A constant is a number that is invariant.* Within the category of constants, there are two types that might be called absolute constants and parameters. An absolute constant is always the same regardless of the model or the context, such as

$$387, -8, \pi, \text{ or } 2\tfrac{1}{4}$$

Parameters and variables are closely allied. They are differentiated not by what they represent but by their function in a particular situation. A *parameter* is constant throughout a model or problem but may vary between problems or models. It differs from a variable in that it is expected to remain constant for short periods of time, at least, so that its value can be utilized for prediction or evaluation of variables. The same item, such as the average savings rate (s), which is defined as total savings divided by total income, or the wastage rate (w), which is the number of students who do not go on to the next year of schooling divided by the enrollment in the current year, may be a variable in one problem and a parameter in another. The wastage rate, for example, might be a parameter in a five year projection model of school enrollment because it would be expected to remain constant over that period. However, it would be a variable in the description of an action program designed to change the wastage rate because it would be expected to change in response to the various actions contemplated.

As the name implies, *a variable does not have to have a fixed value even within a given problem.* A variable such as class size might, for example, have values of 25, 27, 28, 33. There are several groupings into which variables can be classified: independent and dependent, policy and target, and exogenous and endogenous. These three pairs are not mutually exclusive.

The distinction between *independent* and *dependent* variables can be seen in the following example. An equation relating the number of students (S), the student-teacher ratio (R), and the number of teachers (T) could be set up in several forms. If the number of students were fixed at 1,000, the equation might read:

$$R = 1,000/T \tag{1}$$

In this equation T is considered an independent variable and R a dependent variable. The student-teacher ratio, R, is dependent on the variation of the number of teachers, T; as the number of teachers increases, the student-teacher ratio decreases. Of course, mathematically, the roles of R and T could easily be reversed. A simple transformation of equation (1) yields:

$$T = 1,000/R \qquad (2)$$

In this formulation R is the independent variable and T the dependent. Which is the best formulation depends on the actual problem being dealt with. If the student-teacher ratio is decided upon first and teachers hired to meet that requirement, R is logically the independent variable; if the number of teachers is decided upon regardless of the student-teacher ratio, T is logically the independent variable.

Policy and *target* are terms given to some variables in a planning context. Depending upon the goals of the planner and the nature of his control over that which is being planned, the designation of variables as target or policy is circumscribed. A policy variable is one whose value can be affected directly by the decision-making body undertaking the planning. Referring to the previous example, the board of education has control over the number of teachers employed. The number of teachers employed is then considered a policy variable. But the board of education does not have control over the number of students enrolled in its district. That number will vary with time and demographic conditions and cannot be considered a policy variable by the board of education. However, in higher education and private elementary and secondary school systems, the number of students enrolled is at the discretion of the directors of these institutions. Thus, the number of students and the number of teachers are both policy variables in this case.

A target variable is simply a variable whose value is set at some target or desired level. In this example the student-teacher ratio may be considered a target variable and set at some value such as 30/1. Setting a target puts constraints on other variables such as the number of teachers and the number of students. The nature of these constraints can then be studied. Alternately or concurrently, the effect of changes in various policy variables on the target variable can be investigated.

One can also distinguish between *exogenous* and *endogenous* variables. An exogenous variable is one which is not affected by the system or model being studied. The number of students in a public elementary school system is exogenous to the educational problem posed above.[2]

In other words, the value of an exogenous variable is a cause and not an effect of the values of other variables in the system. Endogenous variables are ones whose values are affected by the system. The student-teacher ratio is determined by the independent variables and is therefore endogenous. Endogenous variables can embody aspects of both cause and effect in a model. For example, in a comprehensive model of a school system, the number of teachers can be an effect of the number of students to be educated and a cause of the size of the educational budget.

The above discussion demonstrates that any given variable can be classified in a variety of manners. The number of teachers was seen to be an independent variable, a policy variable, and an endogenous variable under different schema. Similarly, the student-teacher ratio was classified as dependent, target, and endogenous. The fact that variables do not always fall on opposite sides of the dichotomies indicates that it is not redundant to have three groupings for classifying variables.

Consistency

Given these various types of variables and constants, certain limitations on the manner in which they can be entered into a model exist. In order to come up with a unique value for each of the variables, there have to be as many equations in the model as there are variables. If the number of variables is greater than the number of equations, the model is said to be *underdetermined*, and there will be an infinite number of values that will fulfill the conditions of the model, thereby extremely limiting the model's usefulness. For example, for the single equation system with two variables relating number of teachers (T) to number of students (S)

$$T = S/30 \tag{3}$$

there are an infinite number of combinations of values of T and S that will fulfill the equation: For any value of T we pick (10, 17, or 700) there will be a value of S that fulfills the equation (300, 510, 21,000).

If we add another equation with no new variables, say:

$$S = 1,500 \tag{4}$$

thereby enlarging the system to one of two equations and two variables, the possible solutions are reduced to one, which in this case is $S = 1,500$ and $T = 50$. When the number of equations equals the number of variables, the system is said to be *determined*. However, if there are more equations than variables, the system is *overdetermined*. For example, if we add the equation

$$T = 20 \tag{5}$$

we have three equations (3, 4, and 5) and only two variables (T and S). Usually in an overdetermined system not all of the equations can be solved; the equations are inconsistent with one another.[3]

Functions

At this point we introduce the concept and notation of functional relationships. A *function* such as:

$$Y = f(X)$$

which is read Y equals f of X, indicates that the value of the variable Y is a function of, or depends upon, the value of the variable X.[4] This should not be confused with Y equals f times X.[5] Other notations are also often employed for a functional relationship such as:

$$g(X), F(X), \text{and} f_1(X).$$

The dependent variable may be dependent upon more than one variable, in which case each of the independent variables is listed inside the parentheses and separated by commas:

$$T = f(S, C, Y) \tag{6}$$

This suggests that the number of teachers (T) is a function of or depends upon the number of students (S), the number of courses (C), and average teachers salary (Y). In these most abstract forms the functions tell us nothing about the exact relationships involved.

The function specified in equation (6) can be specified more precisely, for example:

$$T = \frac{S}{a} + bC - \frac{Y}{c} \tag{7}$$

where a, b, and c are parameters.

Equation (7) specifies the form of the relationship (for example, the effect on T of a change in C is equal to some parameter b times the change in C) whereas equation (6) specified only the direction of the relationship and the variables involved. We can go one step further and evaluate the parameters a, b, and c as:

$$T = \frac{S}{30} + 20C - \frac{Y}{5,000} \tag{8}$$

This exactly specifies the relationship between T and the independent variables S, C, and Y. Given the number of students, the number of courses, and the average teacher salary, we can easily determine the number of teachers. As will be seen in Appendix II, estimating parameters (such as a, b, and c in the above equation) of functions is one of the main ways in which statistics are utilized in economics of education.

Graphing of Equations

Theoretically, any equation can be represented by a curve on a graph. In practice we cannot draw the curves for equations with more than three variables because each variable requires a dimension. For convenience we limit the presentation to two-dimensional graphs. To plot an equation with one or two variables, a four-quadrant diagram is laid out as seen in Figure I.1. Traditionally, the horizontal line is called the X-axis, and the vertical line is called the Y-axis, and the point where the lines cross is the zero value of both X and Y. Any point on this graph represents a value of X *and* a value of Y. Points to the right of the Y-axis (quadrants I and IV) represent positive values of X and points to the left (quadrants II and III) represent negative values. Points above the X-axis (quadrants I and III) represent positive values of Y and points below the X-axis (quadrants III and IV) represent negative values of Y. Point A in Figure I.1 represents a value of X of $+4$ and a value of Y of $+3$. That is, point A is 4 units to the right of the Y-axis (representing $X = +4$) and 3 units above the Y-axis (representing $Y = +3$). Similarly, point B represents $X = +7$ and $Y = +1$. In the same manner, points C, D, and E represent the following combinations of

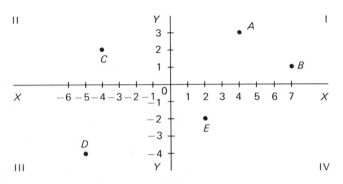

Figure I.1   Four Quadrant Diagram

values of X and Y where X is the first value and Y the second value in each parenthesis: $(-4, +2)$, $(-5, -4)$, and $(+2, -2)$.

The specific curve (or line) representing an equation that can be found by plotting several points representing pairs of values that fulfill the equation. For example, if the equation is $Y = X$, the values $Y = 2$ and $X = 2$ fulfill the equation as do $Y = 0$ and $X = 0$, $Y = -5$ and $X = -5$, and $Y = +7$ and $X = +7$. Each of these is a pair of values for which the equation is true. The curve in Figure I.2 represents

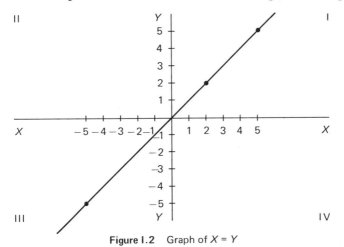

Figure I.2   Graph of $X = Y$

the graph of the equation $Y = X$. In graphing an equation it is often useful to construct a table of values of X and Y. Take the equation $Y = X^2 - 5$. A table, such as Table I.1, is constructed by picking a

Table I.1
Values of $Y = X^2 - 5$

X	Y
-5	$+20$
-2	-1
-1	-4
0	-5
1	-4
2	-1
3	$+4$
5	$+20$

series of arbitrary values of X, substituting each value of X into the equation and solving for Y. For example, take $X = +5$. When $+5$

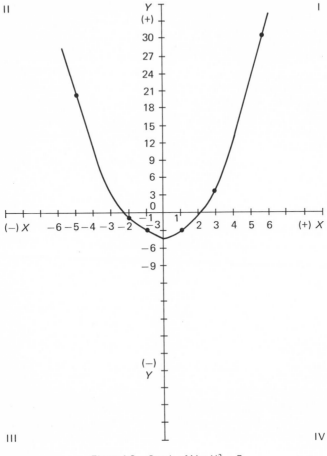

Figure I.3   Graph of Y = X² − 5

is substituted for X, the equation becomes $Y = 5^2 - 5 = 25 - 5 =$ 20. Thus, when $X = 5$, $Y = 20$. Similarly, when $X = 0$, $Y = 0^2 - 5 = -5$; when $X = +2$, $Y = +2^2 - 5 = -1$; and when $X = -2$, $Y = (-2)^2 - 5 = -1$. Once the table has been constructed, the pairs of values can be plotted on the graph and the curve sketched in. As can be seen in Figure I.3, the minimum value of Y when $Y = X^2 - 5$ is -5, while Y seems to have no upper limit and X appears to have no limit on either the positive or negative side.

DERIVATIVES

Simple Derivatives

A derivative is used when it is of interest to know the change in one variable associated with the change in another variable. This concept, taken from calculus, is utilized extensively in economics. It is used, for example, in calculating elasticities in demand theory, profit maximization in the theory of the firm, the tradeoff between factors of production in the production of a good in production theory, and growth itself in growth theory. The information embodied in the derivative can also be found by graphing a relationship between two or more variables. However, the use of derivatives does away with the time consuming (and often inaccurate) process of drawing graphs. In this section we shall define derivatives, both formally and intuitively. Then we shall present some examples of their use in the economics of education and some simple rules for determining them.

A derivative can be defined in two different but equivalent forms.

Derivative = the value of the slope of a line tangent to a curve

$$= \textit{the limit of } \frac{\Delta Y}{\Delta X} \textit{ as } \Delta X \textit{ approaches zero,}[6] \textit{ i.e.,}$$

$$\lim_{\Delta X \to 0} \frac{\Delta Y}{\Delta X} \textit{ which is represented by } \frac{dY}{dX}.$$

A *tangent is a line that touches a curve at a particular point but does not intersect it,* such as the line *nn* in Figure I.4. The *slope* of a straight line is a number that indicates its steepness. *Slope is defined as the ratio of the change in Y to the change in X between any two points on the line.* Referring to Figure I.4, the slope of line *nn* between points *C* and *A* (or any other two points) is 2/3. In this case *Y* changes from 20 to 40, a change of $+20$, while *X* changes from 30 to 60, a change of $+30$. The ratio of this change, $+20/+30$, is 2/3. Since 2/3 is the value of the slope of line *nn* and *nn* is tangent to curve *mm* at point *C*, 2/3 is the derivative of the curve at that point.

The second definition of the derivative, the limit of $\Delta Y/\Delta X$ as ΔX approaches zero, *i.e.,* $\lim_{\Delta X \to 0} \Delta Y/\Delta X$ is perhaps the one which best describes the derivative but which many find the hardest to grasp. It says that the derivative is the value of $\Delta Y/\Delta X$ as ΔX approaches zero. That is, it is the value of $\Delta Y/\Delta X$ as ΔX is made smaller and smaller. The reasoning here is as follows. Note that the value of the slope of the tangent does not describe the actual change in the curve *mm* for a given change in *X*. If the value of *X* increases by 30 units

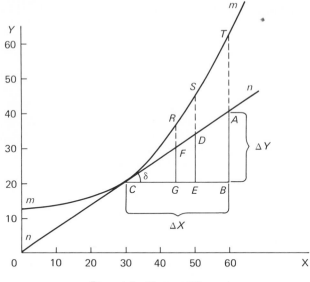

Figure I.4   Slope and Tangent

of X from point C, the value of Y on the curve mm is 60 (point T). Thus, when we changed X by $+30$, Y changed by $+40$ or in other words, $\Delta Y/\Delta X$ was actually 40/30 or 4/3 rather than the value we found for the slope of the tangent, 2/3. It is because of this difference that we say that the slope of the tangent tells us the relative rate of change of Y and X only *at a given point.* As we can see by looking at line CB, as we make the value of the change of X smaller and smaller (BC to EC to GC), we find that the corresponding change of Y along the tangent line (nn) gets closer and closer to the actual change on the curve mm (TB versus AB, SE versus DE, and RG versus FG).

As ΔX becomes very small, approaching but never quite reaching zero, ΔY as seen on the tangent line comes closer and closer to the change in Y as seen on the curve.[7] At the limit, when the change in X is so small as to be effectively zero, the change in Y as seen on the tangent line and as seen on the curve are equal so that the value of the slope of the tangent is the derivative.

If a particular function is being investigated, the derivative indicates the value of the slope of the tangent at any point on the curve representing the function. For example, suppose that average student examination scores on a particular standardized test (S) were the following function of teacher's verbal ability (V):

$$S = V^2 + V + 4 \tag{9}$$

The graph of equation (9) is seen in Figure I.5. The derivative (dS/dV) would tell us the effect of an increase of one point in the teacher's verbal ability on the score of his students. The derivative at any point can be found by drawing the tangent. For example, at $V = 7$, the value of the slope of the tangent is equal to 15.[8] This means that when a teacher has a verbal score of 7, the rate of change between the score of his students on the test and his verbal score is 15 to 1. We can go through the same procedure and find the value of the slope of the tangent at any point. However, there is a generalized method for obtaining the value of the slope of the tangent.

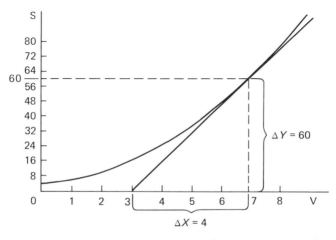

Figure I.5   Graph of $S = V^2 + V + 4$

Through the employment of a few simple rules for finding the derivative, the value of the slope of the tangent at any point is immediately known. The basic rules are:

Rule 1   *The derivative of a constant term is zero.*

    a. $Y = 74$ b. $M = \pi$ c. $Y = 32.75$

$$\frac{dY}{dX} = 0 \qquad\qquad \frac{dM}{dX} = 0 \qquad\qquad \frac{dY}{dX} = 0$$

Rule 2   *The derivative of a variable is a term whose coefficient is the original coefficient times the original exponent and whose exponent is the original exponent minus 1.*[9] For example, the derivative of $Y = aX^m$, dY/dX, is $m \cdot aX^{m-1}$. That is, the new coefficient $(m \cdot a)$ of variable X is the old coefficient (a) times the original exponent (m) and the new exponent ($m - 1$) of the variable is the old exponent (m) minus 1.

d. $Y = 32X^1$ (*i.e.*, $32X$)

$$\frac{dY}{dX} = 32 \cdot 1X^{1-1} = 32X^0$$

$$= 32.1 = 32$$

[since $X^0 = 1$]

e. $T = 7aX^3$

$$\frac{dT}{dX} = 3 \cdot 7aX^{3-1}$$

$$= 21aX^2$$

Rule 3   *The derivative of a series of factors is equal to the sum of the derivatives of each of the factors.* For example, the derivative of $X^2 + 3X$ is equal to the derivative of X^2 plus the derivative of $3X$, *i.e.*, $2X + 3$.

f. $S = V^2 + V + 4$

$$\frac{dS}{dV} = 2 \cdot V^{2-1} + 1 \cdot V^{1-1} + 0$$

$$= 2V^1 + 1V^0 = 2V + 1$$

g. $M = \dfrac{1R^2}{a} + 13bR + 63$

$$\frac{dM}{dR} = 2 \cdot \frac{1R^{2-1}}{a} + 13bR^{1-1} + 0$$

$$= \frac{2R^1}{a} + 13bR^0 = \frac{2R}{a} + 13b$$

All that is necessary to find many derivatives is the ability to utilize these three very simple rules.[10]

Second Derivatives and Maximization

Example (f) under Rule 3 yielded the general form for the value of the slope of the tangent of the equation diagrammed in Figure I.5. We now are able to derive from the formula for the derivative that if $V = 7$, the derivative is equal to 15 (the derivative dS/dV is equal to $2V + 1$; so when $V = 7$, the derivative equals $2(7) + 1$ or 15), just as we found geometrically. Using the same formula, we can also determine that the derivative has a value of -1 when $V = -1$ and 7 when $V = 3$. As may have been noted, the value of the derivative of this function becomes larger and larger as V increases. The rate or the direction of change of the derivative of a function is also of interest in many problems. This is found by taking the derivative of the derivative. If the function is

$$Y = X^b \tag{10}$$

its derivative, dY/dX, is bX^{b-1} (as we know from following Rule 2). The value of the *derivative of the derivative* (or *second derivative*), written

$$\frac{d^2Y}{dX^2} \quad \text{or} \quad \frac{d\dfrac{dY}{dX}}{dX}$$

tells us whether the algebraic value of the derivative is increasing (second derivative is positive), decreasing (second derivative is negative), or constant (second derivative is zero). For equation 10, the second derivative is $b(b-1)X^{b-1-1}$ or $(b^2-b)X^{b-2}$ as can be derived by taking the derivative of $dY/dX = bX^{b-1}$ (utilizing Rule 2). For all values of X, the second derivative tells us the rate of change of the derivative.

We shall now apply these new techniques to a concrete problem in the economics of education. As discussed in Chapter 6, the optimum size of a school is an important problem. The optimum size for a public school is defined as the size for which the average cost per pupil is lowest, *ceteris paribus*. Suppose the function relating per pupil costs (C) and number of students (S) were

$$C = aS^2 + bS + c \qquad (11)$$

The first derivative of this equation indicates the change of costs relative to a change in student numbers, which is the interpretation of the tangent of the curve at any point. Note that in Figure I.6B, the lowest C occurs at the point where the tangent is horizontal. If we can determine the value of S (the number of students) where the tangent is horizontal, we have solved our problem. What is the value of the tangent when it is horizontal? As can be seen, there is no change at all in C for a small change in S along a horizontal line. Therefore, the value of the tangent is zero when it is horizontal. So, in order to find the minimum cost point, we set the derivative equal to zero and solve for S. That is, we find the S for which the derivative is zero. The derivative of (11), $dC/dS = 2aS + b$, equals o when $2aS + b = 0$. Solving that for S, $S = -b/2a$.

We have now found a value of S at which the tangent is equal to o. We do not know, however, whether this is a minimum cost point (as in Figure I.6B) or a maximum cost point (as it would be in Figure I.6A). This is where the second derivative (the derivative of the derivative) comes in. The second derivative of the equation is the derivative of $dC/dS = 2aS + b$, which is $2a$. If a is negative, the second derivative is negative for all values of S. That is, the slope or tangent of the function is always decreasing in value as S increases, as seen in Figure I.6A. The tangent starts at a very high value at J, decreases but is still positive at K, is zero at L, becomes negative at M, and is even more negative at N. In such a case, we have found a maximum rather than the minimum we were seeking. However, if a is positive, the second derivative is positive and therefore always increasing, which implies, as seen in Figure I.6B, that we have indeed found a minimum cost point. Thus, the second derivative being positive means that the equation is at a minimum when the tangent is equal to zero. As was pointed out earlier, one can determine from the graph the information desired: whether the equation is at a minimum or maximum point. However, the use of the first and second derivative does away with the necessity to graph the equation at all.

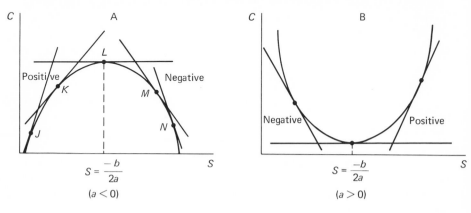

Figure I.6   Graphs of $C = a S^2 + b S + c$

Partial Derivatives

When a variable, say, educational expenditure (E), is dependent on two or more variables, say, enrollment (S) and teacher salaries (T)

$$E = f(S, T) \quad \text{or} \quad E = 500S + 200T$$

one determines *partial derivatives* rather than derivatives. That is, we can determine *the change in the dependent variable for a small change in one of the independent variables* only. We must assume that the other independent variables are held constant. For all equations, as many partial derivatives exist as there are independent variables. In this case two partial derivatives can be found: $\partial E/\partial S$ and $\partial E/\partial T$, where the symbol ∂ represents "the partial derivative." These are, respectively, the change in expenditure for a change in the number of students, all other variables (in this instance teacher salary) held constant, and the change in expenditure for a change in teacher salaries holding all other variables constant. They could also be read as the partial derivative of E with respect to S and the partial derivative of E with respect to T. The same rules hold here as for full derivatives. Variables other than the one whose partial derivative is being found are treated as constants since they are by assumption being held constant. Therefore $\partial E/\partial S = 500$ because for a change in S, $200\,T$ is a constant just as 200π would be; $\partial E/\partial T = 200$ for similar reasons. These tell us that total expenditures increase by 500 for each additional student (holding salaries constant) and by 200 for each dollar added to the average teacher salary (holding number of students constant).

LOGARITHMS

The utilization of logarithms in the economics of education is very limited in range. We will therefore present only a very short general description of logarithms and describe their implications in the context within which they are most often used in our area of concern.

An expression such as 10^2 ($10^2 = 10 \times 10$) is composed of a base (10) and an exponent (2). Any positive number can be expressed in terms of a base and an exponent. Utilizing a base of 10, the following hold:

$$10 = 10^1$$
$$100 = 10^2$$
$$1{,}000 = 10^3$$

In each case the exponent of 10 indicates the number of times the base is multiplied by itself. Most numbers, of course, will require fractional exponents: for example, $136 = 10^{2.134}$ and $75 = 10^{1.875}$. *The exponent to which 10 must be raised to equal a given number is called the logarithm of that number.* Thus 3 is the logarithm of 1000 and 2.134 is the logarithm of 136.

The preceding may be generalized as follows: if $n = b^x$ then $x = \log_b n$ (this is read as the logarithm of n to the base b is equal to x). In addition to 10, e ($e = 2.71828$) is commonly used as a base.[11] Logarithms utilizing e as the base are referred to as *natural logarithms* (often abbreviated as ln rather than log) while base 10 logarithms are called *common logarithms*. The values of logarithms to the bases 10 and e can be found in any book of mathematical tables. The great value of logarithms is in their ease of manipulation and their graphic interpretation.[12]

Logarithms have the interesting property of having *equal* differences

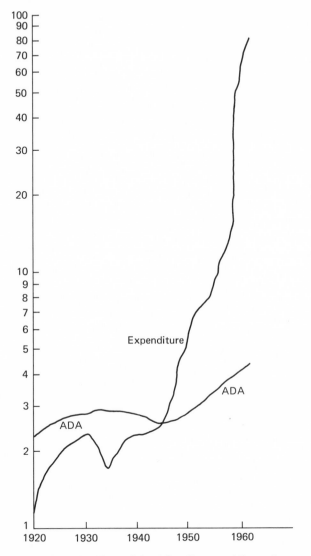

Figure I.7   United States School Enrollment and Expenditure

between them representing *proportional* differences in the original variable. For example, the sequence:

| 10 | 20 | 40 | 80 | 160 |

is represented by the logarithms of those numbers:

| 1 | 1.301 | 1.602 | 1.903 | 2.204 |

Each of the logarithms is .301 greater than the previous one. Thus, equal absolute differences in logs (.301) represent equal proportional differences in natural numbers (100%). This property is very useful for compound growth problems because a straight line representing logarithmic values implies a constant proportional change, *i.e.*, a constant rate of growth. Thus, a graph of a logarithm of a variable over time will show whether the rate of growth of the variable has been increasing (curve becomes steeper), constant (straight line), or decreasing (slope of the curve declines). In Figure I.7 which is drawn on a semilogarithmic scale so that plotting normal numbers yields a logarithmic scale in the vertical direction (whereas the horizontal axis is non-logarithmic), we see that the rate of growth of expenditure on elementary and secondary schooling has been much greater (the curve is much steeper) than the rate of growth of attendance. Average daily attendance has had a steady rate of increase since the end of World War II, a rate greater than before the Depression.

When it is suspected that the relationship between two variables might be a proportional one, the relation would be formulated with the use of logarithms. For example, if it were hypothesized that equal percentage increases in student numbers would lead to equal *absolute* decreases in average cost per pupil, that might be formulated as:

$$C = -a \log S$$

where C is average per pupil cost and S is the enrollment. Thus, when S increases by 10 per cent, C decreases by a fixed amount, not by a fixed percentage.

Appendix II Statistics[1]

INDICES

Index numbers are a widely used statistical tool. Some index numbers are simple and others are quite complex. They are often utilized when comparisons are to be made because they force attention onto percentage rather than absolute differences. The most common type of index relates values of some factor over time. For example, given the number of college graduates in various years (column 1 of Table II.1) an index of college graduates can be constructed. This is done

Table II.1

College Graduate Index

Year	(1) Number of College Graduates (in thousands)	(2) = (1) × $\frac{1}{392}$·100 Index Value (1960 = 100)
1900	27	7
1920	49	12
1940	186	47
1950	432	110
1954	291	74
1956	309	79
1958	363	93
1960	392	100
1962	418	107
1964	499	127
1966	551	141
1968[a]	685	175

[a] Estimated.
Source: Bureau of the Census, *Statistical Abstract of the United States: 1969*, 90th ed. (Washington, D.C.: U.S. Government Printing Office, 1969), p. 121.

by first selecting one year as the base year, the year to which all others will be compared. A division of the values for all other years by the value of the base year yields an *index*. Such an index would have a value of 1 for the base year. In practice, most indices use a value of 100 for the base. Indices having 100 as their base are constructed in

Notes to Appendix II will be found on pages 392–393.

the same manner as indices with 1 as their base except that the quotients are multiplied by 100. For example, choosing 1960 as the base year, the number of graduates for that year becomes 100 (392 = 100). All other values are then adjusted by the following factor, 1/392 × 100, yielding the index values appearing in column 2. The value of the index for each year can be interpreted as that year's percentage of the base year's size. For example, 1940 has an index of 47, which means that the number of graduates in 1940 was 47 per cent of the number of graduates in 1960. This simple percentage interpretation is applicable only to comparisons with the base year.

Indices are useful not only for comparing values in a time sequence but also for making comparisons at a given point in time. A quite common use of an index is to compare the various states of the United States. As seen in Chapter 2, the average value for the United States as a whole can be taken to be the base value. This assures a spread of values below and above 100. If the base chosen were a state with an extremely high (low) value, almost all the index values would be below (above) 100. There is no theoretical reason for having an even spread, only an esthetic one.

PROBABILITY AND SAMPLING

Probability is the base on which statistical analyses are built. Therefore, we begin with a brief introduction to the ideas of probability. Although several approaches to the concept of probability are available, an intuitive approach is adopted here. If someone were to inquire what was the chance of a tossed coin landing with its head side up, you would probably instinctively answer one-half. Indeed, you would be correct. The chance or probability of a head in such an experiment is one-half. Obviously, the coin will either turn up a head or a tail. Therefore, the probability of a head, one-half, does not describe the necessary outcome of one particular toss of the coin. What it does describe is the proportion of heads that will turn up in a large number of trials of the experiment. If a coin is tossed twice, the probability of a head turning up on each toss being one-half implies that we expect one head. This does not suggest that the coin could not come up heads both or neither of the two times. Rather, it suggests that if the action of a coin being tossed twice were repeated many times, the average number of heads for each of the pairs of two tosses would be one. Thus, *probability* is the *expected average occurrence when an action is repeated many times.*

Formally, probability can be defined as follows:

$$P = \lim_{n \to \infty} \frac{x}{n}$$

where P is the probability, x is the number of occurrences of the desired event (say a head turning up), n is the number of trials of the experiment (tosses of a coin), and $\lim_{n \to \infty}$ symbolizes the value of x/n as n becomes very large, approaching infinity. For example, in ten tosses of a coin, there might be four heads ($x/n = 4/10$). In 100 tosses there might be 55 heads ($x/n = 55/100$). As the number of tosses increases, the value of the ratio x/n approaches the probability which in this case is $1/2$. One can find the probability of a particular event in practice by taking the ratio of the number of possible ways the event being considered could occur to the number of possible occurrences, provided that each outcome is equally likely. For example, there is one head on a coin and one tail, so the probability of a head is $1/2$ because there is one way for a head to turn up and there are two possible occurrences. Similarly, a die has one 5 on it and six possible events to a toss (1, 2, 3, 4, 5, or 6), so that the probability of a 5 turning up on a toss of a die is $1/6$.

Many events about which a probability figure is quoted cannot be repeated. A rat turns either left or right at his first exposure to a given wall; a baby is either a boy or a girl; a youngster enters college either immediately following high school or he does not. Therefore, these experiments cannot actually be repeated many times to find the average occurrence. However, one can perform the experiment with many different subjects and in that manner approximate a set of exact replications of the experiment.

A great deal of statistics deals with estimating probabilities when an experiment is repeated many fewer than an infinite number of times. In achieving this and other estimations, random samples are utilized. A *sample is a subgroup of some population where a population is any group.* Of course, one could find an average value of some characteristic of a population by measuring that characteristic for each member of the population. One can, however, estimate the value of a characteristic through statistical methods, utilizing the measurement of the characteristic of a portion of the group. Because it costs time and resources to measure anything, there is a positive value derived from alleviating the necessity of measuring every number of the population.

A *random sample* is simply *a sample that is selected so that every member of the population has an equal chance of being selected.* This can be accomplished by a blind chance drawing or consulting a table of random numbers, which can be found in most volumes of mathematical or statistical tables. The randomness is very important. If, for example, one wanted to find the average height of a group of 50 students and asked them to line up according to age, taking as a sample the first ten students, the selection would not be random at all but according to some attribute (in this case, age) of the children. The average height found from such a sample would not be a good estimate of the average height of the total population involved.

In order to save on sample size (since, as mentioned, each observation has an economic cost), *stratified random samples* are often utilized. That is, the population is divided according to certain attributes, say, age and sex, and the same proportion is selected from each of the subgroups. It has been found that one can achieve good estimates of the desired attribute of a population utilizing a stratified random sample of a much smaller size than a simple random sample. Of course, the attributes upon which one stratifies must be ones hypothesized to have some influence on the variable whose average is being estimated. If one is estimating reading ability of college students, it would probably not help to stratify on the basis of shoe size.

CHARACTERISTICS OF DISTRIBUTIONS

The results of a sample are often diagrammed in what is known as *a frequency distribution, a plotting of the number of cases of each value found in the sample* and a connection of these points (see Figure II.1). The sample represented by Figure II.1 consists of the following observations of, say, height:

$$
\begin{array}{ccccc}
66 & 67 & 68 & 69 & 72 \\
67 & 67 & 68 & 70 & 73 \\
67 & 68 & 69 & 71 & 74 \\
67 & 68 & 69 & 71 &
\end{array}
\qquad (1)
$$

Many different statistics can be employed to describe such a distribution. These can be classified as measures of central tendency, dispersion, and skewness. Each presents a different picture of the group. Measures of *central tendency* include the mean, the median, and the mode. *They describe what are loosely called "average" values.* The *mean* is simply *the sum of the values for each member of a group divided by the number in the group.* $(\sum x/n)$.[2]

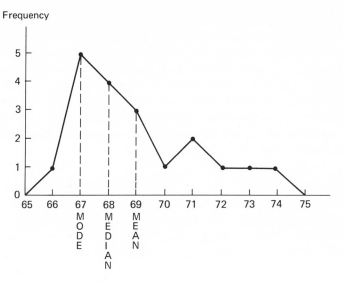

Figure II.1   Frequency Distribution

The *median* is the second statistic describing central tendency. *This is the value that has as many observations below or equal to it as above or equal to it.* If there are an even number of observations, the median value is half way between the two middle values. For example, for six observations, the median value would be equal to one-half the sum of the third plus the fourth highest value. The median may or may not be the same as the mean. For the group of individuals whose heights are listed in (1), the mean height is 69 inches (1311 1/19), but the median height is 68 inches (there are nine who are taller than 68 inches and nine who are equal to or shorter). The last measure of central tendency considered is the *mode*, which is defined as *the value that occurs most frequently.* In this example, 67 inches is the mode because it occurs five times, which is more than any other value. There are many different samples that could have the same measure of central tendency (mean, median, mode, or even all three), samples that are very different in composition.

In practical problems the mean is the most often employed and useful measure of central tendency. When people loosely speak of an "average" value, they generally are referring to the mean. There are some cases, however, when the median or the mode is a better representation of the central tendency. For example, the median puts much less weight on extreme values than does the mean. Since one very high or very low value can drastically affect the mean but not the median, the median is often a better indication of the middle item in a distribution. The mode is the statistic that, for example, a shoe salesman would be most interested in because it is the modal shoe size which requires the largest stock.

Two more statistics often utilized for describing a sample or a population are the variance and the standard deviation. Both of these are measures of the *dispersion* of the observations. That is, *how closely is the sample grouped around the mean?* One could imagine two samples

$$75 \quad 75 \quad 75 \quad 75 \quad 75 \quad 66 \quad 57 \quad 57 \quad 57 \quad 57 \quad 57 \qquad (2)$$
$$68 \quad 67 \quad 67 \quad 67 \quad 66 \quad 66 \quad 66 \quad 65 \quad 65 \quad 65 \quad 64 \qquad (3)$$

that both have means of 66 but are quite different from one another. *The variance is found by squaring the deviations (or differences) from the mean value of the factor being investigated (e.g., if the value of the observation is 75 and the mean is 66, the deviation is 9), summing these squared deviations, and then dividing by the number of observations minus one.*[3] The *standard deviation*, which is utilized more often than the variance, *is the square root of the variance.* The standard deviation of group (1) is 2.14; of group (2) is 8.22; and of group (3) is 1.08.

A final type of description of a sample or distribution is its symmetry. If a distribution is *symmetrical*, its mean, mode, and median coincide as shown in Figure II.2. On the other hand, the distribution may be skewed to the left, as shown in Figure II.2B, or the right, as in Figure II.1. One particular symmetrical distribution is extremely important in statistics: the *normal distribution*. The normal distribution is a theoretical frequency distribution that accurately describes the

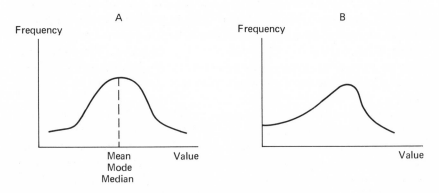

Figure II.2   Symmetry

actual distribution of many different things: height, weight, I.Q., the number of heads of ten coins tossed repeatedly, several estimates of the length of a table, and many, many other things show normal distributions. The normal distribution is derived from the theory of probability and because of that, it is extremely useful in probability problems.

The normal distribution's usefulness is a result of its property of having a specific proportion of its area within a given number of standard deviations from its mean. Because the area under the normal curve represents all of a sample, the area between any two values represents the proportion of the sample lying between those two values, which is equivalent to the probability of any random observation falling between the two selected values. For example, 68.26 per cent of the area under the normal curve is within one standard deviation on either side, 95.44 per cent within two standard deviations on either side, and 99.74 per cent within three standard deviations. This is true for all normal curves regardless of their means or standard deviations. Taking a more concrete case, for the sample of heights the mean is 69 inches and the standard deviation is 2.2. Therefore, one could predict that 68.26 percent of the observations would be between 66.8 (*i.e.*, 69 − 2.2) and 71.2 (*i.e.*, 69 + 2.2) inches if the distribution of height for the population sampled were normal.[4] This attribute of the normal curve makes it possible to determine whether observed relationships are real or merely due to chance, as we shall show below when the testing of significance is discussed.

CORRELATION AND REGRESSION

The principal tools of statistics used in the economics of education literature are correlation and regression analyses. Both are based on probability and often utilize sampling. A correlation or regression is known as *simple* when two variables are involved and *multiple* when there are more than two variables. Although correlation and regression analyses can be executed on functions containing linear or non-linear variables, this appendix will consider only the linear case. Correlations will be introduced before turning to an investigation of regressions.

Correlations

Simple Correlation

A correlation coefficient (r) measures the degree of linear association between two variables. A linear association is one which, when graphed on a four-

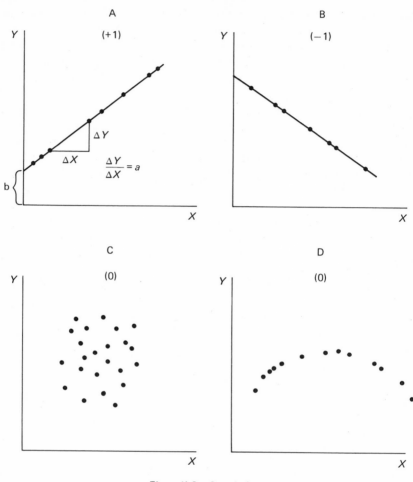

Figure II.3 Correlations

quadrant diagram, yields a straight line. The general equation for any straight line is:

$$Y = a + bX$$

where X and Y are any two variables and a and b are parameters.

The plot of that equation is a straight line with an intercept (the value of Y when X is equal to zero or, in other words, the point where the line crosses the Y-axis) equal to a, and a slope (the change in Y,

ΔY, for a given change in X, ΔX or, in other words, the angle at which the line cuts the Y-axis) of b as seen in Figure II.3. Thus, the relationship between the two variables must be a linear one.

However, the requirement of linearity is not so restrictive as it appears at first blush. Many non-linear relations can be transformed into a linear form. For example, a relation such as $Y = aX^b$ can be transformed into a linear relation by taking the logs of both sides, which yields $\log Y = \log a + b \cdot \log X$. That is, if one makes the following transformations—$Y' = \log Y$; $a' = \log a$; and $X' = \log X$—the equation would be exactly like the model for linear equations: $Y' = a' + bX'$. Similarly, a relation such as $Y = a + bX^2$ is linear if one calculates the value of X^2 for each value of X, calls that X'', and substitutes X'' for X^2 so that the equation reads $Y = a + bX''$, which also is clearly linear.

Suppose that several pairs of values of two variables X and Y, when plotted against one another, fell on a straight line as in Figure II.3A. This is a *perfect positive correlation*: as one variable increases by a given amount, the other increases by a specific amount determined by the slope. One can also have a *perfect negative correlation*: as one variable increases by a given amount, the other decreases by some specific amount, as in Figure II.3B. The coefficient of correlation for a perfect positive correlation is given a value of $+1$ and for a perfect negative correlation a value of -1. On the other hand, there may be no relation at all between the two variables. Such a case is depicted in Figure II.3C. Here the correlation between X and Y is 0. There can also be an obvious correspondence between the two variables and still have a zero correlation. Figure II.3D depicts such a case. The correlation is zero because the relationship is not linear in that when X increases, Y just as often decreases as increases.

The evaluation of the degree of correlation utilizes the criteria of *least squares*. Because correlation measures the degree that two variables are linearly related, the coefficient of correlation (r) is determined by comparison of the actual scatter of points to the straight line that most closely fits the points on a graph. The choice from the infinite number of straight lines that could be drawn is made on the criterion of minimizing the square of the vertical errors, which are called the deviations.[5] Other criteria could be employed in making such a choice. This one has proven to be quite versatile in its implications. Thus, the straight line that minimized the squares of the vertical errors (as seen in Figure II.4) is found, and the coefficient of correlation is basically a measure of how close the actual points match that line. The closer the

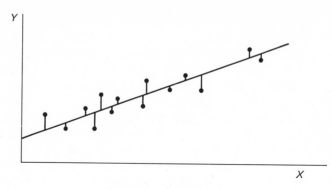

Figure II.4   Least Squares

points are to the straight line, the nearer to $+1$ or -1 is the correlation coefficient. In addition to correlations between the actual values of variables, one can also find the correlation between the rankings of variables. This procedure is known as *rank correlation* and is often chosen when great confidence cannot be put in the exact values of the data or when the data are not in quantitative form (*e.g.*, very high, high, medium, low, and very low). Under such circumstances, the data are ranked and the rankings, rather than the original data, are correlated.

Multiple Correlation

Two aspects of multiple correlation will be discussed: partial correlation and the coefficient of multiple determination. *Partial correlation is the correlation between two variables under the assumption that account has been taken of the influence of other variables. The partial correlation coefficient is the portion of the variance of one variable associated with the variance of a second variable holding some other variable or variables constant.* For example, one might try to correlate the amount of wheat grown on an acre with the amount of rainfall in various years. But a more revealing investigation is to hold the number of hours of sunshine constant while undertaking that correlation. Since sunshine is most likely correlated with both rainfall and wheat grown, it is quite useful to eliminate, or hold constant, this effect on the size of the wheat crop when finding the correlation of rainfall and wheat crop size. Such a correlation would be verbalized as the partial correlation of wheat crop size with rainfall, holding sunshine constant. The partial correlation coefficient is written: $R_{12.3}$, $R_{12.34}$, $R_{12.345}$, and so on (the correlation between variables 1 and 2 holding variable 3 constant, holding variables 3 and 4 constant, holding variables 3, 4, and 5 constant, etc.).

In addition to partial correlation, one can also calculate the *coefficient of multiple correlation* (R).[6] This is the degree to which one variable is correlated with a whole set of other variables. That is, using the above example, R could be the degree of correlation between size of wheat crop and the combination of rainfall and sunshine.[7]

Regression

The statistical tools of correlation and regression do not intrinsically demonstrate causality between variables. By themselves these tools can indicate only whether there is a relationship between the variables. Causality can be inferred only from a statistical analysis when the formulation of the relationship is based on a theoretical foundation. The distinctive attribute that differentiates regressions from correlations is that the former provides a measure of the quantitative effects of one variable on another, in addition to a measure of the degree of association.

Simple Regression

Although there are several types of regressions, only the most common type, linear regression, will be discussed here. Simple regression analysis (only two variables involved) is closely related to the simple correlation analysis just discussed. The basic difference is the objective: *Correlation analysis is designed to find the degree to which the pairs of* X *and* Y *observations fit a straight line, whereas regression analysis is designed to define the straight line* (by finding the values of the parameters of the linear equation, that is, finding the values of a, the intercept, and b, the slope, in the equation for a straight line, $Y = a + bX$). Through the regression procedure, the mathematical details of which shall not be presented here, estimates are made of the parameters of an equation such as

$$Y = a + bX + u$$

> where u is the error term, that is, the vertical distance between the actual points and the line that minimizes the sum of the squares of those errors.

For example, if Y is income and X is years of education, the values of a and b might be calculated to be 4,000 and 200 respectively. In such a case the regression analysis would predict that an individual with eight years of education would have an income of \$5,600 (*i.e.,*

4,000 + 8·200 = 5,600). If the given individual actually had an income of $5,000, the error, u, is equal to $600.

The degree that the regression line fits the actual sample is summarized by the *coefficient of determination*, r^2.[8] *Mathematically, r^2 is the square of the coefficient of correlation, r. Conceptually, it is the portion of the variance in the dependent variable "explained" by the independent variable.*

Multiple Regression

The regression procedure can be extended to cases with many independent variables such as that represented by:

$$Y = a + b_1X_1 + b_2X_2 + \cdots + b_nX_n + u$$

Here, too, one can estimate the values of all the bs and the a, thereby completely estimating the relationship between the independent variables and the dependent one. Each of the *regression coefficients (bs)* estimated through the multiple regression analysis *represents the relationship between the dependent variable and an independent variable, holding all other independent variables constant.* If, for example, the relationship to be estimated is that between an achievement test score, age, and I.Q. score for each individual, it could be formulated as:

$$A = a + b_1Y + b_2IQ + u$$

where A is the achievement test score, IQ is the child's IQ score, Y is his age in years, and u is an error term.

Given the values of these variables for a group of children, the values of the bs and a can be estimated. Then, to predict an achievement test score, one need merely substitute the values of each of the independent variables into the equation that has been estimated. For example, if $a = 27$, $b_1 = 2.5$, and $b_2 = .3$, then a twelve-year-old with an IQ of 110 would be predicted to have an achievement score of 90 ($27 + 2.5 \times 12 + .3 \times 110$). If the particular child actually scored 93, u, the error term, would be 3 for that observation. The bs represent the effects of each of the variables taken separately. That is, b_1 is the effect of a change in Y holding IQ constant. Similarly, b_2 represents the effect of a change in IQ holding Y constant.

There are two tests, in particular, that help in the interpretation of the "goodness" of the hypothesized relationship as a representation of the actual relationship between the variables considered. The first is the R^2 or coefficient of multiple determination, which is derived from R the coefficient of multiple correlation. The R^2 tells what proportion of the variance in the values of the dependent variable is "explained" by the independent variables. That is, it tells how much of the differences in, to go back to the example above, achievement scores is explained by the independent variables, IQ and age, and how much is not explained. Thus, the higher the R^2 the better the equation predicts the value of the dependent variable from information on the independent variables.

In addition, one can test whether or not each independent variable's coefficient, b_i, is significantly different from zero.[9] If a given b_i is not significantly different from zero, then the variable of which it is the coefficient is not a significant explanatory variable. That is, if it were excluded, the amount of the variance in the dependent variable explained would not be significantly reduced. Several times in this discussion the term *significant* has been employed. In statistics significant has a specific technical meaning. *Whether a coefficient is significantly different from zero is determined by what is known as a t-test. The t-test compares the standard error of the b to the value of the b and determines whether a coefficient of that size with a standard error of the given amount is different from zero merely because of chance quirks of the given sample or due to an actual difference.*[10] Specifically, the test determines (if the coefficient is significantly different from zero, for example) that 95 per cent (or any other predetermined percentage) of the time a coefficient of that size and standard error will actually be different from zero rather than due to chance. That is, the probability of a coefficient of that size, given the variable's standard deviation, being due to chance is less than 5 per cent. This is determined through reference to a standard distribution curve similar to a normal curve called a Student's t curve.[11]

Dummy Variables

Regression analysis is quite versatile in spite of the requirement of a linear relationship between the dependent and independent variables. A variable may be non-linear but may be entered into a relationship in a linear form as was seen above. For example, relationships represented by the curves in Figure II.5 can all be entered in a linear form. In addition, non-quantitative variables can be utilized. For example, race, sex, place of residence, and type of education are all variables not easily represented by numbers. Of course, one could represent male by 1 and female by 2 or 10, but what is represented by the one or nine units that separate male and female? Is a female twice or five times "as much" as a male? To handle such variables a

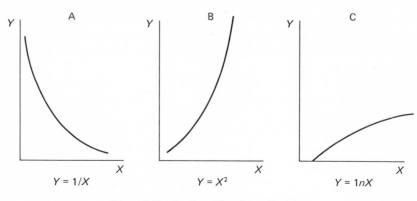

Figure II.5   Graphs of Non-linear Variables

system known as *dummy variables* has been developed. *A dummy variable is one evaluated at either 1 or 0 depending upon whether some particular condition is fulfilled.* For example, one might have a variable for sex, S, which is equal to 1 when the individual is a male and 0 when it is a female. Including such a variable in the regression equation would determine the effect of sex on the dependent variable. Thus, if the value for its co-efficient were 3.8, the interpretation would be that males had, other things being equal, 3.8 more units of the dependent variable than do females.

In addition to one dummy variable representing some qualitative factor, there are many cases when a set of dummy variables must be employed. For example, if it were hypothesized that the type of second-ary school one attended had an effect on achievement test scores, more than one dummy variable would be required because four types of secondary school can be specified: technical, commercial, academic, and comprehensive. In such a case we would use three variables; say X_1, X_2, and X_3, where X_1 would equal 1 if the individual attended a technical secondary school but would be 0 in any other case. Similarly, X_2 would be 1 if the school were commercial and 0 otherwise, and X_3 would be 1 if the school were academic and 0 otherwise (as seen in Table II.2). Notice that there are four types of schools but only three variables. That is because each coefficient of each variable is being compared to the situation of being in the omitted category. Just as in the earlier example of a sex dummy variable the coefficient showed the effect of being male compared to being female, so, here, each of the coefficients of X_1 through X_3 shows the effect of being in that category compared to being in the omitted category, having attended a comprehensive secondary school.[12] Thus, the equation might be:

$$A = a + b_1X_1 + b_2X_2 + b_3X_3 + u$$

and the values of a, b_1, b_2, and b_3 might be 65, -15, -10, and $+25$. If the individual attended a comprehensive high school, the values of X_1, X_2, and X_3 would all be 0 so the predicted value of A would be 65, the value of a. If the individual had attended a technical school, his

Table II.2

A Set of Dummy Variable Values

	X_1	X_2	X_3
Technical	1	0	0
Commercial	0	1	0
Academic	0	0	1
Comprehensive	0	0	0

predicted score would be 50 (since in this case X_1 is 1 and X_2 and X_3 are 0, the predicted value of A is $a + b_1$ or $65 - 15$). Similarly, if the secondary school were a commercial (or an academic) school, the predicted score would be 55 (or 90) since X_2 (or X_3) would be equal to 1 while all the other Xs would be zero. Of course, one can also have dummy variables and ordinary variables in the same equation. Thus, the equation to predict achievement test scores could have the dummies for type of secondary schools as well as variables for IQ and age of the child. Under those circumstances, a b_1 of -15 would imply that the predicted effect of having gone to a technical secondary school would be an achievement test score 15 points lower than that of one who had attended a comprehensive secondary school, IQ and age being held constant.

Depending upon one's hypotheses, there are cases in which it is more appropriate to use a separate regression for each category of a variable than to use dummy variables. If one hypothesized that the effect on achievement test scores of IQ differed by sex, in a hypothesized function $A = f(IQ, S)$, then the use of a dummy variable for sex, as $A = a + b_1IQ + b_2 S$ where S is a dummy equaling 1 for males, would not be appropriate. Such an equation suggests that IQ's effect is independent of the effect of sex. Rather, two equations

$$A_1 = a_1 + b_3IQ \qquad \text{(Males)}$$
$$A_2 = a_2 + b_4IQ \qquad \text{(Females)}$$

should be utilized, one for each sex. In this way, b_3, the effect of IQ on achievement for males, can be different from b_4 the effect of IQ test scores for females. Of course, it is costly to run additional regressions, so the additional cost must be weighed against the improvement in the model, if any.

We have shown that variables can be entered into regression equations in many different forms. In practice, the researcher typically selects the simplest form for a first trial. He then often tries some more complicated forms to see whether the latter explains more of the variance in the dependent variable than does the simpler form (*i.e.*, is the R^2 higher). Thus, the form of a relationship assumed best to describe the events being studied is often a result of several trials. However, the form finally utilized must have some intuitive appeal or there at least must not be any evidence suggesting that formulation is not inappropriate.

Selected Bibliography

GENERAL ECONOMICS TEXTS

HARRISS, C. LOWELL. *The American Economy: Principles, Practices, and Policies.* 6th ed. Homewood, Ill.: Richard D. Irwin, 1968.

LIPSEY, RICHARD G., and PETER O. STEINER. *Economics.* 2nd ed. New York: Harper and Row, 1969.

McCONNELL, CAMPBELL R., *Economics: Principles, Problems and Policies.* 4th ed. New York: McGraw-Hill, 1969.

REYNOLDS, LLOYD G., *Economics: A General Introduction.* 3rd ed. Homewood, Ill.: Richard D. Irwin, 1969.

SAMUELSON, PAUL A., *Economics: An Introductory Analysis.* 8th ed. New York: McGraw-Hill, 1970.

SUITS, DANIEL B. *Principles of Economics.* New York: Harper and Row, 1970.

USE OF NATIONAL INCOME CONCEPTS IN EDUCATION

BENSON, CHARLES S., *et al. State and Local Fiscal Relationships in Education in California.* Sacramento: California State Senate Fact-Finding Committee on Revenue and Taxation, 1965.

BENSON, CHARLES S., and JAMES A. KELLY. *The Rhode Island Comprehensive Foundation and Enhancement State Aid Program for Education.* Providence, R.I.: Rhode Island Special Commission to Study the Future Field of Education, 1966.

BLOT, DANIEL, and MICHAEL DEBEAUVAIS. "Educational Expenditure in Developing Areas: Some Statistical Aspects." In *Financing of Education*

355

for Economic Growth. Paris: Organization for Economic Co-operation and Development, 1966.

HARRIS, SEYMOUR E., *Higher Education: Resources and Finance.* New York: McGraw-Hill, 1962.

HARRISON, FORREST W., and EUGENE P. McLOONE. *Profiles in School Support: A Decennial Overview.* Washington, D.C.: U.S. Government Printing Office, 1965.

JAMES, H. THOMAS, JAMES A. KELLY, and WALTER A. GARMS. *Determinants of Educational Expenditures in Large Cities of the United States.* Stanford: School of Education, Stanford University, 1966.

PALM, GUENTER., "International Comparisons of Educational Outlay: Problems and Approaches." *International Social Science Journal* 20, (1968): 98–108.

SEERS, DUDLEY, and RICHARD JOLLY. "The Treatment of Education in National Accounting." *Review of Income and Wealth* 12, (1966): 195–208.

SHENKER, JOSEPH. "A National Comparative Study of the Patterns of State and Local Government in Financing of Higher Education." Unpublished Ed. D. dissertation, Teachers College, Columbia University, 1969.

SUPPLY AND DEMAND APPLIED TO EDUCATION

FELDMAN, PAUL, and STEPHEN HOENACK. "Private Demand for Higher Education in the United States." In *The Economics and Financing of Higher Education in the United States.* Washington, D.C.: U.S. Government Printing Office, 1969.

FOLGER, JOHN K., "The Balance Between Supply and Demand for College Graduates." *Journal of Human Resources* 2 (1967): 143–75.

GALPER, GARVEY, and ROBERT DUNN. "A Short-Run Demand Function for Higher Education in the United States." *Journal of Political Economy* 77 (1969): 765–77.

MORTON, ANTON S. "Supply and Demand of Teachers in California." *Socio-Economic Planning Science* 2 (1969): 487–501.

APPLICATION OF THE THEORY OF THE FIRM TO EDUCATION

BUCHANAN, JAMES M., and NICOS E. DEVLETOGLOU. *Academia in Anarchy: An Economic Diagnosis.* New York: Basic Books, 1970.

DANIERE, ANDRE. *Higher Education in the American Economy.* New York: Random House, 1964.

JENNY, HANS H., "Pricing and Optimum Size in a Nonprofit Institution: The University." *American Economic Review* 58, (1968): 270–83.

JENNY, HANS H., and G. RICHARD WYNN. "Short-Run Cost Variations in Institutions of Higher Learning." In *The Economics and Financing of*

Higher Education in the United States. Washington, D.C.: U.S. Government Printing Office, 1969.

PEACOCK, ALAN T., and ANTHONY J. CULYER. *Economic Aspects of Student Unrest.* Occasional Paper No. 26. London: Institute of Economic Affairs, 1969.

SIEGEL, BARRY N. "Towards a Theory of the Educational Firm." Mimeographed. Eugene: University of Oregon, Center for the Advanced Study of Educational Administration, 1966.

SOUTHWICK, LAWRENCE, Jr. "Cost Trends in Land Grant Colleges and Universities." *Applied Economics* 1 (1969): 167–82.

EDUCATIONAL PRODUCTION FUNCTIONS

BLAUG, MARK. "The Productivity of Universities." Universities and Productivity Background Papers, Universities Conference, 1968, pp. 19–28.

BLAUG, MARK, and MAUREEN WOODHALL. "Productivity Trends in British Secondary Education, 1950–63." *Sociology of Education* 41, (1968: 1–35.

BOWLES, SAMUEL. "The Efficient Allocation of Resources in Education." *Quarterly Journal of Economics* 81 (1967): 189–219.

CORREA, HECTOR. "Quantity versus Quality in Teacher Education." *Comparative Education Review* 8 (1964): 141–45.

HETTICH, WALTER, "Equalization Grants, Minimum Standards, and Unit Cost Differences in Education." *Yale Economic Essays* 8 (1968): 3–55.

KATZMAN, MARTIN. "Distribution and Production in a Big City Elementary School System." *Yale Economic Essays* 8 (1968): 201–56.

RATE OF RETURN TO EDUCATIONAL INVESTMENTS

ASHENFELTER, ORLEY, and JOSEPH D. MOONEY. "Some Evidence on the Private Returns to Graduate Education." *Southern Economic Journal* 35 (1969): 247–56.

BECKER, GARY S. *Human Capital: A Theoretical and Empirical Analysis, with Special Reference to Education.* New York: Columbia University Press for National Bureau of Economic Research, 1964.

BLAUG, MARK. "The Rate of Return on Investment in Education in Great Britain." *Manchester School of Economic and Social Studies* 33 (1965): 205–51.

CARNOY, MARTIN. "Rates of Return to Schooling in Latin America." *Journal of Human Resources* 2 (1967): 359–74.

HANOCH, GIORA. "An Economic Analysis of Earnings and Schooling." *Journal of Human Resources* 2 (1967): 310–29.

HUNT, SHANE J. "Income Determinants for College Graduates and the Return to Educational Investment." *Yale Economic Essays* 3 (1963): 305–57.

MERRETT, STEPHEN. "The Rate of Return to Education: A Critique." *Oxford Economic Papers* (New Series) 18 (1966): 289–303.

ROGERS, DANIEL C. "Private Rates of Return to Education in the United States: A Case Study." *Yale Economic Essays* 9 (1969): 89–136.

———. "Student Loan Programs and the Returns to Investment in Higher Levels of Education in Kenya." *Economic Development and Cultural Change* (forthcoming).

WEISBROD, BURTON A., and PETER KARPOFF. "Monetary Returns to College Education, Student Ability and College Quality." *Review of Economics and Statistics* 50 (1968): 491–97.

EDUCATIONAL COST-BENEFIT STUDIES

BORUS, MICHAEL E. "A Benefit-Cost Analysis of the Economic Effectiveness of Retraining the Unemployed." *Yale Economic Essays* 4 (1964): 371–429.

CAIN, GLEN G., and ERNST W. STROMSDORFER. "An Economic Evaluation of Government Retraining Programs in West Virginia." In *Retraining the Unemployed*, edited by Gerald G. Somers. Madison: University of Wisconsin Press, 1968.

CARROLL, ADGER B., and LOREN A. IHNER. "Costs and Returns for Two Years of Postsecondary Technical Schooling: A Pilot Study." *Journal of Political Economy* 75 (1967): 862–73.

CORAZZINI, ARTHUR J. "The Decision to Invest in Vocational Education: An Analysis of Costs and Benefits." *Journal of Human Resources* 3 (1968): 88–120.

HANSEN, W. LEE, and BURTON A. WEISBROD. *Benefits, Costs and Finance of Public Higher Education*. Chicago: Markham Publishing Company, 1969.

RIBICH, THOMAS I. *Education and Poverty*. Washington, D.C.: The Brookings Institution, 1968.

SPIEGELMAN, ROBERT G., *et al*. *A Benefit/Cost Model to Evaluate Educational Programs*. Menlo Park, Calif: Stanford Research Institute, 1968.

WISEMAN, JACK. "Cost-Benefit Analysis in Education." *Southern Economic Journal* 32 (1965): 1–12.

ECONOMIC GROWTH AND PLANNING AND EDUCATION

ADAMS, DON, and ROBERT BJORK. *Education in Developing Areas*. New York: McKay, 1969.

BLAUG, MARK. "Approaches to Educational Planning." *Economic Journal* 77 (1967): 262–87.

BOWEN, WILLIAM. "Assessing the Economic Contribution of Education: Appraisal of Alternative Approaches." In William Bowen, *Economic Aspects of Education: Three Essays*. Princeton: Princeton University Press, 1964.

BOWMAN, MARY JEAN, and C. ARNOLD ANDERSON. "Concerning the Role of Education in Development." In *Old Societies and New States*, edited by Glifford Geertz. New York: The Free Press, 1963.

CORREA, HECTOR. *Quantitative Methods of Educational Planning*. Scranton, Pa.: International Textbook, 1969.

FEI, JOHN, and GUSTAV RANIS. *Development of the Labor Surplus Economy: Theory and Practice*. Homewood, Ill.: Richard D. Irwin, 1964.

GARMS, WALTER A. "A Multivariate Analysis of the Correlates of Educational Efforts of Nations." *Comparative Education Review* 12 (1968): 281–99.

HARBISON, FREDERICK, and CHARLES MYERS. *Education, Manpower and Economic Growth*. New York: McGraw-Hill, 1964.

JOLLY, RICHARD. *Planning Education for African Development*. Nairobi: East African Publishing House, 1969.

Organization for Economic Co-operation and Development. *Mathematical Models in Educational Planning*. Paris: Organization for Economic Co-operation and Development, 1967.

TICKTON, SIDNEY G. "Long-Range Planning: A Case Study." In *Financing Higher Education: 1960–1970*, edited by Dexter M. Keezer. New York: McGraw-Hill, 1959.

FINANCING EDUCATION

BENSON, CHARLES S. *The Cheerful Prospect*. Boston: Houghton Mifflin, 1965.
———. *The Economics of Public Education*. 2nd ed. Boston: Houghton Mifflin, 1968.

BOWEN, WILLIAM G. *The Economics of the Major Private Universities*. Berkeley: Carnegie Commission on Higher Education, 1968.

BURKHEAD, JESSE. *Public School Finance*. Syracuse: Syracuse University Press, 1964.

HARRIS, SEYMOUR E. *Higher Education: Resources and Finance*. New York: McGraw-Hill, 1962.

JOHNS, ROE L., and EDGAR L. MORPHET. *The Economics and Financing of Education*. 2nd ed. Englewood Cliffs, N.J.: Prentice-Hall, 1969.

MAXWELL, JAMES A. *Financing State and Local Government*. Washington, D.C.: The Brookings Institution, 1965.

ROGERS, DANIEL C. "Financing Higher Education in Less Developed Countries." *Comparative Education Review* 15 (1971): 20–27.

SHELL, KARL, *et al.* "The Educational Opportunity Bank: An Economic Analysis of a Contingent Repayment Loan Program for Higher Education." *National Tax Journal* 21 (1968): 2–45.

The Economics and Financing of Higher Education in the United States. Washington, D.C.: U.S. Government Printing Office, 1969.

EFFICIENCY IN EDUCATION

Committee for Economic Development. *Innovation in Education: New Directions for the American School.* New York: Committee for Economic Development, 1968.

COOMBS, PHILIP H. *The World Educational Crisis: A Systems Analysis.* New York: Oxford University Press, 1968.

GOODLAND, JOHN, JOHN O'TOOLE, Jr. and LOUISE TAYLER. *Computers and Information Systems in Education.* New York: Harcourt, Brace and World, 1966.

HARTLEY, HARRY. *Educational Planning-Programming-Budgeting: A Systems Approach.* Englewood Cliffs, N.J.: Prentice-Hall, 1968.

KERSHAW, J. A. and R. N. McKEAN. *Systems Analysis and Education.* Santa Monica, Calif.: The RAND Corporation, 1959.

Organization for Economic Co-operation and Development. *Efficiency in Resource Utilization in Education.* Paris: Organization for Economic Co-operation and Development, 1969.

PFEIFFER, JOHN. *New Look at Education: Systems Analysis in our Schools and Colleges.* New York: Odyssey Press, 1968.

SCHRAMM, WILLIAM, *et al. New Educational Media in Action: Case Studies for Planners.* Paris: International Institute for Educational Planning, 1967.

COMPETITION IN EDUCATION

BUCHANAN, JAMES M. and NICOS E. DEVLETOGLOU. *Academia in Anarchy: An Economic Diagnosis.* New York: Basic Books, 1970.

DANIERE, ANDRE. *Higher Education in the American Economy.* New York: Random House, 1964.

FRIEDMAN, MILTON. *Capitalism and Freedom.* Chicago: University of Chicago Press, 1962.

PEACOCK, ALAN T., and ANTHONY J. CULYER. *Economic Aspects of Student Unrest.* Occasional Paper No. 26. London: Institute of Economic Affairs, 1969.

PEACOCK, ALAN T., and JACK WISEMAN. *Education for Democrats.* Occasional Paper No. 25. London: Institute for Economic Affairs, 1964.

ROWLEY, CHARLES K. "The Political Economy of British Education." *Scottish Journal of Political Economy* 16 (1969): 152–76.

SIZER, THEODORE R. "The Case for a Free Market." *Saturday Review* (1969).

GENERAL ECONOMICS OF EDUCATION

BENSON, CHARLES S. *The School and the Economic System*. Chicago: Science
Research Associates, 1966.
BLAUG, MARK. *Economics of Education: A Selected Annotated Bibliography*. New
York: Pergamon Press, 1966.
HÜFNER, KLAUS. "Economics of Higher Education and Educational Plan-
ning: A Bibliography." *Socio-Economic Planning Science* 2 (1968): 25–101.
MACHLUP, FRITZ. *The Production and Distribution of Knowledge in the United
States*. Princeton: Princeton University Press, 1962.
SCHULTZ, THEODORE W. *The Economic Value of Education*. New York:
Columbia University Press, 1963.
VAIZEY, JOHN. *The Cost of Education*. London: Allen and Unwin, 1958.
————. *The Economics of Education*. London: Faber and Faber, 1962.
WEISBROD, BURTON A. *External Benefits of Public Education*. Princeton:
Industrial Relations Section, Princeton University, 1964.

BOOKS OF READINGS IN ECONOMICS OF EDUCATION

ANDERSON, C. ARNOLD, and MARY JEAN BOWMAN, eds. *Education and Economic
Development*. Chicago: Aldine, 1965.
BEREDAY, GEORGE Z. F. and JOSEPH LAUWERYS, eds. *Educational Planning:
The World Yearbook of Education, 1967*. New York: Harcourt, Brace and
World, 1967.
BLAUG, MARK, ed. *Economics of Education I*. Baltimore: Penguin, 1968.
————. *Economics of Education II*. Baltimore: Penguin, 1970.
BOWMAN, MARY JEAN, *et al.*, eds. *Readings in the Economics of Education*. Paris:
United Nations Educational, Scientific, and Cultural Organization,
1968.
LEVIN, MELVIN R., and ALAN SHANK, eds. *Educational Investment in an Urban
Society: Costs, Benefits and Public Policy*. New York: Teachers College
Press, 1970.
MUSHKIN, SELMA J., ed. *Economics of Higher Education*. Washington, D.C.:
U.S. Government Printing Office, 1962.
ROBINSON, E. A. G., and J. E. VAIZEY, eds. *The Economics of Education*. New
York: St. Martin's Press, 1966.

Notes

CHAPTER 1

[1] For a discussion of the views of these and subsequent writers see George F. Kneller, *Education and Economic Thought* (New York: John Wiley and Sons, Inc., 1968).

[2] Fritz Machlup, *The Production and Distribution of Knowledge in the United States* (Princeton: Princeton University Press, 1962), p. 9.

[3] Burton A. Weisbrod, *External Benefits of Public Education* (Princeton, N.J.: Industrial Relations Section, Department of Economics, Princeton University Press, 1964).

[4] Non-market production is any activity that is not sold or bought but is productive nonetheless.

[5] In exceptional cases where there is great risk (*e.g.*, the space program) or where bold innovations and initiative beyond the level to be anticipated from the business community are required (*e.g.*, the Tennessee Valley Authority), government acts as a co-producer or primary producer. Such instances of government enterprise are rare.

[6] The following discussion raises only those points pertinent to education. For a broader analysis of the factors calling forth greater governmental participation in production see Otto Eckstein, *Public Finance*, 2nd ed. (Englewood Cliffs, N.J.: Prentice-Hall, Inc., 1967), chapter 1.

[7] Under certain conditions even air has a cost, for example, in a mine or a submarine.

[8] Many laws of economics are still valid in the absence of rational behavior. For a detailed analysis of this point see Gary Becker, "Irrational Behavior and Economic Theory," *Journal of Political Economy* 70 (1962).

[9] See Chapter 3 for a rigorous analysis of the functioning of the market.

[10] For an analysis leading to the confirmation of this assertion see Lloyd G. Reynolds, *Economics*, 3rd ed. (Homewood, Ill.: Richard D. Irwin, Inc., 1969), chapters 17–19.

[11] Gardner Ackley, *Macroeconomic Theory* (New York: The Macmillan Company, 1961), pp. 14–15. See Appendix I, pp. 321–328 for further discussion of models, theories, and functions.

[12] Many large models have been developed, one being the Federal Reserve–M.I.T. econometric model of the United States economy which consists of approximately 70 basic equations. For a simple description of this model see the *Federal Reserve Bulletin* (January 1968): 11–40.

[13] See Appendix II.

[14] For an interesting illustration of conflicting views on the functioning of competitive markets and the subsequent role to be assigned to government see Milton Friedman, *Capitalism and Freedom* (Chicago: University of Chicago Press, 1962); John Kenneth Galbraith, *The Affluent Society* (Boston: Houghton Mifflin Company, 1958); and John Kenneth Galbraith, *The New Industrial State* (Boston: Houghton Mifflin Company, 1967).

[15] Shane J. Hunt, "Income Determinants for College Graduates and the Return to Educational Investment," *Yale Economic Essays* 3 (1963), and Daniel C. Rogers, "Private Rates of Return to Education in the United States: A Case Study," *Yale Economic Essays* 9 (1969), versus Giora Hanoch, "An Economic Analysis of Earnings and Schooling," *Journal of Human Resources*, 2 (1967), and Orley Ashenfelter and Joseph D. Mooney, "Some Evidence on the Private Returns to Graduate Education," *Southern Economic Journal* 35 (1969).

CHAPTER 2

[1] For a discussion of these four national income concepts see, for example, Richard G. Lipsey and Peter O. Steiner, *Economics*, 2nd ed. (New York: Harper and Row, 1969), pp. 513–15.

[2] Transfer payments are payments to individuals for which no services are currently rendered. They can be payments from the government (for example, interest on government debt, veterans' payments, and welfare) or from business firms (for example, charity).

[3] Charles S. Benson, *The Economics of Public Education* (Boston: Houghton Mifflin Co., 1961), p. 62.

[4] See Appendix II, pp. 339–340, for a general discussion of indices.

[5] Prior to the base year, 1958, the GNP deflator inflates rather than deflates because a dollar purchased more prior to 1958 than in 1958.

[6] See Chapters 7 and 8 for further discussion of this point.

[7] The methodology inherent in interstate analysis can also be applied to intercountry comparisons, once certain statistical problems are overcome. For an analysis of these problems see Guenter Palm, "International Comparisons of Educational Outlay: Problems and Approaches," *International Social Science Journal* 20 (1968).

[8] For an analysis of how such measures are constructed see The Advisory Commission on Intergovernmental Relations, *Measures of State and Local Fiscal Capacity and Tax Effort* (Washington, D.C.: U.S. Government Printing Office, 1962).

[9] See, for example, Seymour E. Harris, *Higher Education: Resources and Finance* (New York: McGraw-Hill, 1962), Chapter 25; and Joseph Shenker, "A National Comparative Study of the Patterns of State and Local Governmental Financing of Higher Education," unpublished Ed.D. Dissertation, Teachers College, Columbia University, 1969.

[10] Current expenditures include all amounts spent at all levels of administration—state, county, and local—for administration, instructional services, plant operation and maintenance, fixed charges, and other school services (attendance, health services, transportation, food services, and so on). It also includes the cost of operating the state and county departments of education, contributions to retirement systems and/or social security, and federal, state, and local funds expended to cover deficits of school lunch and milk programs.

[11] The rank correlation between the two indices is .225 and is insignificant at the .05 confidence level. (For a discussion of correlation and significance refer to Appendix II.)

[12] The first group consists of Alabama, Colorado, Delaware, Hawaii, Indiana, Maryland, Nebraska, Texas, Virginia, Wisconsin, and Wyoming; the second group consists of Alaska, Connecticut, Illinois, Kansas, Louisiana, Maine, Massachusetts, Mississippi, Missouri, Montana, Nevada, New Jersey, New Mexico, North Carolina, Pennsylvania, Rhode Island, South Carolina, South Dakota, Utah, and Washington.

[13] See Chapter 11 for a discussion of federal efforts in financing education.

CHAPTER 3

[1] To obtain this result the nature of the income and substitution effects are reversed. A lower price for one good or service means that if the same bundle of goods and services is purchased, some money will now be left over. Consequently, the consumption of the item whose price declined, and possibly other items whose price did not change, can increase. Furthermore, this item is now a better competitor with the set of items fulfilling the same need and may be substituted for any or all of them.

[2] For the small class of goods known as *inferior goods*, defined as goods whose importance in the budget increases as income decreases, an opposite effect to that seen for *normal goods* can be expected. Although no athletic goods are in this category, a typical example of an inferior good is the consumption of such a basic food as rice. Poor people throughout the world consume larger quantities of rice than their richer brothers. As income goes up, people may diversify their diets and therefore consume less rice and more of other items. But as income falls and the burden of poverty increases, the other items may be bypassed and larger amounts of rice may be bought. This is a function of both the price and nutritional qualities of rice, which make it one of the basic sustainers of human life.

[3] Considerations of the cost of time should enter the analysis of the demand of all goods, not only education. In many cases these opportunity costs are such a small proportion of total costs that they can be ignored without too great a bias. For example, in the purchase of an automobile or home, opportunity costs in terms of shopping time are a small proportion of total cost. For an attempt to incorporate the cost of time in all consumer decisions see Gary Becker, "A Theory of the Allocation of Time," *Economic Journal* 75 (1965).

[4] Theodore W. Schultz, *The Economic Value of Education* (New York: Columbia University Press, 1963), p. 28.

[5] The literature on the supply of labor is replete with references to a *backward bending supply curve*. The curve may be backward bending (exhibiting an inverse relationship between price and quantity) above a certain price because at a high enough wage (price) the supplier may feel that he has acquired sufficient wages to finance his needs and now prefers to substitute leisure for additional work. (See Chapter 5, pp. 113–115, for further discussion.)

[6] See Lloyd Reynolds, *Economics*, 3rd ed. (Homewood, Ill.: Richard D. Irwin, Inc., 1969), pp. 83–86 for a discussion of a classic exception, the cobweb situation.

[7] See Appendix I, pp. 329–335, for a discussion of differentiation.

[8] (See Appendix I for an explanation of the rules of differentiation used in step b.)

a.   Solve for P: $100 = 200 - 20P$

$$-100 = -20P$$
$$-100/-20 = P$$
$$5 = P$$

b.   Calculate dQ/dP: $dQ/dP = 0 + 1(-20)P^{1-1}$
$$= -20P^0$$
$$= -20 \cdot 1$$
$$= -20$$

c.   Substitute values for dQ/dP, P, and Q into the formula:

$$e_p = -(-20) \cdot \frac{5}{100} = \frac{100}{100} = 1$$

$$-\frac{24-18}{\frac{1}{2}(24+18)} \div \frac{18-24}{\frac{1}{2}(18+24)} = -\frac{6}{21} \div \frac{-6}{21} = 1$$

[10] e_a using point B as the base:

$$\frac{-(18-24)}{18} \div \frac{(24-18)}{24} = \frac{1}{3} \div \frac{1}{4} = \frac{4}{3} = 1.33$$

e_a using point C as the base:

$$\frac{-(24-18)}{24} \div \frac{(18-24)}{18} = -\frac{1}{4} \div -\frac{1}{3} = \frac{3}{4} = .75$$

[11] Marginal revenue is easily determinable if total revenue is known. Because it is the incremental revenue from added production, it can be calculated by subtracting the total revenue for producing x units from the total revenue for producing $x + 1$ units, or by taking the first derivative of total revenue with respect to quantity. (See Appendix I, pp. 329–335, for a discussion of derivatives).

[12] Marginal cost is derived from total cost in the same manner as marginal revenue is derived from total revenue. For a detailed derivation of total, average, and marginal cost curves see Appendix B at the end of this chapter.

[13] For a discussion of indifference curve theory see Paul A. Samuelson, *Economics*, 8th ed. (New York: McGraw Hill, 1970), pp. 421–26.

[14] One can explain the purchase of more than one unit of a good or service at a constant price by noting that units preceding the final one yield more satisfaction than their cost.

[15] Because the hypothetical consumer in this analysis is but one member of the overall market, we can assume that individual consumer changes will not be large enough to affect market prices. However, if all consumers undertook similar shifts at the same time, the prices of the goods or services under consideration would change. Such a change could easily be incorporated into the analysis by requiring that marginal utility changes exceed price changes.

[16] Some labor costs are fixed in the short run. An example is an elementary school teacher with an annual contract.

CHAPTER 4

[1] Andre Daniere, *Higher Education in the American Economy* (New York: Random House, 1964); Barry N. Siegel, "Towards A Theory of the Educational Firm," mimeographed, a paper presented to the annual meeting of the Western Economic Association, August 1966; Hans H. Jenny, "Pricing and Optimum Size in a Nonprofit Institution: The University," *American Economic Review* 58 (1968); Hans H. Jenny and G. Richard Wynn, "Short-Run Cost Variations in Institutions of Higher Learning," in *The Economics and Financing of Higher Education in the United States*, A Compendium of Papers Submitted to the Joint Economic Committee, Congress of the United States (Washington, D.C.: U.S. Government Printing Office, 1969).

[2] The Campbell and Siegel model and other demand for education models are criticized for the use of enrollment data as a proxy for demand. Enrollment appears to be a market equilibrium datum since it is determined by the interaction of demand and supply forces. However, since the aggregate supply of educational openings in colleges usually exceeds the demand (there are unfilled places in some schools), aggregate enrollment appears to be almost entirely demand determined and as a result is an acceptable proxy for demand.

[3] Refer to Appendix II, pp. 349–354 for a further discussion of this statistical technique.

[4] Refer to Appendix II, p. 347.

[5] Absolute numeric changes yield proportional changes when converted into logarithms. Consequently, the regression coefficients are also elasticities since *elasticity* is defined as the proportional change in quantity for a given proportional change in income or price. An additional property of a logarithmic linear relationship is constant elasticity throughout the range of the function analyzed. Constant elasticity, in turn, implies that point and arc elasticities are equal. (See Appendix I, pp. 335–337 for a discussion of the properties of logarithms.)

[6] Two alternate demand models have been proposed for explaining the demand for higher education in the United States. Paul Feldman and Stephen Hoenack in their article, "Private Demand for Higher Education in the United States," in *The Economics and Financing of Higher Education in the United States* (Washington, D.C.: U.S. Government Printing Office, 1969), introduce variables measuring the student's performance on aptitude tests, unemployment and earnings data, and regional dummy variables as explanators of demand. Harvey Galper and Robert Dunn in their article, "A Short-Run Demand Function for Higher Education in the United States," *Journal of Political Economy* 77 (1969) incorporate the effect of military service on the demand for higher education.

[7] By the 1969–70 academic year this surplus received wide attention in newspaper reports of the limited number of college teaching positions open to prospective college faculty.

[8] Now widely adopted. See in particular T. W. Schultz [7] and Gary Becker [1]. A useful defense of the approach is given by Mark Blaug [2].

[9] See Chapter 7 of present volume for a discussion of investment and education as an investment good—Eds.

[10] Mark Blaug also argues for such an assumption [3]. This article appeared after we had completed this paper.

[11] We use the 18–24-year old age group because it seems to contain about 80 per cent of the undergraduate population. See A. Cartter and R. Farrel [4, p. 120]. We were not able to obtain data by age of the institutionalized population. For our methods of estimating the "eligibles," see the appendix at the end of the paper.

[12] B. A. Jaffe and Walter Adams [5] have found that there has been no trend for a full century in the proportion of people going on to college after high school. Their findings are based upon backward projections from 1940 and 1960 census data on educational levels achieved by various age groups, a method quite distinct from ours.

[13] It is assumed that other financial costs will tend to vary directly with the consumer price index.

[14] Note, we have not adjusted our income concept for size of family or size of household. While it is true that larger families with given incomes will have more difficulty in sending their children to college, we believe that much of this difficulty is resolved by sending children to less costly schools and by throwing a larger burden of finance upon the student himself. Studies of aggregate enrollment demand are therefore not likely to pick up a large effect from variations in family size. On the dubious statistical relationship between family size and family support for students, see John Lansing, Thomas Lorimer, and Chikashi Moriguchi [6, p. 32].

[15] See M. Blaug [3, pp. 171–72] for a similar opinion.

[16] Any function, for example $R = f(Y, P)$, is homogeneous to degree X if when all of the independent variables are multiplied by a constant, C, the resulting function is C^X times the original function—$F(C^X Y, C^X P) = C^X f(Y, P)$. —Eds.

[17] See the appendix for the sources and procedures used in the various estimates.

[18] The years were 1927, 1931, 1935, 1939, 1947, 1951, 1955, 1959, and 1963.

[19] The *Digest of Educational Statistics* [8] contains a breakdown for recent years, but not for earlier ones.

[20] The first report in the series had a slightly different title; see "Teacher Supply and Demand in Degree Granting Institutions, 1954–55," *NEA Research Bulletin*, XXXIII (December 1955). The series had been under the directorship of Ray C. Maul, and the most recent is *NEA Research Report 1965-R4*.

[21] These data are not precisely comparable, but should be sufficient to illustrate the principle. Maul's data on new teachers is drawn from questionnaires to the colleges hiring new teachers, while his data on the employment of new doctorates is drawn from questionnaires to the graduate schools granting the doctorates.

[22] R. E. Dunham, P. S. Wright, and N. O. Chandler, "Teaching Faculty in Universities and 4-Year Colleges, Spring 1962" (OE-53022-65). Preliminary data were presented in a paper, "Doctorates among Teaching Faculty," at the annual meeting of the American Educational Research Association, February 11, 1965. This study is commonly referred to as COLFACS.

[23] See "A New Look at the Supply of College Teachers," *Educational Record* (Summer 1965).

[24] "Teacher Supply and Demand...," NEA Research Report 1959-R-10, pp. 50–54. The same model was also used in the 1961 report, but did not appear in the later reports.

[25] "Projections of Educational Statistics to 1973–74" (OE-10030, 1964), p. 26.

[26] The ratio, in terms of full-time staff equivalents, ranges from a low of 10:1 to a high of 16:1 in somewhat random fashion, but averages 14 for the decade to 1973–74. In terms of total instructional staff at the rank of Instructor or above, the OE projection ranges from 14:1 to 27:1, averaging 18:1. As Table 4.5 indicates, this is lower than the average of the last decade. See "Projections of Educational Statistics...," *op. cit.*, pp. 8, 24.

[27] The choice of the appropriate replacement rate is so critical to the model that it is surprising that no very serious attempts have been made to verify it. A difference of one percentage point makes a difference of about 40,000 teachers over a decade. Various assumptions have been used by different model builders —*e.g.*, 5 per cent by the Fund for the Advancement of Education in *Teachers for Tomorrow* (1955); 5 per cent by Brown in *The Market for College Teachers* (1965); 4 per cent by Berelson in *Graduate Education in the United States* (1960); and 3 per cent by Wolozin in "How Serious is the Faculty Shortage?" *Challenge* (June 1965).

[28] Memoranda on "Estimates of Demand for and Supply of Higher Educational Staff," Higher Education Personnel Staff, U.S. Office of Education, October 26, 1956, and January 4, 1965.

[29] Ideally, one would like to use full-time equivalents for both measures, but national enrollment data are not available on this basis, despite the fact that the Higher Education Facilities Bill of 1963 uses a full-time equivalent enrollment formula for the distribution of Title I funds.

[30] Bolt, Kolton, and Levine have recently published a model for scientific fields which is in close agreement with the above. Their estimate for scientists, based on a review of National Register data for recent years and on an assumption that scientists retire at age 65, is: death rate—.009; retirement—.006; total—.015. See "Doctoral Feedback into Higher Education," *Science* (May 14, 1965), 918–28.

The retirement assumptions in my estimate are that 4 per cent of faculty aged 60–64 voluntarily retire each year, and that from age 65 on, teachers on the average retire from teaching one year after mandatory retirement age is reached. This is the equivalent of assuming that one-third retire at the mandatory age, one-third continue (probably at another college) for one year, and one-third for two years. An alternative assumption that 10 per cent of teachers age 60 and above will retire each year would give a current rate of .0098.

[31] See A. M. Cartter and R. Farrell, "Higher Education in the Last Third of the Century," *Educational Record* (Spring 1965), for the development of this and alternative projections of enrollment.

[32] See "Projections of Educational Statistics...," *op. cit.*, pp. 12–16, for OE forecasts; and National Science Foundation, *Comparisons of Earned Degrees Awarded 1901–62—With Projections to 2000* (Washington, 1964), p. 54. The author's "A New Look at the Supply of College Teachers," *Educational Record* (Summer 1965), compares these with other doctoral projections. For periods up to ten years ahead, P may be taken as an exogenous variable, determined by the level of fellowship support, the capacity of graduate schools, etc. In projection doctoral degrees, however, I have assumed that, after 1974, P_t is a function of E_{t-1}, the value of the functional coefficient being .0058. From 1964 through 1974, the value of this coefficient is approximately $(.0047 + .0001t)$. This model produced reliable estimates of doctorates for the years before 1964 and a projection that falls reasonably between the low estimates of the Office of Education and the high estimates of the National Science Foundation. For the 1974–85 period, it is very close to Lindsay Harmon's "Reference Series." See "Memorandum on Projected Doctorate Production," National Academy of Sciences (January 29, 1965).

[*Addendum:* Since this note was written, perhaps as a reaction to criticism of "bearish" doctoral projections, the Office of Education has revised its estimates. Their 1973–74 projection, for example, has risen from 24,300 doctorates to 32,500, a one-third increase. Their 1965–74 decade projection is now only 1 per cent below my estimate, instead of 15 per cent. See "Projections of Educational Statistics to 1974–75" (OE-10030-65), p. 21.]

[33] If one were collecting data from colleges and universities, it would be more appropriate to express the supply-demand identity as follows:

$$bP_{t-1} + aD_{t-1} + sD_{t-1} = sD_{t-1} + (c + m + r)D_{t-1} + qf(E_t - E_{t-1}) \tag{3a}$$

This differs from equation (3), in that aD_t is shifted to the lefthand side, since it is technically part of the supply of doctorate-teachers, and a new term, sD_{t-1}, appears on both sides of the equations (s being defined as the percentage of teachers who shift teaching positions from one college to another in any year); when aggregating, sD_{t-1} cancels out. According to COLFACS data, $s = .114$ in 1962/63.

[34] I would estimate that half of science students and at least 90 per cent of non-science students would prefer—other things being equal—to enter college teaching. The fact that only about 20 per cent of the former and 75 per cent of the latter do become teachers upon receiving their degree is attributable to the economically attractive alternatives at the time of graduation. Therefore, b is assumed to be sensitive to relative salaries in academic and non-academic occupations. In the economists' terms, I would assume that b is price (*i.e.*, salary) elastic and that q is relatively price-inelastic.

[35] This might be compared with Brown's "quality-constant supply" function, which uses different (and I believe unlikely) assumptions. *Op. cit.*, Ch. 2.

[36] One quick answer is that government and industry can absorb all the additional doctorates produced. This may turn out to be so, but if it does occur, doctorates in non-educational employment will experience an increasing

rate of growth. For example, if the educational system followed the path indicated by the constant-quality model, then doctorates entering non-teaching employment would grow from the present level of about 7,500 per year to 26,000 in 1975 and to 54,000 by 1985. Over the last ten years, the total number of employed non-teaching doctorates has grown about 4 or 5 per cent per year; over the next twenty years, it would expand at the rate of about 10 per cent per year.

[37] Take the retirement rate (r) as an example; over the next five to ten years, it will probably average from a low of only .47 per cent in biochemistry to a high of 3.71 per cent in classics. Judging from the present age distribution of teachers, the combined mortality and retirement rate for the next several years will be about 2.5 per cent in the humanities, 1.7 per cent in the biological and physical sciences, 1.6 per cent in engineering, and 1.9 per cent in the social sciences.

[38] See Allan M. Cartter, "The Economics of Higher Education," in *Contemporary Economic Issues*, ed. Neil W. Chamberlain (Homewood, Ill.: Richard D. Irwin, 1969), p. 161.

[39] See Humphrey Doermann, *Crosscurrents in College Admissions* (New York: Teachers College Press, 1968), p. 58, Table II-5.

[40] For example, such a program has been proposed recently for the public colleges and universities of California by the Assembly Speaker. See *Los Angeles Times*, June 24, 1969, pt. 1, p. 3.

[41] Doermann, *Crosscurrents...*, pp. 9 and 42–44.

[42] A monopolist might have the power to charge different groups of consumers different prices. By charging a high price to those able and willing to pay it and a low price to those not able and willing to pay the high price, the monopolist generates greater demand and profit than would be realized with a "middle" price.—Eds.

[43] See Joseph M. Burns and Barry R. Chiswick, "An Economic Analysis of State Support for University Education," *Western Economic Journal* (March 1969), pp. 84–95.

[44] In this article, the term *administrator* includes members of the governing boards (*e.g.*, trustees) and academic administrators (*e.g.*, presidents and deans).

[45] See A. Alchian and R. Kessel, "Competition, Monopoly, and the Pursuit of Pecuniary Gain," in *Aspects of Labor Economics* (Princeton, N.J.: Princeton University Press, 1962).

[46] Doermann suggests that these are relevant alternative policies for universities (Doermann, *Crosscurrents...*, pp. 11 and 42–44).

[47] Assuming that schooling is a "normal" good, the substitution and income effects of a price change operate in the same direction.

[48] The changes discussed here and below would be mitigated to the extent that private universities were not passive. For example, some of the additional revenue obtained by private universities from incoming wealthy students could be used for scholarships for high quality poor students.

[49] The magnitude of the changes depends on the extent of the price change and the elasticity of demand for schooling at each type of institution, for each of the income-ability groups. The elasticities depend, in part, on tastes and the availability of substitutes.

[50] This is based on the assumption that graduated tuition is instituted to reduce the cost to the state of financing higher education. See *Los Angeles Times*, June 24, 1969, pt. 1, p. 3.

[51] On this point, see Doermann, *Crosscurrents...*, p. 39.

[52] For a similar view, see William Bowen, "University Finance in Britain and the United States: Implications of Financial Arrangements for Educational Issues," *Public Finance*, 18:1 (1963), p. 55 and pp. 57–58.

[53] Ibid., pp. 45–83.

[54] The apparent difficulties of the University of California during the past few years support the validity of this assumption.

[55] An exception to this, however, would be control over scholarship recipients if the aid were tied to the consumption of a particular commodity, or if it were dependent upon the student's nonacademic performance. As an example of the former restriction, some colleges require that scholarship recipients reside in the school's dormitories.

[56] Comments by students during the recent controversy over tuition at the University of California indicate that this view is widely held.

[57] See Cartter, "The Economics of Higher Education," pp. 158–64.

CHAPTER 5

[1] It is not difficult to find elements that may enter into production that do not fit easily into any of these three categories, such as sunlight and rainfall on the positive side and hurricanes and earthquakes on the negative side. One rationale for excluding such factors is that they are often not controllable by man.

[2] The labor force participation rate is defined as the sum of those unemployed but seeking employment and those employed divided by the total population. Those under the age of sixteen, members of the armed forces, and institutionalized individuals are omitted from this calculation.

[3] The discussion in this section assumes a closed economy, *i.e.*, the absence of foreign trade.

[4] The tradeoff or marginal rate of transformation between desks and blackboards can be seen by drawing a tangent to the production possibility frontier at any point and determining its slope. (See Appendix I, p. 329, for a definition and discussion of the terms tangent and slope.) Since the production possibility frontier is a curve, the slope of the tangent and hence the tradeoff differs at every point. The tradeoff at point E on Figure 5.1 is at the rate of 100 desks for 50 blackboards, or 2 to 1. At point H it has increased to 168 desks for 42 blackboards, or 4 to 1.

[5] One of the products in a two-product example could be thought of as representing all other goods. In this manner the two-product example is not so limiting as it might initially appear.

[6] For definitions of slope and tangent see Appendix I, p. 329.

[7] Again, the discussion is immediately generalizable to three or more factors of production.

[8] Economies and diseconomies of scale may be partly responsible for the U-shaped cost curves discussed in Appendix B of Chapter 3. Economies of scale would bring down average cost as quantity increased, and diseconomies would lead to increasing cost with expansion.

[9] This view is supported by the recent (1970) decentralization of the New York City Board of Education into several semiautonomous units. If this decentralization is successful, the diseconomies of scale argument is in a sense refuted.

[10] An exception to this rule is discussed below.

[11] Decreasing marginal returns to a factor is also one of the explanations of the rising part of the variable and total cost curves presented in Appendix B of Chapter 3. As more and more labor and materials are added to a fixed amount of capital (fixed factors), less additional output is generated, and average variable and average total costs become higher.

[12] This would be true if participation rates rather than hours worked were plotted on the horizontal axis. That Table 5.1 shows hours worked increased as wages increased over time is due to the increase in population size.

CHAPTER 6

[1] For an extensive defense of the validity of quantifying educational output see a more recent article by Woodhall and Blaug dealing with productivity in British secondary education (Maureen Woodhall and Mark Blaug, "Productivity Trends in British Secondary Education, 1950–1963," *Sociology of Education* 41 (1968): 1–35). By using the same methodological approach developed in their earlier work, Woodhall and Blaug conclude that educational productivity in secondary schools has declined during the period under study.

[2] The parabolic relationship, which takes the form $Y = X^2 - X$, is a mathematical representation of curve *aa* in Figure 6.1. It indicates that as enrollment increases, average costs decline up to point E and increase thereafter.

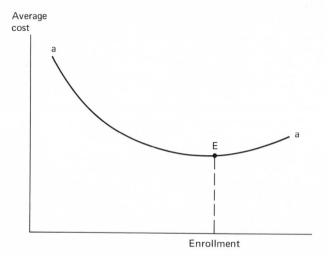

Figure 6.1   Parabolic Cost Curve

This property of cost curves is discussed in greater detail in Appendix B of Chapter 3.

[3] University Grants Committee, *Returns from Universities and University Colleges in receipt of Treasury Grant: Academic Year 1938–1939*. S.O. Code No. 70/152/0/39 (London: H.M. Stationery Office, 1940); *Returns from Universities and University Colleges...1952–1953*. Cmnd. 9130 (London: H.M. Stationery Office, 1954); *Returns from Universities and University Colleges in receipt of Exchequer Grant:...1962–1963*. Cmnd. 2456 (London: H.M. Stationery Office, 1964).

[4] *Higher Education. Report of the Committee appointed by the Prime Minister under the Chairmanship of Lord Robbins. 1961–63*. Cmnd. 2154 (London: H.M. Stationery Office, 1963). *Higher Education. Appendix One to the Report of the Committee appointed by the Prime Minister under the Chairmanship of Lord Robbins. 1961–63: The Demand for Places in Higher Education*. Cmnd. 2154-I (London: H.M. Stationery Office, 1963). *Higher Education. Appendix Two (A)...Students and Their Education*. Cmnd. 2154-II (London: H.M. Stationery Office, 1964). *Higher Education. Appendix Three...Teachers in Higher Education*. Cmnd. 2154-III (London: H.M. Stationery Office, 1963). *Higher Education. Appendix Four...Administrative, Financial and Economic Aspects of Higher Education*. Cmnd. 2154-IV (London: H.M. Stationery Office, 1963).

⁵ See Callahan, R. E., *Education and the Cult of Efficiency* (University of Chicago Press, 1962) for a spirited attack on the whole concept of "efficiency in education." Other educationists have argued that the special features of the "education industry" make a steady or declining rate of productivity inevitable. If so, this fact needs to be openly recognized. Instead, a perfectionist attitude to the problems of measurement in education has led to the almost total neglect of the subject of academic efficiency.

⁶ Central Statistical Office, *National Income Statistics Sources and Methods* (London: H.M. Stationery Office, 1956), pp. 38, 356, provides a brief discussion of the official methods of measuring the output of education and other government services.

⁷ Notice that what is needed is an educational rather than a general price deflator.

⁸ Balogh, T., and Streeten, P. P., "The Coefficient of Ignorance," *Bulletin of the Oxford Institute of Economics and Statistics*, XXV, 2 (May, 1963), p. 102.

⁹ For a review of the literature on productivity, see Blaug, M., *A Selected Annotated Bibliography in the Economics of Education*, 2nd edition, to be published this year by Pergamon Press.

¹⁰ See Vaizey, J., *The Economics of Education* (London: Faber and Faber, 1962), pp. 77–88; Harris, S. E., (ed.), *Economic Aspects of Higher Education* (Paris: OECD, 1964), pp. 28–40, and his *Higher Education: Resources and Finance* (New York: McGraw-Hill, 1962), pp. 557–66. See also an illuminating study by Clark, H. F., *Cost and Quality in Public Education* (Syracuse University Press, 1963).

¹¹ Correa, H., *The Economics of Human Resources* (Amsterdam: North-Holland Publishing Co., 1963).

¹² Fabricant, S., *Trend of Government Activity in the U.S. since 1900* (Washington: National Bureau of Economic Research, 1952); Lytton, H. D., "Recent Productivity Trends in the Federal Government," *Review of Economics and Statistics*, XLI, 4 (November, 1959), pp. 341–59, and "Public Sector Productivity," *ibid.*, XLIII, 3 (August, 1961), pp. 182–84.

¹³ Hirsch, W. Z., *Analysis of the Rising Costs of Public Education* (Washington: Joint Economic Committee, 1959), Study Papers, No. 4.

¹⁴ The study is administered by the University of Pittsburg for the U.S. Office of Education. For a description of the project see Flanagan, J. C., *et al.*, *Project Talent: Designing the Study* (Pittsburgh: University of Pittsburgh, 1960) and the most recent report on the research, Flanagan, J. C., *et al.*, *The American High School Student* (Pittsburgh: University of Pittsburgh, 1964).

¹⁵ University Grants Committee, *Report of the Committee on University Teaching Methods*. Chairman: Sir Edward Hale. (London: H.M. Stationery Office, 1964), p. 107.

¹⁶ Williams, B. R., "Mr. Rowe and University Efficiency," *Science and Freedom*, No. 16 (October, 1960), p. 10. See also "Capacity and Output of Universities," *The Manchester School of Economic and Social Studies*, XXXI, 2 (May, 1963), pp. 185–202.

¹⁷ Robbins Report, Appendix IIA, cited footnote 2 above, pp. 125–38.

¹⁸ The average length of all university courses, according to the Robbins Report, is about 3.7 years. Robbins Report, Appendix I, cited footnote 2 above, pp. 153–156. We have assumed some shortening of the average length of undergraduate courses since 1938 due to the decline in the proportion of medical students. The average length of course of those who drop out was calculated using the different wastage rates of each year of study. Robbins Report, Appendix IIA, cited footnote 2 above, p. 130.

¹⁹ See P.E.P., *Graduate Employment* (London: P.E.P., 1956); Craig, C., *The Employment of Cambridge Graduates* (Cambridge University Press, 1963); and the

report by the University Grants Committee, *First Employment of University Graduates, 1961–1962* (London: H.M. Stationery Office, 1963).

[20] For a discussion of the proportion of extra lifetime earnings properly attributable to higher education, see Blaug, M., "The Rate of Return on Investment in Education in Great Britain," forthcoming in *The Manchester School of Economic and Social Studies*, XXXIII, 3 (September, 1965).

[21] It may be objected that we are employing a question-begging definition of "culture" but all the labels have been used only for convenience. In fact, one attempt to rate university students with respect to "cultural level," defined in terms of scores in specially designed tests, would give greater weight to graduates of pure science than of arts subjects. See Richmond, W. K., *Culture and General Education* (London: Methuen, 1963), pp. 109–19.

[22] Robbins Report, Appendix III, cited footnote 2 above, p. 21.

[23] Maintenance grants paid by the government or local education authorities cannot be included because they are transfer payments and not costs. To use expenditure on grants alone as a measure of input would be to underestimate the value of students' time, since not all students receive grants, while to add this amount to earnings foregone would mean double-counting.

[24] Robbins Report, Appendix IV, cited footnote 2 above, p. 153.

[25] See Bowen, W. G., "British University Salaries: Subject Differentials," *Economica*, XLIII, 120 (November, 1963), pp. 341–59.

[26] See, for instance, University Grants Committee, *University Development 1952–57*. Cmnd. 534, p. 71.

[27] Robbins Report, Appendix IV, cited footnote 2 above, p. 152.

[28] Carter, C. F., "The Economics of Higher Education," *The Manchester School of Economic and Social Studies*, XXXIII, 1 (January, 1965), p. 2.

[29] See University Grants Committee, *Returns from Universities and University Colleges in receipt of Treasury Grant: Academic Year 1959–1960*. Cmnd. 1489 (London: H.M. Stationery Office, 1961), pp. 17–19, and Robbins Report, Appendix III, cited footnote 2 above, pp. 65–66.

[30] An alternative approach would have been to make some estimate of the value of research output and include inputs allocated to research in the index. At the postgraduate level it is particularly difficult to separate the two functions meaningfully.

[31] The statistical analysis consists of first deriving indices of inputs (Tables 6.7 and 6.8) from a set of expenditure data (Tables 6.3 through 6.6). The final productivity figures (Table 6.9) are then derived from the input indices and the indices of output (Table 6.2).—Eds.

[32] Feinstein, C. H., "Production and Productivity in the United Kingdom, 1920–62," *London and Cambridge Economic Bulletin*, No. 48 (December, 1963), pp. xii–xiv.

[33] Deakin, R. M., and George, K. D., "Productivity Trends in the Service Industries, 1948–63," *London and Cambridge Economic Bulletin*, No. 53 (March, 1965), pp. xvi–xx.

[34] *Ibid.*, p. xviii.

[35] Pennsylvania State University, "Abstracts and Bibliography of Studies in Class Size" (mimeographed, 1958).

[36] The dogma that smaller classes are best has a venerable history; "In Babylonian Talmud, Baba Bathra 21A [the middle of the third century] the rule was established by Rabbi Rabba, an authoritative sage of his era: 25 students are to be enrolled in one class. If there are from 25 to 40 an assistant must be obtained." Quoted by Harris, S. E., *Higher Education: Resources and Finance* (New York: McGraw-Hill, 1962), p. 530. It is probably true that there are discontinuities in the relationship between size of class and quality of education: less than 20 students, for example, may yield definite benefits but after,

say, 30 students there is very little difference between 40 or 50. This question of discontinuities remains to be investigated.

[37] The Department of Education has just announced its sponsorship of a research and documentation center for programmed learning in the University of Birmingham which will have responsibility for coordinating research and disseminating results.

[38] University Grants Committee, *Report of the Committee on University Teaching Methods.* Chairman: Sir Edward Hale. (London: H.M. Stationery Office, 1964), p. 118.

[39] These failures have been so well recognized that they are topics of the daily press. For some insights see Christopher Jencks, "Is the Public School Obsolete?" *The Public Interest* (Winter 1966), pp. 18–28.

[40] Some of the most extensive are: Thomas I. Ribich, *Education and Poverty* (Washington, D.C.: The Brookings Institution, 1968). Robert Spiegelman, *et al.*, "Cost-Benefit Model to Evaluate Educational Programs, Progress Report," Stanford Research Institute (March 1967), and "A Benefit/Cost Model to Evaluate Educational Programs," Stanford Research Institute (January 1968). Clark C. Abt, *et al.*, "Design for an Elementary and Secondary Cost Effectiveness Model," Contract OEC 1-6-001681-1681, Report on the Mathematical Design Phase for U.S. Office of Education (February 1967). Jacob J. Kaufman, *et al.*, "An Analysis of the Comparative Costs and Benefits of Vocational Versus Academic Education in Secondary Schools," Contract OEG-1-6-000512-0817, Preliminary Report for the U.S. Office of Education (October 1967).

[41] The sparsity of knowledge in all of these areas is demonstrated in James S. Coleman, *et al.*, *Equality of Educational Opportunity* (Washington, D.C.: U.S. Department of Health, Education, and Welfare, 1966), Chapter III; and Samuel S. Bowles and Henry M. Levin, "The Determinants of Scholastic Achievement," *The Journal of Human Resources* (Winter 1968), pp. 3–24. For a discussion of the problems in doing cost-effectiveness analysis in education, see Samuel S. Bowles, "Towards an Educational Production Function," a paper presented at the Conference on Research in Income and Wealth, University of Wisconsin (November 15, 1968); and Henry M. Levin, "Cost Effectiveness Evaluation of Instructional Technology: The Problems," a paper prepared for the Commission on Instructional Technology (Washington, D.C.: November 1968).

[42] See Robert Spiegelman, *et al.* (1968), p. 54.

[43] This is a rigorous mathematical description of isoquants of the type appearing in Figure 2 of Chapter 5.—Eds.

[44] The elimination of class size as a parameter of achievement is based on the fact that no rigorous study has shown a consistent relation between class size and achievement within the ranges of class size under consideration. For evidence that even drastic reductions in class size and student/teacher ratios show little effect on standardized achievement scores, see David J. Fox, "Expansion of the More Effective School Program," Evaluation of New York City Title I Educational Projects 1966–67 (New York: Center for Urban Education, 1967), pp. 32–44.

[45] The derivation of this solution is assumed to be familiar to the reader. Others may refer to Paul A. Samuelson, *Foundations of Economic Analysis* (Cambridge, Massachusetts: Harvard University Press, 1961). For a formal proof see H. Hancock, *The Theory of Maxima and Minima* (New York: Dover Press, 1960).

[46] The approach taken here is similar to that suggested by Glen Cain and Harold Watts in "Problems in Making Inferences From the Coleman Report," Institute for Research on Poverty, Discussion Paper 28–68 (Madison, Wisconsin: 1968).

[47] "The Education of Negroes and Whites," unpublished doctoral dissertation (Department of Economics, Massachusetts Institute of Technology, 1968).

[48] These estimated payoffs represent approximate slope coefficients for linear relationships between student's verbal score and the specific teacher characteristics, extracted from an equation in which other relevant explanatory valuables were also included in the relationships. Teacher's degree level and other traits showed no statistically significant association with student achievement. See Hanushek's discussion of possible specification biases; *op. cit.*

[49] Henry M. Levin, "Recruiting Teachers for Large-City Schools," (mimeo: The Brookings Institution, 1968). To be published by Charles E. Merrill.

[50] These costs were obtained by applying the teacher's experience and verbal score salary coefficients from Table 6.12 to the production coefficients in Table 6.11. It was assumed that the additional effort would have to be maintained for the first five years of schooling in order to obtain the sixth grade results shown in Table 6.11. Therefore, the present values in Table 6.13 represent additional expenditures for the previous five years compounded at a 5 per cent rate of interest and divided by an average class size of 30 in order to obtain a per student figure.

[51] The additional costs are probably biased downwards because the original salary data from which costs are estimated did not include fringe benefits.

[52] The high payoff to verbal score is not very surprising given the relatively modest intellectual performances—on the average—of teachers in the elementary schools. In fact, while school salary schedules provide higher remuneration for more experience, they offer no incentives to those with greater verbal proficiency. The dull and the superior are treated as equals. As long as the general market for college graduates rewards verbal performance while the schools do not, we can expect that individuals with greater verbal skills will opt for non-teaching careers. See Henry M. Levin, *op. cit.*, chapters 3, 6, and 7.

[53] That is, our production estimates do not satisfy the conditions of the second order partial derivative set out for equation (1) above.

[54] On the other hand, experience of teachers is related to the social class of the student body. That is, the schools characterized by the highest teacher turnover or the least teacher experience are those attended by children who are drawn from the lowest social strata. If the social class of the students is less adequately measured for Negro than for white students, the relatively higher student achievement that is apparently attributable to teacher experience may merely reflect the higher social status of Negro students in schools with low teacher turnover. It is obvious that the teacher experience-student achievement relation between races needs further investigation before we can be more nearly certain of its proper interpretation.

[55] See Henry M. Levin, *op. cit.*, chapter 3. One notable exception to this pattern is that the few teachers who entered the profession during the depression years, 1930–40, showed test scores as high as those of the new teachers.

[56] Gerald Kahn, *Current Expenditures Per Pupil in Public School Systems, 1958–59* (Washington, D.C.: U.S. Office of Education, Circular No. 645, Government Printing Office, 1961), 6.

[57] Lester B. Herlihy and Walter S. Deffenbaugh, *Statistics of City School Systems, 1939–40* and *1941–42* (Washington, D.C.: U.S. Office of Education, Government Printing Office, 1945), 15. (For this earlier year, the second and the third size classes were divided at 30,000 instead of 25,000.)

[58] See Werner Z. Hirsch, "Expenditure Implications of Metropolitan Growth and Consolidation," *Review of Economics and Statistics*, XLI (Aug. 1959), 232–40 (especially 239–40); and "Determinants of Public Education Expenditures," *National Tax Journal*, XIII (March 1960), 29–40.

[59] Of 37,019 public school districts that existed in the United States in 1961–62, 84.2 per cent had enrollments of less than 1,200 and 75.7 per cent had less than 600. United States Office of Education, *Digest of Educational Statistics* (Washington, D.C.: U.S. Government Printing Office, 1963), 29.

[60] Henry J. Schmandt and G. Ross Stephens, "Measuring Municipal Output," *National Tax Journal*, III (Dec. 1960), 369–75.

[61] Of the 18 school district areas, only 13 provide both elementary and secondary schools. Each of the remaining five is a combination of an elementary district and the secondary district to which they send their pupils. Thus, all 18 units are made to cover grades one to 12 or kindergarten to 12 for the sake of comparability, but when some units are a multiple of districts while the others are single districts the meaning of the analysis becomes more doubtful.

[62] There is also a recent study by the Committee for Economic Development which stresses the advantage of a larger school system. It suggests that educational advantages continue to accrue until a combined school system (kindergarten to 12 or one to 12 years) has "perhaps 25,000 students" and that there are financial advantages of many kinds in even larger units. The Committee for Economic Development, *Paying for Better Public Schools* (New York, Dec. 1959), 64.

[63] There is no great significance to this particular figure. It was observed that $6,000 was not very far above average salaries for the majority and using that figure would have eliminated too many schools. On the other hand, $7,000 was too far up in the salary scale. The mean of the average salaries for the 109 schools was $5,662. Teacher salaries alone certainly cannot be an adequate measure of the standard of a school. It was assumed, however, that salaries are in general significantly associated with the quality of teachers and often even with other provisions offered in a school.

[64] These are largely input measures. An ideal approach to the measurement of school quality would be to consider *output* rather than *input* inasmuch as our prime concern in education is not with what we invest in schools but with what we get out of them. However, unavailability of output measures (not to mention difficulties in agreeing upon output substances) and variation in intelligence and socioeconomic background among pupils make such a project extremely difficult.

[65] All school expenditures include both operational and capital outlays, but not debt services, since including the latter would be a double counting for loan-financed capital outlays. The percentage figures are computed from the data available in the *1960–61 Summary of Annual Reports of School Districts* (Wisconsin Department of Public Instruction), 9–10.

[66] James B. Conant, in his noted study of American high schools, emphasizes the need for more diversified high school programs. He strongly recommends that students be provided with adequate elective programs in mathematics, languages, science, English, and social studies and that a seven- or eight-period school day be organized to allow students more flexibility in taking these courses. See James B. Conant, *The American High School Today* (McGraw-Hill, 1959), 41–76.

[67] As was noted in Table 6.15, the number of credit units for smaller schools was related to programs covering a two-year period. In these schools, some courses are offered only in alternate years. To the extent that these two-year arrangements limit the alternatives available for pupils, comparison of the figures shown here does not fully account for their differences.

[68] The fall in pupil-teacher ratio from 24.1 to one to 21.4 to one suggests also that a rise in enrollment at this level introduces more advanced courses where class sizes are typically small until a further increase in enrollment gives the teachers a fuller load.

[69] Henry J. Otto and Fred von Bergersrode, "Class Size," in Walter S.

Monroe, ed., *Encyclopedia of Educational Research*, (New York: Macmillan, 1950), 212–16. (The authors, however, feel that for elementary schools smaller classes are still preferable to larger classes.) See also John I. Goodland, "Room to Live and Learn: Class Size and Room Space as Factors in the Learning-Teaching Process," *Childhood Education*, 30 (Apr. 1954), 355–61; and Herbert F. Spitzer, "Class Size and Pupil Achievement in Elementary Schools," *The Elementary School Journal*, 55 (Oct. 1954), 82–86.

[70] Of a number of conceivable variables, the teacher's salary seems preferable as an indicator of teacher qualifications, even to the composite of academic degree and experience. Two persons with the same degree and years of experience can be rated differently as teachers and such differences are likely to be reflected in their salaries. It may be argued that living costs are higher in larger cities where there are more larger schools and a part of the salary differential between large and small schools may be considered a corrective of local price variation. Most of the schools included here, however, are in places of less than 50,000 in population, and price variation, if any, cannot be significant.

[71] Obviously, some of the unexplained portion of the variation in average per pupil expenditures is attributable to other causal forces not included in the analysis and perhaps, to some degree, to deficiencies of the variables included. Our assumption of linear functional relationships (between per pupil cost and variables other than size) and possible errors and arbitrariness in the reporting of data would undoubtedly have some effects also.

[72] From our regression equation,

$$\frac{\partial X_1}{\partial X_2} = -.402 + 2(.00012 X_2). \quad \text{Thus, when} \quad \frac{\partial X_1}{\partial X_2} = 0$$

$$X_2 = \frac{.402}{.00024} = 1,675.$$

[73] From our equation, the change in the average per pupil operating expenditures (X_1) to result from the change in enrollment (X_2) from 200 to 500 would be:

$$\Delta X_1 = [-.402(500) + .00012(500^2)] - [-.402(200) + .00012(200^2)]$$
$$= -95.40.$$

[74] The concept of returns to scale deals with a given technology. Thus, in using the present analysis as the basis for future projection, we must assume that the educational methods and policies remain largely unchanged.

[75] The Committee for Economic Development, *op. cit.*, 6.

[76] Wisconsin Department of Public Instruction, *Transportation Facts 1962–63* (Madison, Wisconsin, March 1963). The figures are computed from the data available on pages 12–13.

[77] *Ibid.*, 11. The study presents the following illustration of a typical contract for a bus with a daily mileage of 60 miles:

Fixed charge per day for:

Depreciation	$ 4.50
Driver Salary	6.25
Insurance	.50
Garage Rental	.75
	$12.00

Variable charge per bus mile for gas, oil, grease, repairs, maintenance, etc. 10¢ (per mile) × 60 . . . . $ 6.00

Total charge per day $18.00

CHAPTER 7

[1] See Chapter 5, pp. 102–103, for an elaboration of this point.

[2] Gary Becker, *Human Capital: A Theoretical and Empirical Analysis, with Special Reference to Education* (New York: Columbia University Press for the National Bureau of Economic Research, 1964).

[3] If the transaction costs are T and T is independent of the size of the loan, the transaction cost per dollar for a $10 loan is $T/10$ whereas it is $T/10{,}000$ for a $10,000 loan.

[4] See equation (1), p. 158.

[5] Communist Bloc countries, which formerly were doctrinally opposed to interest rates as a particularly odious manifestation of capitalism, now realize this.

[6] PDV is often referred to simply as present value.

[7] $$PDV = \frac{F}{1 + r} = \frac{\$110}{1 + 1.00} = \frac{\$110}{2} = \$55$$

[8] $$PDV = \frac{F}{1 + r} = \frac{\$110}{1 + 0} = \frac{\$110}{1} = \$110$$

[9] For example,

$$PDV = \frac{F_1}{(1 + r_1)^1} + \frac{F_2}{(1 + r_2)^2} + \cdots + \frac{F_t}{(1 + r_t)^t}$$

[10] Expected value is the summation of the products of the value of each possible outcome times the probability of its occurrence. See Appendix II, pp. 340–342, for an explanation of probability.

[11] The symbol $\sum_{t=1}^{n}$ (read as the summation from t equals 1 to t equals n) is a notation that is a shorthand for the sum of several terms differing only in the value of t, where t takes on all values from some lower level (in this case 1) to some upper level (in this case n). For example, if $n = 3$,

$$B/C = \frac{\sum_{t=1}^{3} \dfrac{F_t}{(1 + r)^t}}{\sum_{t=1}^{3} \dfrac{C_t}{(1 + r)^t}} = \frac{\dfrac{F_1}{(1 + r)^1} + \dfrac{F_2}{(1 + r)^2} + \dfrac{F_3}{(1 + r)^3}}{\dfrac{C_1}{(1 + r)^1} + \dfrac{C_2}{(1 + r)^2} + \dfrac{C_3}{(1 + r)^3}}$$

[12] For example, an investment that has a cost of $150 today and has benefits of $100 at the end of each of the first two years would have a B/C of 1.25 at a 5 per cent and 1.08 at a 15 per cent discount rate.

[13] Many projects funded by the government are never successfully concluded. Others cost much more than originally planned. The development of the SST aircraft is certainly an example of the latter and may yet be an example of the former. The risk of either or both of these happening should be part of the interest rate utilized for government projects.

[14] There are computer programs that automatically undertake this process and yield the internal rate of return.

[15] See Chapter 5, p. 102 for a discussion of this concept.

[16] To the extent that the assumption that wages equal the marginal product of labor is not true (see the discussion in Chapter 5, pp. 116–117), this theory will not hold. In addition, some believe that increased education does not imply increased productivity. Rather, it is suggested, educational qualifications act merely as a device for screening job applicants. For further discussion see Ivar Berg, *Education and Jobs: The Great Training Robbery* (New York: Praeger for the Center for Urban Education, 1970).

[17] Becker, *Human Capital*, pp. 29–30.

CHAPTER 8

[1] See J. R. Walsh, "Capital Concept Applied to Man," *Quarterly Journal of Economics* 49 (1935), 255–85.

[2] See Chapter 11, pp. 308–309, for a discussion of two possible loan programs applicable to higher education.

[3] Herman P. Miller, "Annual and Lifetime Income in Relation to Education: 1929–1959," *American Economic Review*, L (December, 1960), 962–86.

[4] H. S. Houthakker, "Education and Income," *Review of Economics and Statistics*, XLI (February, 1959), 24–28.

[5] Theodore W. Schultz, "Capital Formation by Education," *Journal of Political Economy*, LXVIII (December, 1960), 571–83.

[6] Gary S. Becker, "Underinvestment in College Education?" *American Economic Review*, L (May, 1960), 346–54; and Theodore W. Schultz, "Education as a Source of Economic Growth" (Economics of Education Research Paper, August 15, 1961) (Mimeographed), and "Education and Economic Growth," *Social Forces Influencing American Education*, ed. H. G. Richey (Chicago, 1961). It should be noted that Schultz uses a short-cut method to derive his rate of return estimates.

[7] United States Bureau of the Census, *1950 Census of Population, Special Report*, P.E. No. 5B, *Education*, Table 12.

[8] The mean income figures used in this study were estimated by weighting the mid-values of each income size class by the numbers of income recipients in each size class, for each age-level of schooling category. A value of $20,000 was used for the mid-value of the open ended class. Houthakker used a "representative" income in his weighting, in order to take account of the skewness. However, such a procedure superimposes the skewness of the entire distribution upon each age level of schooling category; this leads to serious problems, particularly at the younger age levels, where the resulting mean income values will substantially overstate the "correct" values.

[9] This is an oversimplification, but it did not seem worthwhile to deal with this in a more detailed fashion.

[10] It is unfortunate that such data are not collected since the earnings of male workers below age fourteen are assuredly not zero. Thus opportunity costs are understated to some extent.

[11] "Capital Formation by Education," *op. cit.*

[12] These opportunity cost figures tend to be slightly lower, on a per student basis, than those of Schultz, which average $583 for high school and $1,369 for college, on an annual basis.

[13] *Ibid.*

[14] Average college tuition and fees amounted to $245 in 1949 (see Ernest V. Hollis, "Trends in Tuition Charges and Fees," *Higher Education*, XII [June, 1956], 70). Actually, a figure of $245 was used; this figure was estimated from data on tuition and fees collected, reported for 1949–50 in *Biennial Survey of Education, 1955–56* (Washington: Government Printing Office, 1957), chap. iv. See sources to Table 8.2.

[15] Schultz simply assumed that these costs were 5 per cent of income foregone at the high-school level and 10 per cent of income foregone at the college level. The absolute figures derived from Schultz's work were used in these calculations even though the income foregone figures differed somewhat.

[16] Calculated from United States Department of Health, Education, and Welfare, National Office of Vital Statistics, *United States Life Tables, 1949–51* (Special Reports, Vol. XLI, No. 1 [Washington, 1954]). No attempt was made, however, to adjust for the incidence of unemployment, largely because of the difficulty of disentangling unemployment from non-labor-force status in the

data, which show all males classified by the receipt or non-receipt of income rather than by labor-force status.

[17] Houthakker, *op. cit.*, calculated from Tables 1 and 2, pp. 25–26.

[18] Several of the education-age categories were adjusted for taxes by applying the average effective tax liability by size of income group to the midpoint of the size group to determine the mean tax paid. In general, the average effective tax rate derived for an education-age category was almost identical with that calculated by Houthakker.

Admittedly, the use of the average tax liability ignores the effects of age differences, family size, and so on, but it did not seem worthwhile to adjust for these factors, even to the limited extent that such adjustments could be attempted.

[19] The main criticisms of this whole approach have been expressed most fully and forcefully by Edward F. Renshaw, "Estimating the Returns to Education," *Review of Economics and Statistics*, XLII (August, 1960), 318–24.

[20] Becker, *op. cit.*, has made some adjustments for differences in ability, but his method of doing so is not yet available. Differences in intelligence at different levels of schooling are given in Dael Wolfe, *America's Resources of Specialized Talent* (New York: Harper & Bros., 1954), pp. 142–49.

[21] This point is discussed in T. W. Schultz, "Investment in Human Capital," *American Economic Review*, LI (March, 1961), 1–17.

[22] For another dissenting note see John Vaizey, *The Economics of Education* (London: Faber & Faber, 1962), chap. iii.

[23] It is interesting to note that most states require compulsory school attendance at least to age fourteen (in effect, to the end of Grade 8).

[24] *Op. cit.*

[25] *Op. cit.*

[26] The differences shown here differ somewhat from those that are derived from Miller and Houthakker because of differences in the assumed shapes and levels of the age-income profiles.

[27] Opportunity costs are reflected in the figures showing "additional" lifetime income inasmuch as the income of the person in school is set at zero while his income-earning counterpart receives a positive income; the difference appears in the cost-return stream and measures opportunity costs. However, the other private costs of schooling are omitted in this calculation.

[28] The differences shown here differ somewhat from those derived from Houthakker because of differences in the assumed shapes and levels of the age-income profiles.

[29] For a fuller treatment of this point see J. Hirschleifer, "On the Theory of Optimal Investment Decision," *Journal of Political Economy*, LXVI (August, 1958), 329–52.

[30] For an excellent analysis of some of the conceptual differences between private and social returns see Mary Jean Bowman, "Social Returns to Education," *International Social Sciences Review* (forthcoming), and Burton Weisbrod, "Education and Investment in Human Capital," *Journal of Political Economy: Supplement*, LXX (October, 1962), 106–23.

[31] J. B. Walsh, "Capital Concept Applied to Man," *The Quarterly Journal of Economics*, February 1935; Milton Friedman and Simon Kuznets, *Income from Independent Professional Practice* (New York: National Bureau of Economic Research, 1945); Gary S. Becker, "Underinvestment in College Education?" *American Economic Review*, May 1960.

[32] This was not always the basis. A sex differential, *i.e.*, an additional salary amount for male teachers, was in effect until adoption of Equal Pay schedules in 1911. Position differentials applied to secondary teachers (*i.e.*, junior high teachers received higher salaries than elementary, and high school teachers

more than junior high), until adoption of the single salary schedule or preparation pay plan in 1947. The preparation differentials have provided, since 1958, $400 or $800 above the basic schedule for one or two years of postbaccalaureate study.

33 In the future—by Sept. 1, 1966—the fifth year of preparation will be mandated also for elementary teachers, for whom the baccalaureate presently suffices for certification. A significant difference will, nevertheless, exist between elementary and secondary teachers even when the fifth year is mandated for both groups: the fifth year will not be a prerequisite for employment of elementary teachers, as it is for secondary teachers of academic subjects, but may be acquired during five years of classroom teaching. The monetary significance of this difference will be brought out in the analysis later of the effect of foregone earnings on value of income from the preparation differentials.

34 In 1960, only 58 of the 1,212 new elementary teachers entered with more than the baccalaureate; only 5 of the 257 new secondary teachers entered with more than the fifth year. After three years of teaching service elapse, a substantial proportion have more than minimum preparation. Among elementary teachers on Salary Step 4, 54 per cent had more than baccalaureate preparation; among secondary teachers on Step 4, almost 30 per cent had the sixth year. (Data derived from Oct. 31, 1960 salary distribution, in Morrissey, *op. cit.*, pp. 9, 11–13.)

35 In 1947–50, over 20,000 teachers were registered, almost triple the number in prior years. In 1957–60, almost 25,000 teachers were registered, three out of every four teachers employed; this was about twice as many as had registered in other years since 1951. (Data derived from Board of Education, City of New York, *Sixty-First Annual Report of the Superintendent of Schools, School Year 1958–1959, Statistical Section*, pp. 320, 333.)

The duration of the peak attendance periods corresponds with the three years "normally" required for a person "attending in-service courses to accumulate 30 hours of course work" (*ibid.*, p. 291).

36 Scholastically, the evidence appears to be in the other direction. In December 1961, the Board of Examiners and of Superintendents recommended that teachers be required to follow "a consistent pattern of required courses" in qualifying for the preparation differentials. The tenor of the recommendations indicated less than complete satisfaction with existing in-service courses. (New York City Board of Education, *Staffing Our Schools Today and Tomorrow*, A Report of the Board of Superintendents and the Board of Examiners, December 1961, pp. 61, 86.)

A few months later, some indication of deficiencies in the In-Service Program appeared in the announcement that irregularities had been discovered in attendance records for in-service courses. The Board President designated a subcommittee to look into "the entire area of in-service training and courses" with the Superintendent (*New York Times*, Feb. 9, 1962, p. 31, c. 1).

37 "Present value" is used in the sense in which it is conventionally used in the mathematics of finance: the value at the present time of a sum of money due at a determinable future date—in other words, the value now of a salary which the teacher will receive *n* years hence.

38 New York City Board of Education, *Staffing Our Schools*, Report of Board of Superintendents and Board of Examiners, *op. cit.*, p. 90.

39 Jacob Mincer, "Investment in Human Capital and Personal Income Distribution," *The Journal of Political Economy*, Vol. 64, No. 4 (August 1958), p. 284.

40 Harold F. Clark, *Life Earnings in Selected Occupations in the United States* (New York: Harper and Brothers, 1937), pp. 10, 20.

41 At that date, the basic salary schedule consisted of $4,800 (the starting

or minimum salary) at Step 1. Annual length-of-service increments in various amounts, ranging from $200 to $450, brought the maximum salary to $8,650 at Step 14.

42 Friedman, *op. cit.*, p. 179.

43 Mincer hypothesizes in his theoretical model that "all individuals have identical abilities and equal opportunities to enter any occupation." The assumption is not strained for potential public schools teachers. "Equal opportunities" are available to undertake postgraduate studies and to prepare for elementary or secondary teaching; tuition-free training for both is offered in City and State colleges. According to some educators, "identical abilities" or at least equivalent abilities are required for either elementary or secondary teachers.

44 Discounted at the 10 per cent rate, the earnings advantage for the baccalaureate teacher is almost $5,400. Between the teacher entering with the sixth year and the teacher entering with the fifth year, the difference is about $1,200—in favor of the teacher entering with the fifth year. Discounted at the 10 per cent rate, the advantage becomes almost $2,800.

45 With respect to two teachers, each with the sixth year of preparation, the one who began teaching with that much preparation earns about 10 per cent less than the teacher who began with the baccalaureate and acquired two years of postgraduate preparation during a six-year in-service period. (Discounted at the 10 per cent rate, the earnings deficiency would be about 19 per cent.)

46 Friedman and Kuznets, *op. cit.*, pp. 87, 133–34.

47 In the elementary schools, there were teachers in excess, assigned to fill vacancies elsewhere. In secondary schools, teachers were in short supply, as measured by the number and rate of vacancies. The highest vacancy rate, almost 45 per cent, was in the junior high schools. In the high schools, vacancy rates were almost 17 per cent. In terms of subjects, English and Mathematics accounted for more than half the vacancies in junior high schools. General Science, Social Studies, Fine Arts accounted for almost another third.

Similarly, in the academic high schools, almost 40 per cent of vacancies were accounted for by English and Mathematics. Another 30 per cent was accounted for by Social Studies, Biology and General Science, Physics and General Science, Chemistry and General Science, Health Education-Women.

(Figures computed from New York City Board of Education, Division of Personnel, Bureau of Appointment, "Condition of Day School Organizations Depicting Authorized Positions and Personnel Condition by Rank, Subject, and License, as of October 31, 1959," pp. 7-10, 12–14.)

48 For the history of grievances under the single salary system and under previous plans based on different types of salary differentiation, see Friedman, *op. cit.*, chaps. 1–3 and Appendix I.

49 In the basic schedule, the salary minimum became $5,300 (formerly $4,800) and the maximum $9,170 (formerly $8,650). The fourteen-step salary progression was maintained, but the amounts of the annual increments were changed, as were the intermediate salary steps. Preparation differentials remained $400 and $800.

50 On April 1, 1964, increases of around $130 will be granted at every salary step except the first; the minimum will remain $5,300 and the maximum will become $9,300. On July 1, 1964, increases of around $200—at every salary step except the first—will leave the minimum at $5,300 and bring the maximum to $9,500, in the basic schedule.

51 The promotional differential applies to all academic, vocational, and junior high school teachers, including those teachers of business, technical, or special subjects for whom the fifth year of preparation is not mandated.

It is available also to other teachers, with either an approved Master's degree, or 30 semester hours beyond the baccalaureate. For the latter, however, not less than 36 semester hours (which may be graduate and undergraduate, combined) must be in one subject-matter area. How many teachers are now in this category is not known. Prospectively, large numbers will be. Since the new certification requirements stipulate a concentration of at least 24 semester hours in a specific academic discipline, it may be anticipated that another 12 semester hours of specialization would very likely be acquired by teachers as they qualify subsequently, in-service, for the preparation differentials.

[52] The summary was produced by a joint research project of the Federal Reserve Bank of Boston and the Massachusetts Division of Employment Security under the direction of Edwin C. Gooding, and entitled: *The Massachusetts Retraining Program.* Supplemental data were obtained through interviews.

[53] "Manpower Development and Training Act of 1962," *U.S. Code Congressional and Administrative News*, West Co., St. Paul, Minn., April, 1962, pp. 439–50, 474–502.

[54] The question naturally arises as to whether redistribution of income is an objective of the MDA. The wording of the Act indicates that redistribution is only incidental, and not meant to be a major objective of the program. However, in so far as new workers are placed in the workforce redistribution is inevitable in the Lorenzian sense. A moderate amount of redistribution also occurs as the result of paying subsistence allowances, and other costs of retraining, with public funds.

[55] *U.S. Code Congressional and Administration News*, "Legislative History: Manpower Development Act," West Publishing Company, 1962, pp. 474, 475.

[56] From a social point of view, gains in total income would be a satisfactory measure of benefits. However, benefits to an economic efficiency objective must be measured as gains in productivity. Only if policy makers are indifferent between transfer payments and earned income can changes in total income be used as a measure of benefits from retraining. And, the wording of the Act, "in order to...reduce the costs of unemployment compensation and public assistance," makes it clear that policy makers are *not* indifferent.

[57] A mailed questionnaire was sent to the control group and responses recorded in Exhibit III of the *Massachusetts Retraining Program.*

[58] Editors' note:

$$PV = \sum_{t=1}^{35} \frac{1}{(1 + r)^t}, \quad i.e., \quad \frac{1}{(1 + r)} + \frac{1}{(1 + r)^2} + \frac{1}{(1 + r)^3} + \cdots + \frac{1}{(1 + r)^{35}}.$$

CHAPTER 9

[1] This can be derived from the simple neoclassical production function $Y = f(K, L)$, utilizing only the assumption that factors are paid their marginal product:

$$\Delta Y = MP_K \, \Delta K + MP_L \, \Delta L \qquad (a)$$

Equation (a) states that the addition to output is equal to the addition to each of the factors of production times their marginal products, which is reasonable since the definition of marginal product is the additional output associated with an additional input. Simple algebraic manipulation (divide all terms by Y and multiply the first and second terms of the right hand side of the equation by K/K and L/L, respectively) yields:

$$\frac{\Delta Y}{Y} = \frac{\Delta K MP_K K}{KY} + \frac{\Delta L MP_L L}{LY} \qquad (b)$$

Since $\Delta Y/Y$, $\Delta K/K$, and $\Delta L/L$ are the growth rates of Y, K, and L, respectively, we can write:

$$G_Y = \frac{G_K MP_K K}{Y} + \frac{G_L MP_L L}{Y} \qquad (c)$$

However, capital and labor are paid their marginal products. Therefore, the marginal products times the stocks are equal to the total payments to capital and labor. Consequently, the terms $MP_K K/Y$ and $MP_L L/Y$ are not shares of capital and labor in total output. If a is substituted for capital's share of total output and b is substituted for labor's share of total output, the neoclassical growth equation becomes:

$$G_Y = aG_K + bG_L \qquad (d)$$

[2] For example, if $b = 3/4$, the following would hold:

G_K	G_L	G_Y	$G_Y - G_L$
4%	0%	1%	1%
4	1	$1\frac{1}{4}$	$\frac{3}{4}$
4	2	$2\frac{1}{2}$	$\frac{1}{2}$

[3] The distinction between a percentage and a percentage point is an important one to keep in mind. In this case 1.5 percentage points is 50 per cent of the total growth rate—three percentage points.

[4] W. Arthur Lewis, "Economic Development with Unlimited Supplies of Labor," *Manchester School of Economic and Social Studies* 22 (1954), and John Fei and Gustav Ranis, *Development of the Labor Surplus Economy: Theory and Practice* (Homewood, Ill.: Richard D. Irwin, 1964).

[5] See Chapter 5, pp. 115–117 for a detailed discussion of marginal products.

[6] For some models applicable to education see Organization for Economic Co-operation and Development, *Mathematical Models in Educational Planning* (Paris: Organization for Economic Co-operation and Development, 1967).

[7] Hansen's article is reproduced in Chapter 8.

[8] The extended family system is one in which several generations of a family live together and responsibility for even distant relatives is felt. This can be contrasted to the norm in many countries in which only the husband, wife, and minor children (nuclear family) live together.

[9] If "a" refers to the architect, "arch" to the amount of architectural work accomplished per hour, "d" the draftsman, and "drafting" the amount of drafting work accomplished per hour

$$\frac{\text{arch a}}{\text{arch d}} > \frac{\text{drafting a}}{\text{drafting d}}$$

[10] "Citizenization," Africanization, or Nigerianization is the process of replacing non-citizens, non-Africans, or non-Nigerians in jobs with citizens, Africans, or Nigerians.

[11] The following discussion draws on Mark Blaug, *A Cost-Benefit Approach to Educational Planning in Developing Countries* (International Bank for Reconstruction and Development Report No. EC-157, December 20, 1967).

CHAPTER 10

[1] Frederick Harbison and Charles Myers, *Education, Manpower, and Economic Growth* (New York: McGraw-Hill, 1964). For other such attempts see Mary Jean Bowman and C. Arnold Anderson, "Concerning the Role of Education in Development" in Clifford Geertz (ed.), *Old Societies and New States* (New York:

Free Press, 1963); Walter Garms, Jr., "A Multivariate Analysis of the Correlates of Educational Efforts of Nations," *Comparative Education Review*, 12 (1968); and David McClelland, "Does Education Accelerate Economic Growth," *Economic Development and Cultural Change*, 14 (1966).

² See, for example, The Master Plan Survey Team, *A Master Plan for Higher Education in California: 1960–75* (Sacramento: California State Department of Education, 1960); Indiana State Policy Commission on Post High School Education, *Report of the State Policy Commission on Post High School Education* (Indianapolis: State of Indiana, 1968); and North Carolina State Board of Higher Education, *Planning for Higher Education in North Carolina* (Raleigh: North Carolina State Board of Higher Education, 1968).

³ Elementary school was eight years until 1966.

⁴ Insofar as the income benefits redound to the person making a contribution to knowledge this is covered under education by my method, but this is a negligible part of the whole effect.

⁵ Mean incomes before tax, by age and years of school completed, estimated from these data are given by H. S. Houthakker in "Education and Income," *The Review of Economics and Statistics*, February 1959, p. 25.

⁶ Scores on the Army General Classification Test (AGCT) are approximately equivalent to the more familiar "IQ." The average score of the whole population is 100. About 34 per cent make scores between 80 and 100 and another 34 per cent between 100 and 120. Nearly everyone scores between 40 and 160. Dael Wolfle, *America's Resources of Specialized Talent*, the Report of the Commission on Human Resources and Advanced Training, Harper and Brothers, 1954, pp. 143, 145, 146, 182.

⁷ Wolfle, *op. cit.*, especially pp. 152–54.

⁸ Race, and inherited wealth and family position, are also interrelated with education and earnings, and contribute to income differentials. However, the influence on the income differentials derived from the Census of property income, whether or not related to inherited wealth, is probably small. These income data include property income only if actually received in money, and that very incompletely. An offsetting factor is inclusion, also incomplete, of transfer payments. My interest is in measuring differentials in earnings from labor.

⁹ The importance of parents' education stands out in the following table. It gives the educational status, as of October 1960, of men 20 to 24 years old classified by the amount of education received by their fathers.

		Education of son *(per cent of men 20 to 24 years old whose* *fathers had education specified)*			
Education of father	*Total*	*Did not graduate from high school*	*High School graduate, no college*	*Some college, did not graduate*	*Graduated from or currently enrolled in college*
Did not graduate from high school	100.0	42.6	34.1	7.8	15.5
High school graduate, no college	100.0	10.3	36.1	17.4	36.3
Some college, did not graduate	100.0	6.5	23.8	15.8	53.9
Graduated from college	100.0	4.0	8.2	10.1	77.8

Father's education is, of course, intercorrelated with family income, but additional detail shows that each of the two, separately, was of great importance in determining the education received by sons. For example, among families with an income of $7,500 to $9,999, the percentage of sons with some college attendance was 32.9 for sons whose fathers did not graduate from high school,

57.7 for sons whose fathers graduated from high school but did not attend college, and 82.9 for sons whose fathers attended college (with or without graduating). Among sons whose fathers did not graduate from high school (who comprised over three-fifths of all sons) the percentage with college attendance was 12.6 where family income was under $5000, 23.1 where income was $5,000 to $7,499, 32.9 where income was $7,500 to $9,999, and 40.8 where income was $10,000 or more.

The highest percentage, 88.6, was for sons with fathers who had attended college *and* had a family income of $10,000 or more. Among sons whose fathers did not graduate from high school *and* had a family income less than $5,000, not only was the percentage with some college attendance as low as 12.6 but the percentage not completing high school was as high as 53.9.

Source: Series P-20, No. 110, Bureau of the Census, July 24, 1961.

[10] Reasons for not attending college stated by young people or parents are given in Census Bureau Series, ERS (P-27), No. 30, August 1961.

[11] The need for *some* downward adjustment of the reported income differentials in the use to which I shall put them may be clearer if it is approached from a different standpoint. As the general educational level moves up, the fraction of the population that has received any given amount of education (say, 12 years) presumably is drawn on the average from a lower segment of the ability distribution of the population; the average high school graduate today presumably has less "natural" ability than the average high school graduate a generation ago. Reducing the reported income differentials adjusts for this, although how accurately is, of course, uncertain. It may be observed, however, that Wolfle denies that (as of 1954) past increases in college enrollments resulted in any lowering of the average quality of college students. He also cites a study by Frank H. Finch indicating no decline in test scores on a standardized intelligence test by students in certain high schools over a 15-year period—a result ascribed to improved instruction in the lower grades. (Wolfle, *op. cit.*, pp. 173–74.)

[12] Denison has subsequently found some data that tend to substantiate the use of a 60 per cent figure. See Organization for Economic Co-operation and Development, *The Residual Factor and Economic Growth* (Paris: Organization for Economic Co-operation and Development, 1964), pp. 86–100.—Eds.

[13] The procedure assumes that percentage earnings differentials (measured before taxes) associated with education have not changed in the period covered. If they have increased my procedure would overstate the contribution of education to past growth while if they have decreased it would understate the contribution of education. What little evidence is available suggests that there may have been some small increase in percentage differentials since 1939 but perhaps not in the longer run. Evidently demand for labor has shifted toward a requirement for more education at about the same rate as the labor supply has become better educated. Most of the evidence is given by Herman P. Miller in "Annual and Lifetime Income in Relation to Education: 1939–59," *American Economic Review*, December 1960, pp. 962–85.

[14] Census Series P-20, No. 91, provides two projections. Series A, which assumes a more rapid increase in educational attainments than the alternative series, was used.

[15] These indications are: (1) While the proportions in the younger age groups reporting graduation from high school and college correspond roughly to available information about actual graduations, in the higher age groups these proportions greatly exceed the actual proportions graduating at the time persons of their age were completing school. (2) Comparison of the 1940 and 1950 Censuses for the same age "cohorts" indicates a pronounced upgrading of educational achievement between the two dates. For example, in each age

group up to those 55–59 in 1950, the proportion of the group reported as high school graduates or better rose about 3 percentage points. (In higher age classes it also increased but by a smaller percentage of the total age group.) If the explanation lies in "self-promotion" in reporting, and if "self-promotion" by a given cohort is of similar amount in every decade, then overstatement would increase with age, and in the older age groups be large. Alternative explanations of the 1940–50 differences imply better reporting in 1950, continued education in adult life, or differential death rates by educational level, but I am not convinced that they can explain much of the apparent incomparability.

[16] The adjustment, if accurate, provides a series that is based on similar overstatement of educational achievement in all years, yielding correct percentage changes, not a "true" statement of educational achievements.

[17] A similar adjustment to that just described was applied to this series. Direct comparison of 1940 and 1950 Census data indicated an increase of 10.44 per cent as compared with 9.07 per cent obtained by the projection procedure. Per cent changes in each decade were raised by the difference of 1.37 percentage points.

[18] Since the data on days of schooling were not based on projections of Census Data, no bias adjustment was required. (A 1940–50 test confirmed that any bias indirectly resulting from the bias associated with years of schooling was negligible.)

[19] Computed as $100 - 100[(100.0)/(110.3)]$.

[20] In 1958 males 25 and over represented 57.3 per cent of the labor force; males under 25, 10.0 per cent; females 25 and over 25.9 per cent; and females under 25, 6.8 per cent. The proportion of females completing any grade through high school is, and seems to have been back at least to the Civil War, higher than the comparable percentage for males. There has probably been little difference in trend. Since their average age is also lower, women in the labor force are considerably better educated than men in the labor force. Even the proportion having completed college is higher. In April 1957 the median number of school years completed by women in the labor force aged 18 to 64 was 12.1 as compared with 11.3 for men. (See *Current Population Reports*, Census Bureau, Series P-50, No. 78.) The increasing proportion of women in the labor force would in itself tend to raise the rate of improvement in the average educational level of the labor force, but this effect is offset by the fact that the average age of women in the labor force has been rapidly rising and, presumably, reducing the educational differential in favor of females.

Although use of data covering only adult males in the computations is a limitation in appraising the effect of education on growth, it turns out to be an advantage in pursuing another objective—derivation of an index of labor input adjusted for quality change.

[21] My calculations also assumed that (say) doubling the number of days spent in school during a year raised the quality of labor as much as doubling the number of years without changing the days per year. Numbers given in Table 10.2 allow the reader to experiment with the effects of a change in that assumption.

[22] It may also be noted that the rate of increase in the average number of days or years spent in school by members of the labor force, not weighted by school grade, declines more sharply than my measure.

[23] This figure is based on a comparison of the average income obtained by applying the income differentials of Table 10.1 to the 1980 Census "A" projected distribution of years of school completed for all persons 25 to 29 years of age with the average income obtained by applying them to the same distribution when everyone is moved up one year.

[24] The figure of one-third used for child workers in the following chapter is one-third the earnings of *adult males*, and refers to workers under 20 years of age. A higher fraction is appropriate for the present calculation.

[25] The calculation is net only with respect to the elements considered, which do not include any possible adverse effect on the rate of investment (this is considered immediately below) or any stimulus to the rate of advance in knowledge.

[26] This underlies the fact that the ratio of column 5 to column 4 in Table 10.2 rises markedly over time.

[27] Gary S. Becker, *op. cit.*, p. 349. Professor Theodore W. Schultz is also studying the costs and returns from education. Parts of his study appeared in the *Journal of Political Economy* for December 1960 and the *American Economic Review* for March 1961.

[28] The question, what governs the growth of the capital stock, is considered in chapter 12.

[29] The propriety of charging all the costs of education as an "investment" expense in computing a rate of return, rather than allocating at least part to consumption, is not crucial in my discussion. However, if the discussion were to turn from the "average" student to the desirability of more education for such separate categories as women not intending to work, or students planning despite low prospective earnings to enter occupations offering opportunity for service to God or humanity, or providing pleasant conditions or prestige, the distinction between educational expenditures as "consumption" and as "investment" would become necessary. My personal view is that the non-economic benefits of providing education through the college level at least for those who (a) want it enough to live, if necessary, at a standard of living formerly thought appropriate to a student, and (b) can benefit from it, are so large that its contribution to growth is very nearly "free."

[30] *Higher Education for American Democracy*, a report on the President's Commission on Higher Education, Volume I, Establishing the Goals, pp. 39-41. New York: Harper & Brothers, 1948. The Commission came to its conclusions after correlating (1) scores indicating the mental ability of our general population (Army General Classification Test scores) and (2) scores indicating reasonable expectations of completing college programs successfully (American Council on Education Psychological Examination—1942 college edition).

[31] *Change/Challenge/Response: A Development Program for New York State*. Office for Regional Development, Albany, 1964.

[32] *Technical Manpower in New York State*, Volume 1, Chapter II, Table D. Forthcoming publication of N.Y. State Department of Labor.

[33] Ray C. Maul, *Teacher Supply and Demand in Universities, Colleges, and Junior Colleges, 1961-62 and 1962-63*. Research Report 1963-R3, National Education Association, Washington 36, D.C.

[34] Printed by the Government Printer, January 1965, 20 pp.

[35] The East African Community is an organization consisting of Tanzania, Uganda, and Kenya designed to facilitate economic trade and development.—Eds.

[36] Julius Nyerere, *Education for Self-Reliance* (Dar es Salaam: Government Printer, 1967).—Eds.

[37] George Tobias, *High-Level Manpower Requirements and Resources in Tanganyika 1962-1967* (Dar es Salaam: Government Printer, 1963).—Eds.

[38] Gross Domestic Product (GDP) is a national income statistic similar to Gross National Product (GNP).—Eds.

[39] A rather ominous development is beginning to emerge, which, if unchecked, will cause Tanzania to fail to meet its 1980 manpower self-sufficiency target

by a serious margin. This failure will occur in the most strategic category of high level manpower and the one most heavily dominated by expatriates. These are the science/maths based occupations produced by the universities. All of these require an H.S.C. with a science bias, with sufficient passes to qualify for university entrance. In 1968 the input needed to stay on schedule for the outputs to 1980 was 296 H.S.C. (science bias) passers. Although the Ministry of National Education brought forward a large number of science candidates for the examination only about *half* were able to qualify for university entrance or 254 in all, which was 42 less than required. Worse yet, only 217 of these actually entered university, a loss of a further 37 or a total shortfall of 79 under the number scheduled in order to achieve the 1980 target. The 1969 H.S.C. results have recently been announced. By an odd, and sad, coincidence the number of H.S.C. (science bias) passers (university qualifier level) was again 254. So the 1968 experience bids well to be repeated. If this keeps up, without effective remedial action by the Ministry of National Education, the cumulative shortfall by 1980 in these crucial occupations will be between 800 and 1,000 and this will be approximately 20 per cent short of the total requirements by 1980.

[40] *Government Policy on Employment of Non-Citizens in Tanzania* (Guidelines and Procedures to Assist Employers of Non-Citizens in Handling their Training Requirements under the Revised Immigration Regulations), Government Printer, May 1966, 17 pp.

CHAPTER 11

[1] *U.S. News and World Report*, December 9, 1968, p. 11.

[2] Prior to World War I, custom duties and taxes on liquor and tobacco were the major sources of federal revenue. Personal income taxes and business taxes were levied during the Civil War and again briefly in the 1890s, but each time they were repealed soon after enactment.

[3] Salary increases should not be confused with absolute salary levels. Absolute teachers' salaries are still below most professional occupations requiring a similar educational background.

[4] An additional aspect of tax revision is that of consolidation. It is uneconomic for two or three levels of government each to levy the same tax, thereby duplicating accounting and auditing chores. One level of government—usually the highest—should levy the tax with the rates adjusted to provide the required revenue. This revenue can then be redistributed throughout the federal system in proportion to responsibility for providing public services. Tax sharing, to be discussed in the next paragraph, is a step in this direction from the disbursement side, but need not entail any tax consolidation.

An additional feature of tax consolidation is the elimination of interstate and interlocality competition for industry based on preferential income and corporate taxation. Competition of this type is a hindrance to an efficient national allocation of resources.

[5] An interesting example of a flat grant is the recently adopted Bundy Law in New York State, whereby in 1969 accredited private universities received $400 for each baccalaureate or master's degree awarded and $2,400 for each doctorate. The intent of this program, the first of its kind on the state level, is to help maintain a balance between public and private universities.

[6] Graduate instruction requires a higher faculty/student ratio, a higher proportion of the faculty at the professorial level, and greater expenditures to induce and complement broad research activities that are a concomitant part of graduate training.

[7] *Educational Opportunity Bank*, A Report of the Panel on Educational Innovation to the U.S. Commissioner of Education, the Director of the National Science Foundation, and the Special Assistant to the President for Service and Technology, August 1967, p. 1.

[8] Howard R. Bowen, *The Finance of Higher Education* (Berkeley, Cal.: Carnegie Commission on Higher Education, 1968), p. 35. President Nixon has recently proposed to Congress, in his Higher Education Opportunity Act of 1970, that the federal government provide grants and loans to students from low income families for use at institutions of higher education. In addition, the act proposes that the federal government provide direct financial assistance to states and institutions for meeting the additional costs of starting new programs to teach critically needed skills in community colleges and technical institutes. (*New York Times*, March 20, 1970, p. 28.)

[9] The discussion in this section draws upon the concepts developed in Chapter 5. The importance of the problem justifies any duplication that may exist.

[10] *Webster's New World Dictionary of the American Language*, College Edition (New York: The World Publishing Co., 1966).

[11] There is some evidence that parental concern and interest in their children's schooling is one of the prime factors contributing to achievement on subject matter examinations. In this sense decentralization has economic as well as political implications.

[12] See Richard Judy, "Simulation and Rational Resource Allocation in Universities," in Organization for Economic Co-operation and Development, *Efficiency in Resource Utilization in Education* (Paris: Organization for Economic Co-operation and Development, 1969), p. 262.

[13] Harry Hartley, *Educational Planning-Programming-Budgeting: A Systems Approach* (Englewood Cliffs, N.J.: Prentice-Hall, Inc., 1968).

[14] See John Goodlad, John O'Toole, Jr., and Louise Taylor, *Computers and Information Systems in Education* (New York: Harcourt, Brace and World, 1966) for a description of 27 school programs utilizing computer services.

[15] Examples of such principles are: equal opportunity regardless of means, and the "sanctity" of the teacher-pupil relationship uncolored by monetary considerations.

[16] See Milton Friedman, *Capitalism and Freedom* (Chicago: University of Chicago Press, 1962), chapter 6. For a brief synopsis of these views as applied to school decentralization, see Friedman's column in *Newsweek*, November 18, 1968, p. 100.

[17] "The Case for a Free Market," *Saturday Review*, January 11, 1969, p. 34.

[18] The Office of Economic Opportunity has funded a project to establish such a scheme in selected localities in Massachusetts on an experimental basis. This experiment is projected to begin in the fall of 1971 and to continue for five to eight years. (See *New York Times*, June 4, 1970, p. 1).

[19] Sizer, *op. cit.*, p. 42.

[20] Alan T. Peacock and Anthony J. Culyer, *Economic Aspects of Student Unrest*. Occasional Paper No. 26, The Institute of Economic Affairs (London, England), 1969, pp. 17–18.

APPENDIX I

[1] For elaboration and further discussion of the topics discussed here see J. Parry Lewis, *An Introduction to Mathematics for Students of Economics*, 2nd ed. (New York: St. Martin's Press, 1969) or Parts I and II of Michael J. Brennan, *Preface to Econometrics*, 2nd ed. (Cincinnati: South-Western, 1965).

[2] The number of teachers employed may affect school enrollment if they live in the district in which they teach and have children of school age.

[3] If equation (5) were $T = 50$, the system would be consistent.

[4] The variable (or variables) inside the parentheses is said to be an "argument" of the function.

[5] No hard and fast rule exists for avoiding such confusion. Whether a function is intended can be determined only from the context.

[6] The symbol, Δ, is the Greek letter delta and $\Delta Y/\Delta X$ is read as delta Y divided by delta X.

[7] The change in X can only approach but not reach zero because at ΔX equal to zero, $\Delta Y/\Delta X$ is undefined.

[8] At $V = 7$, $\Delta S/\Delta V = 60/4 = 15$.

[9] In the term aX^m, a is a coefficient of the variable X and m is an exponent of X. A coefficient is a number by which the variable is multiplied. An exponent is simply the power to which a base (or number or variable) is raised. Raising a number to a power is multiplying the number times itself a given number of times. In the term 10^2, 10 is the base which is being raised to a certain power prescribed by the exponent, 2. $10^2 = 10 \cdot 10$; $X^3 = X \cdot X \cdot X$; and $3^5 = 3 \cdot 3 \cdot 3 \cdot 3 \cdot 3$.

[10] Two other rules that we shall not generally need are: The derivative of a product of two functions $Y = UV$ where $U = f_1(X)$ and $V = f_2(X)$ is given by

$$\frac{dY}{dX} = U\frac{dV}{dX} + V\frac{dU}{dX},$$

and the derivative of a quotient of two functions $Y = U/V$ is given by

$$\frac{dY}{dX} = \frac{V\dfrac{dV}{dX} - U\dfrac{dV}{dX}}{V^2}.$$

[11] e is defined as the limit of $[1 + (1/n)]^n$ as n approaches infinity. It has the unusual property of having its derivative equal to itself. That is, $de^x/dX = e^x$.

[12] Three simple rules are relevant.
Multiplication is achieved by adding logarithms:

$$\log (X \cdot Y) = \log X + \log Y$$

Division is achieved by subtracting logarithms:

$$\log (X/Y) = \log X - \log Y$$

Raising to a power is achieved by multiplying:

$$\log (X^n) = n \log X$$

APPENDIX II

[1] For elaboration and further discussion of the topics presented here see John E. Freund, *Modern Elementary Statistics*, 2nd ed. (Englewood Cliffs, N.J.: Prentice-Hall, Inc., 1960) or Part IV of Michael J. Brennan, *Preface to Econometrics*, 2nd ed. (Cincinnati: South-Western, 1965).

[2] The Greek letter, Σ (called capital sigma), denotes the summation of all the values of the term that follows it.

[3] The formula for the variance is

$$\frac{\Sigma(x_i - \bar{x})^2}{n - 1}$$

where x_i are the individual observations, $\bar{x}$ is the mean, and n is the number of observations.

[4] In fact, 79 per cent of that sample were within the specified one standard deviation from the mean. The difference between 68+ per cent and 79 per cent is due either to chance variations of samples or to the actual distribution being non-normal.

[5] The square of the deviations or errors is used partly to make all values positive, a procedure that prevents positive and negative errors from cancelling each other out.

[6] The difference in the notations for the partial correlation coefficient and the coefficient of multiple determination is that the former is subscripted.

[7] The value of R is to a certain degree dependent on the number of variables involved relative to the number of observations, called the *degrees of freedom*. In precise work a correction for the degrees of freedom must be made.

[8] This is often written as R^2. However, we reserve the use of R and R^2 for multiple relationships in order to emphasize the distinction between simple and multiple correlations and regressions.

[9] A hypothesis to be tested, such as the coefficient of a variable is equal to zero, is known as a *null hypothesis*.

[10] The standard error of a regression coefficient is a measure of the standard deviation of the coefficient's variable relative to the coefficient of multiple determination.

[11] The following test is made: If the coefficient were actually zero, find the range of values of the coefficient which would occur in 95 per cent (or any other percentage—the higher the percentage the more stringent the test) of all samples and see if the coefficient from the given sample is within that range. For samples greater than 30 observations, the range would be between 1.96 standard deviations (1.96σ) below the actual value and 1.96 standard deviations above the actual value as seen in Figure II.6 (that is, -1.96σ to $+1.96\sigma$

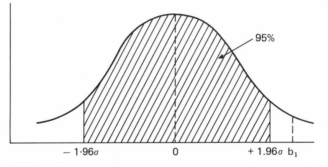

Figure II.6   Normal Distribution

since the value is hypothesized equal to zero) for a Student's t distribution. If the value of the coefficient is greater than $+1.96\sigma$ or less than -1.96σ, there is only a 5 per cent chance of that happening if it is actually zero. For a sample of less than 30 observations, the range in slightly larger. Therefore, the original hypothesis that the coefficient is zero is rejected, and it is said that the coefficient is significantly different from zero at the 95 per cent confidence level. Of course, one can just as easily make the test at the 99 per cent, 90 per cent, or any other confidence level.

[12] See Daniel Suits, "Use of Dummy Variables in Regression Equations," *American Statistical Association Journal* 52 (1957): 547–51 for more detailed discussion of the use of dummy variables.

Index

395